ENERGY TRANSITIONS IN CENTRAL AND EASTERN EUROPE

This book examines the mutual interplay of climate and energy policies in eleven Central and Eastern European countries in the context of the EU's energy transition. Energy security has long been prioritised in the region and has shaped not only national climate and energy policy, but also EU-level policy-making and implementation. Whilst the region shares economic, institutional and historical energy supplier commonalities it is not homogenous, and the book considers the significant differences between the preferences and policies of these member states. Chapters also explore the effect of the EU on member states that have joined since 2004 and their influence on the EU's energy and climate policies and their role in highlighting the importance of the concepts of security and solidarity. The book highlights the challenges to, and drivers of, energy transitions in the region and compares these with those in global energy transitions.

Tomas Maltby is a Reader in International Politics in the Department of Political Economy at King's College London. His research focuses primarily on the development of climate and energy policy. This includes work related to agenda-setting, policy making, the drivers of and obstacles to energy transitions, climate obstructionism and the politics of air pollution.

Matúš Mišík is an Associate Professor at the Department of Political Science at Comenius University Bratislava. His research focuses on energy security in the EU. He is the author of *External Energy Security in the European Union* (2019) and has published articles in journals including *Nature Energy*, *Energy* and *Energy Policy*.

CAMBRIDGE STUDIES ON ENVIRONMENT, ENERGY AND NATURAL RESOURCES GOVERNANCE

Cambridge Studies on Environment, Energy and Natural Resources Governance publishes foundational monographs of general interest to scholars and practitioners within the broadly defined fields of sustainable development policy, including studies on law, economics, politics, history, and policy. These fields currently attract unprecedented interest due both to the urgency of developing policies to address climate change, the energy transition, food security and water availability and, more generally, to the progressive realization of the impact of humans as a geological driver of the state of the Earth, now called the "Anthropocene."

The general editor of the series is Professor Jorge E. Viñuales, the Harold Samuel Chair of Law and Environmental Policy at the University of Cambridge and the Founder and First Director of the Cambridge Centre for Environment, Energy and Natural Resource Governance (C-EENRG).

Energy Transitions in Central and Eastern Europe

THE POLITICAL ECONOMY OF CLIMATE AND ENERGY POLICY

TOMAS MALTBY
King's College London

MATÚŠ MIŠÍK
Comenius University Bratislava

CAMBRIDGE
UNIVERSITY PRESS

CAMBRIDGE
UNIVERSITY PRESS

Shaftesbury Road, Cambridge CB2 8EA, United Kingdom

One Liberty Plaza, 20th Floor, New York, NY 10006, USA

477 Williamstown Road, Port Melbourne, VIC 3207, Australia

314–321, 3rd Floor, Plot 3, Splendor Forum, Jasola District Centre, New Delhi – 110025, India

103 Penang Road, #05-06/07, Visioncrest Commercial, Singapore 238467

Cambridge University Press is part of Cambridge University Press & Assessment,
a department of the University of Cambridge.

We share the University's mission to contribute to society through the pursuit of
education, learning and research at the highest international levels of excellence.

www.cambridge.org
Information on this title: www.cambridge.org/9781108477130

DOI: 10.1017/9781108755672

First published 2024

A catalogue record for this publication is available from the British Library

A Cataloging-in-Publication data record for this book is available from the Library of Congress

ISBN 978-1-108-47713-0 Hardback

TM: For Ellie and for my parents

MM: For Matilda and for Nada

Contents

Figures

Tables

Preface

As with any similar endeavour, the writing of this monograph was a long-term project, and longer than planned as two crucial events impacted the process of writing as well as the book's contents. The Covid-19 pandemic significantly changed our plans (and deadlines) due to the disruptive period and also the significant effects on energy and climate policy within the EU and Central and Eastern Europe, and globally, necessitating revisions and updates to our drafts. Russia's full-scale invasion of Ukraine in February 2022, and preparations for this in late 2021, led to a multidimensional energy crisis in the EU – radically driving up prices and posing a significant threat to security of supplies. This necessitated further revisions to explore the initial effect on the EU's climate and energy policy, including the new objective to quickly phase out all imports from its primary long-term energy supplier. This represents a paradigm shift in EU energy policy, with energy security elevated to the highest of priorities, and unprecedented policies following. Suddenly, the countries of Central and Eastern Europe were not outliers in warning about security of supply risks associated with Russia. Renewables increasingly began to be framed not only as a climate policy but as a tool to deliver energy independence, including in some Central and Eastern European countries. Energy transitions in the region remain at a relatively early stage, but there are indications that events since 2020 have served to accelerate them.

We are grateful to many people who helped during the process of writing this book: numerous colleagues, at our home institutions, conferences, workshops, within other writing projects and the many formal and informal meetings that included discussions on topics included in this book. Our thanks also to the Cambridge University Press team, especially to Matt Gallaway for his support and patience with our delays.

Acknowledgements

Matúš Mišík would like to thank the Slovak Research and Development Agency, which supported work on this book with grant no. APVV-20-0012 (EU Green Recovery in the Post-Covid-19 Period).

Abbreviations

bcm	billion cubic metres
BEMIP	Baltic Energy Market Interconnection Plan
CCS	carbon capture and storage
CEE	Central and Eastern Europe
CO_2	carbon dioxide
COMECON	Council for Mutual Economic Assistance
COP	Conference of the Parties
DG	directorate general
EBRD	European Bank for Reconstruction and Development
EC	European Commission
ECJ	European Court of Justice
ECSC	European Coal and Steel Community
EEPR	European Energy Programme for Recovery
ENTSOG	European Network of Transmission System Operators for Gas
ERDF	European Regional Development Fund
ETS	Emissions Trading System
EU	European Union
EUGAL	European Gas Pipeline Link
EURATOM	European Atomic Energy Community
FSRU	floating storage regasification unit
G20	Group of Twenty
GDP	gross domestic product
GFANZ	Glasgow Financial Alliance for Net Zero
GHG	greenhouse gases
GW	gigawatt
HBP	Hornontrianske bane Prievidza (Slovak coal mining company)

IAEA	International Atomic Energy Agency
IEA	International Energy Agency
IGA	intergovernmental agreement
IKL	Ingolstadt-Kralupy-Litvinov (Czech oil pipeline)
IMF	International Monetary Fund
IPCC	Intergovernmental Panel on Climate Change
ISO	independent system operator
ITO	independent transmission operator
KEXIM	South Korean Export-Import Bank of Korea
LNG	liquified natural gas
LTC	long-term contract
MEP	Member of European Parliament
MFA	Ministry of Foreign Affairs
Mtoe	millions of tonnes of oil equivalent
MW	megawatt
NATO	North Atlantic Treaty Organization
NDC	Nationally Determined Contribution
NECP	National Energy and Climate Plan
NGO	non-governmental organisation
NIMBY	'not in my backyard' (concept)
NPP	nuclear power plant
NSS	national security strategy
OECD	Organisation for Economic Co-operation and Development
OKD	Ostravsko-karvinské doly (Czech coal mining company)
OPAL	Ostsee-Pipeline-Anbindungsleitung (German gas pipeline)
OSCE	Organization for Security and Co-operation in Europe
PCI	Project of Common Interest
PGE	Polska Grupa Energetyczna (Polish energy company)
PGNiG	Polskie Górnictwo Naftowe i Gazownictwo (Polish oil and gas company)
PHARE	Poland/Hungary for the Reconstruction of the Economy
PWR	pressurised water reactor
RRF	Recovery and Resilience Facility
SEA	Single European Act
SoS	security of supply
TANAP	Trans Anatolian Natural Gas Pipeline
TAP	Trans Adriatic Pipeline
TEN-E	Trans-European Networks for Energy
TSO	transmission system operator

UCG	underground coal gasification
UK	United Kingdom
UN	United Nations
US	United States

Introduction

This book explores how the European Union (EU) has attempted to balance its energy security objectives in the twenty-first century, an attempt to achieve security of supply, reasonable prices and ambitious climate goals. Specifically, it focuses on how these challenges have played out in the countries of Central and Eastern Europe (CEE) in the context of their accession to the EU, as members are both subject to and shape the EU's agenda and legislative outputs. We show how a general prioritisation of security of supply concerns has constrained and at times enabled energy transitions in the region, and how a consistent concern with import dependence of Russia was discursively adopted by the wider EU in the late 2000s, and as a policy goal from 2022.

In the EU, a fundamental energy transition is under way. In 2019 wind and solar generated more electricity than coal for the first time. By 2022 these renewable sources had also overtaken gas and nuclear, generating almost a quarter of the EU's electricity (Jones et al., 2023). This book explores energy transitions within CEE countries and the effect of, and effect on, the EU's energy transition as a whole. The year 2022 marked a paradigm shift in EU energy policy (Mišík and Nosko, 2023a). In 2021 a quarter of the EU's energy mix was comprised of Russian fossil fuels, and the EU was significantly dependent on Russia for its coal, gas and oil imports. Russia launched a full-scale invasion of Ukraine on 24 February 2022. By March the European Commission (EC) proposed reducing imports of Russian energy to zero 'well before 2030' (European Commission, 2022a). Before the end of the year the EU had replaced 80% of Russian pipeline gas, and in doing so reduced Russian gas import dependence from over 50% to just over 10% (von der Leyen, 2023).

The current energy crisis started in 2021 due to – among other factors – high fuel demand connected to the post-pandemic recovery (Le Billon et al., 2021) and was exacerbated by the February 2022 Russian invasion[1] of Ukraine (Bricout et al., 2022;

[1] Russia invaded Eastern Ukraine in 2014.

Steffen and Patt, 2022). This put energy security high on the agenda for many countries world-wide (Żuk and Żuk, 2022a), including the EU and its member states (Mišík, 2022). The European Commission has long proposed policy and regulatory solutions focused on energy efficiency and increased domestic renewable energy sources, and did so in response to these crises too (European Commission, 2020a, 2022a). Due to the nature of EU energy policy integration – particularly member states' sovereignty over their energy mixes[2] (Thaler and Pakalkaite, 2021) – member states have chosen different ways to secure their energy supplies (Mišík and Nosko, 2023b).

The energy transition is uneven. Whilst some member states in recent years doubled down on decarbonisation efforts and increased deployment of renewables, others opted for solutions that challenge the EU's goal of reaching carbon neutrality by 2050 (European Council, 2019a). In 2022 EU countries reactivated twenty-six coal plants, most visibly seventeen in Germany, also prolonging the lifespan of some (IEA, 2022a). Similarly, Poland proposed 'to essentially pause the ETS [Emission Trading System]' to support electricity generation from domestic coal for energy security reasons (von Homeyer et al., 2022, p. 131), and in January 2023 the Bulgarian parliament voted to renegotiate the country's coal phaseout plans with the Commission (Reuters, 2023).

With the decision to rapidly wean the EU off Russian fuels, some EU member countries considered using coal as a replacement for increasingly scarce and expensive natural gas (Kuzemko et al., 2022). Coal, despite the high costs of carbon allowances within the Emission Trading System, remained relatively cheap, and importantly several EU countries had significant coal reserves and were able to produce it domestically (JRC, 2021), in contrast to predominantly imported oil or natural gas. Coal then has been recently considered by several member states as a suitable source for electricity generation (but also heating) and a guarantor of energy security (Zakeri et al., 2022). Moreover, coal has been used world-wide also to cover increased electricity demand supporting economic recovery following the Covid-19 pandemic, and in 2021 coal use was larger than in the pre-pandemic year of 2019 (IEA, 2022a), contributing to record emissions in 2021 (IEA, 2022b), after a pandemic-driven decline in 2020 (Kikstra et al., 2021).

Whilst the EU maintained an emissions reduction trajectory between 2019 and 2021 (EEA, 2022), the energy crisis that emerged in 2021 raised the question for governments whether to prioritise – at least in the short term – security of supply goals and the effect this may have on longer-term energy transition objectives[3] (Sarrica et al., 2016; Tutak and Brodny, 2022). Natural gas had previously been considered by many EU countries, especially western states, as a non-problematic energy source helping them to bridge the gap between the current high carbon fossil

[2] A competence reiterated in the 2007 Lisbon Treaty.

[3] The EU's 2030 goal of cutting greenhouse gas emissions by 55% and its 2050 net zero target.

fuel–based energy systems and a low-carbon future based on renewables and nuclear energy (Caglar, 2022; Gatto, 2022; Gürsan and de Gooyert, 2021).

Such an energy transition is necessary to avoid, or reverse, irreversible changes to our climate (Hoegh-Guldberg et al., 2019; Jankó et al., 2020). The effects of climate change are increasingly apparent, including within Europe, with wide-ranging effects on health, water and food security, conflict and migration (Leimbach and Giannousakis, 2019). Production and consumption of energy is closely implicated; in 2010 the energy supply sector was responsible for 35% of emissions (IPCC, 2014). Energy and climate policies are therefore closely interlinked within a wider framework of energy transitions, to decarbonise energy production and consumption whilst maintaining security of energy supply and reasonable energy prices (Bonsu, 2020; Iyer et al., 2017). A growing interlinkage between energy and climate policies has occurred at the EU level, where these two policies have become priority agendas since the mid-2000s (Skjærseth, 2021; Skjærseth et al., 2016); with interconnected objectives related to the energy trilemma (Šprajc et al., 2019): supply security and solidarity, a single internal energy market, and a focus on energy efficiency and decarbonisation.

Energy (supply) security and sustainability became an increasingly important objective from the mid-2000s (Eikeland, 2011; Kulovesi and Oberthür, 2020; Maltby, 2013; Tsiropoulos et al., 2020). Yet for many states within the EU, until 2022 threats to supply security had not been considered high, with internal market legislation and funding considered to be improving resilience to potential disruptions, bolstered by the emerging transition to domestic renewable energy sources. Even when discussing energy infrastructure diversification or security of supplies within the EU, the solutions were predominantly internal – improving interconnections between member states (Selei and Takácsné Tóth, 2022) or creating rules that will enable member states impacted by insufficient energy supplies to request emergency supplies from fellow member states (Trokoudi, 2017). Despite diversification objectives the EU's energy import dependency decreased by just 0.3% in 2020 compared with 2005 (Eurostat, 2023a). In the same period dependency on Russian gas increased from 38% (Anderson, 2008) to 43% (European Commission, 2021a). Internal market measures were based on assumptions of gas sufficiency within the EU, that only its distribution among member states could be problematic. During 2022, many western and northern countries – including Germany and Finland – started to look for emergency measures to improve access to new sources of natural gas from third countries including through new liquefied natural gas (LNG) terminals (Kurmayer, 2022a; Vanttinen, 2022).

However, for Central and Eastern European states (Bulgaria, Croatia, Czechia, Estonia, Hungary, Latvia, Lithuania, Poland, Romania, Slovakia and Slovenia) energy security is not a new issue. It had been a priority for them before EU accession during three rounds of eastern enlargement in 2004, 2007, and 2013 (Epstein and Jacoby, 2014) and during their first years of membership

(Mišík, 2010), even before the 2009 gas supply disruption that highlighted energy security issues in, and related to, the region (Maltby, 2013; Mišík, 2019; Stulberg, 2015). This book focuses on the CEE region and contributes to the literature by examining the energy transitions underway in the EU, and this interplay between energy and climate policies. CEE has been – despite these countries' interest and high-profile interventions in energy security (and climate policy for some) – an under-researched region.

Our main research question asks: What explains the shape, process and extent of energy transitions in CEE? To answer this question, a set of three sub-questions has been developed: (1) What drives energy and climate policies development in the CEE region? (2) What effect does this region have on EU energy and climate policy? and (3) How do these developments within CEE and the EU link with the global context of energy transitions? Derived from the conceptual framework these questions are broadly linked to the role of three different factors that shape energy and climate policy preferences: (1) modes of climate and energy governance, (2) foreign policy and (3) societal factors. Two main arguments are presented in the book. First, that energy security is a dominant issue for the CEE region with climate policy a secondary concern; second, that CEE countries are more heterogeneous, and climate and energy policies are considerably more contested within the region than is often claimed. The interlinkage between energy and climate policy is central to the book and guides the analysis in the individual chapters.

1.1 HOW DOES THIS BOOK DIFFER FROM EXISTING WORKS?

The research presented in this book fills an important gap in the literature. Beyond isolated book chapters and journal articles, relatively little has been written that addresses the interlinkage between climate and energy policy within CEE, despite the region becoming increasingly important in shaping EU policies (see, for example, chapters in edited volumes by Andersen et al. 2017 or Szulecki 2018). The existing book-length literature to date has tended to focus on energy (Birchfield and Duffield, 2011; Tosun et al., 2015), including specific sector areas like renewables (Dekanozishvili, 2023) or natural gas (Mete, 2020a). Other books have focused on climate policies (Boasson and Wettestad, 2013; Dupont, 2016; Jordan et al., 2010) individually and either at the EU level (Goldthau and Sitter, 2015; Herranz-Surrallés et al., 2022) or by looking at one or a small selection of member states (Kopp, 2015; Mišík, 2019). This is the case not only with monographs (for example, Boersma 2015), but also with textbooks (see, for instance, Pollak et al., 2016). Although academic journals between 2004 and 2019 showed growing interest in the region, articles examining policy (i.e., written within social science disciplines) constituted only a small group, while the scholarship was dominated by articles written within (natural) science disciplines (Oravcová et al., 2022). Moreover, energy security was covered only minimally in articles on energy in CEE, particularly relative to the importance of this topic for the region, and the influence of the region on the EU.

Although a book-length text offers much more space to examine the complex nature of energy and climate policy, this monograph acknowledges the challenge of taking a more holistic view and therefore concentrates on a single under-researched region: CEE and its member states while covering both energy and climate policy. This approach permits a focus on energy policy in the context of a transition to a decarbonised energy system, the climate policies of the EU and its member states, as well as the co-constitution of policy between these two levels. This book thus contributes to existing literature in terms of its regional and policy scope, and engagement with the issue of energy policy in the context of transition and climate change policy (Dupont and Oberthür, 2015; Oberthür et al., 2022). While the monograph discusses the re-prioritisation of security of supply over climate of several EU member states since 2021, it embeds this within broader and longer-term EU energy transition developments. It is, indeed, the interplay between energy security and climate policy – presenting a much larger and more long-term challenge for CEE countries than for the rest of the EU – that is at the core of this monograph.

The book highlights three dimensions. First, in focusing on energy policy the book considers the important interplay with climate policies of CEE countries that have not been subject to book-length analysis. The monograph provides an analysis of energy transformation, changing energy policy in the context of national and EU climate policy objectives, and the interlinkages between them, rather than treating the policy areas as discrete. Second, the effect of both the EU on its member states and the member states on the energy policy development of the EU is considered, thus the Europeanisation of these newer CEE member states as well as their increasing influence on the EU's energy and climate policies. Such a regional perspective permits the coverage of different issues connected to energy and climate policies and the interplay between the EU and member state levels. Third, the book provides an analysis of these two policies and their mutual interplay that is crucial for understanding the constraints and opportunities, and perception of these, within the CEE region. Energy policy is a shared competence between the EU and the member states as defined in the Lisbon Treaty (Roeben, 2018). Whilst the EU sets rules in different areas of energy and climate policies (for example, environmental standards, liberalisation rules, level of renewables, some dimensions of energy security, energy safety), the member states still have competences when it comes to developing their national energy policies (particularly in connection to their energy mixes) and have a central position in defining the scope and pace of further energy and climate policy integration.

1.2 THE MAIN OBJECTIVE AND ARGUMENTS OF THE BOOK

The main objective of the book is to analyse the energy and climate policies of CEE countries, and explain how they have affected, and been affected by, EU policy.

In doing so we consider this region from a European and global perspective, exploring the specificity of the area, but also the way changes in the political economy of energy policy and climate change in the region reflect – and therefore help us to understand – broader dynamics. We build on existing research on energy challenges and transitions that are of a transnational nature, and which cut across policy and issue areas. In doing so the analysis provides insights on a set of issues whose importance is crucial to understanding the future of energy and climate policy in the region, the EU and beyond. We also extend analysis beyond the narrowly state-centric, to explore the relationship between member states and the EU, between states and energy companies, the variations of state-controlled/owned and state-involved energy companies, and the role of societal and other non-governmental actors.

The first argument presented highlights the role of energy security for CEE countries. The region's historical connection to Russia, its main energy supplier at least until 2022 and in the case of Hungary and Slovakia also beyond, has been embedded in physical infrastructure and political institutions, resulting in a degree of path dependency (Ćetković and Buzogány, 2020). Fossil fuel dependence has been perceived as a source of vulnerability, and energy has been framed as a key security issue long before the 2021 energy crisis highlighted the importance of energy security for the whole EU (Binhack and Tichý, 2012; Lehtveer et al., 2016; Szulecki and Kusznir, 2018). General, though not universal, fears of energy supply disruption and Russian political interference have stimulated some regional cooperation and efforts to diversify energy supplies (often co-financed by the EU), as well as providing the catalyst for vocal and at times effective lobbying to reinforce energy security cooperation at the EU level. In contrast, climate policy has often been considered by many CEE countries an issue of secondary importance, undermining economic development and potentially a direct challenge to achieving energy security. This has been translated into a cautious approach to climate change mitigation in European and international forums.

The second argument is that in spite of implicit and in some cases also explicit assumptions of many existing studies (for example, Austvik, 2016; Jordan and Moore, 2020) the EU's CEE states are not a homogenous group and have divergent energy and climate preferences and policy priorities. Poland is often the most visible member state, and often a 'speaker' for the region, contributing to a degree of east-west divide on certain issues (von Homeyer et al., 2022). Although it is possible to identify certain common positions of these countries when it comes to the main issues connected to energy and climate policies (for example, the importance of energy security and a rather reserved attitude towards environmental issues; Skjærseth, 2018), these countries have developed a much more diverse set of preferences when it comes to the specificities of these policies.

Moreover, CEE countries are differentiated by the extent to which they support or oppose issues of energy security and climate policy. Therefore, the book claims that CEE countries remain arguably a diverse – even an increasingly diverse – set of countries. Energy dependence and threat perception vary in the region, as do attitudes to concrete issues connected to climate policy. Broader political dynamics are also at work, which go beyond the borders of the region. The opening of electricity and gas markets to competition as part of the EU's internal market restructuring has played a major role, and issues of redistribution and climate justice between 'the East' and 'the West' in Europe mirror those between the Global North and the Global South in international climate negotiations (Eicke et al., 2021). Our research considers the regional groupings within the EU that are active, including the Visegrad Group (Czechia, Hungary, Slovakia, Poland) and the Baltic States (Estonia, Latvia, Lithuania).

1.3 ENERGY POLICY OF THE CEE COUNTRIES

Whilst energy technologies and sources have fluctuated in popularity, there is also significant path dependency and continuity in energy policy within the CEE region despite changes in governments. An objective of the book is to explain the drivers and challenges associated with energy transitions and placing them in a historical context. This allows for an analysis that moves beyond a snapshot description of the contemporary period and balancing different energy security challenges in the 2020s to a broader understanding of the evolution of climate and energy politics and systems in the CEE region. For example, in several member states a drive for energy 'independence' has been a long-term goal despite changes in government (for example, in Czechia, Poland, Slovakia and Lithuania), as have broader climate and energy objectives (though strategies to shape EU policies on these issues have evolved).

The book analyses several energy sectors. Natural gas plays a key role when it comes to the energy security of CEE countries (Kotek et al., 2023; Selei and Takácsné Tóth, 2022). Renewable and nuclear energy sources and related issues of decarbonising and decentralising electricity systems in a transition away from coal also play a key role (Janda, 2018; Mezősi et al., 2020). Whilst oil is included in our analysis this energy source has a secondary importance within the region. Although CEE countries have specific energy policy preferences, they were not particularly active in shaping EU energy policy development immediately after their EU accession, starting in 2004. This changed dramatically following the 2006 (and particularly 2009) gas supply disruptions (Bocquillon and Maltby, 2017; Mišík, 2015). CEE countries' interests were linked to a sense of vulnerability due to a lack of gas market competition, with Gazprom often the monopoly supplier, vulnerability to supply disruptions, few connections to other gas markets and relatively high energy prices.

However, CEE countries' responses to energy challenges have differed. Russian natural gas supply disruptions affected many EU countries, but it was those from CEE that were disproportionately affected in 2006, while a repeat in 2009 left countries such as Slovakia and Bulgaria without access to natural gas for almost three weeks (Kratochvíl and Mišík, 2020). The energy crisis that emerged in 2021 and was exacerbated by the Russian invasion of Ukraine affects all EU members and put energy security at the forefront of EU's energy policy (Steffen and Patt, 2022). The response of CEE countries to the crisis has varied, with most of them supporting EU's effort to cut itself off from Russian energy supplies; however, Hungary has taken a negative stance towards EU-wide positions (for example, when it comes to tougher sanctions towards Russia; Barigazzi and Kijewski, 2022; Rankin, 2022) that earned it the nickname 'Russian Trojan horse' in the past (Orenstein and Kelemen, 2017).

These 'wake up calls' shaped CEE countries' preferences and participation in EU policy, with a general preference for deeper integration to address what they considered to be energy insecurity (Mišík, 2016), and contributed to energy security becoming a priority at the EU level, which accelerated markedly in 2021, to an extent reflecting the concerns of CEE. Poland has been particularly active in energy security proposals (Roth, 2011; Szulecki, 2020), with the Energy Union concept originating with the Polish Prime Minister (Tusk, 2014). Other countries, for example, Czechia, have been actively diversifying their energy sources since the 1990s. The Baltic States have had different, mostly cost-related, energy challenges, although they have also been subject to gas flow interruptions by Russia as their only supplier since the 1990s (Mišík and Prachárová, 2016).

I.4 CLIMATE POLICY AND THE CEE COUNTRIES

Support for more ambitious climate goals is not a dominant feature for the CEE region. Many countries in the region generally associate these with high potential costs for industry, electricity producers and households; link their implementation to substantial job losses; and often oppose EU climate policies (Von Homeyer et al., 2022, p. 132). There has often been a high degree of consensus between governments, political parties, industry and the general public on this opposition, with proposals in favour of burden sharing, and compensation and side-payments for agreeing to climate policy (Skjærseth, 2015). However, we can identify divergent preferences among CEE countries regarding energy efficiency and renewable policies, and preferences regarding the Emissions Trading System. Poland has opposed climate policy goals, partly due to the significance of domestic coal in its energy generation (Bocquillon and Maltby, 2017). Czechia and Slovakia have also been critical of the EU's climate policy goals to protect their domestic industries. On the other hand, although not often showing direct support, the Baltic States were less critical of the EU's climate policy and Lithuania has been supportive of ambitious climate proposals (Green Growth Group, 2013).

The book highlights and explains energy system changes, including the emerging role for renewable energy within the context of material energy systems, ideas regarding energy transitions and energy (in)dependence, and state–civil society relationships; these facilitate and at times provide obstacles to energy policy transitions. We will demonstrate that energy transitions vary considerably within the region in terms of pace and character. However, the energy crisis since 2021 indicates the potential for a catalyst to a revolution rather than evolution in the EU's energy transition towards renewable energy sources as the need to increase domestic energy production for energy security reasons is prioritised by the Commission (European Commission, 2022a), many member states, but also the public (Steffen and Patt, 2022).

For several reasons the CEE region is of importance for our understanding of broader issues connected to the development of EU energy and climate policies, as well as for understanding global energy transitions. First, CEE countries are playing an increasingly important role in the EU's climate and energy policy-making, and to understand the EU's 2020 and 2030 climate and energy policy, as well as decarbonisation objectives for 2050, requires an understanding of the national policies including those of the CEE region. In an EU consisting of twenty-seven member states a group of eleven countries can have an important influence – whether they work in unison, in regional sub-groups, or join different like-minded groups with the older member states. The difficulty of adopting the goal of carbon neutrality by 2050 that was first rejected by four CEE countries (Mišík and Oravcová, 2021a) illustrates well the importance of even a small number of member states in EU's climate and energy policy decision-making. An examination of CEE countries sheds light on the development of the policies in question at the EU level.

Second, challenges faced by the CEE countries – especially those connected to balancing energy and climate issues – are mirrored at the global level. Understanding the CEE experience highlights challenges at the global level and provides lessons regarding how to (or not) approach these. Like emerging economies globally, there is a concern in CEE that climate change mitigation and energy transitions will impose inequitable and unsustainable economic costs, and damage prospects for economic development. In the region the picture is further complicated by the often-central role of foreign policy and security of supply concerns in decision and policy-making. Overall, our analysis of the climate and energy policies and drivers of their development between 2004 and 2023 contributes to an under-researched area. The region has been only at the margins of academic interest, and a discussion about the region and its role within the EU and energy transitions relates to general observations about the nature of energy transition at large.

1.5 STRUCTURE OF THE BOOK

The monograph develops its main arguments and answers to its research questions in three main sections. Chapter 1, in the first part of the book, focuses on a general overview of the development of energy and climate policy within EU and CEE that provides basis for further discussion on the trade-off between these two policies within the book. The chapter outlines the energy and climate objectives of the region, and EU, and policies developed to achieve these, as well as trends and statistics progress towards these. As both policies are crucial for the transition towards a decarbonised economy, this empirical chapter paves way for further analysis in the book and provides general overview of the situation within the EU and the CEE region whilst embedding them in the context of global energy transitions.

The conceptual framework is set out in Chapter 2, from which the key drivers of climate and energy policy are established, and research questions for the book are derived. Drawing from existing literature, we argue that several key factors account for national climate and energy policies, and explain the extent of the region's climate and energy policy homogeneity and heterogeneity. Such an approach enables us to identify the differences between individual CEE countries – for instance, the role of ideas can be used to describe the different understandings of what constitutes energy security issues, and the solutions to these. Some, but certainly not all, countries in the region securitise this issue (e.g., Lithuania and Poland; Sattich et al., 2022; Szulecki and Kusznir, 2018) and frame energy security as a national security challenge, highlighting the foreign policy implications of climate and energy policy and influencing both domestic and EU policy choices. The energy landscape (Bouzarovski, 2009; Bridge et al., 2013) is a set of interconnected social, material and cultural elements, and climate and energy policies are mediated by the political economy of states – within this landscape we draw upon several broad conceptual perspectives on energy transitions, institutional change and understandings of security.

These provide an analytical toolbox to address the interplay of political interests, institutional forces and governance practices within a material and historical context, that of post-socialist EU members from the CEE region with particular energy mixes, infrastructure and foreign policies. Using this toolbox, we explain how key aspects of the energy transition challenge they face – security, economic and environmental – are interpreted and framed, and how national policy and its implementation is shaped. We then explain how the CEE region has in turn shaped, and been shaped by, the EU. This chapter also discusses the methods and data used.

The second part of the book presents three basic types of explanations of different policy preferences related broadly to issues of institutions and governance, foreign policy and societal factors. In its three chapters, this part discusses challenges facing the region and important commonalities between the analysed states. By examining key political and economic factors that determine climate and energy policy (energy governance, foreign policy and societal factors) this part also highlights nationally specific factors that result in a non-homogenous region in terms of climate and energy policy preferences. The book locates itself in the conceptual debates related to explaining national climate and energy policy-making, energy transitions and understandings of security. Chapter 3 looks at the process of restructuring of energy governance in CEE countries, focusing on common patterns and differences in terms of market opening, competition and patterns of ownership. Here it maps efforts towards the liberalisation of the energy sector and explains the enduring variation in political and economic institutions across countries. The challenge of liberalising energy markets while ensuring energy security is discussed in more detail, looking in particular at the implications for the complicated relationship with Russia. Finally, the chapter asks to what extent this restructuring, however incomplete, has permitted an opening of the structure of energy governance to include new actors.

Energy supply security has been a crucial energy policy issue for CEE countries at least since the natural gas supply disruptions of 2006 and 2009. This book argues that energy security plays a generally more important role within the CEE region than issues related to climate change. However, Chapter 4 evaluates the interplay between ideas, institutions and the material nature of energy systems in the development of energy policy. In doing so it also highlights the social construction of energy security, demonstrating that energy security is not self-evident or correlated within the CEE region with dependency on energy imports from Russia. Individual CEE countries perceive energy supplies as a security issue to a different extent, identifying the source and extent of insecurity or risk differently, and the policy solutions to this as a result. While some, for example, Hungary or Bulgaria, have tended to assume a rather relaxed approach to dependence on Russian energy imports, others – most notably Lithuania and Poland – consider energy security one of their main policy issues. The chapter provides further evidence to the second main argument of the book regarding the heterogenous positions towards energy and climate policy of member states in the region.

Chapter 5 focuses on the specific role of social movements and NGOs in energy policy-making in the CEE region. This is structured through a series of case studies that highlight contemporary energy policy issues, specifically with relation to energy pricing, issues of equity and energy poverty, nuclear energy, shale gas and renewable energy. The chapter examines how these issues are framed, justified and legitimised, and the extent of broader societal participation and support. To provide context this chapter considers the developing role of civil society in the region, including legacies of socialism; the historical and contemporary role for societal input into general policy-making; changes in state–civil society relations; and the development of NGOs and interest groups and their influence on climate and energy policy. To contribute to the explanatory value of the monograph, this chapter also analyses in detail three factors developed within the theoretical chapter – the role of ideas, institutions and material nature of energy systems. The chapter examines their impact on the energy transition of the CEE region from a state–civil society relations perspective. It studies these issues in four sub-sections: fuel/energy poverty, the shale gas debate and the role of opposition on environmental grounds, nuclear energy and public participation, and local and community energy initiatives.

The third part of the book focuses in Chapter 6 on the impact of CEE countries on the development of climate and energy policies at the EU level. It is argued that states in the region demonstrate some shared preferences and utilise regional groupings to promote these at the EU level. However, groupings are often ad hoc/issue-based rather than regional. In highlighting both the convergence and divergence, this book then considers the pace and direction of EU climate and energy development since EU enlargements starting in 2004. The chapter discusses the contribution of CEE countries to the development of EU policy – from Polish efforts to create 'Energy NATO' in 2006 (Roth, 2011), CEE countries' efforts to improve energy security following the 2006 and 2009 gas disruptions, and the 2014 Energy Union proposal (Tusk, 2014) to the reaction to the Russian invasion of Ukraine in 2022. The chapter argues that the security dimension was given the priority by CEE countries at the EU level (Bocquillon and Maltby, 2017; Mišík, 2015). They brought the issue of (mainly external) energy security to the EU table during the accession negotiations and immediate post-accession period; however, their preferences were often not shared by older members (Mayer, 2008). The 2006 and 2009 gas supply disruptions shifted the focus towards energy security in the region, and at the EU level. From 2021 the EU's dependency on, and vulnerability to, energy imports from Russia was brought into sharp focus. Both internal (related to internal market development and increased interconnectedness) and external (related to supply sources and routes) energy security has been highlighted by the CEE countries as issues to be dealt with at the EU level.

In Chapter 7 the book goes beyond the discussion on the region and EU and provides an examination of how specific positions of CEE countries towards energy and climate policy fit within the global energy transition. The chapter highlights the ability of regional experience to provide insights into global energy transition issues, and the lessons the region can offer for discussion about how to approach the pathways towards carbon-neutral economies. A link is created between our findings from the CEE region and international energy transitions and climate and energy policy, demonstrating that many challenges of countries in CEE are not unique when placed in an international context. As the region has to adapt to EU climate and energy policies, but is at the same time able to shape these, it provides insights into the process of developing and implementing decarbonisation policy. The EU has also been widely considered, and self-identifies, as an international climate change policy leader, so our analysis of how EU enlargement has shaped EU 2020, 2030 and broader climate and energy policy is a contribution to understanding the EU's international role and future prospects. This chapter provides a conclusion through the argument that the experience of CEE countries within the EU and their (limited) ability to influence the community serves as an example for other regional groups and governance systems.

1

The Development of Energy and Climate Policy in the EU and CEE

1.1 INTRODUCTION

Central to this monograph is the examination of the interlinkage and trade-offs between climate and energy policy, as two main components of energy transitions,[1] with a focus on Central and Eastern Europe (CEE). This chapter provides a general overview of the development within this region and at the EU level,[2] introducing the interplay between these policies at both levels. As energy and climate policies are crucial for the transition towards a decarbonised economy, and the stated objective of the EU and its member states, this contextual chapter paves the way for further analysis in the book. It introduces empirical data and trends and provides a general overview of both contemporary developments and the historical context. In examining the key energy and climate challenges, the chapter outlines regional and broader EU objectives, policies developed to achieve these, as well as trends that illustrate the extent of progress towards these objectives, and explains this development with reference to the primary drivers and obstacles. The context to the EU's positioning as an international climate actor (Godzimirski, 2016; von Lucke, 2021) is briefly examined (Chapter 7 focuses on this), along with the emergence of energy security as an EU priority (Szulecki, 2018b) that CEE countries have contributed to. Energy security was re-prioritised by the EU following the Russian full-scale invasion of Ukraine in 2022 (Mišík, 2022); however, for the CEE countries energy policy had generally a priority for more than a decade. Climate change, on the other hand, has been of lower priority for CEE countries, and some – although not all – have opposed the EU's climate ambitions (Brauers and Oei, 2020).

The process of energy transitions within the CEE region follows, and is connected to, the major political and economic transitions since the end of the 1980s

[1] We use plural to underline our multiple countries approach and stress the argument that there is heterogeneity here in terms of the form and pace of the transitions within the CEE region.

[2] We use EU to also refer to the European Community, its identity until 1992.

(Gros and Steinherr, 2004; Ürge-Vorsatz et al., 2006). We discuss the impact of these rapid and significant industrial and political changes on the economy and the environment within the region, considering the political, economic, societal and infrastructural legacies of the socialist period. The region is characterised by significant reductions in carbon emissions and improvements in energy efficiency since the 1990s (Mišík and Oravcová, 2021b). Whilst there is a political dimension to this, with environmental movements an important part of the anti-communist opposition (Fagan, 2004; Szulecka and Szulecki, 2022), uncompetitive industries lost state support and subsidies and struggled to survive when exposed to greater competition, resulting in a marked reduction in industrial production. Decreasing carbon emissions was a silver lining of this process that resulted in economic slowdown, increased unemployment and other negative social consequences.

During the 1990s the European Commission (hereafter the Commission) prioritised environmental issues in the region (Mišík, 2015) as the level of environmental protection was very low due to four decades of communist regimes that saw nature as a source of wealth. Other Commission priorities during this period included energy market liberalisation and ensuring that incoming members had fully adopted the EU's environmental and energy legislation (*acquis communautaire*). The Commission concentrated on the capacity and political will of candidate countries to transpose existing Community rules into their legal systems; the preferences of these countries were not prioritised (Tosun, 2011). Therefore, energy security was hardly discussed during the process of accession, although several CEE countries considered the issue to be a priority. In general, accession negotiations were characterised by the asymmetrical position of the candidate countries vis-à-vis the EU. The prospect of EU membership was so significant, and the EU's conditionality so inflexible, that EU rules were implemented despite the often serious adaptational pressure on the CEE countries, and the associated costs of accession (Haughton, 2007).

After CEE countries joined the EU in three phases (2004, 2007 and 2013), they were formally able to upload their own preferences on energy issues at the EU level. However, these new EU members were initially limited in both their will and capacity to shape (energy) policy. At first they tended to be followers rather than leaders in developing policies, and when they started to pursue their own priorities they were often criticised for following neither formal nor informal 'rules of the game' regarding negotiation styles or decision-making (Copsey and Pomorska, 2014; Roth, 2011). Only in time were they fully socialised into the EU and its mechanisms, allowing them to shape policy development more effectively. The 2006 and 2009 gas supply disruptions acted as focusing events within the EU, highlighting the security of supply concerns that dominated the energy policy preferences of many of the new member states, and spurring the EU institutions to focus on addressing energy security issues, with the energy crisis that emerged in 2021 having a similar though more dramatic effect (Kuzemko et al., 2022; Osička and Černoch, 2022;

Rodríguez-Fernández et al., 2020). Several years into their membership the CEE member states, often with the support of the Commission,[3] also became more active in energy security policy, supporting EU proposals to diversify energy supply, develop solidarity mechanisms and increase funding for energy infrastructure projects (Jonek-Kowalska, 2022; Mata Pérez et al., 2019; Prontera and Plenta, 2020).

Climate policy increased in importance once the EU became a contractual party to the 1997 Kyoto protocol (Skjærseth and Wettestad, 2008), but it was not a priority for the CEE countries. However, post-accession these states began to develop administrative capacity and expertise, to channel political will into a more focused set of policy areas and to shape EU climate policy-making (Bocquillon and Maltby, 2017). In the aftermath of the 2008 financial crisis EU climate policy development to an extent reflected, or at least accommodated, the interests of the CEE region. During this period the EU's climate ambition decreased, influenced by CEE countries (Ćetković and Buzogány, 2019). Climate policy was reprioritised with the adoption of the 2015 Energy Union initiative (European Commission, 2015a) and the 2019 European Green Deal as a response to the EU's Paris Agreement commitments (European Commission, 2021b). Post-pandemic, the EU is attempting to balance the objective of a sustainable and green recovery driven in part by renewables, with a short-term emphasis on security of supply through non-Russian fossil fuels that runs counter to this.

This chapter provides support particularly for the first main argument of this book, that energy security is generally prioritised over climate change in CEE. Post accession, these countries started to vocally support the former while opposing development of ambitious climate goals. This brings us to the second argument presented within this book: CEE is not a homogenous region; the individual countries differ in their positions on the two interrelated policy fields; and the political economy of their climate and energy polices also differs. The chapter identifies the main differences between CEE countries, providing a starting point for further discussion in later chapters. It is important here to stress that this heterogeneity also applied to energy security prior to 2022; countries in the region identified threats and solutions differently, including their relations with Russia and whether they perceive the resource-rich country as a guarantor of or threat to their security. This has changed significantly after the Russian invasion of Ukraine in 2022; however, there remain key differences. For example, Hungary signed a new long-term gas deal with Gazprom in September 2021, is developing a nuclear power plant through Rosatom, and has opposed stronger sanctions (Barigazzi and Kijewski, 2022; Rankin, 2022). Rather than a regional bloc, CEE countries have also often acted alone on energy issues (particularly Poland, and Hungary in the 2020s), through ad hoc groupings and in more stable groups like the Visegrad

[3] Where their preferences and objectives align on issues such as the objective of diversification of energy supplies, including away from import dependence on Russia.

Group – Czechia, Hungary, Poland and Slovakia – or as a group of Baltic States – Estonia, Latvia, Lithuania.

This chapter proceeds with a historical overview of the EU's activities in both energy policy and environmental and climate policy. Although there is a difference between environmental and climate policy, the latter is based on the former and they both have played an important role not only in the accession process of CEE countries to the EU, but also during their membership. The following section presents a broad picture of climate and energy policies, outlining the policy frameworks within which member states from CEE operate. The section highlights the links between climate and energy policy and the development of energy transitions within the EU and beyond. It argues that energy security was a relatively marginal issue for the EU until the 2000s. It also introduces the efforts of the EU to bring its climate goals to the international level, situating the EU as a global climate actor (Minas and Ntousas, 2018; Wunderlich, 2020). Since 2022 the EU's decarbonisation efforts have increasingly been viewed not only through the climate lens, but also as a way to strengthen the EU's energy security by expanding domestic renewable sources of energy.

The third section of this chapter introduces the EU's climate and energy goals, including those set for 2020, 2030 and 2050, and examines how these targets have developed as well as the EU's progress towards achieving them. The fourth section focuses on the CEE countries and outlines their energy transitions, considering climate and energy policy and key changes since they embarked on a path of democratisation and the transition towards liberal market economies. It introduces the historical legacies that continue to influence significantly CEE countries' climate and energy policies and their particular interest in energy security. This section also discusses the impact of EU membership on these policies.

1.2 THE DEVELOPMENT OF THE EU'S CLIMATE AND ENERGY POLICY

Whilst energy security became a priority for the EU in the second half of the 2000s and again in 2022, it had been on the agenda since the EU's foundation. As early as 1951 the European Coal and Steel Community (ECSC) set out the concept of 'Security of Supply' in Community law and presented it as a main objective. In 1957 the European Atomic Energy Community (EURATOM) Treaty led to community policy in the field of nuclear energy, and the potential for central intervention to 'ensure that all users in the Community receive a regular and equitable supply' (Euratom, 1957, para. 57). These two developments provided an early example of 'energy policy tools based on exclusive supranational powers vested in a central authority' (Andoura et al., 2010, p. 2). These were followed by claims by the member states that security of supply was an aim to be achieved through diversification of supplies and decreased import dependence (Council of the EU, 1964). Whilst the

Commission argued that a Community energy policy was necessary (European Commission, 1968), this did not prove persuasive, and energy policy remained in the hands of member states until the late 1990s.

The 1973 'oil crisis' highlighted concerns about the EU's vulnerability to interruptions of the energy supply. The EU already had in place rules concerning emergency stockpiling of crude oil when the crisis broke out; these were further strengthened as a result of the embargo on the United Kingdom and the Netherlands, with strategic oil stockpiles increased to cover longer supply interruptions (McGowan, 2011). However, despite repeated concerns being raised by the Commission about energy security, member states resisted transferring their sovereignty in this area to supranational institutions. Instead, they focused on individual solutions that varied between countries, including indigenous nuclear energy in France, and North Sea oil and gas in the Netherlands and the United Kingdom (Kirchner and Berk, 2010, p. 869). There was little further energy policy development until the Single European Act came into force in 1987 with an objective of an internal market, including in energy (Matláry, 1997). The 1990s saw the development of a nascent energy liberalisation process with the First Energy Package, containing liberalisation directives for electricity (1996) and gas (1998) (Brutschin, 2015). However, the focus was on the internal energy market and market liberalisation, with only limited attention paid to addressing the issue of security of energy supplies.

Emerging energy security concerns were based on the realisation that energy supplies could be disrupted for political reasons, and the concern that the world was approaching an era of 'peak oil' in which supply would enter a terminal decline and be unable to match (ever) growing demand. Orttung and Perovic (2012) highlighted that US oil production peaked in 1970 and then declined steadily until 2008,[4] supporting Hubbert's 1956 peak oil argument (Hubbert, 1956). The former head of the US Department of Energy James Schlesinger concluded in 2005 that there were a number of political and economic problems linked to the 'finite limit to conventional oil [and] the long-term, fundamental problem of oil supply' (cited in Energy Bulletin, 2005).

Realist scholars (such as Klare, 2009) and many governments assumed that there was a resultant risk of competition for access and control of energy resources from unreliable sources or transit routes (Dannreuther, 2013). For example, Russia's 2009 National Security Strategy claimed that 'international policy for the long term will focus on the possession of energy sources' and that 'under the conditions of competition for resources [it] cannot be excluded resolving problems by military force' (Russian Government, 2009). In the United States, President George W. Bush used his 2006 State of the Union Address to argue that 'America is addicted to oil which is often imported from unstable parts of the world' (Bush, 2006), a sentiment repeated

[4] Though between 2008 and 2015 US oil production almost doubled (EIA, 2018).

three years later by President Barack Obama, who stated that 'America's dependence on oil is one of the most serious threats that our nation has faced' (Obama, 2009). The dangers of depending on oil imports were highlighted by President Joe Biden following the Russian invasion of Ukraine; in his 2022 State of the Union Address he asked domestic oil companies to invest more in domestic production (Biden, 2023).

The development of environmental policy within the EU can be traced back to the 1970s (Skjærseth et al., 2016). In 1972 the EU, plus the United Kingdom, Ireland and Denmark, then non-members, agreed at the Stockholm UN conference on the Human Environment that economic growth should be considered alongside environmental protection. This can be considered a turning point for the EU's approach towards the environment and the nascent development of its environmental policy dimension. Progress was slow, however. There was no further development during the 1970s and first half of the 1980s. Climate policy was first explicitly addressed by the Commission in 1985, and by the European Parliament in 1986 (Skjærseth et al., 2016). The 1986 Single European Act enshrined environmental protection within the EU's legal basis with the aim 'to preserve, protect and improve the quality of the environment, to contribute towards protecting human health, and to ensure a prudent and rational utilization of natural resources' (European Community, 1986). The EU was involved in the 1987 Montreal Protocol, a global convention on the ozone layer. This successfully negotiated a ban on chlorofluorocarbon production, which was directly linked to holes in the ozone layer.

The EU has also focused on embedding the concept of sustainable development within EU domestic and foreign policies. One example is in fishing policy, where there has been a significant shift away from the exploitation of fishing stocks to their sustainable management within the EU fishing industry, as well as highlighting a 'global commons' in the policy area at the international level, and promoting the concept through development aid and conditionality in trade agreements with third countries (Vogler, 2017). However, early attempts in the 1980s to establish a climate and energy package failed – with little progress on developing synergies between the policies or addressing the distributional challenges associated with the objective (Skjærseth, 2016).

The 1990s: Energy Liberalisation and the Initial Development of Climate Policy

In 1995, the EU set out three key objectives for energy policy – economic competitiveness, security of energy supply and environmental protection (European Commission, 1995) – yet the focus was primarily on the internal energy market at this stage. The first energy market liberalisation directives (the so-called first energy package) established rules for electricity and natural gas in order to facilitate the development of the internal energy market, and were adopted in 1996 and 1998, respectively (Herweg, 2017). The objective was to introduce meaningful competition in gas and electricity markets, as the tendency was for these to be characterised until the 1990s and beyond by the dominance of vertically integrated state-owned energy companies with monopolistic positions in the market, combining all activities – production, transition and distribution of energy to end customers. By 'unbundling' these different activities and breaking up vertically integrated energy companies, the aim was to foster the creation of a competitive market environment, with lower prices for consumers.

The first set of directives was a result of a compromise between the Commission, which was pursuing a strong liberal agenda aiming to dismantle monopolistic, vertically integrated energy companies and open the energy market to competition, and, on the other hand, member states striving to protect their national champions, often (partly) owned by governments. The results of the first round of liberalisation were, from the Commission's perspective, less than satisfactory as member states managed to protect the interests of their own energy sectors rather than the interests of customers. The slow pace of liberalisation during the 1990s and only limited impact of the first set of liberalisation rules on the electricity and natural gas markets led the Commission to propose the second and third energy packages that were adopted in 2003/2004 (electricity and gas) and in 2009 (both sectors) (Batzella, 2018).

With regard to climate policy, the EU was highly influential during the 1990s in moving the Kyoto Protocol from an outline to an implemented global governance regime (Groenleer and Van Schaik, 2007): a widely accepted leadership position was established, in the absence of a proactive United States, and as a major current and historical carbon emitter and economic power (Vogler, 2017). The 1992 Earth Summit in Rio established the international principle of 'common but differentiated responsibilities', whereby economically developed states would take the lead in combatting climate change (UN, 1992). Chapter 7 discusses the global context and the EU's leadership efforts at the international level in more detail.

Whilst the EU is constituted solely of advanced liberal economies, the 'common but differentiated' principle also applies here – forming an integral part of the Burden Sharing Agreement within the EU's application of the Kyoto Protocol and its Emissions Trading System (ETS). The ETS was adopted by the EU in 2003 as a market-based policy to address climate change, a global first based on capping and trading carbon emissions (Skjærseth and Wettestad, 2010). The EU is constituted of those with strikingly different capacities to implement climate policies, not to mention divergent historical responsibilities for the problem (Wang and Paavola, 2023). The EU's implementation of the Kyoto Protocol set out that 'cohesion' states within the EU were permitted to continue to increase emissions, balanced by major emitters such as the United Kingdom and Germany offering major reductions. This is a central issue in contemporary EU climate and energy policy, as CEE countries continue to lobby for allowances (and other types of concessions) to expand their emissions or limit their reduction as part of 'catching up' economically with the rest of the EU. The book analyses these issues more closely in Chapters 3 and 6, examining the growing influence of CEE countries on EU climate and energy policy.

The 2000s: Energy Security and Climate Policy, and the Trade-Offs between Them

The 2000s saw a dramatic change in approach by the EU towards energy policy issues, with the establishment of energy security as one of its main strategic objectives, with policies, legislation and financial support targeted at addressing this. Until this point divergent member state energy mixes and complacency regarding energy import dependency were key obstacles to the development of a coherent energy security policy. This change was triggered by a combination of rising energy prices, decreasing domestic production and the eastern enlargements that coincided with the gas supply disruptions of 2006 and 2009. For example, although energy dependence was a 'special concern' for the EU as the largest world importer of gas and oil in 2003, it was not considered one of five 'key threats' (European Council, 2003, p. 14).

Energy security evolved into a major issue later in the decade at first due to an increase in energy prices. For example, the price of oil quintupled between 2000 and 2008, while the price of gas increased by a factor of 3.5 (European Commission, 2011a). Energy prices became a serious issue of concern, particularly given forecasts that they would steadily increase from the mid-2010s to 2050 (European Commission, 2011a); oil was predicted to increase in price by 50%, and gas prices were expected to double, leaving them six and five times higher, respectively, than in 2000. Whilst oil and gas prices dropped significantly in the wake of the 2008 financial crisis, the price of energy remained on the EU agenda. Although not an issue restricted to CEE, a 2015 EU study by the Commission concluded that for most CEE countries, energy poverty affected approximately 20% of households, compared with just over 5% of older member states (European Commission, 2015b), and in January 2018 the EU launched an Energy Poverty Observatory to address the more than 50 million households struggling to 'attain adequate warmth [and] pay their utility bills on time' (European Commission, 2018a).

Security of supply concerns also increased, particularly during the second half of 2000s. The EU experienced disruptions of Russian gas supplies in 2006 and 2009 as a result of contractual disputes between Russia and Ukraine, a key transit state for European gas (Stulberg, 2015). Moreover, there were concerns about the depletion of energy sources within the EU, and the rise of new major global energy consumers like China and India, with competition for finite energy resources on the market. As a result, energy security became established on the EU agenda, and strategies were developed to diversify energy supplies and address rising prices, particularly in the 2010s.

During the 2000s climate and energy policies were seen to be in part synergistic and in part requiring trade-offs between each, though often the tendency was to perceive them as, adversarial rather than mutually reinforcing dimensions of energy policy (Correljé and van der Linde, 2006; Kruyt et al., 2009). The 2007 Energy Policy for Europe (European Commission, 2007) established that the main objectives were those of competitiveness, sustainability and security of supply. These goals thus did not differ from those set by the EU a decade earlier. The security element was to be achieved through reducing dependence on imported fuels and ensuring reliable energy supplies at reasonable prices. Meeting the objectives of reliability of supplies and reduced import dependency was seen to require an improvement in both the internal and external dimensions of energy security (European Commission, 2007). The internal element related to developing an interconnected, single internal energy market that could mitigate any supply disruptions by facilitating the sharing of resources within the EU and driving down prices through greater competition, with energy-efficiency improvements and increased use of renewables reducing demand for imported energy. The external dimension of energy security was to be improved through diversified sources of supply and supply routes, and also developing the capacity and legal mandate for the EU to negotiate with a 'single voice' with supply countries (European Commission, 2006). Climate and energy policies were still to a large extent developed in isolation, though both within the EU's Directorate Generals (for example, DG Transport and Energy and DG Environment) and within national ministries (Skjærseth et al., 2016).

The EU began to focus on bringing both policies together, focusing on the interlinkages between them, and the EU's 2008 Climate and Energy package set energy efficiency, renewable energy and emission reduction goals for 2020 – the so called 20-20-20 package (Council of the EU, 2008). Despite being EU members for several years, CEE states had little influence on these objectives, in large part because there was a high degree of consensus within the EU for ambitious climate action and international climate diplomacy. The mandate for the 2009 UN Copenhagen Climate change conference was also not shaped significantly by the newer member states. The EU's international leadership was called into question as it was seen as failing to achieve the stated objective of an agreement to succeed the Kyoto Protocol, with the bloc sidelined by the US and China (Parker and Karlsson, 2018; Wunderlich, 2020).

The 2010s and Beginning of the 2020s: A Growing Convergence of Climate and Energy Policy and Crises Responses

Since the 2006 and 2009 gas supply disruptions, CEE countries focused increasingly on energy security policy. Due to the decrease of domestic energy production,[5]

[5] Denmark was the only net exporter of energy until 2013, when it became a net importer.

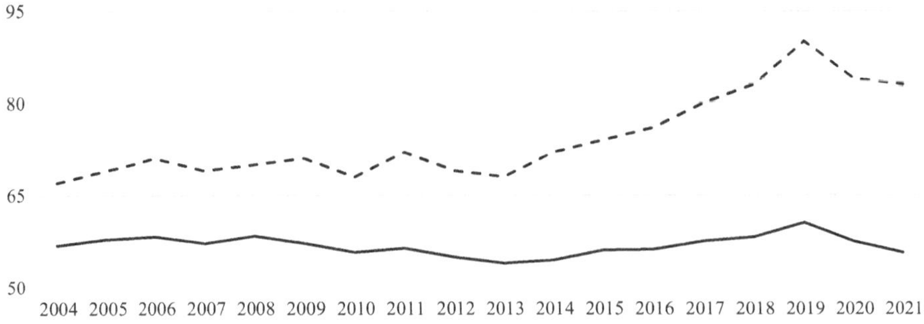

FIGURE 1.1 EU energy import dependency overall (solid line) and natural gas (dashed line).
Source: Eurostat (2023a)

the EU's energy import dependency rose from 57% in 2000. Whilst the financial crisis reduced import dependency for a period, after 2013 it steadily increased, to 61% in 2019 (Figure 1.1; Eurostat, 2023a). For natural gas the increase was more pronounced, with almost 65% of total consumption imported in 2000 and almost 90% in 2019, followed by a pandemic-related decrease (Eurostat, 2023a). The EU's eastern enlargement exacerbated security of supply concerns, with CEE member states disproportionality dependent on gas imports, with an average in 2021 of 82% (Eurostat, 2023a). Whilst the EU imported 45% of its gas from Russia in 2021, many CEE states were completely or largely dependent on Russian gas.

Although the EU imports energy from several countries, Russia was until 2022 the main supplier of crude oil, natural gas and coal (Eurostat, 2023a). Disputes between Russia and transit countries, in particular, Ukraine, have disrupted gas supplies to the EU in 2006 and 2009 (McGowan, 2011) and threatened to do so again during the 2010s (the situation was especially critical during the winter of 2014/2015; Stulberg, 2015). A concern for the EU and particularly CEE states has been the availability and reliability of supplies, and also the reasonableness of prices during the 2000s and 2010s. CEE countries have tended to pay more for Russian gas – their primary, if not only source – than countries in Western Europe despite closer proximity to the source and the assumed lower transportation costs. Lithuania, for example, had the highest prices of natural gas within the EU until 2014, and the situation changed only when an alternative source became available through a newly constructed LNG terminal in the country (Mišík and Pracharová, 2016). As Figure 1.2 shows, there were monopoly suppliers of gas in a number of CEE countries in 2005 – Estonia, Lithuania, Latvia and Slovakia (European Commission, 2023a). Whilst increased competition improved the situation for Lithuania and Slovenia, Estonia remained completely dependent on Russia for gas in 2020, and Czechia, Hungary, Latvia and Slovakia became fully dependent by that point.

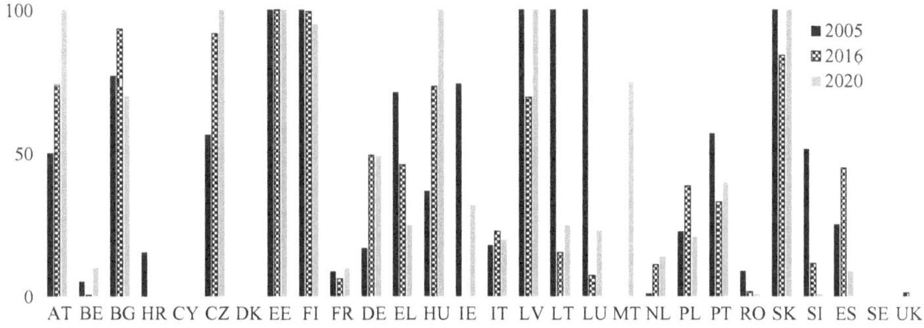

FIGURE 1.2 Supplier concentration index. Note: Non-European Economic Area sources, natural gas, in per cent; data for IE in 2016 and UK in 2020 not available. AT, Austria; BE, Belgium; BG, Bulgaria; CY, Cyprus; CZ, Czechia; DE, Germany; DK, Denmark; EE, Estonia; EL, Greece; ES, Spain; FI, Finland; FR, France; HR, Croatia; HU, Hungary; IE, Ireland; IT, Italy; LT, Lithuania; LU, Luxembourg; LV, Latvia; MT, Malta; NL, Netherlands; PL, Poland; PT, Portugal; RO, Romania; SE, Sweden; SI, Slovenia; SK, Slovakia; UK, United Kingdom.
Source: European Commission (2023a)

The EU's dependency on external energy sources increased as domestic production has declined. From 2010 to 2020, domestic production of natural gas experienced a sharp decrease of 62%, crude oil by 35% and coal by 43% (see Chapters 3 and 4 on the EU's coal phase-out). The only energy source that recorded a significant rise in domestic production was renewables, with an increase of 53% during the ten-year period (Eurostat, 2023b). Therefore, despite increased energy efficiency and utilisation of renewable energy sources, the EU's energy import dependency changed only minimally in the period between CEE countries becoming members (see Figure 1.1). The only significant change can be observed in 2020 and 2021, connected to the temporary decrease of energy consumption caused by the Covid-19 pandemic.

In 2013 the Commission continued to stress the EU's vulnerability because of 'the reliance on imported and insufficiently diversified energy sources, the political instability of several energy-producing and transit countries, [and] global competition over energy sources' (European Commission, 2013a, p. 5). In 2014, the Commission's 'In Depth Study on European Energy Security' highlighted the 'challenge' and increased 'risks to security of supply' that accompanied the EU's increasing dependency on gas imports, and noted that this was particularly the case for CEE states with concentrated imported gas supplies (see Figure 1.2, European Commission, 2014a). The risk, first, was that a disruption of supplies could not be mitigated by reserves or supplies from neighbouring countries – particularly for Bulgaria, Romania and Hungary (and Greece). The Baltic States, Croatia, Slovakia, Slovenia and Poland were also considered to be exposed to potential disruptions (European Commission, 2014a, p. 9). Another problem was that isolated markets with monopoly gas suppliers would have less leverage in gas contract negotiations with suppliers and would pay more for gas than competitive markets in the west of Europe.

In Chapters 3 and 6 this book explores the role of CEE member states in shaping the EU's responses and its strategic goals, including specific measures to address energy security concerns: a 2014 energy security strategy and further legislative proposals after 2016 on security of supply and agreements with third countries. The EU increasingly discussed the mutually reinforcing dimensions of increasing climate, security of supply and prices, through increasing reliance on renewables to reduce the huge cost of energy imports (European Commission, 2018d).

As noted earlier, the EU developed a set of domestic climate-related targets since the 2000s and was active in international climate diplomacy, using domestic policy implementation to claim legitimacy and expertise and to project itself as a leader by example (Kilian and Elgström, 2010; Wunderlich, 2020), considered in Chapter 7. However, the late 2000s financial crisis exacerbated divisions within the EU, and globally, between those actors that framed climate policy as an opportunity for green growth, an ecological modernisation framing of the policy solutions, and those that argued that climate policy hindered economic development. The Commission used the former frame, arguing that the transition to a low-carbon society was both feasible and affordable (European Commission, 2011b). The required investment in technology and infrastructure was considered to be more than offset by job creation, technology export and reduction in dependence on imported oil and gas. The EU's 2021 Covid recovery instrument was framed similarly when it argued that '[t]he green transition ... contributes to the Union's climate targets, fostering sustainable growth, creating jobs and preserving energy security' (European Parliament and the Council, 2021a).

Others view addressing climate change as something that comes with significant costs, and represents a trade-off – undermining economic growth, and for at least some states in CEE undermining the opportunity to catch up with Western EU levels of economic development by penalising their industries, including their energy sectors. For example, in 2014, Ewa Kopacz, the Polish prime minister, stated, 'I realise how important environmental concerns are ... but my government will not accept increases in the costs of energy in Poland and the impacts to the economy' (cited in Foy, 2014). This book explores the extent of these divisions between CEE states, but also within them – it is not uncommon for environmental ministries to propose significantly divergent policies and levels of ambition to economic and financial ministries, something also reflected at the EU level (Skovgaard, 2014). These frames are also dynamic, over time and between and within states.

Since 2010, countries in CEE have also become more active and influential in shaping EU climate policy (see also Chapter 6). The Polish government, for example, vetoed the Commission's initial 2011 Energy Roadmap for 2050

(Wettestad, 2014) and Council conclusions on the 'Low Carbon Roadmap for 2050' twice in 2012 (euractiv, 2012), and joined another three CEE countries in vetoing the 2050 decarbonisation goal at the June 2019 European Council (European Council, 2019b). Poland did not commit to implementation of the 2050 goal finally agreed upon by the other member states in December 2019 (European Council, 2019a). During the second half of the 2010s the Commission launched several important initiatives. The Energy Union of 2015 further interlinked climate and energy policy and was a key priority for the Juncker Commission. A 2019 'Clean Energy Package' updated climate targets, and within this a Governance Regulation (2018/1999) required member states to develop integrated national energy and climate plans. These included a role for the Commission in monitoring and reviewing these plans for alignment with the EU's collective goals (Crnčec et al., 2023; Mišík and Oravcová, 2022).

The European Green Deal of 2019 focused on climate issues, with energy security challenges in the background (European Commission, 2019a; Panarello and Gatto, 2023). However, the Covid-19 pandemic brought to the fore a dilemma that had parallels with the economic crisis a decade before: whether to fuel the post-pandemic economic recovery by supporting development of renewable sources of energy or to restart the economy with the help of fossil fuels (Kuzemko et al., 2020). This dilemma continued post 2022; however, here the division line did not follow the West/CEE logic – several members from the western part of the EU opted to include coal (most significantly, Germany; *Financial Times*, 2022; Geiger, 2023), as did Czechia. However, Poland's coal use was stable, and Slovakia did not change its coal phase-out 2023 deadline. Simultaneously, the EU has promoted a green recovery, including making access to post-pandemic funding in the €720 billion Recovery and Resilience Facility conditional on spending 37% on climate initiatives (Crnčec et al., 2023). The EU's 2030 climate and energy targets have been repeatedly revised upwards, following the successful achievement of the 2020 targets. The 2022 REPowerEU plan linked rapidly phasing out Russian fossil fuel imports with increased ambition for 2030 renewables and energy efficiency targets.

Internationally, the EU's focus was on exporting norms of sustainable development, particularly in developing countries. The EU used the Cartagena Dialogue for Progressive Action, begun in 2010, to develop partnerships and shared interests with those from developed and developing countries, building on its long-established objective, as a mediator of interests between the two and leveraging its trade and development policies particularly with African, Caribbean and Pacific countries (Vogler, 2017). Whilst its international climate leadership was questioned in the late 2000s, following the perceived failure of the 2009 Copenhagen conference (Parker et al., 2017), the EU re-established an influential co-leadership role that shaped a Paris Agreement which significantly reflected its interests (Wunderlich, 2020). These included mitigation and adaptation commitments – the latter with promises of redistribution of funds to assist developing countries with the effects of already occurring climate change. It also played a key role in the formation of a 'high-ambition coalition' of states pushing beyond the globally agreed objective. Oberthür (2016) described the EU's new role in international climate change politics as a 'leadiator', proactive in bridge and coalition building, in both multilateral fora and bilateral negotiations. Leadership ambitions in the policy area continue, in negotiations to implement the Paris Agreement since 2015, closely linked to a form of exemplary leadership through maintaining the implementation of ambitious domestic climate targets (Oberthür and Dupont, 2021).

1.3 THE EU'S PROGRESS TOWARDS ITS CLIMATE AND ENERGY POLICY GOALS

The EU's 2008 Climate and Energy Framework set three main targets for 2020 connected to climate and energy policy: a 20% share of renewables in community's energy mix, a 20% reduction of greenhouse gases emission compared with 1990 and a 20% increase in energy efficiency (European Council, 2008). In 2011, the Commission used an 'energy roadmap' to set a long-term decarbonisation objective of reducing emissions by 80–95% by 2050, including 'almost totally' decarbonising the power sector through the use of renewable and nuclear energy (European Commission, 2011a). The EU's renewables constituted 8.5% of its energy mix in 2004, but by 2020 had almost tripled to 22%, beating its 2020 target (Figure 1.3), and compared with a global share of 5.1% (IEA, 2022c). As with emission reduction targets, the collective 20% renewable target comprised of burden sharing between states, targets based on their capacity and starting points. Energy transitions in the region have proceeded at very different paces.

Latvia and Croatia started in 2004 from a position where the use of renewable energy was already high (at 33% and 24%, respectively), and Romania, Slovenia and Estonia also had substantial renewables pre-accession (16–18%). For these countries hydropower has played a major role in their energy systems since the 1970s. In contrast, others started from a low base: Hungary, Poland, Slovakia and

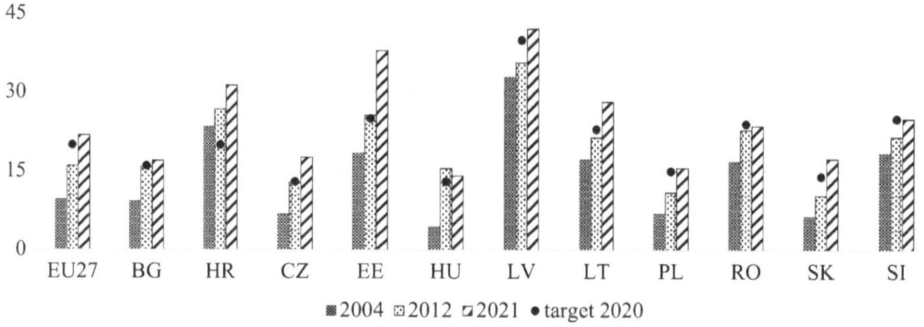

FIGURE 1.3 Share of renewable energy in gross final energy consumption, in per cent.
Source: Eurostat (2023c)

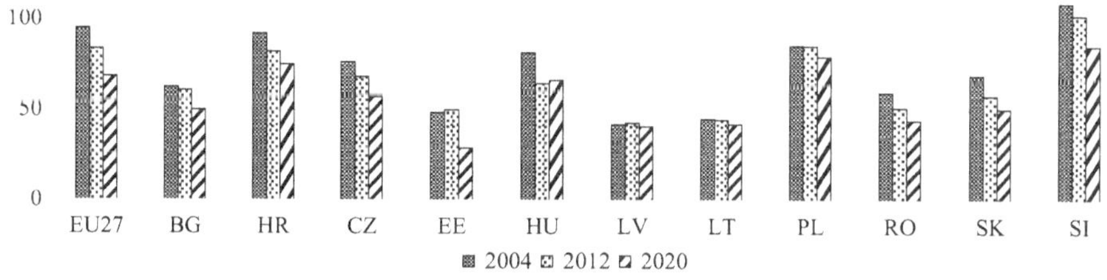

FIGURE 1.4 Greenhouse gas emissions reductions since 1990, in per cent.
Source: Eurostat (2023d)

Czechia all had less than 7% in 2004 (Hungary with just 4.4%). As a result of this and the technical and economic capacity to develop renewables, the EU set targets in the region ranging from 13% for Hungary and Czechia to 40% for Latvia. Moreover, the transition towards decarbonised energy production has varied substantially within CEE. Bulgaria, Slovakia and Czechia almost doubled their share of renewables in the energy mix between 2004 and 2012, and Hungary even tripled theirs (Eurostat, 2023c; see Figure 1.3). The energy transitions challenges are significant, demonstrated by the fact that Poland, Latvia, Cyprus, Slovenia, Slovakia and Czechia all experienced a decrease in their renewables share between 2015 and 2016.

Although all CEE members reached their renewable goals in 2020, most visibly in the overperformance of Estonia, Croatia and Lithuania, Romania decreased its share below the target in 2021. A focus of the later chapters is in explaining these energy transitions, which have been driven by different government incentives, different constellations of public and private actors, and the promotion of different renewable energy technologies. The EU also exceeded its emissions reduction target of 20%, reaching 32% by 2020 (see Figure 1.4). Whilst all CEE countries reduced emissions, the pace of reduction varied significantly – Latvia's, Lithuania's and Poland's emission reductions were far less than other member states in the region between 2004 and 2020. However, a European Court of Auditors report in 2017 stated that emissions reduction targets for 2030 and 2050 'will not be achieved without significant additional efforts' (ECA, 2017), concluding that further measures were required to set a pathway to the 2050 target. A 2030 framework was agreed in 2014 (European Council, 2014), moving to targets of 27% for renewables,[6] a 40% emissions reduction and a 27% increase in energy efficiency (see also Chapter 3).

1.4 AN INTRODUCTION TO ENERGY TRANSITIONS IN CEE

This chapter now shifts its focus to CEE countries that joined the EU during three rounds of so-called eastern enlargement (2004, 2007 and 2013).[7] Here we introduce

[6] The share of renewable energy in gross final energy consumption.

[7] Bulgaria, Croatia, Czechia, Estonia, Hungary, Latvia, Lithuania, Poland, Romania, Slovakia and Slovenia.

an analysis of the influence of post-socialist transitions on CEE countries, their political systems and economies and the link with their energy transitions. This section introduces the CEE countries' energy security preferences relative to those on climate change, providing preliminary support for the main arguments of the book. During the 1990s most climate policy issues within the region were connected to environmental policy, an important part of the accession process. Energy security was, on the other hand, not present in the accession talks, and the energy chapter of the negotiations concentrated on internal energy market rules. Although CEE countries tried to pursue their energy security preferences after they became EU members, it was the 2006 and especially the 2009 gas supply disruptions that provided windows of opportunity for them to upload these preferences to the EU level. The year 2022 highlighted energy security issues within the EU and especially in the CEE region that – despite energy infrastructure diversification efforts over the previous fifteen years – remained significantly dependent on Russian energy supplies.

Political and Economic Transitions of Central and Eastern Europe

The countries of CEE underwent crucial political and economic change from the end of the 1980s (Pickles and Smith, 1998). The end of communist rule and establishment of democratic regimes in CEE were part of the 'third wave' of democratisation that spread throughout the world since 1970s and meant a significant increase in the number of democratic states worldwide (Huntington, 1993). Two main transformations took place in this period – economic and political – and EU membership aspirations were a significant factor in the paradigmatic changes to political institutions, rules, norms and the characteristics of both state-society and state–private sector relations (Haughton, 2007, p. 243).

Some CEE countries had previous experience of democracy (like Czechia and Slovakia from the inter-war period when they coexisted in a common state); others were part of the Soviet Union (the Baltic States) or Yugoslavia (Croatia, Slovenia) and gained independence at the beginning of the 1990s. This variety of historical legacies shaped the character of the political transition during the 1990s and beyond, and influenced CEE countries' economic transitions. The EU played a central role in the process of democratisation, and the CEE countries were united in the desire to become members. Accession was widely seen not only as a 'return to Europe' but as a symbol of return to normality and a firm rooting in the democratic world (Kopecký and Mudde, 2002; Sadurski, 2004).

Following the end of communism, the role of political institutions and limited civil society had to be completely redefined. While the former had to be revised to follow democratic standards (for example, free and fair elections, the separation of powers between the executive, legislature and judiciary), the latter had to be developed almost from scratch with a few exceptions such as the environmental movements that played a role in the independence movements (Podoba, 1998;

Szulecka and Szulecki, 2022). New rules governing the relationship between the government and the civil society had to be established. While the environmental movement was particularly strong at the end of the 1980s, it lost much of its transformational power at the beginning of 1990 as the economic transformation and its negative consequences became more prominent (Pavlínek and Pickles, 2000). The economic transition, as with the contemporary energy transition, proceeded at different speeds. Some countries, such as Czechia and Slovenia, were considered to be forerunners; others, such as Croatia and Slovakia, initially did not fulfil even the basic political criteria for starting accession negotiations (Fisher, 2006).

The economic transition was connected to EU membership. One of the Copenhagen criteria that created a framework for the accession process was a functioning market economy, able to cope with competition within the single market. The other two were the stability of institutions, and administrative and institutional capacity to cope with the EU membership obligations (Dimitrova 2002). Based on these three main criteria a set of thirty-one chapters[8] were developed, with specific requirements in individual sectors based on EU legislation. However, the accession process was criticised for lack of clarity (Schimmelfennig and Sedelmeier, 2005). There was a clear power asymmetry between the EU and the candidate countries as 'there was very little left open to negotiation beyond the odd temporary transitional arrangement' (Haughton, 2007, p. 235). The countries interested in accession had to assume a rather passive position and adopt legislation requested by the Commission. The transposition of EU legislation was a complex and difficult task, and the Union developed a system of 'carrots and sticks' to facilitate the process (Schimmelfennig, 2005). Countries that progressed with the negotiations according to the plan were rewarded with advice, financial support and the promise of membership, while those that diverged from it were punished by prolonging the process, with annual reports acting as a pressure – shaming or rewarding the candidates (Dinan, 2014).

The main economic challenge for the countries in the region was adaptation to market pressures and international competition – issues unknown to economies operating within the Council for Mutual Economic Assistance (COMECON), which was comprised of communist countries under the leadership of the Soviet Union. Due to this limited exposure to international competition, where the focus was on trade within the bloc and the export of raw materials, countries of the 'Eastern bloc' suffered from technological underdevelopment and dependence on Western technologies in several sectors, including energy – for example, equipment necessary for extraction of energy sources (Högselius, 2012). The emergence of a market economy and pressures connected to international competition thus presented significant challenges for CEE countries during the 1990s, and the ability of these countries to adapt to new economic conditions varied.

[8] Current enlargement negotiations consist of thirty-five chapters.

For example, in Hungary the reforms were successful mostly because of an efficient administration and strong support by political elites, political parties and the public (Gros and Steinherr, 2004). However, this early success did not guarantee the continuous and linear development of economic and political institutions (Sedelmeier, 2005).[9] Due to the insufficient progress of several CEE countries in accession negotiations during the 1990s, the Luxembourg European Council of 1997 opened negotiations with only five candidates from the region (Czechia, Estonia, Hungary, Poland and Slovenia), while the other five (Bulgaria, Latvia, Lithuania, Romania and Slovakia) had to wait until the 1999 Helsinki Council to be officially invited to start accession negotiations. Despite this division, all candidates except for Bulgaria and Romania managed to conclude the negotiations by the end of 2002.[10] Accession treaties were signed in April 2003, and ten countries formally approved joining the EU by September of the same year (most by referendum). Consequently, eight countries from Central and Eastern Europe entered the EU on 1 May 2004 together with Malta and Cyprus. Bulgaria and Romania joined on 1 January 2007, and Croatia on 1 July 2013.

Energy and environmental issues were an important part of the pre-accession negotiations between CEE countries and the EU during the 1990s and early 2000s. However, the focus of these was not on energy security – a topic that interested these countries most – but on more technical issues connected to nuclear safety, transfer of environmental standards and adaptation of the EU rules (Mišík, 2015). Energy policy issues were part of chapter 14; environmental issues were included in chapter 22. Both topics overlapped with other issues that were dealt with during the accession negotiations, especially those connected to the internal market.

Environmental and Climate Policy in Central and Eastern Europe

Environmental issues were closely connected to the change of regimes within the CEE region as environmental groups constituted an important section of the anti-communism opposition (Pavlínek and Pickles, 2000). The environment during the socialist period was largely considered a source of resources rather than something to preserve and protect, and as Szulecka and Szulecki note, the political system at the time 'displayed a complete disregard towards the natural environment as a separate system (of beings and values)' (2017, p. 5). Environmental movements were

[9] While Hungary was a regional forerunner during the 1990s thanks to its liberal reforms and successful political as well as economic transition, the country since 2010 has experienced democratic backsliding with Prime Minister Viktor Orbán coining the term 'illiberal democracy' (Buzogány, 2017).

[10] Accession negotiations with these two candidate countries were formally concluded in December 2004; official membership negotiations with Croatia started in 2005 and ended in 2011. The start of the negotiations was postponed due to insufficient cooperation of the Croatian authorities with the International Criminal Tribunal for the Former Yugoslavia (Maldini and Pauković, 2015).

seemingly apolitical as they did not directly challenge communist regimes on ideological grounds, and therefore were tolerated by the totalitarian communist systems. However, these movements created an important foundation for developing societal groupings. As sites of critical questioning of policies, arenas of non-conformity were created (Szulecka and Szulecki, 2022). Environmental movements thus created an important foundation for the development of protest movements and a nascent civil society. These issues are analysed in detail in Chapter 5, which focuses on societal factors in the energy transitions of CEE.

Environmental policy problems in the region were often highlighted within Western Europe; however, as Carmin and Vandeveer (2004) point out, there were also positive practices within the region – for example, relatively high levels of recycling and low levels of automobile use – that were downplayed within the dominant discourse about the region's environmental status. The expectation that the CEE countries would became environmental leaders because of their strong position at the end of the 1980s did not, nevertheless, materialise, and these countries joined the 'followers' group when it comes to environmental and climate policy at the EU level (Carmin and Vandeveer, 2004). However, there was heterogeneity within the CEE countries' climate policy preferences – despite similarities when it comes to the 'big picture' concerning climate policy, there are differences between individual CEE countries that will be examined within the analytical Chapters (3–5) and in Chapter 6 focusing on these countries' impact on the EU.

The economic transitions were a significant factor with regard to environmental issues, as economic restructuring accounted for significant emission reductions (Mišík and Oravcová, 2021b). Heavy industries – technologically outdated, state-subsidised, inefficient and focused on support for the military machinery of the Warsaw Pact – were not able to cope with international competition, which led in many cases to their scaling down or closure. These energy-intensive industries were energy-inefficient – to produce one unit of GDP, these countries used 30–50% more energy than their counterparts in Western Europe (Kramer, 2004). A decline of heavy industries contributed to both economic recession and a decline in living standards, but also to environmental improvement within the region.

Political transformation also had a direct influence on environmental policy of the CEE countries. The decentralisation of political authority, an important part of the political transition, created new levels of authority at the sub-national level. Key environmental policy functions – like monitoring or licencing – were transferred in many CEE countries to this newly developed level (Carmin and Vandeveer, 2004). However, this suffered from instability and frequent changes to its design, which limited the capacity to address environmental issues, a problem exacerbated by the challenges of developing the role of civil society in politics. The early 1990s were also marked by an effort of international donors to support not only the development of democratic institutions and civil society within the region, but also environmental development.

The EU developed two pre-accession support funds that had environmental policy among their objectives. The Poland/Hungary for the Reconstruction of the Economy (PHARE) programme was originally focused on development of democratic institutions and economic transition; however, over time it significantly increased its environmental budget (within its twinning projects) and became an important driver of environmental reforms within the whole region. Projects focusing on the environment, conservation, water management and also energy efficiency counted at the end for 9% of the programme's budget (B&S Europe, 2015). The LIFE programme, 'the EU's financial instrument supporting environmental, nature conservation and climate action projects', was much more focused on the environment, and participation was opened to EU accession countries in 1999 (European Commission, 2023b). This was designed to help the accession countries to implement environmental legislation and to finance nature conservation.

CEE countries made considerable progress during the accession negotiations in environmental policy (Kramer, 2004). However, environmental policy suffered from a problem that was typical for the whole policy-making process connected to the EU's eastern enlargement – whilst compliance was very good at the formal level (even exceptional, see Börzel and Sedelmeier, 2017), CEE countries often failed to implement and enforce policy (Falkner and Treib, 2008).

Energy Security Policy

As with other sectors of CEE countries' economies, the energy sector also underwent a radical change during the transition period of the 1990s (Ürge-Vorsatz et al., 2006). Two main issues shaped the development of energy policy within the region: historical legacies causing high levels of energy dependency on Russian supplies and very low energy efficiency caused by focusing on heavy, energy-intensive industries. The close relationship between CEE countries and the Soviet Union during the communist period included the energy sector. Some of these countries were Soviet satellites (Poland, Czechoslovakia), while others (the Baltic States) were part of the Soviet Union, and some had a much looser relationship, such as part of the former Yugoslavia (Croatia, Slovenia). However, in most cases, major energy supply infrastructure had been developed during the 1960s and 1970s, supplying CEE countries and also providing a means to exert Soviet control (Högselius, 2012). For this reason, the infrastructure (both oil and natural gas) was one-directional, providing a direct link from the Soviet Union (in the east) to the CEE region and the EU to the west. As a consequence of such policies, the share of natural gas, supplied to a significant extent by Russia, in energy mixes of CEE countries remained relatively high (Ürge-Vorsatz et al., 2006). Limited mutual interconnectivity within the region as well as sparse connections to the rest of the Europe were some of the main reasons for the gas supply disruption that occurred in the second half of 2000s.

CEE countries started their political and economic transition at the beginning of the 1990s with high levels of dependency on Russian supplies.[11] However, those countries without significant domestic resources were sensitive to changes in supply patterns. Czechoslovakia decided at the very beginning of the 1990s to diversify its oil supplies by developing a new oil pipeline connecting the country to Western Europe, which was finished only after the break-up of the country in 1996. The pipeline supplied around 40% of oil demand and helped to prevent several potential energy crises caused by disrupted supplies via the Druzhba oil pipeline running through Ukraine and Belarus (Černoch et al., 2012). The situation in the Baltic States was even more difficult during this period. In the early 1990s the Soviet Union used the energy supplies as a means to prevent the Baltic States from breaking away from the Soviet Union and becoming independent states, and several energy supply disruptions were experienced as a result (Grigas, 2013a). Bouzarovski and Bassin (2011) have argued that there is a post-socialist energy legacy in CEE, reflecting a past Soviet and ongoing Russian objective to act as a 'hydrocarbon superpower', projecting political and economic power and influence through energy exports.

Although energy security was an important issue for CEE countries, not all paid the same level of attention to this issue. Slovakia, for example, was not initially active in diversifying its energy sources and was therefore one of the most severely affected by the 2009 gas supply disruption (together with Bulgaria). The country started to diversify only after the EU gave priority – and financial incentives – to this agenda. Such an approach is rather typical for the countries of the region that, on the one hand, understand the need to diversify energy supplies, but, on the other hand, do not have the political will or capacity to invest in this area (Mišík and Nosko, 2017). However, there are also several exceptions – for example, this book will discuss in Chapter 4 the case of an LNG terminal in Lithuania, developed individually after failing to secure EU support that required regional cooperation as a prerequisite for funding.

CEE countries tried to place energy security on the EU's agenda in the pre-accession period (Mišík, 2015). However, due to their asymmetrical position vis-à-vis the Commission, typical for this period (Haughton, 2007), they were unable to promote their preferences effectively and mostly followed the Commission's lead – and requirements (Schimmelfennig and Sedelmeier, 2005), which focused on developing energy ministry administrative capacity, on legal systems to transpose the energy legislation and on safety issues connected to several nuclear power plants in the region. Here negotiations mostly focused on the Commission's objective of closing nuclear power plants, which were considered unsafe due to their design

[11] An exception was Romania, which produced a significant part of its oil as well as gas consumption domestically. In 1990 Romania produced 5.5 millions of tonnes of oil equivalent (Mtoe) of oil and 22.9 Mtoe of natural gas, which covered a significant share of its 16.8 Mtoe and 28.8 Mtoe gross consumption, respectively, figures that increased by the 2010s (European Commission, 2017d).

similarities with the Soviet-style nuclear reactors responsible for the 1986 Chernobyl accident. Three plants were – because of their design – objects of such efforts: Kozloduy in Bulgaria, Ignalina in Lithuania and Jaslovské Bohunice in Slovakia (see also Chapter 4). The EU used accession conditionality along with financial aid for decommissioning to force their closure (van Oudenaren, 2001).

These countries had to replace missing generation capacity, and in the case of Lithuania this was achieved by increasing Russian gas imports. Debates regarding nuclear power are prominent in CEE countries with nuclear power plants or those such as Poland that aspire to develop the technology. For instance, in Bulgaria, a new nuclear power plant planned since the 1980s that was cancelled by the government in 2012 on the grounds of expense and lack of necessity was supported by the public in a non-binding 2013 referendum, and in 2018 was again discussed by the government (Barber, 2018).

The only major energy policy–related issue where candidate countries successfully requested modification of the original EU position in accession negotiations was related to emergency stocks of crude oil and petroleum products. Here CEE countries entered into substantive negotiations with the Commission and managed to win concessions in the form of transition periods to complete their emergency stocks (Tosun, 2011). The first energy liberalisation package was transposed by CEE countries before accession (Moravcsik and Vachudova, 2005). Although the second liberalisation package was adopted after formal approval of CEE countries' membership in the EU, they were not present at the negotiation table as the negotiations were concluded before they formally joined (Herweg, 2017). Therefore, these countries presented their internal energy market preferences only during the preparation of the third round of energy liberalisation process, and demonstrated a plurality of preferences and then implementation records (Bocquillon and Maltby, 2017). These issues are analysed in Chapter 3.

After becoming EU members, CEE countries tried to bring energy security issues to the EU level, though were limited in their success until the 2006 Russian gas supply disruption (Bocquillon and Maltby, 2017). Poland, at the time the most active new member state from the CEE region (Copsey and Pomorska, 2010), tried to push through several ideas connected to energy policy and especially energy security. The most important was a proposal for an 'Energy NATO' with the aim of creating a system of legally binding solidarity at the EU level in the case of energy supply shortages, though this was resisted by many member states that did not see this as a priority and opposed such a step (Roth, 2011). The 2006 and particularly the 2009 gas supply disruptions influenced the EU's agenda by demonstrating vulnerability to supply insecurity. CEE countries then had a more receptive environment in which to attempt to influence EU energy security policy, including the financing of infrastructure, solidarity mechanisms and a greater role for the Commission in monitoring and regulating energy contracts (Maltby, 2013). Chapter 4 analyses the foreign policy issues connected to CEE energy transitions.

1.5 CONCLUSION

This chapter has outlined the growing importance of climate and energy policy for the EU, and the increasing overlap between the two areas. Energy transitions are being driven by the policy responses to both climate and energy security concerns, and by the EU's policy and legislative responses, which have also been shaped by the structural and strategic effect of the EU's 'Eastern' enlargement. Whilst the region is broadly characterised by a focus on energy security and relatively less concern with climate policy, countries within the region are increasingly active and influential in both EU policies, and this increasingly means shaping as well as following the EU's desire for global leadership, particularly on climate issues. Despite three decades of independence, political, economic, societal and infrastructural post-socialist legacies still affect CEE countries; as we have highlighted, the EU's concern with energy security is to a considerable extent a result of pipeline-derived gas dependence on Russia.

We have introduced a central feature of this book's analysis, that this is a region that demonstrates how understandings of climate and energy security vary, in terms of the extent to which they are threatened; the source of such threats, risks and vulnerabilities; and the solutions to climate and energy challenges. The region is characterised by a heterogeneity of policy objectives, economic development (with regions of Slovenia wealthier than the EU average, and of Romania and Bulgaria amongst the poorest), policy implementation from renewable energy leaders (Latvia) to laggards (Slovakia), and from antagonistic to positive relations with their main energy supplier, Russia. The analytical chapters of the book explore these factors and evaluate their importance in explaining energy transitions in the region.

The following chapter outlines the theoretical framework that drives the empirical analysis. The energy landscape (Bouzarovski, 2009; Bridge et al., 2013) is a set of interconnected social, material and cultural elements, and climate and energy policies are mediated by the political economy of states – within this landscape we draw upon several broad conceptual perspectives on energy transitions, institutional change and understandings of security. The book is structured around three dimensions, which form our three central Chapters (3–5). The conceptual perspectives are applied to each. First, we consider the governance of climate and energy, second the effect of foreign policy on climate and energy policy – in terms of national, economic and environmental – and finally we focus on societal factors. In doing so we evaluate the role of state, private and NGO actors, markets and state-market relations, institutions (change and continuity), foreign policy and the materiality of infrastructural systems. Such an approach enables us to identify the differences between individual CEE countries – for example, the role of ideas can be used to describe the different understandings of what constitutes energy and environmental security issues, and the solutions to these. Chapter 6 then shows how CEE countries influence energy and climate policy at the EU level, and Chapter 7 develops links between the experience of CEE and global energy transitions.

2

A Conceptual Framework for Understanding Energy Transitions

2.1 INTRODUCTION

The theoretical framework developed within this chapter drives the empirical analysis in Chapters 3–5. We assume that different approaches to energy transitions can be explained by the influence of material, institutional or ideational factors. Such an approach enables us to explore some of the key causal mechanisms in the form, character and extent of CEE energy transitions. The framework also contributes to the identification of key differences between individual CEE countries – for instance, the role of ideas can be used to highlight the different understandings of what constitutes energy and environmental security issues, the risks posed by policy problems, and the favoured solutions to these. Some, but certainly not all, countries in the region have long securitised energy policy, even prior to Russia's invasion of Ukraine in 2022 shifted perceptions more widely within the EU. Key political actors have framed energy security as a national security challenge, highlighting the foreign policy implications of climate and energy policy and dependency on imported fossil fuels. The extent to which it is perceived that energy or climate is a security issue strongly influences domestic policy choices, and preferences on EU policy and legislation.

The book's conceptual framework builds upon several strands of literature: on socio-technical systems, institutional and political change, and securitisation. In doing so it considers the 'energy landscape' (Bouzarovski, 2009; Bridge et al., 2013) as comprised of a set of interconnected social, material and cultural elements that have impact on energy systems transitions. It is also assumed that climate and energy policies are mediated by the political economy of states, and within this landscape we draw upon broad conceptual perspectives on energy transitions, institutional change and understandings of security. These provide an analytical toolbox that highlights and is used to address the interplay of political interests, institutional forces and governance practices within a material and historical context. Here we draw attention to CEE countries as post-socialist EU members, and evaluate the extent to which their energy mixes, energy infrastructure and foreign policies are still shaped by the political and economic legacies of communist regimes and planned economies. Using this toolbox, we explain how key aspects of the energy transition challenge are interpreted and framed by countries of the CEE region, and how national climate and energy policy and its implementation is shaped. We then explain how the region has been shaped by EU membership and in turn shaped the Union (in Chapter 6).

Theory is central to framing and contributing to an explanation of energy transitions in CEE, and the empirical data demonstrates a clear and significant original contribution to the conceptual literature. The book is structured around three dimensions, which form our three central chapters. The conceptual perspectives are applied to each of the three analytical chapters (Chapters 3–5). First, we consider the governance of climate and energy in the following Chapter 3; second, the effect of foreign policy on climate and energy policy – in terms of national, economic and environmental security – is discussed in Chapter 4; and finally, we focus on societal factors in Chapter 5. In doing so we evaluate the role of state, private and non-governmental actors; markets and state-market relations; institutions (change and continuity); foreign policy; and the materiality of infrastructural systems. The conclusions of the individual analytical chapters draw out the wider implications of our analysis of specific case studies, and we demonstrate the connection and contribution to the theoretical underpinnings of the book.

2.2 ENERGY TRANSITIONS LITERATURE

Energy transitions are 'prolonged' processes (Sovacool, 2016, p. 194), 'inherently protracted affairs' in which accelerated energy transitions are unlikely absent 'extraordinary commitments and actions' (Smil, 2008) and where 'unrealistic expectations concerning the pace of future energy transitions' have been held (Smil, 2016, p. 194). Similarly, Sovacool has argued that 'most energy transitions have been, and will likely continue to be, path dependent rather than revolutionary, cumulative rather than fully substitutive' (2016, p. 212), but nevertheless there is the possibility of quicker transitions because of a 'conscious re-design of the economy along lower carbon lines and the managed decline of existing industries' (Newell and Simms, 2021, p. 913). The former Saudi oil minister Yamani once argued that, 'The stone age came to an end, not because we had a lack of stones, and the oil age will come to an end not because we have a lack of oil' (Macalister, 2000). As Sovacool presciently argued: 'Future transitions may also become a social or political priority in ways that previous transitions have not been – that is, previous transitions may have been accidental or circumstantial, whereas future transitions could become more planned and coordinated, or backed by aggressive social movements or progressive government targets' (2016, p. 210).

In the last decade there has been the Paris Agreement (Hoegh-Guldberg et al., 2019) and increasingly ambitious EU targets and legislation (see Chapter 1), within the context of a wave of influential climate protests (Temper et al., 2020) and the realisation that the 2050 net-zero goal will not be achieved without more ambitious mid-term goals. As energy transitions gather pace, the introduction and development of the wind and solar sectors have significant material implications, linked to their fit with existing energy infrastructure in countries, such as transmission and distribution electricity networks (Borozan et al., 2021; Kozlova and Overland, 2022). A focus on the technical and material aspect of energy transitions (Gatto, 2022; Krupnik et al., 2022) reveals a different range of drivers and dynamics of changes in the period of pre and post-accession.

The literature on socio-technical systems, including energy systems, offers an explanation for how the relatively stable configuration of technical and social elements, also subject to considerable lock-in and stability/continuity (Geels, 2010), can be rearranged during transitions (Buschmann and Oels, 2019). Energy infrastructure can last several decades, and constructing gas infrastructure in the 2020s, ostensibly for short- to medium-term objectives, risks locking fossil fuels into the energy system, undermining the possibilities for future changes and postponing decarbonisation and energy transitions (Bessi et al., 2021; Kemfert et al., 2022, p. 582; Li and Taeihagh, 2020, p. 1).

The literature highlights the role of *systemness* – the materiality of energy systems' infrastructure and energy resources – and the role of veto players in undermining system change towards decarbonisation and a market liberal energy system. It has been argued that these challenges can be enhanced by federalist institutions (including the EU) 'by increasing the number of veto points available to supporters of the status quo or opponents of a low-carbon energy transition' (Balthasar et al., 2020, p. 5). The process of energy transitions and the development of renewable energy also has significant material implications, through the incorporation of new technologies to energy systems. Energy transitions require a transformative shift and 'a change in the state of an energy system' (Grubler et al., 2016, p. 18). Not only does the technology for energy generation change, and require investment, but there are significant costs associated with connecting new renewable electricity to the end consumers, both residential and industrial and within and between countries (Child et al., 2019, p. 98). The challenge is also in developing the material and regulatory system to address and combine the intermittency of different renewable energy sources (Hodge et al., 2020). This was among the factors that had contributed to a lukewarm approach to, and in some cases opposition towards, renewables within the CEE region and other parts of the EU. Electricity networks need substantial investment to be upgraded and expanded to allow the connection of a decentralised and diffuse network of renewable energy sources, sited where the potential for electricity generation is greatest – offshore locations for wind, higher altitude regions for onshore wind, southern locations for solar (Ali et al., 2021). These are often more remote locations, far from residential and industrial centres.

In contrast, the continuity or expansion of large-scale fossil fuel power plants requires a more limited and less costly, particularly to incumbent actors, expansion and renewal of existing material aspects of the energy system (Unruh, 2000, p. 822). Other costs include developing the administrative and regulatory capacity to deal with new technology and to oversee the initial subsidies that bring renewables to the market, as well as designing energy markets, including mechanisms for energy storage (Olabi et al., 2021) and compensation for the incumbent (fossil fuel) electricity generators that provide backup to the intermittent renewable electricity generation in the short to medium term (Bublitz et al., 2019; Peng and Poudineh, 2019).

The socio-technical systems literature highlights the role of path dependence in energy systems and institutions, with veto players deeply embedded in (and dependent on) the existing forms and functions of energy systems (Tsebelis, 2002, p. 19). Related to this path dependence, several authors assume that within energy systems there is a mutual dependency borne out of a co-evolution, between energy technologies, institutional arrangements, social practices and actor constellations (Rohracher and Späth, 2013). This can steer a sector or industry or national economy along one path rather than another (Martin and Sunley, 2010), with past decisions significantly influencing future energy system preferences and development, and the cost and capacity for system change through energy transitions. The interactions between governing institutions (policy-makers, regulators), energy technologies and those that operate them are responsible for the transmission and distribution of their outputs – the electricity generated develop through mutual interaction (Murmann, 2006; Sæther et al., 2011; Unruh, 2000). As argued by Davidescu et al. (2018, pp. 613–614), energy systems have 'co-evolved between electricity generation, the networks to distribute it, and the institutional networks of actors governing and regulating the sector'. This complex system is inherently challenging to change especially due to its interconnectedness and the large number of actors involved in individual parts of the system.

Socio-technical systems consist of three interlinked dimensions (Geels, 2005), including a network of actors and social groups. In the electricity regime important actors include utilities, relevant government ministries, large industrial users, and households; a set of formal, normative and cognitive rules guide the activities of such actors – such as laws and regulations, belief systems, guiding principles, and behavioural norms; and material and technical elements that in the case of electricity include resources, grids and generation plants. Existing socio-technical regimes are characterised by path dependence and lock-in, resulting from stabilising mechanisms (Unruh, 2000) such as the vested interests of incumbent actors, existing infrastructure and sunk investments (Verbong and Geels, 2007). The literature on the political economy of socio-technical transitions highlights the role of the state in exercising different governing capacities in steering these transitions (Baker et al.,

2014; Meadowcroft, 2009). This relates to work that considers how space and territory are entangled with the production and articulation of energy transitions (Bridge et al., 2013; Calvert, 2015). We also examine how the *systemness* of energy, for example, that related to historical energy connections to Russia (trade and infrastructural), has created significant socio-technical inertia, manifested as rigidity in social and material structures – the strong persistence of existing form and function. In the case of energy these could include regulators and long-standing energy transmission and distribution actors, function as a barrier to technological change and transition (Rumelt, 1995, p. 103).

It is assumed that radical energy system change can occur as a result of exogenous or endogenous shocks (Smith et al., 2005). For example, the new policies associated with EU accession and then the EU's 2009 Renewable Energy Directive had a significant negative political feedback effect (Béland, 2010), as they required investment in renewable technology and electricity networks, as well as changes in organisational and institutional structures. Similarly, events during 2022 elevated security of supply concerns, with limited short-term increases in coal in some states as a response (for example, Germany; Financial Times, 2022). However, these shocks are not necessarily associated with significant discontinuities in the actors, networks and institutions involved in the regime. By its nature as network infrastructure, the energy sector has a high degree of *systemness*: changing electricity generation technology requires change or adaptation of electricity transmission and distribution (Van der Vleuten, 2004). Wind and solar infrastructure needs to be, but is not yet, compatible with the characteristics of the existing network structure. Institutional path-dependency can also hamper anticipating the extent of policy change, which in turn also has a negative impact on compliance (Treib, 2014, p. 14).

The issue of coal phase-outs relates to the policy and discourse of 'just transitions', the societal challenges of rapid transitions away from fossil fuels (McCauley and Heffron, 2018, p. 2). Within the EU this particularly concerns several regions economically dependent on fossil fuels that require special attention due to the impact of energy transitions on them. Regions with an economy based on coal mining or heavy industry will be disproportionally impacted by the transition to a low-carbon economy. Justice concerns are, however, linked not only to fossil fuel decline (loss of jobs and skill gaps, and of revenues from fossil sources), but also to 'the inequitable distribution of benefits' for marginalised groups (Wang and Lo, 2021, p. 1). The EU developed a mechanism to support 'just' energy transitions of these regions and mitigate the often local and regional costs of phasing out fossil fuels (Kalt, 2021), including coal mining and coal power plants (Carley and Konisky, 2020, p. 575). This is necessary because as Newell and Mulvaney note, these transitions will stress the limits of 'capacity, autonomy and willingness many state and inter-state institutions have to oversee such a 'just transition' in a neoliberal context in which direct control over energy production and consumption is often either shared with or delegated to the private sector' (2013, pp. 132–133).

Another challenge in terms of material energy systems, and of importance to the CEE region despite the decades since independence, are the material legacies of the socialist period, highly energy-intensive industries, with low energy efficiency and high Russian energy import dependency (Ürge-Vorsatz et al., 2006, p. 2283). During the communist period, energy infrastructure was built that created a physical connection between the Soviet Union and its satellites in Central and Eastern Europe (Högselius, 2012). Industry (especially heavy) in the region was developed thanks to inexpensive energy imported from the Soviet Union, creating another level of control over their Soviet states and satellites (i.e., the Baltic States). Miller et al. highlight that energy transitions involve changes, 'not only to energy technologies and prices but also to the broader social and economic assemblages that are built around energy production and consumption' (2013, p. 135). Considering these and power relations of key institutional actors is also crucial to explaining energy transitions.

2.3 INSTITUTIONAL CHANGE AND CLIMATE AND ENERGY GOVERNANCE

The socio-technical systems literature overlaps in some of its assumptions with political science literature on energy transitions focusing on institutions and political struggles, including governance. Unruh, in the socio-technical systems field, argues that large technological systems, such as energy systems, 'cannot be fully understood as a set of discrete technological artifacts but have to be seen as complex systems of technologies embedded in a powerful conditioning social context of public and private institutions' (2000, p. 819). Despite this, there is recognition that the socio-technical system literature focuses insufficiently on politics and the role of both political and social factors in the choice and implantation of energy technology (Geels et al., 2016; Schubert et al., 2015). As Kuzemko et al. note (2016), socio-technical systems literature tends to consider energy governance as a more depoliticised and technocratic process that in turn obscures power relations between the key actors, and the effect this has on both policy-making and policy implementation. These scholars apply historical institutionalism to energy system change, claiming that the path-dependent qualities of institutions make them inherently difficult to change, and analysis of them is central to explanations of energy transition, as mediators between continuity and change (Kuzemko et al., 2016, p. 96). Developments in the literature highlight the importance of considering political struggles – between political parties, incumbent energy actors, regulators and others (Geels et al., 2016) – and regime actors and their abilities to influence climate and energy governance (Geels, 2014). Regime resistance to energy transitions, including by incumbent energy actors – producers, distributors and regulators – 'is realised through the exercise of material, institutional and discursive power' (Ford and Newell, 2021, p. 6).

Political phenomena and institutions are assumed to have continuity with structured change through 'historical processes' and asymmetries of power between actors in the operation and development of institutions. This focuses on the institutional actors involved in policies and the extent to which path dependence shapes policy choices and can constrain change (Pierson, 2000). Coordination is driven by the adaptive expectations between the actors (Rixen and Viola, 2014), and a path-dependent development of particular political institutions, such as regulatory frameworks, can occur due to (1) the central role of collective action, (2) the high density of institutions, (3) the possibilities for using political authority to enhance asymmetries of power and/or (4) the complexity and opacity of politics (Pierson, 2000).

These institutional actors structure political outcomes and influence attempts at institutional change, political institutions and patterns of interests and routines (Immergut, 2006; Steinmo et al., 1992). In doing so, this strand of literature can highlight the (historical) energy landscape: who the important actor groups are, what interests they represent, and their relationship to climate and energy governance. Whilst there is assumed to be a tendency towards policy inertia, policy change does occur – for example, critical junctures in path-dependent institutional structures can disrupt the stability and continuity of policy (EU accession, for example) (Boogaerts et al., 2016). Similarly, paradigmatic shifts in 'the typical ideas, beliefs and principles that guide policy' (Daigneault, 2014, p. 456) can occur either dramatically or more incrementally and gradually (Mahoney and Thelen, 2010). It is important to examine the incumbent climate and energy actors, how their roles are being challenged, and the result of this political process associated with energy transition. Whilst resistance to change is highlighted by many, its success is not inevitable. As Ford and Newell argue (2021, p. 8): 'Incumbents engage in strategies of resistance and accommodation precisely because political work is required to preserve and maintain that privileged position.'

Historical forces are involved in shaping deep-seated structural shifts in systems of provision (Smil, 2003), and a strand of literature considers 'multiple transformations' in terms of focusing on energy reforms expressed via 'institutional norms, social practices and urban spatial formations' (Sýkora and Bouzarovski, 2012, p. 46). Bouzarovski and Tirado Herrero (2017) and Petrova (2014) highlight the institutional tensions and outcomes that arise out of the clash between neoliberal paradigms and entrenched legacies in societies that are transitioning away from a centrally planned economy. Ćetković and Buzogány (2016) apply the varieties of capitalism literature to energy transitions and discuss the dependent market economies of the CEE region. They argue that there is an important role for industrial interests and societal participation, and that some varieties of capitalism 'face less structural [and contextual] constraints than others' with regard to changing energy systems (Ćetković and Buzogány, 2016, p. 652). An important explanatory variable is the role of the state in climate and energy policy and state-market relations, and this is important for not only the extent of liberalisation of markets but also the form and extent of decarbonisation.

The EU is a major factor in considering energy transitions in CEE, and later we consider the role of EU policy and legislation in catalysing the changes in the region. We also draw attention to the extent to which these countries have incorporated EU rules. Administrative capacity or 'institution-building' has been defined as the creation of institutions necessary for the adoption and implementation of the EU's *acquis communautaire*[1] (Dimitrova, 2002). Mahoney and Thelen (2010) argue that change can take the form of 'displacement' of existing rules or 'layering' alongside them, depending on the absence or presence of veto possibilities, with earlier work suggesting a process of conversion whereby institutions change to serve a new purpose (Streeck and Thelen, 2005). Similarly, although member states were necessarily compliant in transposing EU directives to qualify for accession (Spendzharova and Versluis, 2013), this can be followed by policy implementation failures (Falkner and Treib, 2008) and (non)compliance (Treib, 2014). The democratic backsliding that occurred in some CEE member states during the 2010s and 2020s (Hanley and Vachudova, 2018; Holesch and Kyriazi, 2022; Pech and Scheppelle, 2017) was mirrored also in environmental policy. In Hungary this has departed from the pre-accession rules and there has been a backsliding of EU environmental legislation implementation (Buzogány and Cotta, 2022). Others have found in the region that 'the transformative power of "Europe" is no longer the dominant determinant of environmental policy and governance' (Fagan and Buzogány, 2022, p. 1203).

There are also institutional legacies of the socialist period: a tendency towards a closed, hierarchical policy-making process that undermines state capacity (Noutcheva and Bechev, 2008, p. 128), with 'islands of excellence' (Dimitrova and Toshkov, 2009) developed to achieve EU accession amidst a generally 'passive and patronage-based public administration' (Andreev, 2009, p. 388). Limited state capacity in terms of budget and expertise, a tendency towards what the Commission reported in pre-accession Romania – where 'large vertically integrated state dominated energy companies hold monopolies in production, transmission and distribution' (European Commission, 1997, p. 79) – and a circulation of elites (Hiteva and Maltby, 2014) has led to conflicts of interest and informal channels of influence between formally independent actors within the energy system (Maltby, 2015). The co-evolution discussed above has been argued to have undermined state capacity, as the formal independence of regulators and state companies has been weakened by a lack of political, financial and technical autonomy (Hiteva and Maltby, 2014).

Such capacity is also linked to accountability, transparency and input into the policy-making process. A combination of the closed energy policy-making process and limited civil society capacity and involvement is considered to undermine state-

[1] Obligations including legislation.

society interaction in the region (Börzel and Buzogány, 2010), limiting the possibility to 'act as partners of the state in policy-making' (Dimitrova and Buzogány, 2014, p. 142). In some CEE states the main reason is the deliberate exclusion or sidelining of civil society. In others it is a lack of capacity to facilitate this.

2.4 SECURITISATION/POLITICISATION: THE FRAMING OF POLICY ISSUES

This strand of literature can help to explain the priority that different policies receive in the spatial and temporal dimensions – thus the variation between and within states considering the role of ideas and ideologies, and including how energy and climate security are understood differentially by different countries and actors within them. Kuzemko (2014) argues that energy policy is based not simply on material capabilities, but also on the role of ideas within policy and understandings of energy (and also climate), the importance of 'ideational contestation and change' and 'approaches to energy governance' in policy-making. This links to a constructivist view of security, that there are situations in which actors connect energy and climate policy with existential threats – issues of national security, of survival of the state. Linking to the institutional and material factors associated with energy transitions, it is worth noting Newell and Simms' conclusion that 'transitions are not organic and non-linear, but have to be imagined, designed, financed, constructed and socially accepted' (2021, p. 913).

Whilst there are objective indicators of (in)security, this research assumes that to an extent security is constructed, that 'security' can be used to mobilise an audience and transcend regular political practice, and is an exercise in power. According to the securitisation approach, states develop their climate and energy policies in the context of different understandings of the extent to which there is economic, national and/or environmental (in)security (McDonald, 2013). Judge and Maltby (2017) argue that important to understanding energy policy is not just whether there is intersubjective agreement about *whether* energy is a security concern, but also whether there is agreement about *what kind* of security concern it is. This requires examining whether similar kinds of security concerns are present at the national level. Distinguishing between securitisation and riskification (Corry, 2011), this book examines the different ways that climate and energy have been constructed as a security issue in CEE member states. A key role is played by contextual features – namely, established modes of market and state-led energy governance in the extent to which policy issues are securitised/riskified. These social constructions ('discourses', 'frames') are rooted in history and are path-dependent.

The core argument of securitisation studies is that key energy actors are analysed, and instead of examining whether threats exist, analysts should focus on the process through which such security issues are socially constructed. Such an approach has been applied to energy by a number of authors (Judge and Maltby, 2017;

Khrushcheva and Maltby, 2016; Kuzemko, 2014; Maltby, 2015). As Buzan et al. argue, securitisation is 'the intersubjective establishment of an existential threat with a saliency sufficient to have substantial political effects' (1998, p. 25). Rather than an overly formalistic and restrictive focus on existential threats (Balzacq, 2005), most modern security policies are orientated towards less exceptional forms of threat (Stritzel, 2007; Vedby Rasmussen, 2004; Williams, 2008). There is also a broad distinction between security threats that are immediate and urgent, and risks that are longer-term, based on uncertain and more diffuse dangers, with responses to the latter linked to reducing vulnerability and increasing governance capacity (Corry, 2011; van Munster, 2009). As Huysmans argues, '[s]ecuritizing then takes the form of a scattered process ... little security nothings – that is, devices, sites, practices without exceptional significance. Yet, these little security nothings are highly significant, since it is they rather than exceptional speech acts that create the securitizing process' (2011, p. 377).

In this process a securitising actor may attempt to frame an issue in terms of an existential threat to the survival of a referent object. If this actor is successful in convincing a relevant audience that such a threat exists, then the issue is said to be securitised, which can legitimise the adoption of extraordinary measures to deal with these threatening developments. Security claims are then assumed to affect policy, mediated through established power relations and institutional structures, foreign policy and the material energy landscape; these contextual factors shape how energy and climate can be constructed as constituting security or risk issues. Those actors highlighting the security 'threat' posed by heavy reliance on Russian energy imports became more numerous and found a more receptive audience at key points in recent history, including 2009 and 2022.

In the early 1980s, Ullman (1983) argued for the broadening of the definition of security to include an environmental dimension, though Buzan et al. in 1998 claimed that climate change was not yet established as a security issue at the international level (1998). Diez et al. argued that the securitisation of climate change occurred in the 2000s, highlighting the explicit linkages drawn between security and climate in the discourse of major state and international actors such as Germany, the United Kingdom and the United States (Diez et al., 2016). A number of authors have explored how climate change has long been labelled an environmental security issue including at the UN (Detraz and Betsill, 2009), and climate change's threat to traditional national and international security has increasingly been highlighted, in part because of the increased risk of environmentally induced conflict and migration (Barnett and Adger, 2007). Linked to this broadening of the definition of security, Oels (2013) argues that there has also been a shift in the understanding regarding what is threatening about climate change, and what risks are being conceived as governable.

This links to the discussion above of riskification, that it is less about direct causes of harm and has more to do with what Corry, through an analysis of climate change politics, labels the 'possibility of constitutive causes of harm' (2011, p. 235), and what

Diez et al. (2016) note as the *extent* to which climate change is established as a security issue or risk. The EU similarly has repeatedly drawn attention to the link between climate change and national security issues such as conflict, terrorism and violence (European Council, 2016, 2003). Additionally, for the EU, energy security is intertwined with climate policy. According to the Commission, 'The Union's energy security is inseparable from the 2030 framework for climate and energy' (European Commission, 2014b, p. 19). Judge and Maltby (2017) argue that there are technical and political-economic factors central to considering energy policy and securitisation. Technical factors include physical energy infrastructure, source of energy supply and the energy mix. Political-economic factors are related to regulation and market intervention; the (institutional) 'rules of the game'. Here there are varieties of market, deregulated market-based system of energy production, trade and consumption, and subservience of markets to the political objectives of state governance. In this book we interrogate the claim that understandings of security vary between states and over time, and that this plays a key role in explaining agenda-setting and climate and energy policy making.

Post-socialist legacies play an important role when applying the assumptions of the securitisation literature to our research. When examining threats we should consider the institutionalised and the historical experiences of an issue (Balzacq, 2010), and in doing so 'take into account the actors' history, identities, and strategic myths' (Ciută, 2010, p. 317). This is not to say that 'moments' of securitisation are unimportant, particularly when they are connected to dramatic events and rapid political and economic changes. Such moments can act as focusing events that force participating actors to react to developments. However, it is crucial to note that historical context plays a role in conditioning invocations of, and responses to, 'crises' by situated, legitimate actors. As Campbell notes, 'crisis' is a process of social, political and linguistic construction and narration (2002). Political actors can perceive, define, construct and react to 'crises' in a variety of ways. Contradictions and failures can then be selected by policy-makers to contribute towards the construction or continuation of a crisis narrative, which is a 'discursive construction' (Hay, 1996). 'Crises' themselves are then as much discursively constructed as 'security' threats, though distinguished by the more temporary nature of the former. As Hart notes, 'the most important instrument of crisis management is language. Those who are able to define what the crisis is all about also hold the key to defining the appropriate strategies for [its] resolution' (1993, p. 41).

As Dannreuther has claimed, the contested and competing discourses that construct security do not operate in isolation from political economy, which 'has a determining effect on which particular securitization of energy assumes dominance' (2015, p. 467). Political economy also requires a consideration of structural conditions, and 'what actually gets securitized is decisively shaped by material power relations' (p. 468) as well as the path dependency of state-industry relations and socio-political organisation of society, which has an effect on the security logics in place in various countries. Judge and Maltby also highlight 'the key role played by contextual features – namely established modes of market and state-led energy governance' (2017, pp. 180–181).

According to Felix Ciută, and central to the research in this book, energy security is contested; '[e]nergy security clearly means many different things to different authors and actors, and even at times to the same author or actor' (2010, p. 127). Whilst this is true also within states in the EU, it is also the case between them. As a result, collective securitisation outcomes in energy policy have been characterised by this contestation and a lack of consensus, though not necessarily a failure of shared security concerns (Sperling and Webber, 2019). We argue that this allows an identification of the varying understanding and logics of climate and energy security, and the policy solutions to addressing perceived insecurity. In doing so security logics offer an explanation for the limits of integration at the EU level in this policy area. The ability of actors to successfully securitise energy and climate policy in the EU depends on audience acceptance and that the Commission, the European Parliament and the member states reach a sufficient shared understanding of the source of a threat to energy security, the scale of this and an appropriate policy response. The research seeks to identify how energy security is understood by each of the actors we examine, whether this has changed and what logics of security are at play.

2.5 CONCLUSION

The main research questions are: What drives climate and energy policy development in CEE countries? In other words, what explains the shape, process and extent of energy transitions in the region? Several research sub-questions guide the analysis. Derived from the conceptual framework, these questions are broadly linked to the role of three different factors that shape energy and climate policy preferences of CEE countries: (1) modes of climate and energy governance, (2) foreign policy and (3) societal factors. These are analysed in the second part of the book (Chapters 3–5) via three different analytical prisms based on three strands of literature examined in this chapter.

There are several research questions that are considered as we address the central research question of what drives climate and energy policy development in CEE countries. From the literature on energy transitions, modes of energy governance and understandings of security, we derive the following three sets of research sub-questions that drive the research:

1. Material
   a. To what extent has EU accession transformed energy infrastructure and systems?
   b. To what extent does (historical/existing) energy infrastructure provide an obstacle to achieving energy and climate objectives?

2. Institutional
    a. To what extent has EU accession transformed climate and energy governance and policies?
    b. How does the process of energy transitions relate to the broader transition away from a centrally planned economy – a post-communist transition towards greater liberalisation?
    c. What is the role for incumbent energy actors (regulators, energy companies) in the process of energy transitions, particularly in terms of liberalisation, decarbonisation?
3. Ideational – Understandings of security
    a. Are economic, national and environmental dimensions of climate and energy policy prioritised?
    b. To what extent do these frames reinforce or undermine each other?
    c. To what extent is energy and/or climate policy framed as a security issue?

3

Energy Governance

3.1 INTRODUCTION

This chapter looks at the process of restructuring of energy governance in CEE countries driven by the development of the EU internal energy market, focusing on common patterns and differences in terms of market opening, competition and patterns of ownership. It maps efforts towards the liberalisation of the energy sector and offers an explanation for the enduring variation in political and economic institutions across the CEE region. The challenge of liberalising gas and electricity markets while ensuring energy security is discussed, looking in particular at the implications of energy relationships with Russia particularly before the full-scale invasion of Ukraine consolidated the EU's drive to diversify away from Russian energy supplies (European Commission, 2022b, 2022a). Finally, the chapter asks to what extent this restructuring, however incomplete, has permitted an opening of the structure of energy governance to new actors. Applying the analytical framework, it incorporates three basic explanations developed within the previous chapter (ideas, institutions and the material nature of energy system) to analyse energy governance in CEE countries. The chapter, for example, examines the influence of domestic actors as well as EU institutions on energy transitions within the region, and analyses how the energy systems and the co-evolution of institutions, technologies and energy companies influence these processes.

The EU has pursued energy market liberalisation, incrementally opening energy markets to competition since the second half of the 1990s (the so-called First Energy Package). Further legislative changes in the 2000s laid the foundations for the EU's energy transition. This included the 2007 Lisbon Treaty, the 2003/2004 Second Energy Package and the 2009 Third Energy Package, providing a legal and regulatory foundation for such a paradigmatic change (Herweg, 2017). The Energy Commissioner labelled the changes in the EU Internal Energy Market a new 'institutional architecture' (Oettinger, 2011). The objectives were threefold. First, to facilitate the gradual transformation away from a fossil fuel–dominated energy regime towards a more sustainable energy system (LaBelle and Horwitch, 2013), as part of the EU's objective to decarbonise by 95% by 2050, proposed by the Commission in 2011 (European Commission, 2011b). Second, to introduce more competition in the energy market, to aid industrial competitiveness and pricing for citizens as well as other end consumers. Finally, the objective was to increase security of energy supplies by increasing the number of market players receiving energy supplies from different sources (European Parliament and the Council, 2009a).

A key focus of this chapter is to examine the various actors involved in governing energy policy in CEE, and the extent of changes in energy governance within the region, and between these states. The chapter highlights the connection between the liberalisation of gas and electricity markets, the decarbonisation of economy, the implementation of renewables into energy systems, and the actors involved in and effected by this – from political and civil society actors to transmission and distribution system operators and renewable and traditional energy companies.

It is also important to situate the restructuring of CEE countries' energy sectors within the EU accession process (Mišík, 2015). These countries have had to adopt and implement the EU's internal energy market legislation. CEE countries have exhibited heterogeneous preferences here, leading to divergent models of energy governance. The unbundling of former state-owned energy monopolies, the progressive opening of electricity and gas markets to competition, and the creation of independent energy regulators have profoundly transformed the energy governance of member states from the region. At the same time the process of energy liberalisation has been slow, partial and uneven, both in the region and in the EU as a whole (Bouzarovski, 2009; Jamasb and Pollitt, 2005). Isaacs and Molnar (2017) have argued that the increased state intervention in the Hungarian energy sector, a statist model, is also being adopted by other CEE countries. For example, in Lithuania the state has been consolidating parts of the gas and electricity market under its control; in Slovakia the government fully nationalised the main gas company Slovenský plynárenský priemysel (SPP) in 2014; and in Hungary the state has mandated price cuts and increased its stake in oil and gas companies (Weiner and Szép, 2022).

The chapter considers the degree of convergence with a liberal EU model of energy governance, and in Chapter 6 the book explores how CEE member states have attempted to shape the EU's model through uploading their own preferences. The liberalisation of national energy sectors in the EU has led to particular challenges in CEE countries (LaBelle, 2009), fuelling fears of dominance by Russian companies (Butler, 2011), which has been reflected in negotiations over internal energy market legislation – the debate over the so-called Gazprom clause being a prime example of such concerns (Maltby, 2013).

CEE countries have experienced an overhaul of their energy systems following the collapse of the Soviet Union and their transformation from centrally planned to market economies (Aslund, 2013; Gál, 2021). These changes have caused a decline of economic activity in some sectors (especially heavy industry) and related emissions. Energy systems in the region, which used to be characterised by the dominance of monopolistic and publicly owned energy companies, have undergone a process of liberalisation and opening to competition (Butler, 2011). Although this shift is not specific to the region and reflects the rise of a neoliberal paradigm in global energy governance (Helm, 2007; Stern, 1998), in the EU it was guided predominantly by the development of the internal market (Sencar et al., 2014). The effects have been most significant in those countries with centralised political and economic energy structures (Gray, 1995; Ürge-Vorsatz et al., 2006).

Despite the appearance of paradigmatic shifts in energy governance, the energy market changes in the CEE region also exhibit characteristics assumed in the general literature on institutional change: of gradual and incremental change (Mahoney and Thelen, 2010), with pre-existing institutions structuring political outcomes (Steinmo et al., 1992) and influencing concrete political institutions and established patterns of interests and routines (Immergut, 2006).

The chapter is structured as follows. The second section examines the overall development of energy governance in the CEE, focusing on the impact of the historical legacy and studies the dynamics of internal market governance in the region, looking at the natural gas and electricity sectors. While some countries in the region were strong supporters of deep liberalisation, several opposed the Commission's liberalisation drive. The third section discusses the internal energy market regulation's links to energy supply security and the role of CEE countries in the process of its development. The fourth section discusses the governance of sustainable energy transition with a focus on renewable energy sources, but also looks into the more global approach of the EU towards decarbonisation by examining the 2018 Energy Union Governance Regulation and its impact on the CEE region. The fifth section looks at the governance of decarbonisation from a different angle when it discusses carbon pricing and the position of CEE countries on issues related to the EU's Emissions Trading System (ETS).

3.2 STATE-MARKET RELATIONS AND LIBERALISATION

Following the fall of the Communist regimes, state-market relations in the energy sector have changed dramatically in the CEE region, with widespread privatisation. This process was gradual, and, in some cases, privatised energy companies were later re-nationalised. Russia's 2022 Russian invasion of Ukraine highlighted energy security and for some actors reinforced the necessity of state control over strategic energy sources. Changes in state-market relations have been significantly driven by EU internal market development in the 1990s and 2000s. We explore the variation of energy governance in the region, and the extent to which there is a convergence on the Commission's favoured liberal market model.

Gas Market Liberalisation

This section considers the transformation of CEE countries' gas sectors, in particular, the pace and extent to which the EU's Third 'Energy Liberalisation Package' has been implemented. Building on packages in the second half of 1990s and the beginning of 2000s, the third in 2009 required the legal and functional separation of transmission and distribution operations from the economically competitive activities of energy generation and supply (Maltby, 2013). However, there are different options regarding the unbundling of vertically integrated companies for member states. We discuss which of the three available options were chosen and why, and the implications for the governance of gas markets of these choices.

Whereas in the northwest gas region of the EU there was significant progress in the harmonisation of different national markets and some development towards regional gas markets, in CEE the market dynamics remained mostly national, with bilateral export relations with a single supplier changing only slowly (Fernandez and Palazuelos, 2014; see Figure 1.2, Chapter 1). Gas import dependency for many CEE states exceeded 50%, and the gas industry has been predominantly state-owned in some member states such as Czechia, Slovakia and Poland, justified in the latter as a means to achieve economic and national security.

As Fernandez and Palazuelos (2014, p. 495) have argued, since the late 1990s, 'the European Commission has forced changes on players, scenarios and exchange mechanisms through legislative action in order to build a new [liberalised] energy model'. This has been driven largely by two objectives, that of increasing security of supply and reducing prices – linked to economic and national security frames, respectively. This was to be achieved through (1) weakening the power, often monopolistic, of incumbent energy firms; (2) facilitating, financing and mandating the diversification of imports to mitigate the risks of dependence on Russia, particularly in CEE; (3) creating an interconnected single energy market; and (4) changing the pricing structure to eliminate long-term contracts and destination clauses that prevented gas from being re-exported to third countries. The EU's gas trade had been characterised by the large-scale domestic production by two members (the Netherlands and the United Kingdom[1]) and the high dependence on imports from three non-EU countries (Norway, Russia and Algeria). However, in CEE this dependence has been almost solely on Russia.

[1] Though the United Kingdom has been a net importer since 2004.

Until 1990 the Soviet Union's nationalised gas industry controlled the production of Russian gas and its export to CEE, exerting a significant political and economic influence through this. Bouzarovski and Bassin (2011, also Maltby, 2015) have argued that there is a post-socialist legacy in CEE, a positioning of Russia as a 'hydrocarbon superpower', projecting power through dominating gas exports to the region and playing a major role in the ownership of export and transit infrastructure (see also Chapter 1). Gazprom also often controlled significant shares of national energy companies, and through this the part-ownership of distribution to residential and business consumers in CEE. Pre-accession, national energy companies in the region were state-owned, 'national champions' within closed domestic markets. Whilst liberalisation of the markets has since occurred, this has been both incomplete and variegated. A key point has been, even prior to 2022, the changing role of Gazprom within the EU's energy markets. The Commission, based on internal energy market legislation in the Third Energy Package and at the request of Lithuania, launched an investigation into Gazprom in 2011 that included raids on Gazprom offices in ten CEE member states and in 2012 led to the opening of proceedings into contracts between Gazprom and eight CEE states: Bulgaria, Czechia, Estonia, Hungary, Latvia, Lithuania, Poland and Slovakia. The Commission's case concluded that Gazprom had been abusing and trying to protect its monopolistic market position by pursuing 'an overall strategy to partition Central and Eastern European gas markets ... to charge unfair prices in certain Member States' and prevent re-exports of gas (European Commission, 2015c). This was settled in 2017, with Gazprom agreeing to permit resales and indexing gas prices to competitive benchmarks, and changes were legally binding on Gazprom from May 2018 (Chyong et al., 2023).

Electricity Market Liberalisation

There are several characteristics of the CEE electricity sector that, whilst not exclusive to the region, are common: the limitation of new market entrants through the vertical integration of generation, supply and network activities, and the significant extent to which wholesale markets remain national in scope. The low-level cross-border electricity trade has been a feature of the energy landscape, though a significant development of interconnections between members states in the region, linked to the development of the emerging single EU electricity market, has had a major influence on national markets. The first electricity directive, in 1996, had the objectives of introducing competition, disrupting monopolistic electricity companies and integrating markets (Haber, 2018). A second (2003) and third (2009) directive mandated further liberalisation, including a full retail market opening; the unbundling of distribution, transmission and import companies; and greater regulation of access to infrastructure and cross-border trade (Pollitt, 2012).

In developing a single electricity market there is an ongoing process of market coupling, divided into EU regions. For example, Poland is in 'North-West Europe', and Czechia in the '4M Market Coupling' together with Slovakia, Hungary and Romania. The legacies of central economic planning and communist rule can be found in the predominance of state ownership and the enduring regulated pricing despite the process of liberalisation. As with the gas sector, state intervention in electricity is common in the region (Weiner and Szép, 2022).

In contrast to gas market liberalisation, electricity markets were subject to a fourth (2019) and fifth (2021) energy package. These were preceded by the 2014 Council decision, which set an interconnection target of 10% (European Council, 2014) that was increased to 15% by the 2018 Governance Regulation (Official Journal of the European Union, 2018). The aim was to enable transmission of the target amount of electricity to neighbouring countries by 2020 and 2030, respectively, to provide the physical links to facilitate a single market (the European Internal Electricity Market; Escribano et al., 2023; Hawker et al., 2017). The fourth energy package, as part of what was labelled *Clean Energy for All Europeans*, included an Electricity Directive (2019/944/EU) and Electricity Regulation (2019/943/EU). The main three goals were significantly orientated around climate objectives as they aimed at '[p]utting energy efficiency first, achieving global leadership in Renewable energies, and providing a fair deal for consumers', with 'market-based principles for the operation of electricity markets: prices will be formed on the basis of demand and supply' (European Parliament, 2021a). An objective was also to encourage decentralised electricity generation and prosumers/active energy market participants.

The fifth package, *Delivering the European Green Deal*, aimed to align the EU's energy targets with the new 2030 and 2050 climate ambitions, the former to achieve emissions reductions of 55%, and the latter for a climate-neutral EU. An objective was to reform the electricity market design to better accommodate the rapidly increasing quantity of renewable electricity being produced (Peng and Poudineh, 2019). When considering the effects of this process of liberalisation, the third energy package was linked to notable declines in wholesale electricity prices in its early years of implementation (Council of the EU, 2014) with a significant increase in competition in the electricity generation market in countries such as Estonia, Latvia and Croatia (Pollitt, 2019). However, the costs incurred for both businesses and residential consumers later increased due to increases in network charges, taxes and levies (Pollitt, 2019), some related to the cost of subsidising renewable energy.

3.3 SECURITY OF ENERGY SUPPLY LEGISLATION

This section examines EU common rules on security of supplies developed to improve energy security, particularly following the 2006 and 2009 Russian gas supply disruptions, with common supply security rules designed to complement the internal market liberalisation rules. The following section examines security of electricity supply legislation and then two gas regulations.

Security of Electricity Supply

The objective of creating an interconnected single electricity market had a clear security objective, to facilitate increased electricity flows across national borders, with a balance of member states' ultimate responsibility of electricity supply within a regulated EU energy market. In 2017 a key tool was introduced, a *Network Code on Emergency and Restoration* (Regulation 2017/2196/EU), which set out detailed rules and standards for the management on how to respond to power failures. This was shortly followed by the fourth energy package focused on risk prevention, with the regulation on electricity risk preparedness (Regulation 2019/941/EU) making it a national requirement to prepare contingency plans for potential electricity crises and requiring '[m]ember states to cooperate ... in a spirit of solidarity', a shift from a previous invitation to cooperate.

The 2019 Regulation (2019/941/EU) also included 'common definitions, risk assessment methodology and crisis scenarios' to direct the planning for crises and to increase transparency by requiring the sharing of plans. Through the establishment of Regional Coordinating Centres, neighbouring member states were grouped, facilitating greater coordination between them whilst retaining member state sovereignty, with the Commission only invited to comment on plans (Beaussier and Cabane, 2020). In response to Russia's invasion of Ukraine, in June 2022 Germany, Austria, Czechia, Hungary, Poland and Slovakia signed a memorandum of understanding on risk preparedness and solidarity in the electricity sector that explicitly planned for situations where market-based measures fail to provide security of electricity supplies (Kurmayer, 2022b).

The 2010 Security of Gas Supply Regulation (994/2010)

The 2006 and 2009 gas supply disruptions were 'a pivotal turning point in legal thinking about European gas security of supply' (Fleming, 2019, p. 102). They showed not only that several member states in the region were unprepared for supply disruptions (especially Bulgaria and Slovakia; see Chapter 1), but also, as the Commission admitted in its evaluation of the disruptions, that 'a clear strategy as well as concrete instruments were lacking' (European Commission, 2009a, p. 11). In response, the Commission proposed new rules, with a 2010 Security of Gas Supply (SoS) Regulation obliging gas suppliers to ensure an uninterrupted supply of gas to customers defined as 'protected customers' (de Almeida, 2019), a definition that differs between individual member states.

One of the main lessons from the 2009 supply disruption was the need to harmonise national measures in order for all member states to fulfil at least some minimum criteria to avoid free-riding (Rodríguez-Gómez et al., 2016, p. 461). The Commission attempted to find a balance between member state sovereignty and national policy responses that would undermine other member states. The 2010 SoS Regulation introduced the concept of solidarity as a response, something further developed by the 2017 SoS Regulation (Fleming, 2019). An innovation was the N − 1 rule, whereby a member state must diversify its natural gas infrastructure to a level where it is able to maintain gas supplies for its protected customers even if its main supply route (N) is interrupted (−1), to the extent that it could cover seven 'extremely cold days'. Improvement of interconnections in the form of development of (physical) reverse flows was another tool of the regulation, and the Commission developed several funds to finance infrastructure projects (European Commission 2014c; see also Chapter 4).

The 2010 SoS Regulation governed long-term contracts (LTCs) via Article 13 that required national authorities (i.e., ministries) to communicate intergovernmental agreements (IGAs) of over a year with third countries to the Commission (though not publicly). Member states reported altogether 300 LTCs until 2014, with 36% of them being in force for twenty or more years; five countries communicated more than thirty contracts each (European Commission, 2014c). However, member states fiercely guarded their sovereignty to decide their energy mix and choose suppliers (de Hauteclocque et al., 2015), and the Commission's report provided only aggregate, not individual member state data (European Commission, 2014c).

To address this, the Commission introduced a 2012 Decision (994/2012/EU) establishing an information exchange mechanism for intergovernmental energy agreements between member states and third countries – replacing the provisions in the SoS Regulation. However, after reviewing 124 IGAs submitted on the basis of this rule, the Commission concluded that the decision 'in its present form is not considered effective' (European Commission, 2016a, p. 5) as its ex post nature prevented the Commission from effectively enforcing the EU's internal energy market rules regarding LTCs (Herranz-Surrallés, 2017). However, building on prior legislation the Commission managed to push through a more ambitious proposal for oversight of IGAs that included an ex ante mechanism (Batzella, 2021). The resulting Decision 2017/684/EU introduced ex ante evaluations of LTCs and was part of a broader energy security package, including a revised gas supply regulation.

What this new system introduced was an approach used in the European Semester to align member states' policy preferences with those of the Commission. Member states first presented their 'draft' preferences for Commission review, with revisions then requested before their formal approval (Woźniakowski et al., 2021). A very similar ex ante approach was later utilised to align member states' national goals to EU 2030 climate and energy targets that are legally binding at EU but not national level (Mišík and Oravcová, 2022; see also Section 3.4). However, even this new approach of the Commission proved limited as energy actors managed to circumvent common EU rules by switching to other types of gas contracts.

The 2017 Security of Gas Supply Regulation (2017/1938)

The 2017 SoS Regulation introduced new requirements for member states, including risk assessments and the establishment of preventative and emergency plans (Praks and Kopustinskas, 2019). One of the main differences between the two regulations is the inclusion of electricity undertakings among the actors responsible for gas supply security that is 'part of a bigger mission of the Commission to include electricity undertakings and industry more into the scope of the new security of gas supplies Regulation' (Fleming, 2019, p. 104). This is connected to the expected increased role of natural gas in electricity production. The revised regulation also reflected the results of gas supplies' stress tests conducted in 2014 that identified the Baltic States, Hungary, Bulgaria, Romania, Finland and Greece as the most vulnerable to gas supply interruptions (European Commission, 2014d).

This regulation introduced the concept of risk groups and a new solidarity principle that is designed to further improve energy supply security (Kochanek, 2019). These 'risk groups' are clusters of member states with common gas suppliers and supply routes grouped together on the basis of the 2014 stress tests (European Commission, 2014b). The tests showed that 'the performance of the Union in terms of resilience improved remarkably in case[s] of an adequately coordinated response' and that improved regional cooperation was required (Perrone, 2019, p. 12). The idea behind the risk groups was to 'serve as basis for enhanced regional cooperation and agreement on effective cross-border measures' (Fleming, 2019, p. 105). The CEE countries included in two main risk group clusters within the regulation were the Eastern gas supply risk group and the South East supply risk group.

Solidarity was an important principle included in the 2010 SoS Regulation (Goldberg, 2011) and was further developed in its 2017 revision, whereby a member state 'is obliged, under certain conditions, to take measures to ensure the gas supply to protected customers' in other member states that request assistance (Hancher and Marhold, 2019, p. 297). Such solidarity is envisioned to be the last resort and the requesting state must provide fair and prompt compensation. While solidarity is highlighted in the document, the regulation also includes a set of 'exit gateways' for those unwilling to participate: for example, it states that the obligation to provide solidarity is subject to the safe and reliable functioning of the gas system of the country providing solidarity (Fleming, 2019).

Kochanek implicitly argues that CEE member states are the main beneficiaries of the solidarity principles because their energy supplies were much less diversified and connected to the rest of the EU's gas markets (2019). The regulation requires the risk groups to cooperate in the case of regional emergency at the level of transmission system operators (TSOs) – this rule was tested in December 2017 when TSOs successfully reacted to an incident at the Baumgarten gas hub in Austria that threatened gas flows between Slovakia and Austria and between Austria and Hungary, Italy, Slovenia and Croatia (Törőcsik and Selei, 2018). The groups also need to cooperate when developing preventative and emergency measures, with a recommendation to do so in the 2010 Regulation becoming a requirement by 2017.

3.4 GOVERNING SUSTAINABLE ENERGY TRANSITIONS

This section considers the various policy instruments designed to achieve the renewable and energy efficiency targets set by the EU in 2009 (the 2020 Energy and Climate Package) and 2014 (the 2030 Energy and Climate Framework), updated in 2018 with the revised Renewable Energy Directive and through to 2021's climate law and 2022's REPowerEU policy. This section considers the policy measures selected, the pace of introducing renewable and energy efficiency measures, and the obstacles to these. Also considered is the role of electricity systems and their development to accommodate renewable energy installations, including smart grid construction, national and transnational infrastructure development, and the role of distribution system operators and transmission system operators. Path dependency is a crucial impediment to rapid institutional change to match dramatic policy shifts. We find that the obstacles are related to institutional, material, and societal factors, with the legacies of post-socialist economic and institutional transition still influential (Ürge-Vorsatz et al., 2006).

There has been a pattern of renewable energy policy over-compliance and then reversal in the EU (Gürtler et al., 2019; Lockwood et al., 2017), fitting with cases of active environmental policy dismantling in the wake of the financial crisis (Bauer and Knill, 2012; Gravey and Jordan, 2016, 2020). Here we examine the types of renewable support policies, the number of policies in support of renewables (*density*), and the level of support (*intensity*) (Jordan et al., 2013; Knill et al., 2009). Whilst several CEE countries could be crudely characterised as renewable policy 'laggards' (for example, Poland and Slovakia), there have also been 'leaders' that have achieved EU objectives well ahead of schedule. For example, a form of renewable policy dismantling occurred in Bulgaria and Romania, countries that achieved their targets approximately eight years ahead of the 2020 target, but then proceeded to introduce retrospective legislation and to dismantle policy support as the initial pace and cost exceeded projections. Rather than a deeper energy transition, what the legally binding 2020 renewable targets led to in some countries was the mobilisation of significant resistance to going beyond the minimum from the public, politicians and industry – in particular, groups representing established energy companies and sources of energy production (Davidescu et al., 2018).

How renewable energy has been framed by member states is an important consideration in this section, whether it is conceptualised as realising economic, environmental or national security goals or merely as an obligation of EU membership that does not constitute a national priority. In doing so we explore the extent to which security is mobilised and whether the three key frames noted are overlapping or competing in CEE, thus whether there is convergence with the EU's framing of climate and energy objectives as synergistic, mutually reinforcing and coherent.

The 2018 Governance Regulation

The 2018 Regulation on the Governance of the Energy Union and Climate Action (2018/1999) created a link between member states' national climate and energy goals and EU-wide targets. Contrary to the 2020 targets that were partially binding at the national levels, the 2030 energy and climate targets were instead largely binding at the EU level – the EU had to collectively reach them as member states invoked sovereignty to resist the extension of nationally binding renewable energy targets (Kulovesi and Oberthür, 2020). The Governance Regulation's main task was to create a link between national goals and the EU-wide targets to make sure that the latter were met, and the possibility of member state free-riding was limited. The Governance Regulation established an ex ante mechanism that required member states to submit to the Commission their National Energy and Climate Plans (NECPs), which mirrored the Paris Agreement's bottom-up mechanism, and required outlines of 2030 goals and how each member state planned to achieve them. The Commission evaluated these based on a set of benchmarks stemming from existing commitments (Mišík and Oravcová, 2022). The Commission requested, though could not require, that member states that did not contribute – according to its own assessment – fairly to the EU-wide targets increase their commitment levels (European Commission, 2020b). This mechanism was successful in its first cycle in modestly increasing national energy and climate goals, and significantly closing an 'ambition gap' between the EU-wide and national goals found in initial national plans for renewables, though energy efficiency plans still fell short of the EU's legally binding collective target (Vanhercke and Verdun, 2022).

There were five main national goals that the Commission evaluated in the NECPs. These were connected to the main 2030 EU-wide targets: greenhouse gas reductions, increasing the share of renewables, decreasing primary and final energy consumption (energy efficiency) and increasing electricity interconnectivity (Official Journal of the European Union, 2018). Overall, in CEE, member states followed many of the Commission's recommendations to improve the ambition of their climate goals, and some were considered to have gone beyond the minimum required and were 'ambitious' – Slovakia's emissions cuts and Croatia's, Estonia's and Lithuania's renewable targets (European Commission, 2020c). Whilst the Commission concluded that the collective ambition had increased, they criticised the majority of CEE states – with renewable plans for Czechia (European Commission, 2020d), Poland (European Commission, 2020e), Hungary

(European Commission, 2020f), Romania (European Commission, 2020g), Slovakia (European Commission, 2020h) and Slovenia (European Commission, 2020i) all considered 'unambitious' and not representing a fair burden-sharing of the EU's collective target. For Czechia the Commission concluded that 'plans to increase its share of electricity consumption from renewable sources to 16.9% by 2030 [which constitutes] a significant slowdown compared to 2010–2018, despite the massive cost reductions in wind and solar photovoltaic power generation' (European Commission, 2020d, p. 2), and energy efficiency was considered to represent only low to modest ambition. For Slovakia, Romania and Hungary, energy efficiency ambition was also considered 'low' to 'very low'. With the exception of Poland all CEE member states met the energy security related 15% interconnection target.

Governing Renewables

To fulfil the renewables' goal set within the 2020 climate and energy package, the EU set a 20% target for the bloc, with burden sharing between member states based on factors such as GDP and starting points. Directive 2009/28/EC (European Parliament and the Council, 2009a) set different nationally binding renewables targets. These goals were transposed into national legal frameworks and created the basis for an increase of renewables in CEE countries during the following period (Mišík, 2021) and the development of complex and flourishing renewable policies, and Figure 3.1 shows the progress towards national goals between 2009 and 2020. While most of these countries had previously utilised hydropower to a significant degree – with minimal room for further growth – wind, solar and other types of

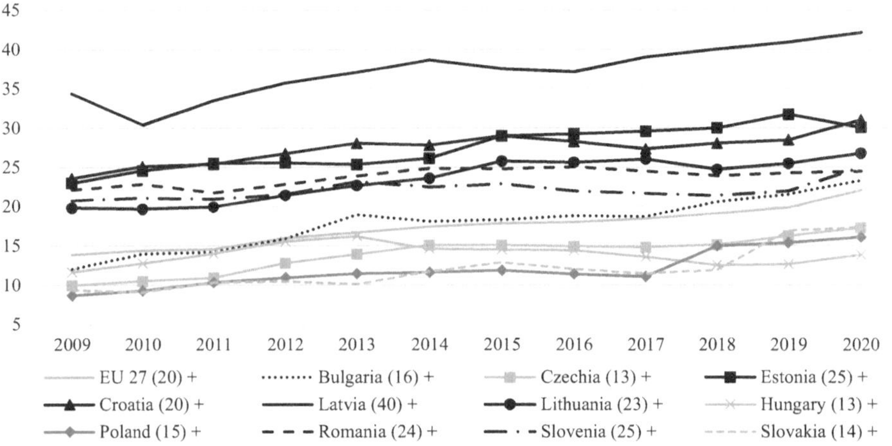

FIGURE 3.1 Share of renewable energy sources in gross final energy consumption. Note: National 2020 goal in parentheses; '+' means that this goal was achieved.
Source: Eurostat (2022a)

renewables were underdeveloped. Therefore, most of the interest (as well as EU financial support) was directed to this area.

All CEE countries reached their 2020 renewable goals, following the use of a variety of policy instruments, such as quota obligations in Poland and Romania or feed-in tariffs in Bulgaria, Czechia, Hungary and Slovakia (Ragwitz et al., 2012). However, this process also brought a set of problems that resulted, in some cases, in renewables policy dismantling due to high costs connected to their support (Gürtler et al., 2019; Mišík and Oravcová, 2020). In Slovakia renewable energy as a share decreased between 2015 and 2018, and Czechia experienced the same reversal between 2014 and 2017 (see Figure 3.1). In Czechia key factors were '(1) an inflexible policy design; [and] (2) the lack of industry exemptions, which caused extensive lobbying by powerful incumbents against the scheme' (Gürtler et al., 2019, p. 8). A third factor was found in a similar pattern of policy dismantling in Bulgaria and Romania, the early achievement of the nationally binding target, with little incentive to go beyond it (Gürtler et al., 2019).

Bulgaria, Czechia and Romania achieved their EU2020 targets seven to eight years ahead of the 2020 target, and Slovakia five years ahead, but all proceeded to introduce retrospective legislation and to dismantle policy support as the initial pace and cost associated with subsidies and the electricity grid exceeded projections. Rather than a deeper energy transition, what has been experienced is the mobilisation of significant resistance from the public, politicians and industry – in particular, from groups representing established energy companies and sources of energy production (Davidescu et al., 2018). Whilst in Bulgaria the effect was a temporary dip, in Romania, renewable energy had a lower share in 2020 than in 2014. In Slovakia, a stagnation of renewables continued until 2019 when changes were made in the methodology used to determine the share of renewables (a significant amount of biomass was added; Mišík and Oravcová, 2020). Overall, there were questions over the extent to which stable and sustainable renewables policies had been established that would allow further growth, and the role for nationally binding targets.

Cetkovic and Buzogany (2020) argue that a key to explaining the development of renewables in the region is foreign policy relations with Russia (and the extent to which it is perceived as a reliable supplier) and alternatives to renewables. These alternatives often relate to preferences on nuclear energy – where a reliance on this as a potential source can absorb funding and political capital at the expense of prioritising renewable technologies. For example, in Lithuania the country's 2018 National Energy Independence Strategy abandoned nuclear plans and focused on renewables (Janeliūnas, 2021, p. 284) as a means to achieve not only climate goals but security of supply through energy independence from Russia.

The challenges of increasing renewables within the CEE region have been very visible in the case of Hungary and Poland, countries that adopted legislation prohibiting the construction of wind turbines close to residential areas, strictly restricting development. In Poland since 2016 no wind turbines were permitted within approximately 2,000 metres of a residential building or national park, effectively restricting development to only 2% of the country (Jackson, 2023). Similarly, Hungary had a ban on wind turbines within twelve kilometres of populated areas, an effective outright ban (Szőke, 2023). Whilst Poland can construct offshore wind farms and has revised the onshore wind farm policy to a limited extent, Hungary as a land-locked country does not have this option. Other countries, for example, Slovakia, have limited the employment of renewables by other means, for instance, by not issuing grid connection permits for these energy sources Similarly, a 2022 Hungarian government decision to prohibit the connection of all new photovoltaic plants to the electricity grid (Makszimov, 2022).

3.5 GOVERNING FOSSIL FUEL PHASE-OUTS: CARBON PRICING

Increasing the deployment of renewables is crucial for climate change mitigation, and related to phasing out fossil fuels, especially coal. While Chapter 4 discusses the energy security aspects of domestic coal and Chapter 6 examines support for coal at the EU level, here we consider the related governance of emissions.

A key driver of energy transitions in CEE is the Emissions Trading System (ETS), regulating the price of carbon emissions and funding energy transitions. The ETS requires over 10,000 factories and power plants in the EU to have a permit for every tonne of CO_2 they emit, with the objective of providing a powerful financial incentive to reduce pollution. This market mechanism uses auctions, with prices set by supply and demand and gradually decreasing permits that drive up costs. The Commission concluded that '[i]nstallations covered by the ETS reduced emissions by about 35% between 2005 and 2019' (European Commission, 2022c). CEE countries benefitted from generous opt-outs provided for countries in the region – derogations that provided free permits during a transition period, exemptions on the grounds of protecting industry and coal-fired power plants and the economies of CEE in general (Skjærseth and Wettestad, 2010). The ETS' National Allocation Plans submitted by CEE countries were initially rejected as being insufficiently ambitious, and countries in the region were forced to significantly reduce their national allowance allocations (Spencer and Fazekas, 2013). However, when the ETS was implemented in 2005 it was found that Poland was among the countries that had over-allocated and been too generous in providing allowances to the ETS industry (Skjærseth and Wettestad, 2008). A 2009 revision of the ETS Directive centralised its functioning at the EU level (Bocquillon and Maltby, 2017). From 2013 existing coal power plants received free allowances, but new plants no longer qualified for this (Egenhofer et al., 2011).

Revenues generated from auctioning ETS revenues are to be allocated to reducing emissions, mitigating or adapting to climate change in the EU or third countries according to Article 10 (3) of the 2009 Directive on the greenhouse gas emission allowance trading scheme (European Parliament and the Council, 2009b). A 2018 reform introduced two funds to accelerate energy transitions. The first was a Modernisation Fund to be used to upgrade energy systems in lower-income member states in CEE, a solidarity measure to compensate the outdated energy sector in the region (Wang and Paavola, 2023), though importantly this excludes coal. The scale of this fund is estimated at €48 billion between 2021 and 2030, depending on the carbon price (European Commission, 2022d), and the CEE states are the only recipients.[2] Linked to relative GDP the major recipients are Czechia and Poland, and this fund supports energy efficiency, storage, renewable energy and modernising energy networks in addition to funding retraining and reskilling in fossil fuel regions.

The second is an Innovation Fund, also funded by the ETS, that will invest approximately €38 billion in renewable, low-carbon and carbon capture and storage between 2020 and 2030 (European Commission, 2022e) and is the successor to a €2 billion NER 300 fund also financed through the ETS (European Commission, 2022f). Aimed at 'highly innovative technologies', much of this is targeted at innovations in renewable energy generation, but also storage and nascent carbon capture technologies. In contrast to the Modernisation Fund this is open to all member states, and the first progress report in 2022 showed that whilst it 'received applications from almost all Member States, projects are developed in many Member States, albeit with a lower representation in Eastern Europe' (European Commission, 2022g, p. 16), with CEE countries appearing to be disadvantaged when identifying and seeking funding from the 'big flagship projects' it is targeted at. Of seventeen selected large-scale projects, only three were in CEE (two in Poland and one in Bulgaria) (European Commission, 2022h).

3.6 CONCLUSION

This chapter examined post-accession climate and energy governance in the CEE region. The internal energy market has been harmonised within the EU, with implementation of the rules of the first two liberalisation packages part of their accession process. Some CEE countries demonstrated divergent preferences on the third liberalisation package as will be explored in Chapter 6, and the implementation of these measures has been influenced by their historical legacies, including state-owned energy monopolies that were affected by the liberalisation process.

Linked to enduring material and political relations with Russia, the energy securitisation process has varied in terms of the extent to which security of supply has been considered threatened, by whom, and with what appropriate policy response. Generally, in CEE there has been support for greater policy integration,

[2] Beneficiary member states: Bulgaria, Croatia, Czechia, Estonia, Hungary, Latvia, Lithuania, Poland, Romania and Slovakia.

to empower the Commission in order to improve their positions towards energy suppliers from third countries. As a result, greater prioritisation was given by CEE countries to the development of common security of supply rules. These included new rules concerning the oversight of intergovernmental agreements and LTCs between EU member states and energy exporters from third countries, particularly Russia. Whilst the region is arguably the main beneficiary of energy solidarity introduced by the Security of Supply regulation in 2010, a divergence of preferences was later seen as Hungary and Slovakia expressed critical positions when solidarity on energy sanctions was high on the agenda from 2022 (Mišík and Nosko, 2023b), as will be discussed in Chapter 6.

The EU's renewable energy legislation has been highly influential, with all CEE states, many from relatively low starting points, achieving their 2020 targets and many being some of the first EU states to do so. However, renewable policy dismantling and limited political will was present in most CEE countries. This has manifested itself in reservations about, and opposition to, ambitious 2030 climate goals and the extent to which renewables are considered as tools to achieve energy independence and security of supply. In Chapter 6 we explore the extent to which these states have attempted and been successful in shaping the EU's climate and energy policy to accommodate their preferences.

4

The Effect of Foreign Policy on Climate and Energy Policy

4.1 INTRODUCTION

Although most CEE countries were traditionally dependent on energy supplies from Russia (and before 1991 from the Soviet Union), this dependency was not considered to be a source of strategic vulnerability in most cases even after these countries embarked on the path towards democracy and market economies at the end of the 1980s (Bocquillon and Maltby, 2017; Högselius, 2012). The main exception was Czechia, which considered dependence on Russian energy supplies to present a security challenge and diversified oil and natural gas supplies during the 1990s as a response (Jirušek et al., 2017). Contrary to Western EU members for which Russia was also an important – but not sole – natural gas and oil supplier, the majority of CEE countries had no other supplier options and therefore were fully dependent for natural gas (and oil) on Russia (Godzimirski, 2013; Herranz-Surrallés, 2016; Siddi, 2017). Energy security has become a crucial energy policy issue for these countries after the natural gas supply disruptions of 2006 and 2009 (Grigas, 2013a; Mišík and Prachárová, 2016), while climate policy emerged on the CEE countries' agenda only in the late 2000s. These disruptions have been combined with increasing gas prices particularly in the late 2000s, selective gas pricing for different member states, and increasingly assertive Russian foreign policy (Khrushcheva and Maltby, 2016). The 2022 Russian invasion of Ukraine provided an impetus for these member countries to double down on their prioritisation of energy security, though not all of the CEE states have supported strict EU sanctions against Russia's energy sector.

By discussing the energy supply structure and foreign policy sources of CEE countries' energy policy preferences, this chapter contributes to the first argument of the book about the prioritisation of energy security over climate policy, which is reflected in CEE countries' policy and investment preferences. To support such an argument, this chapter evaluates the interplay between ideas (securitisation/

politicisation), institutions (climate and energy governance), and the material nature of energy systems (socio-technical regimes) in the development of energy and climate policy of these countries in relation to their external energy supply structures. In doing so it highlights the social construction of energy security (i.e., the impact of ideas), demonstrating that within the CEE region energy security is not self-evident or correlated solely with dependency on energy imports from Russia. Individual CEE countries perceive energy supplies as a security issue to a different extent, identifying the source and extent of insecurity or risk differently.

As a result, their policy solutions to these issues differ, with some states increasing domestic energy production (particularly coal, nuclear energy or renewables), several focusing on external diversification (i.e., new oil and gas interconnectors or liquefied natural gas (LNG) terminals) and others focusing on the promotion of a stronger common EU approach. For example, and as considered further in Chapter 6, Czechia, Hungary and Slovenia assume a rather passive approach at the EU level, whereas others – most notably, Lithuania and Poland, and also Slovakia – consider energy security one of their main domestic policy issues, and prioritise promoting EU-level policy responses to increase regional and national energy security. While natural gas is considered by the EU to be a bridging energy source on the pathway to a net zero future (Hauser et al., 2018; Mete, 2020b), its security dimension has been the focus for many CEE countries. Whilst security of supply is used to justify nuclear use, or aspirations, it is less strongly linked to renewables in CEE as a means for attaining energy independence (Lithuania is an exception). However, there are significant differences between CEE countries in the utilisation of individual energy sources and strategies.

This chapter focuses on how CEE states conceptualise their energy security and what they identify as a challenge or threat to it, considering the tensions between energy policy and climate objectives, in particular. Taking into consideration economic and national security objectives, we examine five areas: (1) EU legislation responding to external gas supply disruptions, (2) pipeline and LNG infrastructure to diversify supply sources away from Russia as a means of achieving energy security, (3) using domestic coal for energy security reasons despite climate goals, (4) renewables as a solution to energy security challenges and (5) the utilisation of nuclear energy driven by climate and security of supply concerns.

4.2 THE EU'S SECURITY OF SUPPLY LEGISLATION

As noted in Chapter 1, the 2006 and 2009 gas supply disruptions showed that several member states in the CEE region were unprepared for such a situation. At the heart of supply security problems in the region were long-term contracts (LTCs) with third countries and no alternative supply options (European Commission, 2014c, p. 19). LTCs have been – and in several cases remain – the main method of gas imports to CEE countries, although EU legislation has driven changes to market-based short-term contracts, for example, in the Czechia and Lithuania, and in Poland from 2020 (for transit) and 2022 (for supply). The end of 2021 exposed shortcomings in the gas market as a swift recovery of demand following the 2020 pandemic-fuelled decrease caused a steep increase in the price of natural gas in the European gas market, prompting a call for a return to LTCs (Khan 2021; Kotek et al. 2023).

In theory LTCs provide a stable environment for both exporter and importer and enable long-term investments in complex, and expensive, import infrastructure. The traditional system often involved a national monopoly gas company negotiating with a monopoly supplier, and for CEE this was usually Russia's Gazprom (Talus, 2012). However, the development of the EU internal energy market and liberalisation of energy markets contributed to the break-up of energy monopolies together with the expansion of gas interconnections and the development of LNG terminals. These enabled CEE countries to increasingly access the global gas market, often at a lower price than Russian gas. A liberalised gas market is, however, in tension with LTCs (de Hauteclocque et al., 2015, pp. 2–3). The 2010 Gas SoS Regulation stated that by 2014 all states should be able to cope with losing their main supplier in which there was often an LTC in place, and this led to upgraded gas interconnections involving Bulgaria, Czechia, Hungary, Poland and Slovakia (Korkmaz, 2018).

Stress tests conducted in 2014 identified the Baltic States, Hungary, Bulgaria, Romania, Finland and Greece as the most vulnerable in the case of future gas supply interruptions (European Commission, 2014d), though by November 2021 a report simulating gas supply disruptions (ENTSOG, 2021) found that the possible cooperation of member states was 'significantly improved' in circumstances of unusually cold winters, with only the Baltic States and Finland remaining vulnerable. The winter of 2022 saw the region unaffected by supply problems despite Russian gas disruptions.

4.3 GAS SUPPLY DIVERSIFICATION

Despite gas supply diversification efforts, most CEE countries at the beginning of 2020s continued to import significant amounts of Russian gas (see Chapter 1 and Table 4.1). This was a result of the legacy of Soviet energy infrastructure (Högselius, 2012). Natural gas and oil supplies were used to keep Soviet control over strategic sectors of CEE economies, to maintain political influence and create centripetal links between the Soviet Union, particularly Russia, and the satellite Soviet and Comecon states (Bouzarovski, 2009, p. 455). After the fall of the communist regimes in CEE, most countries paid little attention to energy and climate issues (Mišík, 2010). The economic transformation put pressure on their economies, and energy supply diversification and interconnections with neighbouring states were not priorities; nor was import dependence generally considered to be a significant security issue before the first gas interruption of 2006. With the exception of the Baltic States

TABLE 4.1 *Natural gas data in CEE countries* (2020, *in Mtoe if not specified otherwise*)[a]

	BG	CZ	EE	HR	HU	LT	LV	PL	RO	SI	SK
Production	0.0	0.2	0.0	0.7	1.3	0.0	0.0	3.4	7.4	0.0	0.1
Net import	2.4	6.3	0.4	1.7	6.6	2.0	0.9	13.6	1.6	0.7	3.6
Gross inland consumption	2.5	7.3	0.3	2.5	8.46	2.0	0.9	17.4	9.7	0.7	4.09
Import dependency (%)	96.4	86.0	106.3	68.8	75.6	98.9	100.1	78.3	16.6	99.4	88.1
Russian import dependency (%)[b]	79	55	12	16	61	27	92	50	24	60	68

[a] BG, Bulgaria; CZ, Czechia; EE, Estonia; HR, Croatia; HU, Hungary; LT, Lithuania; LV, Latvia; PL, Poland; RO, Romania; SI, Slovenia; SK, Slovakia.
[b] Data for 2021.
Sources: European Commission, 2022i; Statista, 2023.

and Czechia, the historical experience of problem-free Soviet and then Russian energy supplies in combination with the need to deal with day-to-day consequences of political and economic transition, including negotiating EU membership (Schimmelfennig, 2001), left most of the CEE countries uninterested in diversification of their energy supplies until at least the early to mid-2000s (Gustafson 2020; Mišík and Oravcová 2021b). Security concerns increased as oil supply disruptions were experienced by Czechia in the 2000s (Jirušek et al., 2020), and Russian oil supplies to Lithuania were cut off in 2006 (Balmaceda, 2008).

The 2006 and 2009 gas supply disruptions had an impact on many CEE energy policies and elevated energy security to a priority issue. CEE governments increasingly engaged in a process of securitisation by linking gas supplies with national security, making claims about the existential threat posed by its main supplier, Russia, potentially using energy as 'a weapon' (Judge and Maltby, 2017, p. 201). It had become increasingly clear that Russia was willing and able to use energy to exert 'coercive economic, diplomatic and political pressure on the CEE countries' (Ostrowski, 2020, p. 2). This had a direct effect on policy. One of the main lessons was the urgent need to diversify gas sources and avoid dependency on a single source. Limited – or non-existent – alternative supply routes exacerbated the impact of the crises in a region where several countries were dependent on gas supplies from one supplier (Gazprom) via a single route (the Brotherhood pipeline). The Baltic States were recognised by the Commission's 2006 energy green paper as an isolated 'energy island' (European Commission, 2006), with no gas connections to other member states, vulnerable to supply disruptions.

Two prime examples of such a situation were Bulgaria and Slovakia. Both were left in January 2009 without any natural gas supplies for almost three weeks, and a lack of infrastructure to provide emergency supplies from neighbouring countries. Whilst Russia had previously been seen as a security guarantor rather than threat in Bulgaria, the supply disruptions challenged this perception (Hiteva and Maltby, 2014) as the 2009 disruption affected Bulgarian hospitals, schools and industry, with an estimated economic cost of €250 million (Energy Regulators, 2010). For Slovakia this came as a shock to policy-makers who thought that the transit status of their country was a sufficient guarantor of their energy security, and where the estimated costs were around €100 million per day for more than two weeks (Mišík, 2019).

Other CEE countries also had to deal with notably decreased supplies, and very low domestic production precluded replacing external supplies with domestic (see Table 4.1). Only Romania and Croatia[1] had sufficient domestic natural gas production to meet demand (Pavlović et al., 2018; Vlček and Jirušek, 2019; see Chapter 5 on shale gas (non)development). Due to the historical legacy of Russian energy supply infrastructure, CEE countries were dependent on gas flowing in one direction, from east (Russia) to west (European countries), so providing emergency supplies from

[1] Croatia joined the EU in 2013, so experienced the 2009 crisis as a non-member.

FIGURE 4.1 Map of main Russian gas transit routes to Europe.
Source: Naftogaz, 2022

Western Europe was not possible (Bouzarovski, 2009; see Figure 4.1). Moreover, the existing gas pipelines (Yamal, the Brotherhood) were not interconnected in a north-south direction so even the fact that the Yamal pipeline was working did not help countries like Slovakia that were fully dependent on the Brotherhood natural gas pipeline. As explored in Chapter 6 countries such as Poland then attempted to shape EU policy and 'collectively securitise energy and enhance non-market solutions' – establishing Russia as a threat to the EU rather than a source of regional or national energy security (Hofmann and Staeger, 2019, p. 325).

Diversification of gas supply sources and routes was an objective for the EU before the 2006 and 2009 supply disruptions (Maltby, 2013), and a number of countries in the CEE region highlighted that import dependence was problematic. National security strategies (NSS) of the CEE countries underlined the need to diversify already in the early to mid-2000s (e.g., Czech Government, 2003: 10; Latvian Government, 2005: 4; Polish Government, 2003: 3; Slovak Government, 2005: 7); however, there was little explicit mention of Russia as the source of insecurity, though Lithuania's 2002 NSS was an exception with its reference to '[o]-verwhelming dependence of the Republic of Lithuania on the strategic resources and energy supplies of one country' (Lithuanian Government, 2002, p. 5). The 2006 and 2009 supply disruptions changed this. Member states in the region began to perceive Russian energy supplies as jeopardising their energy, and even national security after 2006, with the country frequently explicitly referenced (Latvian Government, 2015, p. 4; Lithuanian Government, 2017, p. 4; Polish Government, 2007, p. 6) and implicitly referred to in the NSSs by all other countries in the region except Hungary. In contrast, Hungary signed a fifteen-year gas contract with Russia in September 2021, and in February 2022 and despite tensions between the EU and Russia over Ukraine requested an increase in Russian gas imports (RFERL, 2022).

Different supply routes for CEE countries affected the extent of their disruption (Schmidt-Felzmann, 2011). Poland received – until the construction of an LNG terminal – its gas supplies only via the Yamal pipeline, constructed in the 1990s (Szul, 2011). This became a focal point of the EU in late 2021 when Gazprom decreased its supplies via this pipeline, and in response the flow of gas was reversed to supply Poland from German gas storage (Reuters, 2021a). The Baltic States have their own energy interconnectors with Russia that have been prone to interruptions, which has driven them to take action to reduce import dependence and their isolation as an energy island through energy infrastructure projects (Grigas, 2013a). Lithuania experienced a series of energy supply interruptions following its independence declaration in 1990, with Soviet leaders hoping this would prevent the country from developing a self-sufficient economy (Janeliūnas, 2009). This energy isolation from Europe also applies to electricity for the Baltic countries, and in 2018 there was a commitment to synchronising their electricity networks with the rest of Europe by 2025, explicitly because of the risk posed by dependence on imports from Russia. According to the Estonian Prime Minister Jüri Ratas, 'Connecting the electricity networks of Estonia, Latvia, and Lithuania with Europe will make us less dependent on Russia in terms of energy and will ensure security of supply of electricity' (Ratas cited in Collier, 2018). This is co-financed by a €720 million grant from the EU's Connecting Europe Facility, the largest ever from this funding stream (European Commission, 2020j), and was accelerated in autumn 2022 to a completion target of 2024 (CEE Energy News, 2022).

Slovenian vulnerability to gas supply disruptions is low: the country has a smaller than average share of natural gas in the energy mix (about 10%) due to very low residential gas consumption; has diversified gas supplies including connections to Austria, Hungary and Italy (REKK, 2018, p. 8); and switched most of its supplies from LTCs to market-based short-term supply deals during the 2010s (Agencia za enegrijo, 2017). In 2023 a mid-term gas contract between the biggest natural gas trader, Geoplin, and Gazprom that had been in place since 2018 expired (Crnčec et al., 2021). A previous LTC from 2010 to 2025 was renegotiated and expired at the end of 2017, and since 2023 Slovenian gas imports from Russia have been replaced by Algerian supplies (Slovenian Government, 2022).

Czechia underwent both route and source diversification in natural gas and oil in the 1990s and thus differs from other CEE countries in pursuing this strategy so early. The objective of a new oil pipeline was to connect to the German market; the

Ingolstadt-Kralupy-Litvinov (IKL) oil pipeline that started operating in 1996 was 'a practical manifestation of 1990s Czech political discourse, aimed at strengthening political as well as economic ties to Western Europe' (Jirušek et al., 2020, p. 125). Whilst critics voiced their concerns at the significant and supposedly unnecessary investment, the pipeline supported Czech energy security during the second half of the 2000s when supplies of Russian oil via the Druzhba pipeline were disrupted, and again in December 2009 when Russia stated that oil supplies could be cut following a gas dispute with Ukraine (France 24, 2009). These reductions of oil supplies corresponded with a 'more assertive Czech foreign policy' that included signing a bilateral agreement to build a radar station as part of the US missile defence system, a step strongly opposed by Russia (Nosko, 2013, p. 124). Czechia also diversified its natural gas sources by concluding a twenty-year gas supply contract with Norway in 1997 (Binhack and Tichý, 2012). This strategy significantly shielded the country from the 2009 gas supply disruption and facilitated the emergency supply of gas to Slovakia through a provisional manual reverse flow on the Brotherhood pipeline during the last days of the crisis (Jirušek et al., 2020). Since the expiration of the gas supply contract with Norway in 2017, Czechia has connected its gas market to Germany's via a newly built interconnector.

The lack of physical interconnections was one of the main reasons behind the consequences of the 2009 gas supply disruption. The under-developed energy infrastructure hindered the proper functioning of an internal energy market, as bottlenecks and limited interconnections prevented physical transmission of natural gas to areas suffering from supply disruptions. The Commission stressed that the crisis 'highlighted shortcomings in the gas pipeline network, on which the internal market is based' (European Commission, 2009a, p. 10). Diversification, including building LNG terminals and establishing new gas interconnections, has been driven by increased supply security concerns, and facilitated by significant EU financial assistance (Oravcová and Mišík, 2018).[2] For example, the EU provided €305 million of the €560 million Gas Interconnector Poland-Lithuania project costs in order to end 'energy isolation in the Baltics' (European Commission, 2015d). The European Energy Programme for Recovery (EEPR) was established as a response to the 2008 financial crisis, and with €4 billion of funding was the catalyst for a wide range of projects in the region (European Commission, 2013b). In the Visegrad Group countries, sixteen projects were supported by the EEPR, 'a critical factor in mobilising both public and private resources and in increasing state-to-state cooperation in the region' (Prontera and Plenta, 2020, p. 4). Overall, twenty-four projects supported by the scheme were connected to at least one CEE country by 2020 (European Commission, 2021c).

[2] This includes the European Energy Programme for Recovery (Regulation (EC) 663/2009) and Connecting Europe Facility (via Projects of Common Interest (PCI) list); Delegated Regulations (EU) 1391/2013, 2016/89, 2018/540, 2020/389 and 2022/564.

Despite material differences in natural gas supply structure, there has been strong CEE consensus since 2009 regarding diversification of routes and supplies, something the Russian annexation of Crimea served to reinforce (Butler, 2018), and the invasion of Ukraine by Russia in February 2022 accelerated. As discussed in Chapter 6, these countries brought this discussion to the EU level where the Commission was a strong ally (Maltby, 2013). CEE countries employed several options to diversify their energy supplies after the crisis, and the diversification agenda concerned mainly natural gas infrastructure as this presented the most visible challenge, but it also included other energy sectors, including oil and electricity. We identify four gas diversification strategies ranging from (1) reversing flows on one-directional transit pipelines, (2) building new energy interconnectors, (3) developing liquified natural gas (LNG) terminals and (4) supporting development of major pipelines to new energy sources.

Reversing the Flow of Natural Gas

The first strategy – physically reversing the natural gas flow – was already applied towards the end of the 2009 gas disruption in two of the most affected countries, Bulgaria and Slovakia. Traditional infrastructure provided supplies from the east (Russia), while the reverse flows developed following the 2009 disruption in several CEE countries supported mostly – although not exclusively – the west-east direction of natural gas flow. The Slovak and Czech transmission system operators (TSOs) upgraded a compressor station to supply Slovakia from the western direction from 18 January 2009, enabling emergency supplies of a small volume of gas to Slovakia from Western European energy companies. The station was further upgraded in 2011, with support from the EEPR covering approximately €0.5 million, or 50% of overall costs (European Commission, 2021c; eustream, 2011). Bulgaria also managed to receive alternative supplies from Greece via its LNG terminal towards the end of the crisis using a temporary solution (Kovacevic, 2009). However, the country was cut off from Western European supplies (European Commission, 2009a, p. 11).

Strengthening interconnections with their neighbours became the top energy policy priority of both governments. The Commission supported this objective politically, but also economically, with the condition that all proposed pipelines must be bi-directional to be included among EU Projects of Common Interest (PCIs) that were eligible for EU funding. Other reverse flow projects for existing pipelines were financed in Slovakia, Czechia, Hungary, Poland, and between Lithuania and Latvia (European Commission, 2018b).

New Interconnectors in the Region

The second type of CEE diversification strategies during the 2010s was the development of new interconnectors within the region, to develop a regional energy network enabling CEE countries to receive alternative emergency supplies from several neighbours during a supply disruption and to prevent a repetition of the 2006 and 2009 situations where the EU had enough gas but could not distribute it to where it was needed (Mišík, 2019). Such infrastructure also improves gas market conditions as physical connections are a precondition for internal energy market development and the transfer of price signals over national borders. Besides, the development of gas interconnectors between EU members supports the move away from LTCs and towards market-based supplies, for example, in Czechia and Slovenia (Osička and Ocelík, 2017).

A North-South Energy Corridor to develop connection between the Visegrad Group countries was included among the Commission's 2010 'Energy Infrastructure Priorities for 2020 and Beyond' (European Commission, 2010a) and was later included in several priority corridors within the Trans-European Networks for Energy scheme after its reform in 2013 (Regulation (EU) 347/2013). This provided €5.35 billion for energy infrastructure in the 2014–2020 period, and a further €8.7 billion for 2021–2027 (European Parliament, 2021b). Groups based on priority regional corridors include North-South gas interconnections in Central Europe and the South Eastern Europe corridor (NSI East Gas).[3] These groups are coordinated by the Commission and consist of many energy stakeholders from the member states (including regulators, transmission system operators, and energy companies). Since 2013 the Commission has published a biannual list of PCIs that present projects qualifying for financial support from EU funds and streamlined administrative procedures at the EU level. Proposed infrastructural projects must connect at least two EU member states and contribute to market integration, sustainability, competition and energy security to be included on the list (Article 4 of the Regulation (EU) 347/2013). PCI projects have been key to facilitating upgrades to the European gas network (Rodríguez-Gómez et al., 2016).

Sixty-two regional natural gas projects were included in the first four PCI lists, including twenty-one gas projects involving V4 countries (Prontera and Plenta, 2020). Several more projects have been developed by Bulgaria, Romania, Slovenia and the Baltic States. For example, in 2014 the bulk of projects funded were for addressing the Baltic energy island (two thirds of thirty-four projects that year were for the region), and in 2015 the bulk of projects funded were in the broader CEE region (half of the thirty-five that year; European Commission, 2021c), including

[3] This is the most important for CEE countries as the diversification of natural gas presented the main challenge, however, they are also part of other priority corridors (CEE members only listed): North-South electricity interconnections in Central Eastern and South Eastern Europe (Bulgaria, Croatia, Czechia, Hungary, Poland, Romania, Slovakia, Slovenia), the Baltic Energy Market Interconnection Plan in electricity and gas (Estonia, Latvia, Lithuania, Poland), the Southern Gas Corridor (Bulgaria, Croatia, Czechia, Hungary, Poland, Romania, Slovakia, Slovenia), and Oil supply connections in Central Eastern Europe (Croatia, Czechia, Hungary, Poland, Slovakia).

interconnectors, LNG terminals and feasibility studies. The €300 million Balticconnector between Finland and Estonia (with an annual capacity of 2.6 billion cubic metres [bcm]) entered into commercial use in January 2020, supported by €206 million in EU funding (Klemetti and Mäkinen, 2022), while the €558 million Gas Interconnection Poland-Lithuania (GIPL) was commissioned in May 2022, integrating the Baltic gas island with the rest of the EU's internal gas market, following €266 million in EU funding (European Commission, 2020k). Commission President Juncker stated at the signing of the joint declaration for this project: 'Today's signature is about European solidarity ... Today we have done much more than bringing the energy isolation of the Baltic States to an end. We have brought the region further together. Today we have agreed on European infrastructure that will unite us, instead of dividing us' (cited in European Commission, 2015e).

Beyond gas, Estlink 1 – the first interconnector between the Baltic States and another EU country – was built in 2006, funded by Finnish and Baltic electricity companies (Pakalkaitė and Posaner, 2019). The capacity of Estlink 1 (350 MW) was, however, not enough to cover the increased demand in the Baltic region caused by the EU accession–required closure of the Ignalina nuclear power plant in Lithuania (see Section 4.6 of this chapter). Another cable (the 650 MW Estlink 2) was added in 2014 to provide increased capacity of connection between the countries, with €100 million of the €306-million project cost provided by the EEPR, and another €75 million provided by the European Investment Bank (European Commission, 2010b). Other electricity projects – NordBalt between Sweden and Lithuania, completed in 2015 with €131 million in EU funding from EEPR (Modern Power Systems, 2016) and the Litpol Link between Lithuania and Poland, completed in 2021 with €27 million in EU funding (Ministry of Energy of the Republic of Lithuania, 2015) – were included in PCI lists, in the latter case to kick-start a project planned, but not delivered, since 1992 (Pakalkaitė and Posaner, 2019).

The 2022 PCI list included 98 projects, 67 connected to electricity transmission and storage projects, 20 connected to natural gas. Among these gas projects, 15 were connected to countries of the CEE region (European Commission, 2022j). However, opponents of this list launched legal action against the Commission, claiming that inclusion of natural gas projects in the list is in breach of EU's own climate commitments (Sánchez Nicolás, 2022). The inclusion of these projects gives these projects access to EU funding and priority in permitting processes, though with a risk of locking in rather than phasing out fossil fuel use.

LNG Terminals

The third regional diversification strategy is connected to the development of LNG terminals. These means not only route, but also source diversification as they enable import from the global gas market, decreasing dependence on Russian gas

(Gritsenko, 2018). There have been a range of regional LNG projects proposed, including in Poland, Croatia and Lithuania; a shared Baltic project; and an Estonian-Finnish joint project. Three had materialised by 2023. Lithuania developed a floating LNG terminal in Kleipeda; Croatia established a similar type of terminal on the island of Krk; and Poland opted for a land-based terminal in Swinoujsćie.

The idea to build a common Baltic LNG terminal originated in the second half of the 2000s, and its main aim was to diversify away from Russia as the monopoly gas supplier and provide an alternative to building a gas interconnector with Poland. The 2007 Lithuania National Energy Strategy mentioned this option, and the Commission supported the project on the basis that one LNG terminal would suffice for the whole Baltic region (Pakalkaitė and Posaner, 2019). However, it was not possible to find an agreement on the common project among the Baltic States (Baun and Marek, 2013), and Lithuania pursued its own project (Baltic Times, 2018). The proposed regional project exposed the limits of cooperation between the Baltic States, the predominance of national energy policy and an unwillingness to put into practice the Lisbon Treaty's 'spirit of solidarity', particularly given the different degrees to which each of the states perceived themselves as energy insecure (Maltby, 2015). Latvia, for example, can rely on significant underground storage of gas, and the Latvian government concluded in 2006 that given 'LNG project costs and expected gas prices, it would be a very high fee for the additional security of supply' (Latvian Government, 2006). Whilst Latvia was a strong supporter of a regional LNG project, its view was that this should be located in Latvia. However, Estonia and particularly Lithuania were concerned about the Russian influence on Latvian gas infrastructure through Gazprom or a Gazprom subsidiary such as Latvia Gas (Galbreath and Lašas, 2011) and preferred a different location.

In 2012 the Lithuanian gas company Klaipėdos Nafta signed a ten-year lease starting in 2014 for a floating storage and regasification unit with Norwegian Höegh, after which there is the option of purchasing the floating storage regasification unit (FSRU), though details were not made public (Pöyry Management Consulting, 2018). Lithuania's solo project did not qualify for EU funding since it did not fulfil requirements for the PCI list, lacking a regional energy security dimension. What drove Lithuania's willingness to pay a high price, an estimated $130 million, to decrease dependence on Russian gas was an adversarial relationship borne in part from concerns about the price the country was paying for having a monopoly supplier (Seputyte, 2014). The Lithuanian government took Gazprom to the international arbitration court in Stockholm to pursue a claim for €1.5 billion related to alleged price fixing by the gas company; however, whilst Gazprom was found to have a conflict of interest as supplier of gas and shareholder of Lietuvos Dujos (Lithuanian Gas), compensation was not awarded (LRT, 2019). The floating terminal's capacity – 4 bcm per year – is equivalent to the total gas consumption of all three Baltic States. The Commission's 2014 stress tests concluded (before commencement of the project) that once the LNG terminal would be completed, 'the supply for the protected customers would be ensured in the three Baltic States in all scenarios' (European Commission, 2014e, p. 4). In 2022 the Latvian government stated its intention to build its own LNG terminal, and to also join the Paldiski LNG project with Finland and Estonia 'in the first stage of giving up Russian gas' (ERR, 2022; LETA, 2022).

Critics have argued that Lithuania's LNG terminal failed to further develop the natural gas market by opting for an inflexible LTC contract with the Norwegian company Equinor (previously Statoil; Belyi, 2019). Moreover, the state aid for the terminal, authorised by the European Commission, is envisioned to last for fifty-five years and consisted of investment aid as well as state guarantees to the terminal operator for a loan and aid covering all fixed operational costs (European Commission, 2018b). However, Gritsenko warns that LNG terminals – like other fossil fuel infrastructure – can create a '"technological lock-in" that will commit the region to continued use of fossil fuels due to the existence of path dependent infrastructure' (2018, p. 81). LNG gas was not competitive with the prices of pipeline gas coming from the Russian Federation; as the terminal began operating, there was a rapid decrease of Russian pipeline gas prices for Lithuania in 2014 (Ruble, 2017). Therefore, the Lithuanian government established a system of purchase obligations imposed on private and public undertakings that guarantee high utilisation rates of the terminal (Gritsenko, 2018). The Lithuanian government has paid to insure itself against Russian gas supply disruptions, the price-distorting effect of a monopolistic market, and the potential for economic leverage to be translated into political pressure and influence.

Poland's LNG terminal at Świnoujście was finished in 2016 with a capacity of 5 bcm per year, increased to 7.5 bcm at the end of 2023. The EU co-financed the project, providing €55 million through the EEPR and €224 million through the European Regional Development Fund (ERDF; European Commission, 2019b). The terminal extension was included into the PCI list as 'strengthening security of supply of [the] entire Central and South Eastern Europe', achieving both 'energy independence and EU climate goals' (European Commission, 2019c), implying that gas was a climate-compatible option if it displaced coal. Several different contracts were signed between the terminal's operator (PGNiG) and LNG suppliers, including an LTC with Cheniere Energy for US supplies (Schmidt, 2020). Following the 2006 gas supply disruption there was a clear shift in Polish foreign policy, with the Polish National Security Strategy stating, 'The dependence of Polish economy on supplies of energy resources – crude oil and natural gas – from one source is the *greatest external threat to our security*' (Polish Government, 2007; emphasis added). The LNG terminal project was approved in 2008, and the Foreign Minister in 2012 said that 'the spectre of energy-related blackmail' could be addressed through diversification and 'implementing a competitive energy market' (Sikorski, 2012). The Świnoujście terminal has contributed to perceived increased energy security as it 'underpins the state's energy self-sufficiency [by] granting it access to global LNG markets' (Szabo and Fabok, 2020, p. 6), and was a factor in the decision to not extend a Polish LTC for Russian gas through the Yamal pipeline after 2022 (Weiner, 2019). The terminal is also expected to improve energy security in the region through new interconnectors with Slovakia (co-financed by the EU through the PCI and finalised in 2022) and Czechia (the Stork pipeline, financed by the EEPR and launched in 2012). Construction of the Baltic Pipe pipeline that will connect Denmark and Poland was also supported by the EU under Connecting Europe Facility with €265 million, scheduled to be completed in 2023 (Baltic Pipe, 2021).

Among other LNG projects that have been proposed within the CEE region, only the Krk terminal in Croatia has developed beyond general proclamations. A joint Finnish-Estonian LNG project reached the level of mutual agreement but did not move beyond a discussion of financial issues (Euractiv, 2014). The Croatian LNG project was supported by the EU, with repeated inclusion in lists of PCI projects, support for the feasibility study and construction totalling €124 million. The terminal received EU funding because it aims to supply not only Croatia but, via interconnectors, other member states plus several Balkan states. Due to a lack of commercial interest, the Croatian government offered direct financial support of €100 million. Croatian financial support was approved by the Commission in July 2019 because, according to the competition Commissioner Margrethe Vestager, '[t]he new LNG terminal in Croatia will increase the security of energy supply and enhance competition, for the benefit of citizens *in the region*' (European Commission, 2019d; emphasis added). The terminal was officially inaugurated in January 2021 with a capacity of 2.6 bcm per year. Demonstrating demand for it, the capacity of the terminal was fully booked for the first three years (Innovation and Networks Executive Agency, 2021).

Major New Pipelines

A final gas diversification strategy is new supply routes. None of the CEE countries has been a leader of a major new pipeline project. Bulgaria and Hungary, though, have been partners in consortia developing these, mainly due to their location. However, CEE countries have also opposed pipelines. Nabucco gained the biggest support within the region but has been replaced by more modest alternatives (first Nabucco West and later TANAP/TAP). The positions of CEE countries towards other pipeline projects led by Gazprom varied considerably, with Poland and the Baltic States the main critics – especially of Nord Stream I/II (Goldthau, 2016; Jirušek, 2020).

Nabucco was originally proposed in 2002 and developed by European energy companies in the late 2000s to diversify away from reliance on Russian gas. Although the project received €200 million in support from the EEPR, the project never materialised and the support was terminated (European Commission, 2018b). Among its proposed sources of gas were Iran, Turkmenistan or Azerbaijan (especially from the huge Shah Deniz gas field), with a route for its 31 bcm capacity through Bulgaria, Romania, Hungary, and Austria, which, together with Turkey, signed an intergovernmental agreement in July 2009 (Skalamera, 2018). At the same time, Gazprom started to develop the South Stream pipeline, seen as a direct competitor (Le Coq and Paltseva, 2014) since it would provide route diversification for Russian supplies of natural gas to Europe. Some CEE countries that signed an agreement on Nabucco also signed up to South Stream, and Skalamera claims this had the direct effect of 'undermining Nabucco' (2018, p. 25). Hungary changed its strong opposition to South Stream (Abdelal and Tarontsi, 2013) to supporting the project to 'decrease the risks of transit through Ukraine' (Aalto et al., 2017, p. 401), though this fits a pattern of closer energy relations with Russia, including financial support for Hungary's nuclear programme (explored in more detail section 4.6).

Bulgarian energy policy-making has been significantly shaped by economic and political actors whose preferences have been largely to maintain the historical dependence on Russian energy resources (Maltby, 2015, p. 825). The 2008 draft Bulgarian energy strategy noted the 'critically important' role of LTCs with Russia to stabilise prices and supply (Bulgarian Government, 2008, p. 49), and Bulgaria initially signed up to the South Stream pipeline (plus an oil pipeline and nuclear deal) in 2008 and was further motivated to participate by the promise of transit revenues and gas price discounts in return for its commitment to the project. This was re-affirmed in a 2012 agreement, alongside a new contract for the import of Russian natural gas supplies for Bulgaria (Bulgarian Government, 2012). A direct link between the two agreements was denied by Russia and Gazprom, but both were announced on the same day (Rilska, 2012). This alleged linkage formed part of an investigation by the Commission into companies linked to Gazprom ('Bulgargaz', 'Bulgartransgaz' and 'Overgas') on the basis of potential anticompetitive behaviour, and a wider investigation in the region followed (see Chapter 3).

Slovenia and Croatia also signed agreements on the South Stream pipeline together with Austria, Greece, and Serbia. However, it lacked strong commercial rationale (Baev and Øverland, 2010) and was cancelled in December 2014 following the Commission's insistence on applying EU energy market rules including third-party access to energy infrastructure (Directive 2009/73/EC). Gazprom switched to Turk Stream, which ends in Turkey where EU market rules do not apply (Dastan, 2018). Bulgaria was central to this decision as its representatives expressed hesitation to proceed with the South Stream project without the EU's approval regarding the applicability of internal energy market rules. In 2014 Bulgaria explicitly opposed South Stream, before it was cancelled later that year. Putin accused Bulgaria of 'burying' the project (Jirušek et al., 2017).

The Nord Stream I gas pipeline was developed as a common German-Russian project following the 2009 gas supply disruption, importing 55 bcm per year directly to Germany from Russia. The upgrade of the project, Nord Stream II, would double this capacity and significantly decrease the need to use Ukraine as a transit country. The Nord Stream II development was expected to reduce transit revenues through the Brotherhood pipeline for Ukraine, and for Slovakia; following North Stream I's completion, gas transit dropped by a quarter, from 74 to 54 bcm (eustream, 2021). The Visegrad group wrote to the Commission in November 2015 expressing concern about the 'potentially destabilising geopolitical consequences' of Nord Stream II (Gotev, 2015), though failed to gain concerted wider support. For example, the Bulgarian Prime Minister stated that 'I am in favour both of Nord Stream and of such a gas hub in Bulgaria. Nobody can convince me that an additional gas source is bad for my country' (Borissov cited in Gotev, 2015).

Both Slovakia and Czechia prepared for a situation in which Russian gas would start flowing from the west (Germany, i.e. via Nord Stream) rather than the east (Ukraine, i.e. via Brotherhood). The TSOs of both countries entered negotiations about capacity reservation in the new direction, and Slovakia strongly supported the Eastring pipeline to connect with the proposed gas hub in Turkey once Turk Stream was operational (Mišík and Nosko, 2017). However, Eastring ended in a preparatory phase (a feasibility study was finalised in 2018; Eastring, 2018) and was discontinued after not being included in the fourth PCI list in 2019 and failing to find sufficient commercial backing (Energy Briefing, 2019). A Czech idea to create a direct connection to Austria and thus circumvent Slovakia by developing a direct Bidirectional Austrian-Czech Interconnector met with strong Slovakian opposition and was shelved. Similarly, an upgrade of an interconnector between Czechia and Poland (Stork II) was put on hold due to the Polish concern that the pipeline would be used to ship Russian gas from Nord Stream II (Oravcová and Mišík, 2018).

Poland has been the main opponent of the Nord Stream projects; this position goes back to the preparation phase of the pipeline (Bouzarovski and Konieczny, 2010), and the view that the pipeline was 'politically motivated and a threat to Poland's energy security' as Russia would be in a position to interrupt supplies to Poland via the Yamal pipeline whilst maintaining gas flows to Germany or other Western European consumers via Nord Stream (Heinrich, 2018, p. 65). Moreover, the pipeline was perceived as 'exemplifying special German–Russian relations with profound geopolitical consequences, despite being presented as a purely commercial endeavour' and having a negative impact on Ukraine (Gawlikowska-Fyk, 2019, p. 203). The Polish Prime Minister in September 2020 argued that the pipeline 'explodes the EU's energy policy from the inside ... [and] makes Europe dependent on Russian gas supplies' (Brzozowski, 2020). Poland has used several approaches to voice its criticism towards this pipeline, as further explored in Chapter 6. Following the Russian invasion of Ukraine in February 2022 the approval process of the project on the German side was suspended.

4.4 PROMOTING COAL DESPITE CLIMATE GOALS?

A further strategy has been for CEE countries to maintain domestic fossil fuel production in part due to security of supply reasons, despite the climate policy implications (see the discussion on renewables in the following section and in Chapter 3). Coal power plants, predominantly using domestically mined coal, still have an important place in electricity generation of several CEE countries (see Table 4.2). This connects coal to the broader energy security discourse while at the same time directly contradicts climate policy goals as it is the most polluting source of energy (Burnham et al., 2012). It is necessary to significantly lower the amount of coal in electricity generation by 2030 and phase it out by 2050 in order to meet the EU's Paris Agreement High Ambition Coalition commitment to keep global warming below 1.5°C (Jewell et al., 2019) and the 2021 Climate Law setting a 2050 net zero target (European Parliament and the Council, 2021b). In 2019 all countries in the region committed to a net zero emissions 2050 target except Poland (European Council, 2019), and many (all three Baltic States, Croatia, Hungary, Slovakia and Slovenia) had signed up to the Powering Past Coal Alliance – a further commitment to phase out coal power plants by 2030. Although domestic coal has been considered by several countries from the CEE region as a means to strengthen energy security since 2022, most have not revised their coal policies and use significantly.

Coal at the Centre of Energy Security Discourse?

Coal is central to the energy security discourse of several CEE countries (Sivek et al., 2017). The environmental cost is often considered to be a necessary negative externality, the price to pay for security of supply and/or economic security. This section analyses the interplay between energy security and climate policy objectives regarding the utilisation of domestic coal. Despite climate policy objectives, several CEE countries strongly support their coal industries and defend their right to utilise domestic coal for electricity production (particularly Bulgaria, Czechia and Poland; see below). However, other countries of the region have started to prepare for coal phase-out (see Table 4.2), utilising tools introduced at the EU level like the Initiative for Coal Regions in Transition and the Just Transition Fund. It is important to note that phasing out coal from electricity generation does not mean phasing it out from the economy (given the challenges of decarbonising steel and cement production, for example). While hard coal is mined relatively few European locations (within the CEE region, especially in Poland), brown coal (lignite) is used in both the energy sector and district heating (as well as for individual heating) and is much more widely spread.

Coal is still important for the EU, but in decline. In 2016, 207 coal-fired power plants with 150 GW installed capacity were operating in twenty-one member states

TABLE 4.2 *Coal production and consumption (2020, in Mtoe if not specified otherwise)*[a]

	BG	CZ	EE	HR	HU	LT	LV	PL	RO	SI	SK
Production	3.7	10.2	2.6[b]	0.0	0.9	0.0	0.0	40.0	2.6	0.9	0.2
Brown coal	3.7	8.8	0.0	0.0	0.9	0.0	0.0	8.8	2.6	0.9	0.2
Hard coal	0.0	1.4	0.0	0.0	0.0	0.0	0.0	31.2	0.0	0.0	0.0
Share in gross domestic consumption (%)	20.7	25.4	57.8[b]	4.8	3.4	1.3	0.0	38.9	8.1	14.3	1.2
Consumption	4.3	12.2	2.9[b]	0.4	1.7	0.1	0.0	40.9	3.5	1.0	2.3
Net imports	0.4	1.6	0.0	0.4	0.7	0.1	0.0	0.1	0.8	0.2	2.0
Electricity generation from coal (%)	33.2	38.1	36.7[b]	8.9	10.6	0.0	0.0	68.0	16.8	25.6	6.6
Coal phase-out date	2038	2033	2040[b]	2033	2025	Complete	Complete	None	2032	2033	2023

[a] BG, Bulgaria; CZ, Czechia; EE, Estonia; HR, Croatia; HU, Hungary; LT, Lithuania; LV, Latvia; PL, Poland; RO, Romania; SI, Slovenia; SK, Slovakia.
[b] Oil shale.

Source: European Commission, 2022i, 2023c.

and produced 24% of all electricity consumed (JRC, 2018). Two years later the situation had already changed significantly – there were 166 coal-fired power plants with 112 GW of installed capacity in eighteen countries (JRC, 2021). After Germany, Poland has the second highest number of coal coal-fired power plants (forty-one) with a combined capacity of 28 GW; Czechia is third with fifteen power plants and capacity of 6.5 GW (JRC, 2021). As explored further in Chapter 5, coal mining and coal power plants provide significant employment in many regions, which influences the pace of energy transitions.

While many EU member countries (including those from CEE) have embarked on a path towards a complete coal phase-out by 2025 (for example, Slovakia and Hungary), or 2030 (Croatia, Estonia, Slovenia), several countries in the region consider coal to be part of their long-term energy mixes (especially Bulgaria and Poland). However, the phase-out or significant decrease of coal share in electricity production in many countries including Denmark, Luxembourg and Spain was not as much a result of climate-conscious decisions as structural changes to the coal industry, the depletion of domestic reserves or the emergence of economically viable alternatives (Lehotský et al., 2019). The average age of European coal-fired power plants is thirty-five years, so the retirement of many of them is a technical rather than political issue, and the European coal sector is under commercial pressure to close uneconomical coal mines. Foreign energy policy has also facilitated a faster coal phase-out, as in the case of Hungary.

Coal as a long-term option is often due to energy security concerns. Bulgaria, Czechia, Romania and Slovenia have a high share of coal in their energy (and especially electricity) mixes (see Table 4.2). Poland, the main producer and consumer of coal in the region, is the only EU member state for which the International Energy Agency predicted steady coal demand after 2022 (IEA, 2017). Moreover, Poland did not commit to domestic implementation of the EU's 2050 net zero goal (European Council, 2019a). Whilst several other CEE countries initially also rejected this goal at a June 2019 European Council meeting (Czechia, Estonia and Hungary; Morgan, 2019), they committed by December, and are accelerating their coal phase-outs.

Estonia produces almost all its energy from domestic shale oil sands (Lehtveer et al., 2016), although this is declining after connecting to the Nord Pool market (via the Estlink 1 and 2 cables) and increasing reliance on renewables. Due to this, Estonia has been considered to have the highest level of energy security among the Baltic States as it has the lowest import dependency (Zeng et al., 2017). The prevailing 'sovereignty-based discourse' in Estonia dictates that the government is responsible for providing affordable services including energy by 'maximum use of oil shale', which is 'central for security' (Kama, 2016, pp. 841, 843). Estonian shale is predominantly used in electricity generation. The country managed to receive free emission allowances within the Emissions Trading System (ETS) until the end of 2019, after which dramatic price increases were designed to accelerate a shift to renewables (Kallemets, 2016) and coal use elsewhere. Analysis suggests the ETS has played a key role in the reduction of coal power emissions by 43% between 2013 and 2019 (Rosslowe, 2020), and the role of carbon pricing is likely to increase given the rapidly increasing costs; the price of a tonne of carbon tripled in 2021 alone (Financial Times, 2021).

Energy security is used to legitimise continued support for coal-fired power plants and coal mining, domestically and at the EU level. Pro-coal arguments often stress flexibility that coal-fired plants can offer through balancing the grid and as back-up for intermittent renewables. Contrary to other EU regions, nuclear power is not used in the CEE region for balancing purposes and instead delivers baseload electricity (Loisel et al., 2018). Domestic coal is thus often presented as the only option to cover peak electricity demand without the need to increase the import of (Russian) natural gas (Gonzalez-Salazar et al., 2018). These arguments are used even in cases when significant amounts of coal are imported from Russia, such as in Poland and Slovakia (Mišík and Oravcová, 2020). However, since the energy crisis that began in 2021 the position of coal in CEE countries' energy mix did not change; those CEE members that embarked on a coal phase-out trajectory (such as Slovakia or Hungary) stayed firmly on this path.

Poland

Poland is the prime example of the prioritisation of security of energy supplies over climate issues in relation to coal utilisation within the CEE. The country is also the main supporter of electricity generation from coal within the region. In 2020, most of its electricity came from coal (68%; see Table 4.2) though this has decreased from 96% at the beginning of the 1990s (Eurostat, 2021; IEA, 2016), in part driven by an increase in renewables (especially wind) – responsible for 16% of electricity generation (Eurostat, 2021). An abundance of coal has been considered to be a guarantor of energy security and also of 'the national sovereignty which had so often been abused in the past' (Kuchler and Bridge, 2018, p. 144). The country's National Energy and Climate Plan, submitted to the EU in December 2019, outlined the plan for coal[4] to still generate 56–60% of power production in 2030 (European Commission, 2020l). However, in May 2021 the Polish government agreed with the mining union on a closure of all coal mines in the country by 2049, though not coal power plants (Sokołowski et al., 2022; UN, 2021a).

This political dimension of energy security has been driven by the country's heavy reliance on natural gas and oil imports from the Russian Federation and the Polish efforts to minimise this dependency, as coal reserves have guaranteed low import dependency (Gawlikowska-Fyk, 2019, p. 195; Manowska et al., 2017, p. 193).

[4] Though 13 million tonnes of less expensive coal were imported from Russia in 2018 (Euracoal, 2022).

However, there is increasing societal opposition to coal mining. A derogation from the EU ETS Directive (Article 10c) applied from 2013 enabled Poland (and other countries with high fossil dependency and low GDP, although Poland is the biggest beneficiary) to keep receiving free ETS allowances as support of its energy transition in exchange for investment in the energy sector and diversification of the energy supply. However, rather than facilitating an energy transition, Müller and Teixidó (2021, p. 818) concluded that the rule enabled investment in the refurbishment of existing coal-fired power plants.

The Polish government's position is one of cautious or delayed decarbonisation; Gawlikowska-Fyk argues that the country supports 'a stepwise process with the ultimate goal of *decreasing* carbon intensity – not complete decarbonisation' (2019, p. 198; emphasis in original). The domestic political elite has advocated modernisation of the industry enabling production of 'clean coal' (Kuchler and Bridge, 2018). Carbon capture and storage (CCS; Karimi and Toikka, 2018) and underground coal gasification (UCG; Mocek et al., 2016) have been options examined by the Polish coal industry. However, both options are currently underdeveloped and their public approval is problematic. While the latter has proven to be technically feasible, but has not been applied commercially yet, the former lacks public and commercial support. At the EU level, the Commission concluded in its 2020 report on the implementation of EEPR funds that all CCS projects supported by this scheme had been cancelled (the last one in 2018), arguing that the fund's financial assistance 'was not sufficient to prompt companies to realise commercial-scale CCS demonstration projects' (2020a, p. 1).

Czechia

Czechia has the second highest share of coal in electricity production among CEE countries (38.1% in 2020; see Table 4.2); however, compared with Poland, almost all its domestically produced coal is low-quality lignite (brown coal) mined in open pits (Rečka and Ščasný, 2016). This brings, besides higher emissions, several other environmental issues (pollution by particle matter, visible environmental degradations, etc.) as existing coal reserves are in highly populated areas and exploitation of new resources impacts the local population. These issues were also at the core of Czech complaints against the expansion of the Polish Turów brown coal mine located on the border with Czechia and Germany. In 2021 the Czech government sued Poland at the European Court of Justice, before settling the dispute bilaterally (Żuk and Żuk, 2022b).

The social dimension of coal is important, as it provides what is claimed to be relatively inexpensive energy for different types of heating (individual, district) and employment (see Chapter 5). Expansion of coal mining in Czechia is therefore linked to environmental and social issues, and is also considered to be a domestic source of energy security (Rečka and Ščasný, 2017). Energy security plays a key role within the Czech energy policy discourse, with coal portrayed as a crucial energy source decreasing dependence on imports from third countries (Osička and Černoch, 2017), and which 'represents an important stabilizing factor for the Czech energy sector' given the import dependence of other fuels (Sivek et al., 2020, p. 2). The Czech media, however, mainly emphasise local environmental (pollution) and social (employment) dimension of coal mining as opposition has grown (Osička et al., 2020). While the 2015 revision of the State Energy Policy stressed the security aspect of domestic coal, it also acknowledges environmental risks connected to coal mining for the first time (Ministry of Trade and Industry of the Czech Republic, 2015a). Under the Babiš government (2017–2021) a state commission recommended a 2038 coal phase-out, but there was no commitment to this. However, the Fiala government (2021–) set a 2033 phase-out in 2022 (Government of the Czech Republic, 2022).

Other Countries in the CEE Region

While Poland and Czechia are the main producers and consumers of coal in CEE, coal plays an important role in the energy policies of several other countries. The Slovak Energy Policy published in 2014 argued that domestic coal 'increases the security of electricity supply and lowers Slovakia's energy dependence' (Ministry of Economy of the Slovak Republic, 2014). The low-quality domestic lignite was not economically viable to utilise for electricity generation purposes; therefore, the Slovak government since 2004 subsidised (by approximately €100 million annually; IEA, 2018) a coal power plant (Elektrárne Nováky) and thus indirectly subsidised coal mining in the country (Ministry of Economy of the Slovak Republic, 2015). This support was framed mostly on energy security grounds, although the social dimension of mining was also used as an argument. However, with the depletion of coal sources and a series of closures of old mines, the number of people directly employed in the coal industry was in decline, and economic and environmental concerns trumped the security of supply benefits of coal by 2019, when a decision was taken to discontinue this support and thus effectively phase out domestic coal from electricity production by 2023 (Mišík and Oravcová, 2020).

Energy security had been considered the main reason to use coal power in Hungary, using domestic coal reserves, and the Hungarian National Energy Strategy of 2012 argued that 'for supply security reasons, the eco-friendly utilisation of domestic coal and lignite deposits should play an increasing role in the long term' (Ministry of National Development, 2012, p. 21). However, by 2018 Hungary's deputy secretary for climate stated that '[e]lectricity production based on lignite has no more long-term economic viability in Europe' (Botos cited in Stefanini, 2018a) and in 2019 the Hungarian president announced at the UN Climate Action Summit that the country would close down its only coal-fired power plant in Mátra by 2030 (Patricolo, 2019), and this coal phase-out was later accelerated to 2025.

Other countries in the region have been slower to commit to phasing out the use of coal. Bulgaria, with the third highest share of coal in the region, strongly supports domestic coal. Its 2011 energy policy strategy document set out that 'the existing coal potential of Bulgaria will be utilized to the maximum' as '[t]he significance of the indigenous coal for energy security is indisputable' (Bulgarian Ministry of Energy, 2011, pp. 5 and 11). The 2021 Bulgarian National Energy and Climate Plan claimed that domestic coal can provide electricity for next sixty years, that coal power plants 'guarantee Bulgaria's energy security and the competitiveness of the Bulgarian economy' and that coal is 'a strategic energy resource for the country's energy and national security' (Ministry of Energy, 2021, pp. 24–25). However, pressure from the EU has had an influence. As a condition of receiving Recovery and Resilience Funding, Bulgaria in February 2021 initially included a reference to phasing out coal, and to unlock funding a concrete coal phase-out date of 2038 was set out in a revised plan in October 2021 (WWF, 2021). Uncertainty over the commitment to this was highlighted by the environment minister in January 2023, who argued that '[a]t the moment, with the current and the force majeure circumstances, I do not consider that we are prepared with an alternative [to coal], but we must guarantee energy and national security' (Karamfilova cited in Novinite, 2023).

The emergence of coal phase-outs has been strongly driven by economics. The ETS has exacerbated pre-existing issues related to the commercial viability of coal power and the wisdom of continuing to provide significant government subsidies. The security of supply framing has for some countries diminished recently; however, they tend to use this argument for keeping their coal industries and coal-based electricity generation running until late 2010s. For Bulgaria, Czechia and – especially – Poland, coal-based electricity production continues to be legitimised with reference to energy security concerns.

4.5 RENEWABLE ENERGY: THE NEW 'ENERGY INDEPENDENCE' TOOL?

Renewable energy (electricity) production is crucial for the decarbonisation of energy mix and a sustainable economy. However, renewable energy sources (RES) have increasingly been framed as key to achieve not only climate policy objectives, but also national security goals. Indigenously produced renewable energy is considered to be a tool to increase energy independence and decrease dependence on imported fossil fuels (Sattich et al., 2022), a means to achieve 'both energy independence and sustainability' (Zeng et al., 2017, p. 189). This section looks at the geopolitical dimension of renewables, namely, their ability to provide domestically sourced energy, including electricity, and decrease energy import dependence.

Whilst there are competing frames regarding what dimension(s) of security should be pursued and prioritised, Fischhendler et al. (2015) and Marktanner and

Salman (2011) have argued that advocacy coalitions increasingly promote renewable energy at least in part through framing it in terms of geopolitical benefits. This framing has two dimensions. The first is to make the claim that promoting renewable energy decreases dependency on foreign supplies, in turn increasing security of energy supply and leading to more competitive pricing. Valdés Lucas et al. argue that 'as a domestic and decentralised energy supply, renewable energy sources are less vulnerable to the use of energy as political weapon or to physical attacks' (2016, p. 1034).

The second frame (albeit less commonly present in many CEE countries) is to claim, as the EU-Russia Dialogue did, that renewable energy has potentially positive geopolitical implications, mutually beneficial in terms of trade, technology transfer, and fostering greater cooperation. Overland (2019), however, argues that the geopolitical considerations of renewables are often one-sided, focusing on possible challenges they can bring to international relations. As will be demonstrated in this section, in the CEE region, neither framing is prominent. Indeed, to date only a few CEE countries, including Lithuania – a forerunner of RES development in the region – have prominently framed renewable energy as a means to increase energy independence. However, only after the country gained access to new sources of electricity via new interconnectors was security of energy supply considered sufficient to then base its energy strategy significantly on renewables (Sattich et al., 2022).

Renewables as a Source of Energy Security for CEE Countries

Given the importance of energy security for countries of the CEE, it could be expected that they would use any opportunity to decrease their energy dependence by utilising domestic sources of energy, particularly those countries with a high dependency on Russian energy imports. While CEE countries utilise domestic coal for energy security reasons and this drives nuclear commitments too (even Russia-financed; see later), the link is less clear with renewables where concerns with its cost have been a key feature (for example, in Czechia and Slovakia). Table 4.3 provides an overview of renewables within the energy mixes of CEE countries.

For Latvia and Lithuania renewables present almost the only domestic source of energy; however, several other CEE countries also have a very high share of renewables in their domestic electricity production, although they play a smaller role in overall domestic energy production (for example, Croatia or Romania). After the closure of Lithuania's Ignalina nuclear power plant in 2009, the share of biomass (firewood) in the Lithuanian energy mix almost doubled, and hydro tripled (Štreimikienė, 2016). However, this increase of renewables covered less than one fifth of Ignalina's capacity and therefore new sources of electricity had to be found – including imports from Belarus and Russia. The Baltic States are among the countries with the highest share of renewables among CEE countries and have used them since the 2000s to improve their energy security by diversifying existing

TABLE 4.3 *Renewables in total final energy consumption (2020)*[a]

	BG	CZ	EE	HR	HU	LT	LV	PL	RO	SI	SK
Production (Mtoe)	2.6	5.2	1.8	2.3	3.1	1.7	2.7	12.5	5.8	1.1	2.2
Production share (%)	24.1	22.1	40.1	62.2	29.2	85.0	100	21.5	25.9	31.4	32.4
Share in gross final energy (%)	23.3	17.3	30.1	31.0	13.8	26.8	42.1	16.1	24.5	25.0	17.3
2020 RES target	16	13	25	20	13	23	40	15	24	25	14
2030 RES target (NECP)	27.09	22	42	36.4	21	45	50	21-23	30.7	27	19.2
Electricity production RES (%)	23.6	14.8	28.3	53.8	11.9	20.2	53.3	16.2	43.4	35.1	23.1
Heating and cooling share (%)	37.2	23.5	58.8	36.9	17.7	50.3	57.1	22.1	25.3	32.1	19.4

[a] BG, Bulgaria; CZ, Czechia; EE, Estonia; HR, Croatia; HU, Hungary; LT, Lithuania; LV, Latvia; PL, Poland; RO, Romania; SI, Slovenia; SK, Slovakia.
Source: European Commission (2022i).

energy supplies (Zeng et al., 2017, p. 189). In Lithuania RES development has particularly been driven by an effort to reduce import dependence, and a national target for reaching 12% share of renewables in total primary energy supply by 2010 was set as early as 2002 (Klevas et al., 2007). The security of supply and climate dimension have both been framed as important (Katinas et al., 2014, p. 427).

In 2012 the Lithuanian National Security Strategy focused on promoting renewables as a means to increase supply security (Lithuanian Government, 2012, p. 13), which was repeated in the 2017 Strategy as explicitly reducing import dependence (Lithuanian Government, 2017, p. 15). The 2018 National Energy Independence Strategy (Ministry of Energy of the Republic of Lithuania, 2018, p. 14) aims to increase renewables for the purpose of 'reducing the dependence on fossil fuel imports and increasing local electricity-generating capacities', a sentiment repeated by the energy minister after Russia's invasion. Renewables are also seen as a means to improve prices and supply security as '[t]he rapid development of green energy is crucial not only as a prerequisite for full energy independence but also as the only sustainable way to reduce electricity and heating bills' (Energy Minister Kreivys cited in Patricolo, 2022). In 2022 Lithuania became the first EU country to ban Russian gas imports (Milne, 2022), followed by coal, oil and electricity starting in May, 'in its journey towards energy independence' (Kreivys cited in Peseckyte, 2022).

With one of the highest shares of renewables in the EU, by 2008 the Latvian government was stressing renewables as a means to achieve 'energy independence' in its National Security Strategy (Latvian Government, 2008, p. 9), and reiterated the supply security dimension in the 2011 update (Latvian Government, 2011, p. 8). It continued to stress the role of renewables in increasing the country's energy independence between 1990 and 2017 (Latvian Government, 2020). Similarly, in the 2017 Estonian National Defence Strategy, security of supply is explicitly linked to 'wider use' of renewables (Estonian Government, 2017, pp. 15–16). While the country's 2010 National Security Strategy links renewables to diversifying supplies (Slovenian Government, 2010, p. 44), the Slovenian government's support for further development of renewables has been limited by other environmental restrictions as a large share of the country is included in Natura 2000 programme, which prevents expansion of hydro and wind energy in protected regions (Al-Mansour et al., 2014; Crnčec et al., 2021).

The Romanian government noted the energy security dimension of renewables in its 2007 National Security Strategy by stressing the importance of guaranteeing national security including through an 'increase [in] the production of hydro-energy' (Romanian Government, 2007, p. 46). Similarly, Bulgaria's 2011 National Security Strategy highlighted the role of renewables in the energy mix to 'guarantee energy security' (Bulgarian Government, 2011, p. 39). However, although Bulgaria and Romania reported a rapid increase in renewables share during the 2007–2013 period, this was connected mostly to EU targets. Once these 2020 targets were reached, veto players managed to dismantle renewables policies (Davidescu et al.,

2018; Hiteva and Maltby, 2017, p. 238). The 2020 Romanian Defence Strategy did highlight, though, the 'Russian Federation's aggressive behaviour' (Romanian Government, 2020, p. 6) and separately continued to emphasise the need to reduce dependency on fossil fuels through 'clean green energy' (Romanian Government, 2020, p. 36).

In 2005 the Slovak National Security Strategy discussed 'better use of renewable resources' as a means to 'reduce negative consequences of dependence' (Slovak Government, 2005, pp. 11–12), but although the Slovak Energy Policy claimed that the use of renewables 'increases self-sufficiency and therefore energy security in addition to environmental benefits' (Ministry of Economy of the Slovak Republic, 2014, p. 60), the main discourse surrounding renewables in Slovakia was connected to their perceived high costs (Janda, 2018). Similarly, the Czech Energy Strategy acknowledged that renewables 'decrease dependency on imports' (Ministry of Trade and Industry of the Czech Republic, 2015a, p. 19); however, it also noted that their subsidies have an effect on 'competitiveness and impact on social stability' (ibid.), and overall in 2015 it was considered that they had only 'limited potential'. In Croatia the National Security Strategy made a clear link between renewable sources and addressing 'the sensitivity of the Republic of Croatia to disruptions in energy supply' (Croatian Government, 2017, p. 10).

Szulecki and Kusznir (2018) argued that the Polish position towards the role of renewables as an energy security tool has been ambiguous. Energy security benefits

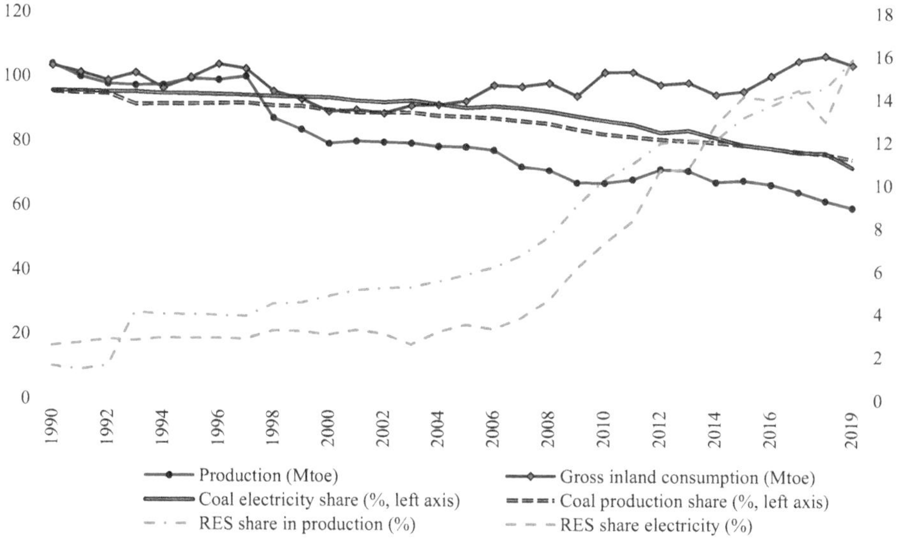

FIGURE 4.2 Renewables and coal in the Polish energy mix (2019). Note: Left axis in Mtoe, right in per cent if not indicated otherwise.
Source: Data based on Eurostat (2021)

were highlighted in the 2007 National Security Strategy (Polish Government, 2007, p. 17) and to an extent in the 2020 version where an aim was '[e]nsuring energy security of the state, based on traditional energy sources, by creating conditions for the development of alternatives' (Polish Government, 2020, p. 34). While renewables are considered to contribute to energy security, this 'role is to be conditional . . . on the generation costs, the technology and whether they are able to fit into the model of the country's economic and business development' (Szulecki and Kusznir 2018, p. 127). However, as shown in Figure 4.2, there has been a significant increase in renewables in Poland since the late 2000s. This is mirrored in a decline in the production of electricity from coal-fired power plants (from 95% to 68% between 1990 and 2020), though coal remains dominant in discourse and practice.

4.6 NUCLEAR ENERGY, PERCEIVED AS A SECURE AND CLIMATE-NEUTRAL ENERGY SOURCE

Nuclear energy is viewed within the CEE region as having two main dimensions. Besides being presented as a carbon-neutral and almost 'green' energy source, it is also considered to support energy security as a domestic source of energy that can reduce dependence on energy imports. Nuclear is considered to be a crucial tool to facilitate energy transitions; the Czech Prime Minister Babiš even queried during a meeting with his Slovak counterpart in 2019 why nuclear was not included among renewable sources of energy (Slovak Government, 2019). Three years later, in early 2022, the Slovak Prime Minister Heger argued that '[n]uclear energy must be part of the energy mix that leads us to climate neutrality' when he met with then freshly appointed Czech Prime Minister Petr Fiala (dpa, 2022). These views from the region played a role in the EU's 2022 decision to include nuclear in the 'green' taxonomy, permitting EU funding for it (see Chapter 6). The long-term nature of nuclear fuel supply contracts is seen as a safeguard of energy security, though this has also been the cause of Commission intervention. For example, the Commission objected to a twenty-year contract between TVEL (a Rosatom subsidiary) and Hungarian company MVM operating the Paks nuclear power plant (NPP), successfully requesting its shortening to ten years due to EU competition rules (euractiv, 2015). Paradoxically, whilst nuclear is justified as a means to increase security of supplies and reduce reliance on imported Russian fossil fuels, most CEE countries (except Slovenia and Romania) are also reliant on importing nuclear fuel from Russia (Szulecki and Overland, 2023; Vlček, 2016). Slovakia imported nuclear fuel from TVEL via air five times during 2022, as nuclear energy was not sanctioned and the sanctioned Russian aviation sector received an exemption for this activity (JAVYS, 2023).

Nuclear technology has a long tradition within the CEE region. The first research reactor commenced electricity production in Bulgaria in 1961, while construction of commercial nuclear power in the former Czechoslovakia began in the late 1950s though was not completed until 1972 (Oudenaren, 2001). The communist legacy has influenced the nuclear industry of CEE countries differently. While former Soviet state Lithuania's Ignalina NPP used the same RBMK-type reactor as elsewhere in the Soviet Union, including in Chernobyl, the communist countries of Eastern Europe (Bulgaria, Czechia, Hungary and Slovakia) used various models of VVER reactors, a type similar to the Western pressurised water reactor (PWR) used in the Krško NPP in Slovenia. The Romanian NPP Cernavodă, which was finalised only after the collapse of the communist regime in 1996, was developed during the 1980s and uses a Canada-type deuterium uranium reactor (CANDU). As a result, Romania and Slovenia experienced a development of their energy systems that was more independent from the Soviet Union, with access to Western nuclear technology. Effects of these differences became visible during the 1990s when EU accession negotiations touched upon the issue of nuclear energy. Several Bulgarian and Slovak and all Lithuanian reactors were considered unsafe, and these countries had to decommission them as a condition of EU membership (Oudenaren, 2001).

Almost all CEE countries have had some experience with nuclear energy. In 2023, six CEE countries had functioning NPPs (Bulgaria, Czechia, Hungary, Romania, Slovakia and Slovenia[5]); Poland has repeatedly considered building NPPs and even briefly started construction during the late 1980s. Until its EU accession mandated closure on safety grounds, Lithuania's NPP supplied up to 95% of its electricity (Vilemas, 1995) and exported energy to the whole Baltic region. Croatia imports nuclear generated electricity (0.4 Mtoe in 2020; 4.8% of all energy needed that year; European Commission, 2022i), though most of it from Krško NPP, which the country co-owns and co-operates with Slovenia (Franki and Višković, 2015). Although there is an effort to diversify sources of nuclear fuel for Soviet-era reactors still functioning in the CEE region (i.e., the VVER type), the alternative suppliers (the US and French companies) lack the capacity to produce enough fuel of this type (Pan, 2023).

Nuclear power in the region has been plagued by financing issues. Czechia halted preparation of its new reactors in NPP Temelín in 2014 after an unsuccessful public procurement procedure (Jirušek, 2020); Bulgaria is also considering development of a new power plant in Belene (on the site of construction terminated in 1990; Tchalakov and Mitev, 2019), although the project was halted in 2012 due to insufficient funds (Radio Free Europe, 2019). After interrupting construction of a NPP at the end of the 1980s (see below), and developing ideas for a new nuclear facility during the 2000s, Poland presented plans to build its first NPP in its strategic energy policy document in 2018 (Ministry of Energy of Poland, 2021). The Baltic States considered building a common power plant (Visaginas NPP in Lithuania) to replace the missing generation capacity after the closure of the

[5] Slovenia shares Krško NPP with Croatia, however, because the NPP is located in Slovenia we included only this country here.

Ignalina NPP in 2009 (Genys and Krikštolaitis, 2017). However, this effort was unsuccessful due to the cost and inability to decide on its location, a similar challenge to the failed plans to build a joint LNG terminal. An exception to these failed efforts is Slovakia, which has the second highest share of nuclear electricity mix in Europe after France (above 50% of electricity generation; see Table 4.4). This increased after Unit 3 of Mochovce NPP started operation in 2023 and will further increase after the expected commencement of Unit 4 in 2024.

Massive public protests in Germany, Italy and Switzerland following the Fukushima nuclear accident of 2011 contributed to policy change to nuclear

TABLE 4.4 *Nuclear power plants in CEE countries*

Country	Electricity production (%, 2020)	Nuclear power plant	Type of reactor	Commercial start	Shut down
Bulgaria	40.8	Kozloduy 1, 2	VVER-440 V-230	1974, 1975	2002
		Kozloduy 3, 4	VVER-440 V-230	1980, 1982	2006
		Kolzloduy 5, 6	VVER-1000 V-320	1987, 1991	2047, 2051[a]
Czechia	36.9	Dukovany 1–4	VVER-440 V-213	1985–1987	N/A
		Temelín 1, 2	VVER-1000 V-320	2000, 2003	N/A
		Temelín 3, 4	N/A	planned	N/A
Hungary	46.3	Paks Unit 1	VVER-440 V-213	1983	2033[a]
		Paks Unit 2	VVER-440 V-213	1984	2034[a]
		Paks Unit 3	VVER-440 V-213	1986	2036[a]
		Paks Unit 4	VVER-440 V-213	1987	2037[a]
		Paks 2 (2 units)	VVER-1200	2029–2030[a]	N/A
Lithuania	0	Ignalina	RBMK-1500	1983	2004
			RBMK-1500	1987	2009
Romania	20.6	Cernavodă 1	CANDU 6	1996	N/A
		Cernavodă 2	CANDU 6	2007	N/A
		Cernavodă 3,4	CANDU 6	2030, 2032[a]	N/A
Slovakia	53.5	Jaslovské Bohunice A1	KS-150	1972	1977
		Jaslovské Bohunice V1 (1,2)	VVER-440 V-230	1980, 1981	2006, 2008
		Jaslovské Bohunice V2 (1,2)	VVER-440 V-213	1985	N/A
		Mochovce 1 and 2	VVER-440 V-213	1998, 2000	N/A
		Mochovce 3 and 4	VVER-440 V-213	2023, 2024[a]	N/A
Slovenia	37.2	Krško[b]	PWR (Westinghouse)	1983	2043[a]

[a] Expected.
[b] Krško NPP was built in collaboration between Slovenia and Croatia during the Yugoslav period and its electricity generation is shared among these two countries – although for Croatia it is included in Eurostat statistics as an import.
Sources: European Commission, 2022i, 2017a; IAEA, 2021.

phase-outs in Western Europe (Bernardi et al., 2018; Müller and Thurner, 2017). In contrast, nuclear technology has been promoted and actively supported by CEE countries despite the nuclear disaster (Elliott, 2013). Western European countries have had historically different attitudes towards nuclear energy than the CEE region. Austria banned nuclear power in a referendum in November 1978 that prevented the already finished NPP Zwentendorf from entering service (Pelinka, 1983), and became one of the most visible critics of nuclear technology (Fawn, 2006; Lofstedt, 2008; Wagner et al., 2015). A referendum in Italy that took place in the aftermath of the 1986 Chernobyl disaster caused the closure of all NPPs by 1990, and plans to reintroduce nuclear energy into the Italian energy mix after 2008 were halted by another (post-Fukushima) referendum in 2011 in which 94% voted against nuclear energy (with a turnout of 57%; BBC, 2011). Post-Fukushima both Germany and Belgium decided to phase out their nuclear reactors (DW, 2011; Renn and Marshall, 2016). There are two projects in the rest of the EU; in France (Flamanville unit 3) and Finland's Olkiluoto 3, which started its test production in January 2022. None were started after 2011.

Compared with low levels of support elsewhere in the EU, the CEE region includes many countries that have very positive perceptions of the nuclear energy. The Fukushima accident did not have a profound impact on nuclear industry in the region; there were no massive protests or popular movements against nuclear energy comparable to those within Western Europe except in Lithuania, as explored in Chapter 5. Elsewhere, public support for nuclear energy continued (Wang and Kim, 2018). Although the Romanian Cernavodă NPP units 3 and 4 project lost initial foreign (French, Spanish and German) partners post-Fukushima, Chinese and later predominantly French backing were found (Intellinews, 2020). The following two sub-sections examine two main factors that are behind this support for nuclear energy within the region: energy security and climate goals.

Nuclear Energy as a Security Safeguard

Nuclear energy is key for many CEE countries wanting to minimise import dependence, though its development in the region was influenced by different factors. While the Bulgarian, Lithuanian and Slovak nuclear sectors were most significantly impacted by the EU during the membership negotiations, the nuclear policies of Hungary and Bulgaria were affected by their governments' close relations with Russia. However, in all cases, energy security played an important role when deciding on the (further) development of the nuclear sector. For example, in 2012 the Hungarian National Security Strategy stated that 'nuclear energy will remain a determining factor for Hungary in the foreseeable future' and linked nuclear technology to energy security (Hungarian Government, 2012, p. 14).

Other countries in the region share similar energy security discourses connected to nuclear energy. Poland considers nuclear energy a guarantee of energy security and supports construction of a power plant with the use of energy security discourse (Wagner et al., 2016). A strong environmental movement in the post-Chernobyl period emerged, and, consequently, 'the Polish nuclear program became a key issue around which domestic dissent mobilized' (Szulecki, 2020, p. 4). The Polish NPP in Żarnowiec ceased in 1990 and all nuclear plans were shelved until the mid-2000s when the discourse connected to nuclear power shifted from discussions focused on safety issues to those framing the 'benefits in terms of energy security' (Ministerstwo Gospodarki, 2014, p. 1), and security was used to justify 'measures going beyond the usual practice of liberal democratic politics' necessary to build the first Polish NPP (Szulecki, 2020, p. 4). This included framing opponents as 'enemies' and involving the secret service in physical protection of planned construction sites against protesters. Examining media narratives surrounding the construction of nuclear power plants in Poland during 2015–2021, Żuk (2023, p. 580) concluded that 'in the vast majority of media reports, regardless of their political sympathies, there [were] no opinions critical of nuclear energy ... [t]he only difference between media messages is that they emphasise different arguments [in favour]'. A 2013 National Security Strategy set out that a key objective is the '[d]-evelopment of resistance against threats to national security' and linked this to '[p]roviding security of nuclear power system in Poland' (Polish Government, 2013, pp. 74–75). However, a final location for the NPPs had not been selected by late 2023, and funding was not in place, making a scheduled completion in the mid-2030s optimistic.

In the Czech case, the 2011 energy strategy proposed to build as many as fourteen new nuclear units, and whilst this number was lowered to between two and four in 2015 (Ministry of Trade and Industry of the Czech Republic, 2015a), 'the perception of nuclear [energy] as a domestic source remains an integral and unchallenged part of the Czech energy discourse' (Osička and Černoch, 2017, p. 11). Nuclear energy has been considered to significantly contribute to energy self-sufficiency, a concept often used interchangeably with energy security in the Czech discourse. Nuclear energy is thus 'perceived as the most appropriate response to' energy policy problems and is constructed within media discourse as a clean, climate policy–aligned, domestic energy source (Kratochvíl and Mišík, 2020). A similar discussion can also be seen within Slovak media and public discourse that is dominated by pro-nuclear government actors and uncritical support for the expansion of the Mochovce NPP. This support was characterised by a lack of transparency and limits to public participation (Mihók, 2020, p. 6). Significant budgetary overruns and delays emerged and the project's budget more than doubled (from €2.8 billion in 2008 to almost €7 billion in 2023) with completion delayed by a decade from the planned date of 2013, demonstrating similar financial and timeline issues as in Finland and France (see, for example, Tromans, 2019).

The paradox of decreasing fossil fuel imports from Russia by utilising nuclear energy based on Russian technology and Russian nuclear fuel is very visible when examining developments within the Bulgarian and Hungarian nuclear sectors. Bulgaria, a country that has often had close political relations with Russia (Baun and Marek, 2013, p. 200), directly awarded a contract to Atomstroyexport, a daughter company of Rosatom, to construct a proposed new nuclear project in Belene in 2006. This was the site where construction began during the 1980s, before being terminated in 1990 as a result of pressure from the Bulgarian Green movement, which became one of the strongest political parties at the end of 1980s (Tchalakov and Mitev, 2019). In March 2012 Bulgaria withdrew from the Russian-backed Belene nuclear power plant project, due to concerns with cost and environmental damage (MacDowall, 2012), and failure to attract investment from Western European companies followed by a referendum in 2013 that failed to reach the turnout necessary to ratify the result in favour of it. As a result, the €7 billion project required a €620 million compensation payment to Russia's state-owned Rosatom group (Hope, 2014). The project was revived in 2018 following a parliamentary decision, with the government reaffirming that it was seeking a strategic investor in 2019 (Reuters, 2019), though in 2021 the government approved expanding the existing power plant with investment from the US company Westinghouse instead (Novinite, 2021).

In 2014 the Hungarian government awarded a contract for Paks 2 NPP – replacing existing units by 2025–2026 – to Russian company Atomenergoproekt. A €10 billion loan from Russian state-owned Vnesheconombank helped to finance the €12 billion project, which is the largest investment in the country and dwarfs other energy projects (Szabo and Fabok, 2020). A Commission state aid investigation was launched as 'the Hungarian State will accept a lower return on its investment than a private investor would do' (European Commission, 2017a, p. 1), but the project was approved after the Hungarian government promised a series of measures ensuring competition in the domestic electricity market. The loan payments were originally supposed to start in 2026; however, in April 2021 a five-year delay was granted by Russia, reflecting estimated delays to its completion (Reuters, 2021b). In August 2022 the Hungarian foreign minister claimed that project, now with a delayed 2030 completion target, 'will ensure Hungary's energy security in the long term and protect Hungarians from wild swings in energy prices' (BBC, 2022a).

In Hungary nuclear power is discursively supported by claims based on an energy security rationale. Besides the short-term goal of creating new jobs connected to the construction of the power plant, the Hungarian government also expected to decrease energy import dependency (Aalto et al., 2017) and make 'a substantial contribution to the maintenance of the security of energy supply' (Ministry of National Development, 2012, p. 28). Moreover, the government framed the contract with Atomenergoproekt as a national security issue, which enabled the documentation connected to the project to be classified for thirty years, limiting public discussion and scrutiny. Expanding nuclear power has been explicitly linked to the decision to bring forward a coal phase-out from 2030 to 2025 by the Hungarian president, who claimed that the country 'will stop producing energy from coal while expanding production of nuclear power plants' (Áder cited in Patricolo, 2019). However, as Aalto et al. argue that as a result since 2010 'Russian actors have consolidated their position in the Hungarian energy sector' (2017, p. 401), which also deepens dependence in other areas, including geopolitical and financial.

Nuclear is seen by Romania as key for security and climate objectives. In its 2007 National Security Strategy (Romanian Government, 2007, p. 46), the government claimed that key to increasing energy security is to 'speed up programs to produce nuclear energy', and in 2016 that '[n]uclear energy is a strategic option for Romania. The extension of nuclear capacity can enhance energy security and lower emissions' (Romanian Government, 2016, p. 3).

After the collapse of the communist regimes in CEE, nuclear facilities within the region became a subject of interest for the international community due to safety concerns. The G7 summit in July 1992 determined that Soviet-era reactors were not fulfilling international standards of nuclear safety and suggested 'replacing less safe plants by the development of alternative energy sources and the more efficient use of energy' (G7, 1992, p. 2). The main publicly presented reason was the fact that some NPPs did not include containment against radiation leakages and could not be upgraded. However, despite international pressure these countries resisted a phase-out due to the importance of their NPPs for economic and energy security (see, for example, Sorbello and Oliva, 2012 discussing the Bulgarian case). To overcome resistance the EU therefore used pre-accession conditionality as well as the promise of decommissioning funds to support the closure of the problematic nuclear power plants (Oudenaren, 2001). This strategy was successful and led to the closure of several nuclear reactors; units 1–4 in Kozloduy, Bulgaria; two units in Jaslovské Bohunice, Slovakia (older VVER models); and all units of the Ignalina NPP in Lithuania (RBMK type). This significantly influenced their energy policy. This was particularly visible in the case of Lithuania, a country that produced almost all its electricity from nuclear power and where the forced closure of Ignalina NPP increased energy import dependency (see below; Balmaceda, 2013; Grigas, 2013b). All other existing reactors in the CEE region were considered to fulfil safety standards after being upgraded. These upgradable NPPs were either based on Western technologies – like the Slovenian and Romanian power plants – or on a newer model of Soviet-technology based VVER reactors (for example, in Czechia and Hungary, and four units in Slovakia).

Bulgaria, Lithuania and Slovakia received financial compensation to decommission these power plants from the international community as well as from the EU (still an ongoing process). Bulgaria also received a non-material compensation immediately after signing the agreement on decommissioning four reactors in Kozloduy NPP in the form of dropping the EU visa requirement for its citizens in 2002 (Tchalakov and Hristov, 2019). The European Bank for Reconstruction and Development (EBRD) manages the biggest fund financed by the Commission and eight European governments (Austria, Denmark, France, Ireland, the Netherlands, Spain, Switzerland and the United Kingdom). Until mid-2018, more than €650 million had been used to decommission the Slovak NPP, with a further €750 million in Lithuania and €1 billion in Bulgaria (EBRD, 2021). Decommissioning is a long process, and in the 2021–2027 period another €552 million will be spent in Lithuania and €118 million in Bulgaria and Slovakia (European Commission, 2018c). In Slovakia, decommissioning includes a smaller A1 NPP in Jaslovské Bohunice that was closed down in 1977 after two accidents (JAVYS, 2019). In its report on decommissioning reactors in all three countries, the European Court of Auditors (2016) estimated overall EU support until 2020 to be €3.8 billion and the overall costs of the decommissioning to be €11.4 billion (including nuclear fuel disposal).

The requirement to shut down these power plants (or several reactors) had an impact on energy security of the affected countries as the missing electricity supplies had to be replaced by electricity imports or increased domestic production. The former strategy often increased dependency on Russian gas supplies. Moreover, Lithuania also started to import electricity from the Russian Federation (Mišík and Pachárová, 2016), while Bulgaria lost its position as the main electricity exporter in the Balkans (Tchalakov and Hristov, 2019). This further increased the role of nuclear power in the energy security discourse of these countries, as well as countries of the region that supported the development of nuclear energy (Augutis et al., 2011; Sorbello and Oliva, 2012; Vlček, 2016). During the 2009 gas supply disruption the Bulgarian president and separately the Slovak prime minister suggested restarting the recently shut down reactors as a solution to problems in the electricity sector caused by the lack of natural gas for power generation (BBC, 2009). This met with a strong negative reaction from the Commission; for example, in the Slovak case it suggested this was a 'clear violation' of the EU accession treaties (Sydney Morning Herald, 2009). Bulgaria also made an official request to restart its reactors already in 2007 due to economic concerns, though the request was declined despite a plea from several neighbouring countries that imported Bulgarian electricity (BBC, 2007).

Nuclear as a Climate-Neutral Energy Source

The second main argument behind support for nuclear energy within the CEE region is connected to the low-emission nature of the technology. NPPs are considered to produce only minimal amounts of GHG and therefore are viewed by some as a suitable solution for transition towards carbon-neutral economy envisioned by the EU by 2050. This argument has continuously evolved through the 2000s and 2010s; however, since it was not connected so closely to the EU accession process as the issue of security of supply, it has had a less prominent place within the nuclear discourse in the CEE region. Only after the 2004 and 2007 accession rounds did climate issues increase on the EU agenda. However, the climate policy role of nuclear energy is not as straightforward as it is often argued within the CEE region, especially when taking into consideration the whole life cycle of NPPs. The supporters of nuclear power often overlook both the front- and back-cycle of the technology – that is, the mining, transport and enrichment of nuclear fuel as well as the transportation and storage of the nuclear waste (Culley et al., 2010). However, as explored in Chapter 6, Hungary, Poland, Czechia, Romania, Slovakia and Slovenia together with France successfully lobbied in 2021 and 2022 for nuclear energy to be included into the so-called taxonomy on green investments (Reuters, 2021c), enabling EU financial support for nuclear projects that met certain criteria.

However, the critical arguments about the carbon footprint of nuclear energy are not part of discussions about this technology within the CEE region. When discussing nuclear, the main challenges are considered to be connected to energy safety and nuclear waste management. These two issues are therefore also the main topics of the European Nuclear Energy Forum, a platform for pro-nuclear EU member states led by Czechia and Slovakia (see Chapter 6). The questionable nature of the climate merits of nuclear technology is not part of the discourse, nor is it prominently raised by critics of nuclear facilities operational within the CEE countries, like Austria (Müller, 2017). Instead a strong link between nuclear energy and mitigating climate change has been created within the energy transition debate in CEE. Nuclear energy is seen as 'a major opportunity for the decarbonisation of global economies' (Prăvălie and Bandoc, 2018, p. 81), being able to reverse the negative consequences of fossil fuel–based electricity generation.

At the policy level, this argument is being repeated not only by the pro-nuclear groups or nuclear power plants owners and operators but also by national governments echoing the energy policy discourses of governments including South Korea (Chung and Kim, 2018), the United States (Bernardi et al., 2018) and the United Kingdom (Corner et al., 2011), where they are used to support the construction of new nuclear installations or prolong the lifespan of existing plants. In the region, countries both with and without NPP utilise this argument; for example, the pro-nuclear Polish governments often present nuclear electricity generation as 'the only way to secure economic growth and CO_2 emissions reductions' (Wagner et al., 2016). The key strategic long-term document Polish Energy Policy until 2040 presents nuclear energy as the key tool for reaching its climate goals the claim is made that '[d]ecarbonisation of the energy sector will be possible through the implementation of nuclear power and offshore wind energy' (Ministry of Energy of Poland, 2021, p. 6).

CEE countries with NPPs also argue in favour of the technology using climate arguments. The Hungarian Energy Strategy until 2030 claims that besides energy security and cheaply produced electricity, the replacement of existing Paks nuclear power plant with Paks 2 is necessary in order 'to move toward the decarbonisation of the Hungarian economy [as] economical and efficient tools of meeting the environmental and climate protection targets' (Ministry of National Development, 2012, p. 29). In the Czech context, the contribution of nuclear energy to climate mitigation is not only the official position of the government, but also one of the top reasons for public support (Frantál and Malý, 2017), alongside its energy security benefits (Siqueira et al., 2019). According to the Czech National Action Plan for the Development of the Nuclear Energy Sector, 'nuclear energy constitutes a key instrument to ensure a gradual decarbonisation of the Czech energy sector and thus contribute to achieving our European and international commitments in the field of climate protection' (Ministry of Trade and Industry of the Czech Republic, 2015b, p. 21).

Similar arguments have been used by other CEE countries. In 2009 the Croatian Energy Strategy stated that '[o]f all the observed measures, nuclear power use is a measure with the greatest potential in decreasing the greenhouse gas emissions' (Croatian Government, 2009, p. 10). For Slovakia nuclear is 'the driving force of low carbon growth' of the national economy (Ministry of Economy of the Slovak Republic, 2014, p. 41), and nuclear energy, together with renewables and decarbonised gases, continued in 2019 to be seen as 'a key to achieving a low-carbon economy' (Slovak Ministry of Economy, 2019, pp. 11–12). Bulgaria also supports further development of nuclear energy as it provides a 'reasonable balance between the available energy resource in the country and the European clean energy objectives' (Bulgarian Ministry of Energy, 2011, p. 5), while nuclear is 'a promising resource for generation of emission-free electricity' (ibid., p. 12). In its National Energy and Climate Plan (NECP), Bulgaria argued that an increased share of nuclear energy was one of the key causes of declining emissions in the country since the 1990s (Ministry of Energy, 2019).

Lithuania presents an exception from countries that have experience with nuclear power within the region when it comes to the role of this energy source in climate mitigation. A referendum in 2012 was against a proposed NPP in Visaginas, and appears to have ended government nuclear plans (Genys and Krikštolaitis, 2017). In its revised energy 'National Energy Independence Strategy' (Ministry of Energy of the Republic of Lithuania, 2018), the Lithuanian government suggests that the development of renewable sources of energy and energy efficiency are the main set of tools to contribute to national climate goals. The position of nuclear energy is limited only to the decommissioning of Ignalina NPP and safety concerns regarding the Belarussian Ostrovets NPP, which is close to Lithuanian borders and is considered by the Lithuanian government to have serious safety issues.

4.7 CONCLUSION

This chapter analysed the mutual interplay between energy and climate policy within CEE from a foreign policy perspective. It explored how energy import dependence, especially for natural gas, influences energy and climate policies and strategies employed to ensure their energy security and fulfil their climate commitments agreed at the EU level. While the first two sections examined the efforts to strengthen domestic markets and increase diversification of gas sources in order to decrease the reliance on a very limited number of sources (usually Russia) and thus improve security of supply, the fourth, fifth, and sixth sections discussed the interplay between energy security and climate issues in the context of foreign policy, including the framing of domestic coal, renewables and nuclear power as means to increase energy security by reducing energy imports, although the climate footprint of these different energy types varies significantly.

The chapter contributed to the main claim of the book about the prioritisation of energy security of CEE countries over climate goals by looking at this issue from a foreign policy perspective. Despite common traits of countries in the region, individual countries approach foreign policy issues in energy and climate area from different perspectives. While some CEE countries focus only on the improvement of energy security, like diversification or the development of common EU or regional gas supplies and rules at the EU level (Lithuania or Slovakia), others prioritise both goals (renewables and nuclear, Slovenia) and some demonstrate a clear preference for security of energy supplies over climate objectives and prioritise coal in direct opposition to climate goals (Poland, and to an extent Bulgaria).

Evidence presented in this chapter points towards securitisation as a key explanation of the development of energy and climate policies of CEE countries. This is connected to their external energy relations, alongside the materiality of energy policy linked to the infrastructure developed during the Cold War. This claim about the ideational influence on policy is substantiated by the stability of preferences of these countries towards more energy security despite changes in the material nature of energy systems (i.e., diversification, increase in domestically produced renewables) as well as the institutional frameworks (development of energy security provisions at the EU level). Governments here have engaged in the process of a securitisation of gas supplies from third countries by linking them to national security, especially after the 2009 gas supply disruption. Those countries that see coal or oil shale as a safeguard of their energy security, such as Poland or Estonia, did not change their perception of their fossil fuel source dependence as a guarantor of energy security despite increased climate policy pressure from the EU.

5

State-Society Relations

5.1 INTRODUCTION

This chapter focuses on the role of civil society in energy policy-making in Central and Eastern Europe (CEE), relating to issues of equity, energy pricing and energy poverty. The chapter examines how these issues are framed, legitimised and contested, and the extent of broader societal participation and support for energy transitions. To provide context, this chapter considers the broader academic debates and empirical data with regard to the developing role of civil society in the region, including legacies of socialism, the historical and contemporary role for societal input into general policy-making, changes in state–civil society relations and the development of non-governmental organisations (NGOs) and interest groups and their influence on climate and energy policy.

Energy transitions are associated with large-scale social (and economic) transformation and are an inevitably conflicted process (Meadowcroft, 2009, p. 337). Whilst the degree of participation permitted and practiced in energy policy varies, the public sphere and civil society is where goals and norms can be articulated, and future visions of energy systems and governance proposed. Social movements play a key role in the struggle for cultural hegemony and the promotion of alternative social practices (Brulle and Norgaard, 2019, p. 904). As a political process energy transitions are shaped by a long-term process of contestation and conflict (for example, local resistance to developments, the 'not in my backyard' (NIMBY) concept; Emmerich et al., 2020). This chapter analyses three factors developed within the theoretical chapter: the effect of ideas, institutions and the material nature of energy systems on the energy transition of the CEE region.

This second section of this chapter introduces changing state-society relations and the role for civil society and social movements in CEE, including related to energy transitions. It explores the concept of energy democracy and the institutional context for community energy projects. Here, returning to the discussion of energy governance in Chapter 3, the extent to which national energy policies in the region are inclusive is considered. This section, moreover, analyses the ideational contestation around support for, and resistance to, energy transitions. Section 5.3 addresses the extent and form of civil society support for renewable sources of energy. This includes an exploration of the ideational framing of the just transition concept and the broader material drivers of energy transitions in CEE. The section thus discusses issues related to the winners and losers of energy transitions in economic terms, including employment opportunities and the extent to which this is offset by fossil fuel–related job losses. The financing of a transition and the extent to which public support for renewables has been mobilised are also discussed. The concluding part of this section highlights the key themes related to state-society relations in the energy transitions of CEE, and draws attention to the main recent trends and potential trajectory of these in the region whilst also pointing out some of the key differences between countries.

Section 5.4 focuses on protests against (and on occasion for) non-renewable energy projects, considering the ideational contestation and framing of energy transitions, along with the material constraints to energy transitions. The involvement of civil society in protests against, and for, nuclear, coal and shale gas and oil projects in CEE is the main focus. The conclusion argues that while energy security is the main concern for the region, public concern regarding climate issues in the form of protests against various fossilfuel–centred projects is visible and influential.

5.2 CHANGING STATE-SOCIETY RELATIONS IN THE CONTEXT OF CEE ENERGY TRANSITION

After briefly setting out the role of civil society and social movements in CEE, including in energy policy, this section explores the concept of energy democracy and the institutional context for community energy projects, and the extent to which national energy policies in the region are inclusive. Also discussed here is the ideational contestation around support for, and resistance to, energy transitions.

The Role of Civil Society and Social Movements in CEE Climate and Energy Policy

Communist regimes had an important impact on the development of the energy sector in the CEE region, and severely affected the ability of these countries' societies to engage in the formation of public policy. Although presenting different types of autocracy, all CEE countries had non-democratic regimes between late 1940s and early 1990s that enabled the creation of only very limited civil society (Bernhard, 1993).

Limited civil society in combination with mandatory membership in government-led organisations (unions, sport clubs, etc.) created a legacy of low participation in NGOs (Meyer et al., 2020). However, there were some seeds of grassroot organisations, mostly environmentally focused (in Czechoslovakia, Poland and the 'Danube Circle' in Hungary) as these were not considered threatening by the communist elite (Podoba, 1998; see also Chapter 4). Paradoxically, these turned out to be crucial in bringing down the communist regimes in some CEE countries and showing 'the power of "civil society" in opposing Communist regimes across the region' (Kopecký and Mudde, 2003, p. 1). For example, in Czechoslovakia 'the green element played such a prominent role in the 1989 'velvet revolution' that it could have been called the 'green velvet revolution' (Podoba, 1998, p. 129). Yet in the 1990s there was little public participation in environmental activities in the region, with NGOs poorly funded, organised and managed (Kopecký and Mudde, 2003). This situation has to an extent endured in the region, with civil society affected by low levels of political participation, and relative disengagement from the public sphere. Foreign NGOs have been active but have largely prospered as organisations independent of mass participation (Mazák and Diviák, 2018).

Electorally green parties perform relatively poorly in the region (Grant and Tilley, 2019, p. 505), with environmental concerns marginalised (Chaisty and Whitefield, 2015). There has been a pattern of lower concern about climate change compared with elsewhere in the EU (European Commission, 2017b, p. 14; 2008a, p. 9; 2005, p. 9). For eleven EU member states, climate change was the most important environmental challenge in 2017, but this included no CEE countries (European Commission, 2017b, p. 14). Similarly, in 2019 and 2021, all countries in the region had a lower-than-average proportion of the population considering climate change as the single most important problem facing the world (European Commission, 2021e, 2019e) and ten out of thireeen countries with the lowest levels of concern were in CEE in 2021 (European Commission, 2021e, p. 10).

There are signs of limited change. The global phenomenon of weekly climate strikes, begun by Greta Thunberg in Sweden in 2018, also engaged citizens in CEE, with climate strikes in all countries (Fridays for Future, 2022). There have also been environmental protests across Bulgaria in 2020 regarding a new biodiversity law (Todorov, 2020); in Poland an NGO led a successful campaign against the logging in Białowieża Forest (Gabbatiss, 2018a); and in Slovakia protests against fracking and gold mining resulted in the prohibition of certain types of mining (Cehlár et al., 2015). In 2021 polling of public opinion showed that when asked for the four most serious problems facing the world, the eleven CEE states were all below the EU average of 49% in listing climate change (European Commission, 2021e). However, taking a slightly longer perspective there has been a trend towards increasing concern that climate change is one of the most serious problems, and where in the EU as a whole there was only a marginal increase between 2015 and 2021, in Bulgaria, Czechia, Estonia, Latvia and Poland this was more significant (see Figure 5.1).

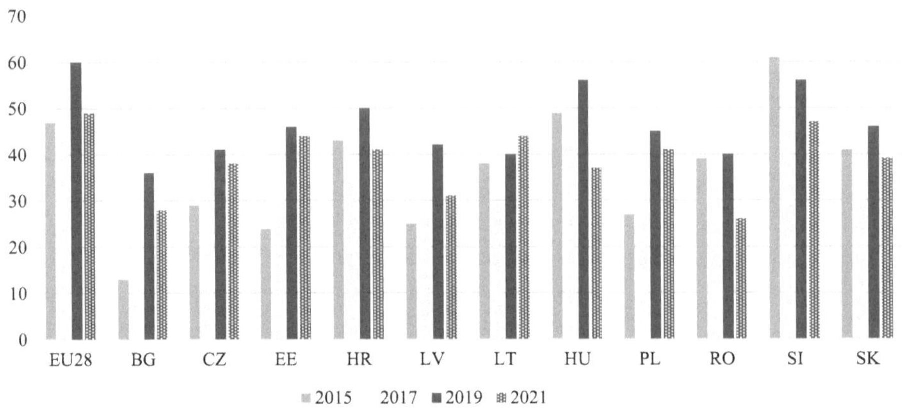

FIGURE 5.1 Public opinion (in per cent) regarding whether climate change is considered one of the four most serious problems facing the world. BG, Bulgaria; CZ, Czechia; EE, Estonia; HR, Croatia; HU, Hungary; LT, Lithuania; LV, Latvia; PL, Poland; RO, Romania; SI, Slovenia; SK, Slovakia.
Source: European Commission (2015f, 2017b, 2019e, 2021e)

Energy Democracy, Community Energy and Inclusive Energy Policy-Making

This section focuses on decentralised policy-making and explores the role of regional and local government and non-government community initiatives. The dominant model of energy systems has traditionally been centralised, with minimal citizen involvement. Energy transitions challenge this. Citizen-led energy initiatives are increasingly considered to be key elements in decarbonising of energy systems (Seyfang et al., 2013), including the role of active 'prosumers' – those citizens who not only consume but produce energy (Szulecki, 2018a). There has been a shift in the EU towards a more decentralised, community energy system (Bauwens et al., 2016), though community energy initiatives are more developed in Western Europe, and particularly in states such as Denmark and Germany (Jänicke and Quitzow, 2016, p. 125). They also have the potential to facilitate greater 'energy justice', in terms of delivering a more equitable distribution of costs and benefits – the affordability, transparency and accountability of decision-making (Fuller and McCauley, 2016; Sovacool et al., 2016). Chatterton et al. argued that social movements are using 'new vocabularies, social and spatial practices and repertoires of resistance' (2013, p. 611), and with regard to energy transitions these include energy democracy, climate justice, energy justice and just transitions.

Linked to Chapter 3, a potential development associated with energy transitions is this broadening out of the range of actors involved in the governance of energy policy to include smaller scale actors, from the individual to cooperatives at the local level. Here, increased energy democracy through 'democratic popular sovereignty; participatory governance; and civic ownership' (Szulecki, 2018a, p. 35) is possible.

An energy system that is lower-carbon, more inclusive and more equitable can potentially be achieved (van Veelen and van der Horst, 2018, p. 2).

New opportunities are developing for active rather than passive citizens in managing energy, available through community energy initiatives (Hewitt et al., 2019, p. 2). There is no clear definition of community energy, and it can also refer to non-profit legal entities that imply participation, wider engagement, and redistribution. They are often hierarchical, with minimal engagement of, and decision-making by, members and redistributing primarily to those in a position initially to invest (Argüelles et al., 2017, p. 36). The institutional framework is key to the democracy of energy initiatives in practice (Creamer et al., 2018; Szulecki and Overland, 2020; van Veelen and van der Horst, 2018). Where this is in place, community energy can drive energy transitions. It has been argued that social acceptance of renewable energy projects is linked to greater inclusion of citizens in terms of participation in deliberative planning procedures but also ownership (Creamer et al., 2018, p. 3). For example, participation in energy transitions through community energy initiatives can facilitate a positive feedback loop in which participants develop (more) positive attitudes towards renewables (Bauwens and Devine-Wright, 2018).

However, in CEE, community energy initiatives remain a niche development (Ćetković and Buzogány, 2016; Kunze and Becker, 2015). The European Federation of Renewable Cooperatives showed that whilst there were approximately 1,900 European energy cooperatives in 2023, only 0.1% were in CEE: two in Bulgaria, two in Romania, two in Croatia, two in Hungary, one in Poland and one in Slovenia (RESCOOP, 2023). A broader categorisation finds a diversity of community energy renewable projects only in Croatia, with a small number of small-scale projects found in Czechia, Hungary, Poland, Slovakia and Slovenia, but none in Bulgaria, Estonia, Latvia, Lithuania or Romania (Capellán-Pérez et al., 2020). In Poland, Hewitt et al. (2019) identified only one officially registered energy cooperative – Nasza Energia – though they argue that even this was a business rather than citizen initiative.

Resistance to cooperatives is argued to be based on the former socialist regime's command and control variety in which members had limited control and decision-making power, such as in Poland (Beckmann et al., 2015, p. 222; Meyer et al., 2020). Similarly, it has been argued that there is a lack of trust in collective agency in CEE, with specific challenges related to legal regimes and governance – for example, the legal challenges in establishing energy cooperatives in Latvia (Vihalemm and Keller, 2016). In Poland, the government has promoted since 2016 energy clusters (*klastry energii*) rather than energy cooperatives, favouring these groupings of individuals, businesses, local government and research institutions – though these are free to be based on fossil fuel energy generation (Hewitt et al., 2019). Such cautious moves towards energy decentralisation are also found in Slovenia where in 2019 the government proposed a legislative change to permit groups of buildings or multi-household residential buildings to establish energy cooperatives through joint solar power plants (The Slovenia Times, 2019).

The EU has been a force for change in terms of encouraging public participation in public policy, including that related to the environment. In addition to co-financing projects through the European Regional Development Fund (ERDF), the EU has created a legislative framework to support community renewable energy development. The 2018 Revised Renewable Energy Directive promotes decentralised energy production and encourages its development through institutional changes to reduce barriers, particularly those facing local projects, and to ensure wide participation of local members. According to the directive, 'renewable energy communities should be able to share between themselves energy that is produced by their community-owned installations' (European Parliament and the Council, 2018, p. 92). In Czechia, there is the example of an Energy Self-Sufficient Municipality, the village of Kněžice, relying heavily on biogas and biomass electricity production co-financed by the EU's ERDF (Dutkevičová, 2013). This is despite national regulatory challenges, including permitting issues that ban wind turbines close to military or residential areas (Dytrych, 2020), and where municipal buildings were prevented from installing solar energy and local generators are prohibited to directly sell to local consumers rather than via large distribution companies (Walsh, 2019, p. 3).

The Czech National Energy and Climate Plan claims that community energy projects deserve 'particular emphasis' due to significant added value in terms of local acceptance of renewable energy sources and access to private capital (Ministry of Trade and Industry of the Czech Republic, 2019, p. 47). However, an April 2020 amendment to the Act on Supported Renewable Energy Sources failed to mention community energy (Dytrych, 2020). As in Czechia, in Hungary legislative barriers have prevented the sale of electricity from community energy projects to the grid at market prices, or the establishment as energy suppliers (Walsh, 2019), with a ban on renewables within twelve kilometres of any settlement (Cicero, 2021). A similar regulation excluded 99% of Polish land from containing onshore wind turbines (PWEA, 2020), though an amendment in early 2023 improved this to some extent, cutting the restriction from 1,500 to 1,700 metres from the nearest residential building to 700 metres (EurActiv, 2023). However, there are signs that civil society pressure, along with that from the EU, has had an effect. Friends of the Earth Hungary is running a pilot community energy project in the village of Pilisborosjenő (Walsh, 2019) and an amendment to the Hungarian Electricity Act introduced the concept of energy communities from 2021 onwards (MTVSZ, 2020).

In 2018 in Croatia the town of Križevci launched a crowd-funding initiative, led by the Green Energy Cooperative, and involving Greenpeace Croatia, to fund a small solar power plant, as part of the objective of becoming energy independent by 2030. This raised the necessary funds to install it on the rooftop of the municipal business centre within ten days. Investors received discounts on their energy bills in addition to annual interest payments in return for the average €500 invested. In 2019 a second crowd-funded campaign met its target within forty-eight hours (Energy Cities EU, 2020). The mayor argues that this had 'improved citizen inclusion' and 'involv[ed] public institutions and citizens' in the energy transition (Dimitrova, 2020, n.p.). Following this, in March 2020, investors and local residents formed a local energy cooperative, Križevci Laboratory for Innovation in Climate (Energy Cities EU, 2020). Such examples of community energy initiatives, demonstrating the potential for broad societal participation and facilitating a more rapid and democratic energy transition, remain in their infancy in the region, though institutional frameworks to support them are gradually being put in place.

5.3 GREEN GROWTH IN CEE

This section explores the ideational framing of the just transition concept and the broader material drivers and constraints of energy transitions in CEE. A key consideration is the material constraint of energy systems and employment in fossil fuel industries, and how the concept of a 'just' energy transition is being framed within the region. A just transition is a driver of energy transitions, when concerns about social and economic effects are taken into account, for example, where funding is provided to those regions and workers in the fossil fuel industry. However, it can also be used as a means to legitimise opposition to ambitious and rapid energy transitions, arguing that an incremental approach or one that occurs only in the future is necessary.

Just Energy Transitions

A key challenge is the necessity to take into account the distributional and social consequences of energy transitions (Geels et al., 2017, p. 1244). Whilst 'the socially transformative potential' of energy transitions has been highlighted (Brulle and Norgaard, 2019, p. 891; also Burke, 2018, p. 1), they will lead to winners and losers, and for a just transition the latter need to be compensated to ensure there is broad social acceptance (Heffron and McCauley, 2018, p. 75).

This can include for example, alternative job opportunities and training for employees in mothballed fossil fuel plants, and subsidies for energy consumers to ameliorate any increase in energy costs (Abraham, 2017). The EU discusses a just transition as a process that is 'strategically planned ... [with] gradual industrial restructuring' (JRC, 2018, p. 4), including in 'coal regions in transition'[1] where there

[1] Pilot projects were underway in 2023 across Europe, including in four CEE counties: Silesia (Poland), Western Macedonia (Greece), Trenčín (Slovakia), Moravia-Silesia, Usti and Karlovy Vary (Czechia), Jiu Valley (Romania), Asturias, Aragón, Castilla-y-León and Castilla-La Mancha (Spain), Brandenburg, Saxony and Saxony Anhalt (Germany).

tends to be a lack of economic diversification (European Commission, 2023c). The concept of a just transition was initially proposed by trade unions (Brown and Spiegel, 2019) and was part of the Paris Agreement in 2015, according to which climate efforts should take into 'account the imperative of a Just Transition of the workforce and the creation of decent work and quality jobs' (UNFCCC, 2016). At the 2018 UN climate change conference in Poland, the EU committed to the Silesia Declaration, which 'underlines that Just Transition of the workforce and safeguarding and creating sustainable employment and decent work are crucial to ensure public support for long-term emission reductions, as well as to enable countries to reach the long-term goals of the Paris Agreement' (Council of the EU, 2018, p. 2). This was a view echoed in 2021 by Timmermans, the Commissioner responsible for Climate Action, who stated: 'We must show solidarity with the most affected regions in Europe, such as coal mining regions and others, to make sure the Green Deal gets everyone's full support and has a chance to become a reality' (European Commission, 2021b, n.p.).

A Just Transition Fund with an enhanced €19 billion budget was included in the Covid Recovery financing package, targeted at 'regions that are the most carbon-intensive or with the most people working in fossil fuels', in order to 'alleviate the socio-economic costs triggered by climate transition, supporting the economic diversification and reconversion of the territories concerned' (European Commission, 2022l). All ten countries in CEE are eligible for funding, with nine regions in Poland and six in Romania (European Commission, 2020m).

Contesting the Concept of Just Transitions

The concept of a just transition is one in which there is an ideational struggle for discursive hegemony. It is something of an empty signifier at present, which simultaneously means speeding up and slowing down energy transitions. Here we see social movements, different governments and other energy actors struggling to shape the concept and associated practices and policies (Brown and Spiegel, 2019).

Brown and Spiegel (2019, p. 159) note that 'the frame of climate justice ... is an "unsettled" term, constantly being (re)negotiated in response to the threat of co-optation'. The concept is contested, as is its implementation. Energy transitions are political processes (Burke and Stephens, 2018), founded on 'a highly contested political terrain' (Angel, 2016, p. 7; also Newell and Mulvaney, 2013). Linking to Chapter 3, Lahiri-Dutt highlights the co-evolution of coal economies with national regulatory authorities and the interlinkage with 'different notions of the meanings, morality and material values of coal' (Lahiri-Dutt, 2016, p. 203). As found in the case of Czechia, an objective of the coal industry is to create cultural and/or community economic identity – as central to the economy, community or security of the state (Lehotský et al., 2019). This is similar to findings about the US coal industry where Bodenhamer (2016, p. 1143) points out that a discourse is used in which the coal industry 'is reified as a powerful political, economic, and social force', and attached to cultural values such as the self-reliance – associated with employment, low(er) energy costs, community values and dignity (Bell and Braun, 2010). In Poland miners 'are respected at higher levels than medical doctors or teachers; 84 percent compared to 74 percent and 71 percent respectively' (Mikulska and Kosinski, 2018, n.p.). This can provide an obstacle to the pace and form of an energy transition.

The term 'just transition' is also one used by actors to defend the status quo, to argue for a very slow transition that significantly constitutes continuity rather than change. There has also been an attempt to frame particular visions of energy transitions as 'just' and to caution against energy transitions. In 2019 Michał Kurtyka, secretary of state in the Polish Ministry of the Environment, and the president of COP24 in Katowice, argued that the yellow vest protest in France 'demonstrates that when planning transformation we also have to think about the social costs, about the taxpayer, who is the energy customer' (PWEA, 2019, n.p.). However, as Jenkins et al. (2020, p. 141) note, a just transition agenda has the 'potential to slow the ambition of change too'. At the UN climate change conference in Katowice in 2018 where the Just Transition declaration was signed, President Andrzej Duda of Poland insisted that their countries could not 'fully give up on coal' (Plumer, 2018).

Poland, Hungary, Slovenia, Slovakia and Czechia have recently had populist governments and the literature has highlighted the obstacle this can provide to energy transitions, with right-wing populist parties associated with more modest emission reductions (Jahn, 2021). Possible causal mechanisms can be found, for example, in post-truth scholarship, which has highlighted a tendency, particularly in populist political parties and governments, to challenge common 'facts', including related to the scale of challenge posed by climate change, and necessary responses (Jasanoff and Simmet, 2017). Several authors have considered the links between right-wing populist parties and climate and energy policy, generally finding that they take a less ambitious if not obstructionist view on energy transitions (Ćetković and Hagemann, 2020; Huber, 2020; Lockwood, 2018), particularly where this is associated with tax increases and participating in and implementing international agreements. Huber et al. (2020) found that both right-wing populist (Law and Justice in Poland), and right-leaning valence populist parties in government (ANO in Czechia) tend to attack supranational elite decision-makers and the scientific consensus on climate change. Whilst climate-sceptic discourse is moderated by a move from opposition to government, climate policy and its implementation still tend to be opposed domestically and at the EU level, the latter of which is discussed further in Chapter 6. In Poland there is also some evidence of increasing societal polarisation, with environmental support linked to party affiliation (Szulecka and Szulecki, 2022). This is found more generally in the EU, that centre-left supporting citizens tend to be more supportive of climate mitigation than those who identify with the centre-right (McCright et al., 2016). In Poland and Czechia in 2020 supporters of right-wing populist parties tended to be less likely to think their government was doing too little on climate change or that climate change was a serious problem, and more likely to have an unfavourable view of scientists (Pew, 2020, p. 24). Research on the European Parliament has found that Polish and Czech members of the European Parliament (MEPs) are among the most frequent opponents of climate policy (Buzogány and Ćetković, 2021).

Lockwood (2018) has noted the link between climate scepticism and support for conspiracy theories and a hostility to climate science. Sustainable energy policies have become an area of increasing contestation, often along ideological lines (Dunlap, 2013; McCright et al., 2016), with attacks on 'elite' scientific knowledge (Fraune and Knodt, 2018) leading to a politicisation of science (Goldman et al., 2017). Braun (2014) argued that the EU's values with regard to climate change had not been internalised by CEE actors, and there is evidence of this amongst politicians in the region who are explicitly climate-sceptic. Some Polish MPs called it the 'fraud of all times' and described climate policy as 'a new religion of politically correct European elites' (Marcinkiewicz and Tosun 2015, p. 199). Similarly, in Czechia, PM Babiš dismissed climate action as the imposition of international elites putting climate 'in the position of a religion' (Novinky.cz, 2019), and the Hungarian Prime Minister Orbán discussed EU climate policy as a 'utopian fantasy' (Kingsley, 2021, n.p.).

Building on the concept of sociotechnical imaginaries linked to populism, future visions can export the problems beyond the 'here and now' reality to future technological development (Gatto, 2022; Ruzzenenti and Wagner, 2018), and related research has argued that 'believing that science will solve environmental problems tends to be associated with lower environmental concern' and lower climate ambition (Tranter and Booth, 2015, p. 160). An example of what Kuchler and Bridge label 'fantasies of technology' – those that either do not yet exist or which are highly ambiguous – include carbon capture and storage (CCS) to create 'clean coal', which can be used to sustain the possibility of a future pathway in which fossil fuels such as coal remain central to a state's economy and culture (2018, p. 139). Sovacool et al. (2011, p. 4669) offered a warning that such a technological fantasy around clean coal can constrain policy-making that could otherwise drive energy transitions, and 'risks delaying more durable measures and diverts resources from more effective alternatives'. Marshall (2016, p. 291) argues that CCS acts as an 'isolating' defence mechanism that 'postpones alternative action, thus preserving some established power relations and values'. Fitzgerald's (2012, p. 439) research found that definitions of clean coal can be so broad that they encompass any technology used to reduce carbon emissions, however limited, and are packaged in a 'clean and green' image promoted using public relations campaigns. 'Clean coal' was prominently discussed by the Polish hosts at the 2018 UN Climate Change conference in Katowice, with President Duda hailing 'efficient coal technologies' for a reduction in emissions and stressing clean coal's compatibility with climate policy (Ruiz, 2018).

Energy Poverty as a Barrier or Driver?

The liberalisation of electricity and gas markets as part of internal energy market legislation is also closely linked to state–civil society relations. The EU has gradually introduced a social dimension to electricity directives (Haber, 2018). For example, the second electricity liberalisation directive (2003) set out that member states had a duty to provide universal right of electricity supply, protecting vulnerable consumers, primarily from disconnection (Dubois and Saplacan, 2010, p. 343), and the third directive (2009) also required member states to monitor and report on progress towards this objective alongside defining and categorising citizens who are 'vulnerable' and/or in energy poverty. This directive also laid the foundations for national action plans to identify and reduce energy poverty for the first time. As such, since 2009 there has been a binding social protection element to EU energy policy. However, there has also been a significant increase in energy prices in CEE, particularly related to the increasing costs in gas and electricity found elsewhere in the EU but also to the removal of state subsidies for some consumers, and significant issues with energy inefficiency (Bouzarovski and Tirado Herrero, 2017, p. 27).

Energy poverty is a major issue in CEE states such as Hungary, Bulgaria and Romania. Despite having the lowest household electricity and gas prices in the EU, relative to the cost of living these are high, and the highest incidence in the EU is in Central, Eastern and Southern Europe (Bouzarovski and Thomson, 2019; Bouzarovski and Tirado Herrero, 2015). A Commission report in 2018 found that '[w]hen compared to the total expenditure, the poorest households in Sweden spent only 3% on energy, while in Slovakia this share was more than 23%' (European Commission, 2018d, p. 2). In 2018 the poorest European households were spending 8.3% of total expenditure on energy, compared to some CEE countries where the corresponding figure was 15–22% (European Commission, 2023d). In the same year over 30% of the population in Bulgaria had arrears on utility bills, with over 10% in Latvia, Croatia, Romania and Hungary (European Commission, 2020n), and in Czechia the most affected are coal-mining regions (Zachová, 2021a). By 2021 nearly a quarter of Bulgarian citizens (23.7%) were affected by energy poverty, followed by Lithuania (22.5%) (Fleck, 2022). Whilst the primary driver is the cost of winter heating, summer cooling is also a source of energy costs in the region (Bouzarovski and Thomson, 2019).

Energy prices have become a priority issue in some CEE countries (Bouzarovski and Tirado Herrero, 2017). Whilst energy transitions are predicted to reduce energy costs (UK Government, 2014), and evidence suggests there is little correlation with electricity prices (Ferris, 2021), the short-term effect, in either reality or perception, can be the increase in energy prices or the disproportionate increase for those in energy poverty as government subsidies for renewable energy are borne by consumers. For example, the Hungarian PM in 2021 argued that climate policy was linked to '[r]aising the prices, having a new regulation, rocketing the prices to the sky, destroying the middle class' as '[c]ommon sense on one side and fantasy on the other one' (Kingsley, 2021). In 2022 energy prices surged in CEE, contributing to the highest inflation since the 1990s, reaching the highest levels in Hungary (25.6%) and over 15% in Czechia, Estonia, Latvia, Lithuania and Poland in March 2023, against the EU average of 8.3% (Eurostat, 2023e). Much of this was felt in higher energy costs as 2022 gas prices were 121% higher than in 2021, feeding through to household bills that more than doubled on average in the EU between the third quarter of 2021 and the end of 2022 (European Commission, 2023e, p. 31), likely exacerbating pre-existing energy poverty, particularly in many CEE countries.

Lamb et al. (2020, p. 22) conclude that there are several ways in which climate policies exacerbate inequalities, including where the financing of policy is passed onto households in an untargeted way (such as electricity prices), where taxation on fuel or appliances is regressive, and where wealthier households disproportionally benefit through policies such as through solar subsidies that reduce energy prices. Dramatic changes in energy prices were experienced across CEE in the 1990s and early 2000s. For example, Bulgaria experienced significant increases in energy prices between 2002 and 2004 when seven electricity distribution companies were privatised (LaBelle, 2017, p. 618). Whilst energy prices stabilised, energy poverty remained a major issue, and energy prices were highly politicised. Protests about the price of electricity in Bulgaria contributed to the government resigning in 2013 (Ganev, 2014), and smaller-scale protests continued in 2019 (Novinite, 2019). In Hungary energy prices increased thirteen-fold between 1992 and 2013 (Bouzarovski et al., 2016), and electricity prices doubled in Hungary between 2002 and 2010, with the price of gas tripling. Energy prices were a key issue in the run-up to the 2014 Hungarian general election, with the government imposing 20% price cuts on energy companies providing district heating, gas and electricity in 2013, with further cuts of 3–7% in 2014 (Bouzarovski et al., 2017, p. 29). This caused excess energy use in the residential sector, and the policy has benefited especially upper-income households, while the poorest part of the population – using firewood for heating – did not benefit from the price cuts (Weiner and Szép, 2022). The Slovakian government's decision to re-nationalise the biggest gas company was also driven by energy prices becoming a major domestic political issue (Isaacs and Molnar, 2017).

The governance arrangements discussed in Chapter 3 are crucial here to a just energy transition in which the costs are distributed fairly and in a way that does not exacerbate significant energy poverty issues in many countries in the region, which 'requires integrated policies that directly address equity and procedural justice, supported by well-functioning institutions and financial alignment towards affordable low-carbon energy services' (Lamb et al., 2020, p. 23). An example is that energy-efficiency measures that would address energy poverty issues have in countries such as Poland and Hungary mainly benefited wealthier households that can afford the balance which is not subsidised by the government; capital is required to address energy poverty in the first place, and the short-term costs of energy efficiency measures (such as insulation) often exclude those who would benefit the most (Bouzarovski et al., 2017, p. 31).

Green Jobs and Financing Energy Transitions in CEE

A 'green growth' industrial agenda has been promoted by governments and industry lobby groups and certain NGOs – framing economic and environmental security as issues that can be tackled together, focusing on the synergies between tackling climate change through renewable energy and energy-efficiency measures and alleviating energy poverty and driving economic growth in the green energy sector (Ürge-Vorsatz and Tirado Herrero, 2012). An alternative to 'green growth' is the claim that fossil fuel power generation and mining is an unavoidable trade-off. The environmental damage and negative health effects are subordinated to objectives to maintain or increase employment and secure affordable and reliable energy supplies (Brown and Spiegel, 2019, p. 155). Chapter 7 explores how these countervailing narratives are present outside the EU despite much pro-climate rhetoric and policy. CEE countries are then not unique in the experience of a 'pace of transition [which] is plagued by political inertia and the residual support it retains, bolstered by narratives of development, growth, and technological progress' (Brown and Spiegel, 2019, p. 155).

Globally, the International Renewable Energy Agency estimated that 12 million direct and indirect jobs existed in the renewable energy sector in 2020, an increase of 4.7 million since 2012 (IRENA, 2021). Some 1.3 million of these jobs were found in the EU. In CEE more specifically there were 287,000 people employed in the renewable energy sector in 2021 (EurObserv'ER, 2023). In comparison, in 2021 the Commission estimated that the coal sector in the EU directly employed 208,000 people, including 158,000 in coal mining; indirectly, coal provided another 130,000 jobs (JRC, 2021). Poland employs half of the EU's coal workforce, followed by Germany and then Czechia, Romania and Bulgaria. Six of the twenty regions employing the highest number are in Poland, and of these the single region of Silesia employed an estimated 82,500 people in 2015 (JRC, 2018). However, between 2015 and 2018 there was a decrease in the number of people employed directly or indirectly in the coal industry (about 29,000 in the former) connected to mine closures. There were thirty-seven fewer coal mines in the EU in 2018 compared with 2015 (90 and 127, respectively); however, the number of member countries in which these are located stayed the same: eleven (JRC, 2021).In 2018 it was estimated that the Polish wind industry supported 12,000 jobs, and that if offshore wind plans were implemented this could grow to 77,000 by 2030 (Harper, 2018). A challenge of a Just Transition is to provide funding and policy to provide retraining and alternative economic opportunities, such as in renewables, in order to limit the social and economic disruption of an energy transition.

Job losses will be relatively high in certain CEE countries, with a single Polish region estimated to lose up to 41,000 jobs and regions in Czechia, Romania and Bulgaria likely to lose over 10,000 jobs each (JRC, 2018, p. 3). An additional challenge relates to the types of jobs lost (Eurofound, 2019, p. 17); in Poland workers in the coal sector receive double the average wage (Scislowska, 2018); in Bulgaria salaries in the mining sector are comparable to finance jobs (Morris, 2021); and in Romania coal mining pensions, reached at the age of forty-five, are 10% higher than average coal miner wages (France 24, 2020a). There is then the question of the extent to which 'green growth' through the expansion of renewable energy could offset these losses to directly and indirectly related coal (mining and power plant) jobs.

The framing of a 'just transition' is relevant here. Some proponents of a gradual or limited energy transition have described coal as having a key role in a 'just transition', for example, with the promise that 'clean coal' could significantly address environmental concerns, as part of a win-win scenario (Brown and Spiegel, 2019, p. 156).[2] This is despite the failure of CCS to be demonstrated as effective and commercially viable. It is estimated that only 13% of European coal generation capacity could be retrofitted with the technology, and this would be at the considerable additional cost of between 35 and 70% (JRC, 2018, p. 82). In Poland, policymakers have framed coal as clean and modern, and a key part of the Polish economy and culture (Kuchler and Bridge, 2018, p. 137). Poland's former prime minister Beata Szydło in December 2016 called for Polish coal 'to be a synonym of development and modernity', arguing that 'there will be no strong Polish economy without a strong mining industry' (Kuchler and Bridge, 2018, p. 136). This framing appears to have had some success. Badera and Kocoń (2014, p. 514) find that in local coal mining communities in Poland, there is far higher awareness of the economic issues (and profit) than of environmental damage. Chapter 6 returns to this and discusses the debates on just energy transitions at the EU level, and what role CEE countries have played in shaping this. For example, the coal industry lobby group Euracoal ('the voice of coal in Europe') has actively involved itself in Just Transition policy, promoting a managed decline (Stefanini, 2018b). In October 2017 Polish Deputy Minister of Energy Michał Kurtyka commented that this initiative provided 'an opportunity to find a place for coal-based technologies in the power mix and economies of EU countries' (Kuchler and Bridge, 2018, p. 144).

Despite this support, the coal industry is in decline across Europe and in the CEE region. This follows further historical decline. For example, in Upper Silesia in Poland in the 1980s, there were 14 coal mines. In 2018 there were two (Sauer, 2019).

[2] This was the case not only in Europe. In 2018 President Trump claimed he had 'ended the war on beautiful clean coal' (*The Washington Post*, 2018), and in Australia, the Resource Minister in 2017 argued, 'We've got the cheap coal. The clean coal technologies are proven' (Murphy, 2017).

Nationwide, there were 70 coal mines employing 400,000 at the end of the communist period, and 20 mines employing 80,000 by 2021 (The Independent, 2021). It is estimated that in 2020, 45% of coal power plants were losing money within the EU (Easton, 2021). Economic pressures led to 27 coal mines closing between 2014 and 2017 in the EU, leaving 128 in operation and 31 earmarked for closure. A wave of coal power plant retirements between 2020 and 2025 is estimated to lead to a loss of 15,000 out of 52,000 jobs within the EU, with another 18,000 by 2030 (JRC, 2018, p. 3). The Commission also estimates 109,000 out of 185,000 coal mining jobs are at high risk in Europe, the vast majority by 2030 (JRC, 2018, p. 3).

There have been different approaches to managing a just energy transition in CEE, but there are signs of a limited shift in the region. The Hungarian government, a country where there are 2,500 jobs in the coal mining and power plant industries (JRC, 2018, p. 21), set an objective of a coal phase-out by 2030 (later accelerated to 2025) accompanied by a €250 million transition plan to both fund renewable energy projects and retrain coal professionals (Open Access Government, 2019), similar to a 2018 Spanish Government plan to also fund early retirement and environmental restoration work (Neslen, 2018). Poland faces a greater challenge, with 112,500 employed in coal-related activities and with 13,000 employed directly in coal power plants. Whilst all Polish opposition parties have committed to a coal phase-out, the deadline of the goal ranged from 2035 to 2050, and is not supported by the Law and Justice government as of 2023. The leader of a Polish miners' trade union – ZZGwP – argues that 'the transformation must be person-centred and not only about the economy' (Collins and Osborne, 2018), and in 2021 a restructure led to a landmark but still conservative agreement between the Polish government and coal unions to phase out coal mining by 2049 (Gündüzyeli and Flisowska, 2020).

In Czechia, the government developed the RE:START strategy for economic restructuring of the main mining regions, Ústecký, Karlovarský and Ostrava, and budgeted €1.5 billion over the first three years, with 20% of this budget coming from European structural and investment funds (European Commission, 2019f). Following this, and to set a coal phase-out date, the Czech Coal Commission was established, with NGO representatives comprising two of the seventeen members. This was set a task of deciding between phase-out deadlines of 2033, 2038 or 2043, and in November 2020 it recommended the middle date (Zachová, 2021b). In the ten days prior to this announcement Extinction Rebellion activists protested outside the Environment Ministry (Bankwatch, 2020). In January 2022 this phase-out was accelerated by a new governing coalition to 2033 'at the latest' (The Independent, 2022). In Slovenia there has also been rapid change. In the country's draft National Climate and Energy Plan in February 2020 the country committed to a coal phase-out by 2050 (Spasić, 2020). A public consultation was launched in March 2021 to consider a government proposal to set 2033 deadline, narrowed down from 2033/2038/2042 options, and despite opposition by the Chamber of Commerce and Industry (CEE Energy News, 2021) this led to a September 2021 commitment to this earlier deadline (Ralev, 2021), followed in November 2021 by a commitment to complete this by 2030 by joining the Powering Past Coal initiative (Government of Slovenia, 2021).

In 2015 the Slovak government decided to continue subsidising electricity generation from coal by approximately €100 million annually until 2030 (Ministry of Economy of the Slovak Republic, 2015). However, in December 2017 the Slovak Minister of Environment announced at the One Planet summit in Paris that the country will terminate these subsidies and thus effectively phase out coal from electricity generation in 2023 (Blondeel et al., 2020). This will also mean closure of country's last coal mine in the Upper Nitra. The commitment since then has been repeatedly confirmed by different Slovak government representatives, and the process of transformation of the Upper Nitra region started in 2019 when a road map for transition of the region was adopted (Government of the Slovak Republic, 2019). While many factors (including economic and environmental) supported this decision, the pressure from civil society contributed to the decision, including a 2018 Greenpeace protest at a coal mine in the Upper Nitra region (Reuters, 2018a).

Authorities in Czechia (2014), Romania (2016) and Poland (2015) requested state aid to finance the closure of coal mines, including the environmental and social costs (JRC, 2018, p. 48). The March 2017 closure of the Paskov mine in Czechia occurred following an agreement between the state and mining company Ostravsko-karvinské doly (OKD) to cover most of the social welfare costs (€23 million of the required €24.9 million) (JRC, 2018, p. 48). Public financial support for energy transitions is strongly supported. In 2017 the strongest opposition was found in Belgium, Poland, Czechia and Romania – though this was only in the range of 13–17% (European Commission, 2017b, p. 62).

The costs of an energy transition could be at least partially offset by any reduction in subsidies for fossil fuels. The G7 and G20 committed to this in 2009 and the EU reaffirmed this in November 2016 with the 'Clean Energy for All Europeans Package' (Lowitzsch et al., 2020). Yet in 2020 the Commission concluded that subsidies had not decreased despite public pledges and remained at an estimated annual level of €50 billion, a 6% increase since 2015. In contrast, only €24 billion was directed to subsidising wind and solar generation (European Commission, 2020b, pp. 5–6). In CEE financial support of fossil fuels increased significantly between 2008 and 2016 in Bulgaria, Latvia, Lithuania and Poland (European Commission, 2023c). In Poland, the Supreme Audit Office in 2017 estimated almost €15 billion had been provided in support for the coal mining sector between 2007 and 2015 (Supreme Audit Office, 2017). Whilst in 2020 sixteen EU member states had plans to phase out fossil fuel subsides, this included only Slovenia, Latvia and Lithuania from CEE (European Commission, 2020b, p. 57).

There has been active state opposition to the decline of fossil fuel–based mining and energy production. In 2019 Estonia, Czechia, Hungary and Poland initially opposed a 2050 net zero emissions target proposed at the June European Council summit (European Council, 2019b). Poland's Prime Minister Mateusz Morawiecki demanded a 'fair' transition to zero emissions, and the Hungarian Prime Minister Viktor Orbán said a goal of carbon neutrality by 2050 'would impose massive burdens on Hungarian industry ... [s]o let's start to talk about money' (Energy Reporters, 2019). The Czech prime minister, Andrej Babiš, called the targets 'ecological hysteria' (Energy Reporters, 2019), in line with a State Energy Policy outlining only a gradual coal phase-out without any specific steps to achieve this (Černoch et al., 2019, p. 143). Whilst all CEE countries supported the net zero 2050 goal by December (European Council, 2019a), Poland did not commit to its implementation (Mišík and Oravcová, 2021b) and by early 2023 only Poland had no coal phase-out goal, even by 2050. Twenty EU member states had committed to a 2030 coal phase-out by 2022, including five CEE states (PPCA, 2022).

5.4 CONTESTING ENERGY TRANSITIONS IN PRACTICE

The social and political struggles around energy transitions are considerable given the costs, benefits and trade-offs associated with them (Pinker et al., 2020). Public acceptance of renewable projects, or of renewable technologies and climate targets in general, is an important factor, but can be nationally and locally specific, related to the variation in energy transitions within countries, and within regions. This section focuses on protests against, and on occasion for, fossil fuel energy projects, considering the ideational contestation and framing of energy transitions, along with the material constraints. Whilst not a focus of this section it is important to note that there have also been some protests against renewable projects in the CEE region. The Hungarian Parliament in December 2016 passed a law banning wind turbines from within twelve kilometres of populated areas, following protests against proposed wind projects around Lake Balaton, with a local environmental NGO protesting against the Environmental Impact Assessment (EJAtlas, 2019a). Similarly, in Volovja reber, Slovenia, environmental opposition led to plans by the state-owned firm Elektro Primorska to develop a wind farm in a nature reserve being abandoned (EJAtlas, 2019a).

Coal Projects

Opposition to new coal developments, either mining or coal power plants, has been an increasing feature in CEE, and many protests have been successful. In Croatia a coalition of local citizens and national and international NGOs (including Friends of the Earth Croatia) protested against the extension of the Plomin coal power station. The plans were announced in 2011, and whilst the Environment Ministry approved the project, in June 2013 the local municipality, Istria County, worked with two NGOs – Zelena Akcija (Green Action) and Zelena Istra (Green Istria) – to file a legal case against the Environmental Impact Assessment. This failed, as did a referendum of those in the Labinština region in 2015. Whilst 94% voted against the project, turnout was less than the required 50%. A further attempt was made by NGOs in a letter to the Commission highlighting that a contract signed between the Croatian electricity company HEP with Japanese (Marubeni) and French (Alstrom) investors breached EU competition law (EJAtlas, 2016). This was coupled with protests, in France and Croatia, against the bank operating as financial advisers. In January 2016, the project was suspended, following the Commission agreeing that it was inconsistent with EU legislation (CEE Bankwatch Network, 2016).

Social movements opposed to mining in Czechia date back to the late 1980s and continued through to the mid-1990s, though these were then dormant until the Czech government proposed expanding coal mining limits in 2005 (Černoch et al., 2019, p. 143). Local referenda in 2005 and 2006 showed strong rejection of mining expansion, and environmental NGOs, mainly Greenpeace and Hnutí Duha (the Czech branch of Friends of the Earth), played a role. In 2007 Litvínov-based NGO Kořeny (Grassroots) was set up, and the mayor of Litvínov in 2012 repealed a provision permitting property expropriation by mining companies (Černoch et al., 2019, p. 143). In Czechia in June 2015 a coordinated set of street protests in twenty-one cities called for maintaining limits on coal mining in North Bohemia, and a group of NGOs (Hnutí Duha and Greenpeace Czech Republic) and the Czech Green party organised as a coalition sharing this goal – 'Limity jsme my' (We are the limits; Friends of the Earth Europe, 2015). In October 2015, the government decided to continue with coal mining, though with limits around populated areas (Business Insider, 2015). The arguments used to support the expansion of coal mining in Czechia have been mostly connected to social issues (providing cheap coal for heating and employment) and also energy security (Rečka and Ščasný, 2018). However, the industry faces financial difficulties. For example, the largest private coal mining company, Ostravsko-karvinské doly (OKD) in Czechia, with 13,000 workers, filed for insolvency in 2016 (Thomas, 2016). Lehotský et al.'s (2019) analysis of media reporting of the coal industry in Czechia found that in discussions about a coal phase-out, the industry is mainly characterised as an economic rather than environmental problem.

Whilst strong rhetorical commitment to supporting the coal industry from the government continues in Poland, the coal industry is also in financial difficulty. As a result, in 2014 the Polish government contracted the Boston Consulting Group to draft a Repair Plan for the state coal company Kompania Weglowa. This outlined the poor prospects for the company and recommended closing four of its fourteen coal mines, with the loss of around 10,000 jobs (Vasev, 2017). However, pro-coal protests from the coal miners' unions led to a reprieve, demonstrating their influence on policy-making. There have also been significant and increasing protests in Poland against coal. In 2009 a local referendum in Brody and Gubin recorded a three-quarters opposition to lignite mining, and in 2014 an eight-kilometer-long human chain stretched between Kerkwitch in Germany and Grabice in Poland, in opposition to the opening of new mines (EJAtlas, 2018). Both municipalities elected mayors opposed to the mining in 2015, and a not-for-profit law firm – the Frank Bold Foundation – submitted a complaint to the UN Aarhus Committee citing a failure to adequately take into consideration local opinion. The project was suspended in 2016. Similarly, a plan for a large 1,000-MW coal power plant in Wola, Silesia, in 2013 led to coordination between seventeen health and environmental NGOs and a joint letter to the coal investor in July 2014 (Polska Zielona Sieć, 2014). A Polish NGO, Towarzystwo na rzecz Ziemi (Society for the Earth), raised concerns about the Environmental Impact Assessment, and in September 2014 the local council adopted a resolution to phase out coal plant investment, followed the next month by the local court revoking its environmental permit.

International and domestic NGOs have contested coal power plants in Poland. In December 2018 Greenpeace demanded that state-owned Polska Grupa Energetyczna (PGE) cease coal investment by 2030 or they would take the company to court, and this was combined with direct action at the Bełchatów power station (the most polluting in Europe) and street protests in Katowice around the UN climate change conference (France 24, 2018). Another protest in Imielin by the group Green Imielin included a petition, a street protest and their own hydrogeological study to oppose a coal mining project, though this was still approved by the regional environmental regulators in October 2018 (Shotter and Huber, 2019). However, in June 2019 plans for a coal-fired power station in Północ were rejected by the Polish Supreme Administrative Court after protests from a coalition of local, national and transnational civil society groups called Stop Elektrowni Północ[3] alongside local farmers and a legal complaint from Client Earth, which initially led the local authority to cancel the permit before the court case (Client Earth, 2019). Public support for a coal phase-out is strong in Poland, with 69% in favour in December 2018 (Kaminski, 2018) and 76% in May 2019 (Xinhua, 2019). In part this is linked to emerging concern with air pollution in Poland. Thirty-six of Europe's fifty most (air) polluted cities are in Poland (WHO, 2022), and a local group, Krakow Smog Alert, founded in 2013, was influential in pressuring the city in 2019 to ban the burning of wood and coal in residential buildings; this was later followed by a government Clean Air Programme to subsidise the replacement of residential coal and wood burners used for heating and cooking (Waldholz, 2018).

Yet coal also has strong support, from those who work in the industry and associated trade unions, from former employees, their families and others who are indirectly employed. In 2010, a protest by 40,000 people against the closure of coal mines in Poland occurred, and in September 2014, Polish coal miners blocked trains importing Russian coal (The Moscow Times, 2014). Beyond this there is a broader

[3] Comprised of a variety of NGOs: National – Association Workshop for All Beings, Wspólna Ziemia; Transnational – ClientEarth Prawnicy dla Ziemi, Greenpeace Polska, WWF Polska; Local – Eko-Kociewie (Stop Elektrowni Północ, 2022).

support derived from coal's cultural and economic role (Brown and Spiegel, 2019, p. 159). In Bulgaria in October 2016 more than 100 coal miners in the south-west of the country refused to come to the surface in a protest against up to 750 planned redundancies (Jamasmie, 2016). The protest delayed the job losses, but the mine closed at the end of 2018 with the loss of the final 400 jobs (Hilton, 2018). An additional protest in November 2018 in Bulgaria, of more than 1,000 workers, sought guarantees from the government to keep the lignite coal mines and power plants in southern Bulgaria open, where 20,000 were employed. Relatedly, the government successfully appealed against a decision from the Commission to impose stricter pollution limits on coal power plants, gaining an exemption from the Industrial Emissions Directive, which brings in stricter limits on the emissions of pollutants from 2021 (Reuters, 2018b). In October 2021 Bulgarian trade unions staged a national protest and put forward a 100,000-signature petition to ensure 'sufficient time' for a just transition (Industriall, 2021). In Romania, thousands of miners protested in Petrosani over multiple days in March 2012 in a protest against planned redundancies and closures of several mines (Reuters, 2012a).

The coal industry has also engaged with civil society to attempt to build support. A façade of increased participation was noted in Poland by Brauers and Oei (2020, p. 6) where at lignite mines meetings were organised and information points installed to involve citizens; however, this was as much if not more about a strategy of developing responses to defend the status quo of the industry and to improve its image. Barnett et al. concluded that engagement with the public by developers can be motivated by 'expert reassurance rather than mutual exchange and engagement' (2010, p. 47). Czech Coal also launched a billboard campaign in 2013 in the Ústi region based on security for the region, featuring images of local residents not employed in the industry but indirectly dependent on it, with a caption 'I also have a job thanks to coal!' (Aktualita, 2013). In Slovakia, the coal company Hornontrianske bane Prievidza (HBP) supported a petition initiated by a mining union to safeguard jobs, its 12,000 signatures including that of the Prime Minister, amidst accusations by the opposition that HBP employees were pressured to sign; the regional government blocked the expansion of the mine (Melichar, 2018).

Whilst there is active civil society opposition to coal mines and power plants in the CEE region, this has also been met with counter-protests. The economics are against coal, though, with government support necessary to keep the coal mining and power generation industry in business (Brauers and Oei, 2020, p. 5), and a growing political shift against coal and its financial support is apparent.

Nuclear Projects

This section focuses on political debates and public participation associated with several nuclear projects in the region. Countries of CEE region have stayed very positively inclined towards utilisation of nuclear energy even after the Fukushima nuclear accident in 2011 (Nosko and Mišík, 2017). The closure of nuclear power plants in Bulgaria, Lithuania and Slovakia was a polarising issue, as governments have had to replace nuclear electricity, and businesses and residents have had to adapt to increasing electricity costs related to new construction of generation capacity (Mišík and Prachárová, 2021). Whilst associated with low energy bills, a legacy of development during the socialist period when energy prices were subsidised, new nuclear plants tend to be overbudget and completed late, with foreign investment often controversial. The public debate on nuclear power in CEE countries is one in which the technology is framed in largely positive terms (Frantál and Malý, 2017; Polanecký and Haverkamp, 2011). An example is in Bulgaria where a 2013 referendum regarding a new nuclear power plant resulted in a 60% vote in favour, though a 20% turnout was too low to be binding and a decision was taken to cease construction.

Similar plans for the expansion of existing nuclear power plants have been ongoing in Czechia for decades, though opposition (including in neighbouring Austria) has been organised since the 1990s primarily around the issue of storage of radioactive waste (Ocelík et al., 2017). However, the government has consistently supported nuclear power plans, including in their 2015 nuclear energy strategy, and promotes the technology as central to energy objectives and competitive in pricing with renewables (Osička et al., 2021). There has been strong though declining public support, from 77% in 2009 (NSE, 2009) to 68% in 2014 (WNA, 2021a) and 61% in 2020 (McEnchroe, 2020). This political and public support is linked to perceptions of the technology as domestic, linked to self-sufficiency and energy security, and as an environmentally sound alternative to coal (Osička and Černoch, 2017). Following the Russian invasion of Ukraine, the support for nuclear significantly grew to 72% in November 2022, with most respondents claiming that the invasion – together with the increased costs of electricity – is behind their support (iDnes, 2022).

In Lithuania, a 2012 referendum ended plans to construct a new nuclear power plant. The plan was based on a collaboration between the Baltic States and Poland that had been planned since 2007. The project, to be based in Visaginas, reached the stage of an initial contract with Hitachi before the consultative referendum defeat, with 63% voting against and only 34% in favour. The public had previously been asked, in 2008, whether to extend the operation of the Ignalina nuclear power plant. Whilst 91% were in favour of this, turnout was below the 50% threshold, and the reactor closures in 2004 and 2009 were a condition of EU accession (Mišík and Prachárová, 2021). In 2014, following Russia's annexation of Crimea, there was broad Lithuanian parliamentary approval to pursue the project. Again, Hitachi signed an initial agreement, with Latvia and Estonia continuing to support it. Yet the 2016 National Energy Strategy delayed the project indefinitely, citing cost concerns (WNA, 2021b), and the Lithuanian government protested against the opening of a nuclear power plant in neighbouring Belarus (Janeliūnas, 2021).

In Hungary in 2009 the parliament voted to build new nuclear power capacity as a replacement of the ageing Paks NPP. A 2011 opinion poll showed 58% were opposed to a new nuclear power plant and just 32% were in favour of expanding Paks (Kovács, 2014), and there were protests against the planned Paks 2 nuclear power plant, (Cook, 2014). In 2016 Greenpeace Hungary and Energiaklub Climate Policy Institute appealed unsuccessfully against the environmental permit (Orbán, 2016). The project has been characterised by a lack of transparency, and in 2015 the government had exempted the project from freedom of information laws for thirty years (Novak, 2015). This is related to a broader issue of the development of civil society and democratic participation of the public in climate and energy policy (Sarlos, 2015) in a context in which the government of Hungary additionally has engaged in a concerted move to restrict the financing and influence of NGOs through an 'anti-NGO law' (the law on the Transparency of Organizations Receiving Support from Abroad) (Neuwahl and Kovacs, 2021). Moreover, the state-backed company overseeing the expansion spent nearly $ 4 million between 2014 and 2017 promoting the project through the media and think tanks (Pivarnyik, 2017). The project is proceeding with Russia's involvement negotiated in 2014 and including a loan of €10 billion, 80% of the estimated project costs (Weiner, 2021). Chapter 4 examined the Paks development in further detail.

The 2014 Polish Nuclear Energy Program aimed for a 2024 completion date for the country's first nuclear plant, but by 2020 this had been delayed to 2033 (Wilczek, 2020). Whilst plans for a nuclear power plant in Poland have been widely discussed, there has been a lack of deliberative democracy, and the debate has been largely state-initiated and state-controlled, to the exclusion of civil society (Wagner et al., 2016). However, nuclear energy in Poland has relatively strong public support, with polling showing 60% in favour in 2006, 50% in 2009, 64% in 2014, and 59% in 2017, with the main driver of support (57%) a concern about energy independence (primarily from Russia; see also Chapter 6; WNA, 2022a). As in the Czech case, Polish public support for nuclear energy has sharply increased following Russian invasion of Ukraine. Support reached a high of 75% in late 2022 (Notes from Poland, 2022).

Whilst in decline, nuclear energy had retained relatively strong public support in the region before the Russian invasion of Ukraine, with positive associations between the technology and both energy independence and low energy prices. Since 2022, support for nuclear energy in several CEE countries grew, most notably in Czechia and Poland. This is in line with increased support for nuclear energy found elsewhere in Europe (Brugidou and Bouillet, 2023). However, as Figure 5.2 shows, the majority of the public in most CEE countries (with Hungary the exception) totally agree or tend to agree that '[t]he war in Ukraine makes it more urgent for EU Member States to invest in nuclear energy' (which is also the average EU opinion), whereas for seven western EU member states this remains a minority position (European Commission, 2022m).

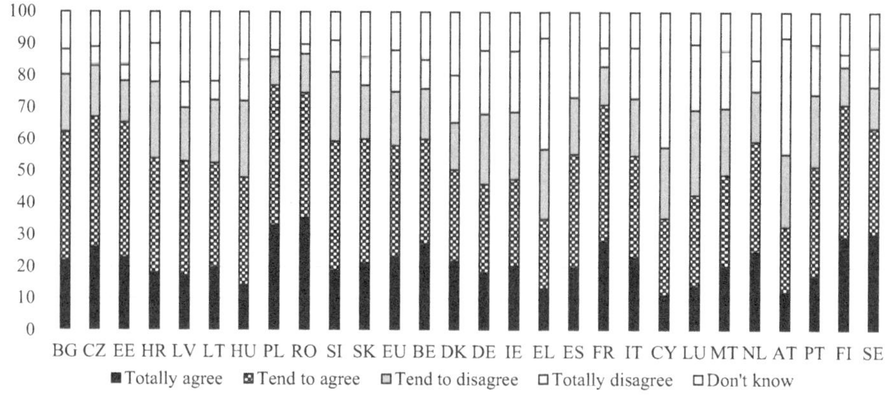

FIGURE 5.2 Public opinion (in per cent) regarding whether the Russian invasion of Ukraine makes it more urgent for EU member states to invest in nuclear energy. AT, Austria; BE, Belgium; BG, Bulgaria; CY, Cyprus; CZ, Czechia; DE, Germany; DK, Denmark; EE, Estonia; EL, Greece; ES, Spain; EU, European Union; FI, Finland; FR, France; HR, Croatia; HU, Hungary; IE, Ireland; IT, Italy; LT, Lithuania; LU, Luxembourg; LV, Latvia; MT, Malta; NL, Netherlands; PL, Poland; PT, Portugal; RO, Romania; SE, Sweden; SI, Slovenia; SK, Slovakia.
Source: European Commission (2022m)

Shale Gas and Oil Projects

As with nuclear energy, shale gas policy and decision-making processes are characterised in the region by a lack of wide-ranging deliberation and broader stakeholder participation, including a failure to involve local government and/or the local community (Wagner, 2015). Protests against shale gas quickly followed the discussion of a 'shale gas revolution' by a number of governments and energy companies. Local and regional protest organisations were established, and these were often supported by national and international NGOs.

Given extensive reserves, much has been made since 2009 of the potential for a shale gas 'revolution' in the EU, echoing that of the United States. Despite high hopes that it would be a 'game changer' for gas markets highly dependent on Russia (Geny, 2010; McGowan, 2014), no commercial fracking had yet occurred towards the end of 2023 in CEE, and there are heterogenous preferences between and within states regarding the issue. The environmental the national security and economic implications of commercially exploiting this domestic energy resource have been subject to a high degree of public and political debate, particularly given the lack of consensus regarding the costs and benefits of shale gas (Sovacool, 2014). Goldthau (2018) notes that key drivers were the economic opportunities of job creation and lower prices, and the imperative to increase security of energy supply particularly by reducing energy import dependence on Russia. This section explores how the technology has been framed and why different policies have been pursued in the CEE region. In doing so it explores the power relationships between actors involved in the process, and considers the role of civil society.

Lis and Stankiewicz (2017) highlight one of the strategies of proponents of shale gas, that of framing it as a technology that is misunderstood by non-experts. It is both complex and technical and also, linking to Chapter 4, it is of strategic security importance, which justifies its elevation beyond what is often considered merely NIMBYism: 'There is a very deep opposition in Polish society against every new investment which upset the status quo' (oil and gas company representative, 2013, cited in Lis and Stankiewicz, 2017, p. 66). This sentiment has also been held by members of the government, with the Polish Minister of Environment claiming, 'The biggest problem in shale gas exploitation is public resistance' (Maciej Grabowski cited in Lis and Stankiewicz, 2017, p. 66). Most countries in the region have shale gas deposits (except for Croatia, Slovakia and Latvia), with the largest estimated to be in Bulgaria, Poland and Romania (European Commission, 2017c). Different approaches to the regulation of shale gas have been taken in Europe and in CEE. These include more permissive (Lithuania, Romania and Poland) and more restrictive (Bulgaria, Czechia) approaches (Van de Graaf et al., 2018, p. 1283).

In Poland, shale gas has been heavily promoted, with a framing by the government that it represents an opportunity to increase environmental, economic and national security (Goldthau and Sovacool, 2016). However, organised opposition to shale gas projects has involved local residents and both national and international NGOs, with strategies of opposition using protests and legal cases (Szulecka and Szulecki, 2022). For example, a social movement called 'Occupy Chevron' blockaded a proposed Chevron shale gas drilling site in Zurawlow, Poland, in June 2013 for 400 days, leading to the withdrawal of the company (Nelsen, 2015). The movement involved local farmers and anti–shale gas activists from Poland and also from abroad (Lis and Stankiewicz, 2017, p. 56). In response to the exit of international firms operating in the sector, the Polish government announced a waiver on tax in the industry from 2015 to 2020 (Reuters, 2013). Despite this, in 2016 the chief executive of PGNiG concluded that '[s]hale gas as such has failed indeed' (Reuters, 2016a), and even the energy crisis that emerged in 2021 did not lead to a recommitment to it. The economics of shale gas has proved to be a major challenge, and in 2018 the Finance Ministry declared that it was unprofitable (TVP World, 2018).

The Bulgarian government framed shale gas as an opportunity to increase national and economic security and in June 2011 granted a licence to Chevron to conduct shale gas tests in the north-east of the country (Reuters, 2012b). However, there was opposition both on environmental grounds and also against the involvement of foreign companies, an 'economic sell-out frame' (Goldthau, 2018, pp. 143–144). Street protests in six cities in January 2012 and opposition from academics, NGOs and a coalition of national and local politicians (LaBelle and

Goldthau, 2014) led to the Bulgarian parliament voting to ban shale gas a few weeks later (BBC, 2012). Similarly, in 2010, the Romanian government signed a deal with Chevron for shale gas exploration. However, there was little consensus on the national security and economic benefits, and civil society opposition built on a movement opposing gold mining at Rosia Montana and used similar nationalist, anti-capitalist and environment protection framing to successfully oppose this (Goldthau, 2018). Mass protests led the company to suspend exploration and extraction activities in Vaslui County in April 2012, and in October 2013 in Pungesti villagers, including local farmers, blockaded the main road for a week (EJAtlas, 2019b). Further protests in April 2014 (Novinite, 2014) led to the suspension of operations prior to a withdrawal from Romania in February 2015 (EJAtlas, 2019b) after Chevron stated that the commercial exploitation of reserves was not viable (Van de Graaf et al., 2018).

Unconventional oil and gas resources have led to what Kuchler (2017) has argued are contested 'post-conventional energy futures', where the promises of domestic energy reserves fail to materialise, drawing public attention to the issue. Oil shale in the region is isolated to Estonia where it has generated electricity since the early twentieth century, and whilst there is growing contestation around the role of the resource, 'energy security assertions have socially normalising and reproductive effects', including with regard to the dominant role of shale oil attached to notions of low prices, self-sufficiency and self-determination (Kama, 2016, p. 833). In the mid-2010s the Federation of Estonian Chemical Industries led by oil shale representatives ran a campaign called 'Our welfare lies in our natural resources!' (Sillak and Kanger, 2020, pp. 105–106). In contrast NGOs have been campaigning for a phase-out – a 'Poxit' (Rahvaalgatus, 2017) – by using a green growth frame based on replacing the 6,000 fossil fuel–related jobs with jobs in renewables (Holmgren et al., 2019). Fridays for Future Estonia successfully took the government to court to stop construction of a new shale oil plant in 2020 on the basis that it was incompatible with the government's Paris Agreement commitments and did not adhere to environmental impact assessment requirements, with the construction licence suspended a year later (Friends of the Earth, 2021). There has been a policy shift, with the new government in 2021 pledging to end state subsides and phase out oil shale mining and all use by 2040, and oil shale for electricity generation from ~85% of the energy mix to zero by 2035 (Reuters, 2021d). In 2022 the government recommitted to this timeline, whilst increasing use in the short term was justified by replacing Russian gas imports. According to the Estonian Minister of Economy, 'Extraordinary measures must be used in exceptional circumstances. Fortunately, we have an alternative fuel' (Riina Sikkut cited in Jack, 2022).

Shale gas (and oil in Estonia) is one of the most politically and publicly contested energy sources and has been since it emerged as an apparent harbinger of low prices and energy independence in the early 2010s. Whilst shale reserves are relatively widespread in the region, few governments have embraced it, and others banned it almost immediately on environmental grounds. The economic promise faded, protests have been widespread, foreign direct investment mostly evaporated, and as of late 2023 no shale gas had been commercially produced in the region.

5.5 CONCLUSION

Energy security remains a dominant issue for the region, and this has affected the extent to which there is public concern, and civil society mobilisation, around environmental concerns and a drive for a more rapid energy transition. However, what is also clear is the direction of travel. Public environmental and climate concern is increasing and there are fossil fuel projects across the region that have been actively opposed by both social movements and civil society organisations (local, national and transnational).

Whilst there is a general tendency in CEE for energy policy to be one in which there is limited transparency, limited engagement with civil society and a prioritisation of energy security that justifies elite-driven policy-making, there are some signs of a shift. The role of citizens in the energy sector has changed. Millions of people in the region are active participants in the energy sector, prosumers generating rather than just consuming energy. In addition, whilst there have been protests against energy transitions in the form of strikes to halt the closures of coal mines, the majority of social movements have coalesced around promoting and accelerating energy transitions. Whilst perhaps smaller in scale than elsewhere in Europe, climate strikes were widespread in the towns and cities of CEE. There has been, to varying extents, a discursive development of governments because of civil society pressure, and indications in policy actions that the pace of energy transitions and fossil fuel phase-outs is increasing. Chapter 7 explores in further detail the idea that the experience of the CEE region is generalisable, with parallels to and lessons for global energy transitions.

6

The Influence of CEE Countries on EU Climate and Energy Policy

6.1 INTRODUCTION

In this chapter we consider the CEE region's effect on the EU's climate and energy policy. We also consider the influence on the understandings of energy security within the EU and the framing of, and responses to, these challenges at the EU level. While acknowledging and even stressing differences between individual CEE countries, this chapter argues that the CEE region can be characterised by a general prioritisation of energy security over climate policy, and a long-standing concern about the influence of, and threat from, Russia. The book at this point examines how different approaches to energy policy and climate change issues are presented at the EU level, and the extent to which CEE countries are willing and able to pursue their specific preferences – within regional and sub-regional cooperation (for example, the Visegrad Group or the Baltic States) or individually.

The chapter discusses the contribution of CEE countries to the development of EU climate and energy policy – such as Polish efforts to create 'Energy NATO' raising the alarm about dependency on Russian energy imports following the 2006 gas supply disruption, the 2014 Energy Union proposal and the 2022 response to Russia's invasion of Ukraine, which reshaped EU's energy policy. Although Poland played a prime role in most of these initiatives, several other CEE countries also attempted to promote their energy security ideas at the EU level. The security dimension was prioritised by CEE countries, with most diplomatic efforts focused on this (Bocquillon and Maltby, 2017; Mišík, 2015). Whilst they brought the issue of (mainly external) energy security to the EU table during their accession negotiations, there was little shared understanding with other member states who considered energy security to be an issue best solved through national policy (Mayer, 2008). The 2006 and 2009 gas supply disruptions shifted the focus towards energy security in the CEE region, and at the EU level (see also Chapter 4). Both internal (market development and interconnections) and external (supply sources and routes) energy security has been highlighted by the CEE countries as issues to be dealt with at the community level. Contrary to climate policy, in which CEE countries played a mostly passive and oppositional role (see Chapters 3 and 5), some have been very active in energy security policy, proposing ideas and initiatives and trying to frame their importance for the EU's security.

This chapter shows that for the CEE states there was some success in placing energy security high on the agenda, particularly in connection to the internal energy market and infrastructural developments. However, whilst countries in the region highlighted the risks and threat of relying on Russian energy imports, there was a lack of collectively held concern, and while Russia's invasion of Ukraine in 2014 shifted this further, it was the full-scale invasion of Ukraine in 2022 and related interruption of Russian gas supplies to the EU that led to a decisive shift in discourse and policy response, facilitated by widespread concern about the use of Russian energy as a foreign policy weapon (European Commission, 2022a; McWilliams and Zachmann, 2022; Osička and Černoch, 2022). Despite the previous gas supply disruptions of 2006 and 2009, the EU's dependence on Russian gas imports increased after 2010, from 31 to 38% by the end of the decade (Eurostat, 2022b). As a result, in 2020 Russia was the largest single supplier of oil, gas and coal to the EU (Eurostat, 2022b). However, within three months of the start of the Russian invasion of Ukraine in 2022 the Commission had proposed making the EU independent from all Russia fossil fuels 'well before 2030' (European Commission, 2022a). The effect was rapid. By September gas imports from Russia had decreased by 74% (European Commission, 2023f).

There has been a process of learning for CEE in terms of how to pursue their policy preferences at the EU level (Copsey and Pomorska, 2010), though we can see differences between CEE countries. While Poland is very active in proposing new policy proposals related to energy security, and Czechia and Slovakia in nuclear energy, others limit their engagement to a more passive support of proposals. Whilst CEE as a region can be considered as supportive of the EU's common approach to energy security and developing a common voice towards energy-exporting countries, Hungary and Slovakia were among the strongest opponents of Russian oil sanctions discussed in April 2022 (Taylor, 2022a). The chapter explores this variation.

Such an active approach has been less present in climate policy. Often CEE countries' actions here have been characterised as reactive to EU policy rather than attempting to set the agenda and develop policy. However, related to emissions trading and the level of ambition of climate objectives and decarbonisation there have been prominent examples of acting either alone or in a coordinated approach to upload climate policy preferences to the EU level, to promote a concern that there is a trade-off – that climate policy goals negatively influence energy security priorities and undermine economic development (Sivek et al., 2017; Szulecki et al., 2016). Whilst Poland is the most visible country among the CEE members of the EU, actively opposing ambitious EU climate targets and leading similar-minded coalitions during EU negotiations, other CEE countries have also supported ambitious climate goals. For example, Estonia and Slovenia were part of a Green Growth Group proposing greater EU ambition (Green Growth Group, 2013).

The chapter discusses the engagement of CEE countries in the EU's energy and climate policy. It starts by providing an overview of these countries' positions pre-accession. The chapter then discusses energy security policy proposals of CEE countries including 'Energy NATO', the Energy Union and collective gas purchases, but also opposition of some to EU sanction proposals towards Russia in 2022 and the coordinated voluntary gas demand reduction during the 2022/2023 winter. In Section 6.3 the chapter examines how CEE countries shaped the internal energy market's natural gas legislation, including their influence on the anti-monopoly investigation against Gazprom. This section also outlines CEE countries' consistent opposition towards the Nord Stream pipelines that had an important internal energy market dimension. Section 6.4 studies how the CEE countries managed to influence the size of the funds that were assigned within the EU for infrastructural projects, including those that were created following the 2009 gas supply interruption (the European Energy Programme for Recovery, Projects of Common Interest), and in response to the Covid-19 pandemic (the Recovery and Resilience Facility).

The chapter shows the interest of CEE countries in issues connected to energy security and their effort to push this agenda to the EU level, though also how understandings of what threatens energy security vary. The last section discusses the divergent position of CEE countries towards the EU's climate agenda that has materialised in their various – and often contradictory – positions on the EU's 2020 and 2030 climate and energy targets.

6.2 JOINING THE EU AND ITS DECISION-MAKING PROCESS

This section discusses CEE countries' activity within the EU after most of these countries became members in 2004. It looks at this issue from a general perspective, thus paving the way for the analysis of CEE countries' activities within the Union in climate and energy policy. In most areas CEE countries were initially followers rather than pace-setters, which has been attributed to the legacy of accession conditionality (Börzel and Sedelmeier, 2017). With length of membership CEE countries became much more active, but also assertive, which materialised in various proposals (for instance, the Eastern Partnership; Copsey and Pomorska, 2014; Neuman, 2017), opposition to policies during negotiations (for example, during the refugee crisis of 2015/2016; Pachocka, 2016; Visegrad Group, 2016), and also opposition to climate policies and the EU's related sectoral targets.

CEE countries were engaged in the EU's climate and energy policies before eight joined in May 2004, mostly in connection to the accession negotiations that began in 1997 (with a few in 1999; Haughton and Malová, 2007). These were, however, considered one-sided with candidates mainly following Commission's requirements and governed by the conditionality process (Schimmelfennig and Sedelmeier, 2004). Contrary to the previous enlargements, the eastern one comprised several rounds (2004, 2007 and 2013) and was not based on ad hoc negotiations with individual accession countries, but a complex system developed to support what was considered the largest and most challenging enlargement (Moravcsik and Vachudova, 2005). At the 1993 Copenhagen Summit a set of fundamental conditions was agreed that candidates must meet in order to be granted membership (Sedelmeier, 2011). These were translated into 'chapters' containing different EU policies and institutional rules that were at the heart of negotiations between candidates and the Commission that guided the accession process. This includes chapters for energy (15) and environment (27).

Within this mechanism a system of 'carrots and sticks' was firmly embedded – countries that followed Commission's recommendations, and fulfilled required conditions, were rewarded (with the membership status being the ultimate reward); those that did not were punished by slowing down or even halting the negotiation process (Schimmelfennig and Sedelmeier, 2004). Conditionality thus created a very strong learning experience for CEE countries that impacted their activities within the EU also after they became full members and its formal influence disappeared (Haughton, 2011). The negotiation process focused not only on transfer of EU rules (the so-called *acquis communautaire*) but also on institution building (Lippert et al., 2001) as the CEE countries undergoing political and economic transition were lacking in strong institutions supporting democracy and a market economy (Sedelmeier, 2012). This was a mammoth task for countries still struggling with the legacy of the communist regime and planned economies. The candidate states from CEE had little room for pursuing their own preferences in this process even when crucial issues were at stake. As the discussion about the closure of nuclear power plants in three candidate states examined in Chapter 4 demonstrated, accession was an asymmetrical process of imposing EU conditions rather than a negotiation.

During the 1990s CEE countries were interested in energy security issues, especially supply diversification, mainly due to their dependency on Russian supplies (Mišík, 2015). Pre-accession Czechia (Binhack and Tichý, 2012) and the Baltic States (Streimikiene et al., 2007) were developing diversification projects (see also Chapter 4), though Slovakia, Poland and other countries were not actively challenging the existing eastward-looking supply structures. Moreover, there were few examples of concessions extracted by CEE countries from the accession process. Emergency oil stocks is one. All candidate countries aspiring for the 2004 enlargement – with the exception of Hungary, which had already fulfilled the criteria – successfully requested a transition period of one to seven years post-accession to increase oil emergency storage to EU required levels due to the high costs

(Tosun, 2011). Internal energy market rules being negotiated just before 2004 (the second liberalisation package) provided minimal opportunity to engage in shaping the outcome of negotiations. Whilst representatives of candidate countries were joining negotiations regularly, the main reason for this activity was to familiarise themselves with the internal workings of the EU's decision-making process without the opportunity to present their own preferences and influence the outcome.

Early in their membership, CEE countries were not very active within the EU decision-making process, mostly reacting to proposals by other members and avoiding positions that would go against the majority. Gradually, a central-eastern grouping emerged (Hosli et al., 2011; Mattila, 2009), but this was not as strong as the south-north division that was the prominent cleavage within the Union (Mattila, 2008). Despite concerns about 'decision-making paralysis' following enlargement, this did not materialise, with the amount of adopted legislation actually increasing in the ten-year period post 2004 (Toshkov, 2017). Immediately after accession CEE states generally continued the modus operandi of following EU proposals (Cirtautas and Schimmelfennig, 2010). In terms of their influence, when voicing opposing preferences, the CEE countries, even united, often failed to influence negotiations or block initiatives (ibid., 190), yet despite pre-accession concerns, new members had an apparently very positive compliance record (Börzel and Sedelmeier, 2017).

Even when the CEE countries started to be active after several years of their membership, their contribution to the decision-making mechanism was not always straightforward. Poland gained a reputation as a difficult member state due to last-minute requests during negotiations or an unwillingness to compromise, which was considered to limit coalition-building (Copsey and Pomorska, 2014). While this was an example of 'non-compliance' with informal rules (negotiation styles), challenges with the application of formal rules were also apparent. This issue was connected to transposition of EU rules to national legislation.

Although member states were necessarily compliant in transposing EU directives in order to qualify for accession (Spendzharova and Versluis, 2013), this was followed by policy implementation failures and (non)compliance in the following five years. Falkner and Treib (2008) examine this gap between good legislative records and formal transposition, and problems with application on the ground, as part of a 'world of dead letters'. Here EU-driven practices were not internalised by becoming part of the actors' mode of operation, transforming policy preferences and enabling substantive change (Dąbrowski, 2012). Formally, these countries fulfilled their responsibilities towards the EU; in practice, the common rules were often not enforced. Work on variations of 'shallow Europeanization' in the newer member states focused on the appearance of compliance and strategic action and identifies cases of 'creative compliance' (Börzel and Risse, 2007) and 'symbolic transformation' (Sotirov et al., 2015). However, later research indicates that these patterns are not universal and that CEE countries' implementation varied (Zhelyazkova et al., 2017).

Over time CEE countries learned the 'rules of the game' (both formal and informal) and became standard contributors to the decision-making process characterised by consensus (Finke, 2017; Heisenberg, 2005). Poland proposed several energy-related policy proposals and has been also very active as a critic of the Commission's climate proposals and targets. Moreover, CEE countries' compliance record has become more similar to those of the rest of the EU overall (Buzogány, 2021) including in environmental policy (Börzel and Buzogány, 2019).

6.3 COLLECTIVE ACTION ON GAS

This section examines the proposals to increase energy security through collective action on gas purchasing. This section argues that ideas were the main driving force of these proposals CEE countries have been active in proposing and supporting initiatives to address the vulnerability of states to the threat of Gazprom's divide and rule tactics, particularly with regard to smaller gas markets.

'Energy NATO'

The first major energy initiative stemming from the CEE region was a proposal to establish the European Energy Security Treaty (also known as 'Energy NATO') by Poland in 2006. The idea behind the initiative was focused on energy security and was supposed to create an energy supply mechanism similar to Article 5 of the NATO treaty – 'all for one, one for all'. This was the first major policy initiative by a CEE member two years after accession and triggered by the 2006 natural gas supply disruption, although Poland was not directly impacted by it. The Treaty's objective was to provide energy solidarity 'through the creation of mutual assistance guarantees' (Roth, 2011, p. 601). The initiative was considered part of a broader Polish effort to establish coalitions within the EU to highlighting threats posed by Russia (Closson, 2009). Poland was significantly dependent on Russian energy supplies, and the development of the Nord Stream pipeline between Russia and Germany directly threatened the development of the Yamal pipeline through Poland that until 2022 was one of the main supply lines of Russian gas to Europe and provided valuable transit fees to Poland.

Following the first gas supply disruption, a joint position was presented in January 2006 by Poland together with Hungary, Czechia and Austria on the diversification of energy supplies to CEE (Jeziorski, 2006). Later in the month Poland, Czechia, Slovakia, Austria, Hungary, Slovenia, Croatia and Romania discussed coordinated strategies to address Russian gas dependence (Geden et al., 2006, p. 20). A month later Poland presented a proposal for a European Energy Security Treaty, to guard against 'potential political pressure exerted with the use of energy instruments' and emphasising 'solidarity' (Council of the EU, 2006a, p. 2). This followed a letter to the *Financial Times* by the prime minister calling for a mutual energy solidarity clause (Marcinkiewicz, 2006). The initiative was supported by the Visegrad Group and the Baltic States, but failed to gain wider support (Taylor, 2006), with Austria and Germany in particular stressing the importance of interdependence and cooperation with Russia, rather than confrontation (Roth, 2011, p. 613).

Western EU member states (especially Germany) accused Poland of dealing with energy security issues that emerged after the 2006 supply disruption in a heavy-handed manner that was in contrast with the prevailing understanding of the interdependent nature of EU-Russia energy relations (Jarosz, 2011). Germany, France, and the United Kingdom were not in favour of solutions that they saw as an effort to isolate Russia (McGowan, 2011). While Poland managed to put the proposal on the March 2006 European Council agenda, it did not receive enough support, though solidarity as an energy policy concept was adopted by the March 2006 Green Paper (European Commission, 2006). Germany presented its own proposal, called 'Energy OSCE', to govern EU energy security according to the model of the Organisation for Security and Co-operation in Europe, thus including not only consumer countries but 'also the producer and transit states and compris [ing] an international energy dialogue' (Götz, 2007, p. 17). Poland, along with fellow Visegrad Group members, emphasised security of supplies and the threat posed by Russia, focusing on solidarity in material terms – in regulations and infrastructure. It was argued by a Polish interviewee that '[s]olidarity, dependence and security' constituted the 'Polish ideas, slogan and vocabulary' within the EU (cited in Maltby, 2014, p. 226). The proposal failed, with the Energy Council mentioning only 'coordination mechanisms' rather than solidarity at that point (Council of the EU, 2006b). However, Article 194 of the Lisbon Treaty (negotiated at the June 2007 European Council summit) included a commitment to energy policy being developed with 'a spirit of solidarity between member states', and Article 122 allows the Council to enact measures in 'a spirit of solidarity' if severe difficulties of supply arise within the energy sector. This was a direct concession to Poland (Youngs, 2009).

There were parallels also with the post-accession efforts of the Baltic States, which, despite divergent energy mixes, were concerned that energy isolation from the rest of the EU was a problem, a threat to either supplies (Lithuania) or price (Latvia). What united the countries was to elevate the problem of being an energy island to the EU level, from the birth of the narrative in the mid-2000s to its adoption by the EU within a few years. In June 2008, the Latvian Energy Commissioner Pielbags stated:

> Without secure supplies in the Baltic Sea region, there is no energy security for the European Union. The region is leading the way in an important shift of thinking in energy policy. A shift that means seeing energy security not just as a national issue, but as a regional concern.... Energy collaboration, solidarity and common goals are an important regional task. And, for the EU, they are imperative.
>
> (Piebalgs, 2008)

From 'Energy NATO' to 'Energy Union'

Following the inclusion of energy solidarity in the Lisbon Treaty, in 2008, the Polish government was successful in getting the (anti)Gazprom solidarity adopted in the Third Energy Package's Gas Directive (2009/73/EC; Eikeland, 2011). This was a dilution from the Polish preference of excluding third countries from access to national energy infrastructure. The Directive included a weaker clause with more national regulatory discretion, following resistance from Italy and Germany (Brutschin, 2015). Although the 2009 gas supply disruption meant a major shock especially for the CEE countries, none of them developed an immediate response to the crisis in a form of a policy proposal at the EU level. As discussed in Chapter 4 their focus was on diversification projects developed or at least partly financed by the Commission. The exception was Lithuania's decision to build its own LNG terminal after not being able to find a common solution with the other Baltic States that would unlock EU financing. As this chapter discusses, CEE countries focused on allocating as much funds as possible within the EU's mechanisms to support energy infrastructure development.

The March 2014 annexation of Crimea by Russia started a process that led to the creation of the Energy Union, a complex 'umbrella' initiative covering all aspects of energy and climate policy within the EU, in 2015 (European Commission, 2015a). While the resulting initiative was complex in nature, the original idea was focused on energy security and the development of a common EU voice towards external energy suppliers, namely, Russia. Shortly after the Crimea annexation, Polish Prime Minister and soon to be the president of the European Council Donald Tusk published an opinion piece in the *Financial Times* highlighting that 'excessive dependence on Russian energy makes Europe weak' and claiming that the EU needed to develop a strong common external energy policy with an energy security focus to counteract Russia, an 'Energy Union' 'based on solidarity and common economic interests' (Tusk, 2014). The best way to start this process, he claimed, was to develop a system of common purchases of gas like that within the nuclear industry. Here, member states must buy their nuclear fuel via the EU's Euratom Supply Agency, and the initiative revived the common purchasing features of the Energy NATO initiative.

Tusk's initiative was expanded upon by the Polish Ministry of Foreign Affairs, which developed a six-point plan of how to strengthen the energy security of the EU (MFA Poland, 2014). These ideas were adopted by Jean-Claude Juncker, the new president of the Commission, who included this initiative under the name 'Energy Union' among five top priorities of his new Commission in February 2015 as a concept broadened out from its initial focus on energy security to also include the internal energy market, energy efficiency, the decarbonisation of the economy, and research, innovation and competitiveness (European Commission, 2015a). The Polish proposals were more concentrated on external energy relations (Austvik,

2016), and whilst these remained important in the Energy Union proposal (Mišík, 2019), the initiative evolved into one which sought 'to reform European energy governance, policy and regional cooperation, streamlining these with long-term climate protection goals' (Szulecki et al., 2016, p. 548). Jean-Claude Juncker stressed the importance of the Energy Union by making it one of main topics of his Commission presidency (2014–2019), but also by creating the position of vice-president of the Commission for Energy Union (filled by Maroš Šefčovič, a commissioner from Slovakia). This approach was supposed to increase the coherence of the Commission's proposals as energy-related initiatives had to be agreed by all impacted Commissioners, including those responsible for energy, climate, transit and agriculture. The Energy Union remained the principal energy and climate policy until it was supplemented by the 2019 European Green Deal with its stronger climate emphasis.

Collective Gas Purchasing, 2022

Several previous energy security policy initiatives included an idea to create a mechanism of collective gas purchases of imported natural gas. This was a response especially to the Russian 'divide and rule' approach to its European customers under which it would deliver gas to individual EU member states under different conditions, including different prices, as noted in the earlier discussion of the Commission's conclusion that Gazprom had engaged in illegal anti-competitive behaviour. Such an approach undermined member states' unity as those that were receiving Russian natural gas under relatively better conditions (for example, Germany) may be against a tougher approach towards exporting states and companies. Transferring the responsibility for gas purchase to the EU level (a specialised agency) would leverage the EU's market power to achieve lower prices. Whilst Tusk's 2014 proposal (Tusk, 2014) highlighted this, and a draft Energy Union document discussed the 'enhancement of the EU's bargaining power, notably through voluntary demand aggregation', including with gas (Crisp, 2015), it was absent from the Energy Union a year later despite support from CEE countries (European Commission, 2015a).

The idea to develop a collective gas purchasing mechanism re-emerged in late 2021 in response to rising gas prices, and again and more decisively during the first half of 2022 after the Russian invasion of Ukraine followed by decreased deliveries of natural gas to the EU and cutting off Poland and Bulgaria completely in April (Holz et al., 2022) – which the Commission President von der Leyen labelled 'yet another attempt by Russia to use gas as an instrument of blackmail' (Abnett 2022). In December 2021 the Commission proposed a system of voluntary joint purchases of gas reserves (European Commission, 2021f), following lobbying from countries including Romania, Greece and Spain (Kurmayer, 2022c). The Commission's proposal for a REPowerEU strategy published less than two weeks after Russia's

2022 invasion argued that '[a] joint European platform for contractualisation of gas supply based on bilateral negotiations with major gas producers would help diversification and smart risk management, hence ensuring security of supplies on favourable conditions for all buyers across the EU' (European Commission, 2022a). This idea was adopted by member states during the March 2022 European Council (European Council, 2022a), and the first meeting on the EU Platform for the common purchase of gas, LNG and hydrogen took place in April 2022.

By autumn 2022 the idea of collective gas purchasing had come closer to reality following belated support from Germany (Kurmayer, 2022c), albeit in watered-down form. The Commission proposed that 'joint purchasing' would be enabled through '[a] voluntary purchasing system, allowing companies to form a European gas purchasing consortium', alongside a mandatory requirement for 15% of gas storage volume. The objective was, first, to 'facilitate a more equal access to new suppliers and international markets [to] give more negotiating weight to European importers' (European Commission, 2022n, p. 3), and, second, to exclude Russian energy. However, the proposed mandatory volume of gas purchased collectively (i.e., 15% of storage) is only approximately 5% of the EU's overall annual gas consumption, far from the ambitious joint purchase of natural gas at the EU level that favoured much larger volumes in order to leverage the EU's collective purchasing power (Mišík and Nosko, 2023b).

Sanctions on Russia

Portela et al. (2021) argue that the EU's sanctions, requiring unanimous member state support and introduced after Russia's invasion of Crimea in 2014, were introduced following initial solidarity amongst member states, and survived a divergence of preferences that emerged soon after, including between CEE states. Those most in favour of a strong response were the Baltic States and Poland, along with Romania (and the United Kingdom and Nordic states). There was a strong normative dimension in which it was recognised that solidarity amongst member states and support for Ukraine's territorial integrity were required (Szép, 2020). However, Bulgaria, Hungary, Czechia and Slovakia (and a number of southern and western member states) were amongst those states that proposed weaker sanctions (Natorski and Pomorska, 2017; Sjursen and Rosén, 2017). For example, the Bulgarian president claimed that '[s]anctions are not a solution to the problem' (Bulgarian National Radio, 2016), and the Bulgarian foreign minister by 2017 argued against the EU consensus that extending sanctions should be automatic, and proposed that a process of 'pragmatic rebuilding of cooperation' was economically necessary (Sullivan, 2016).

Following Russia's 2022 full-scale invasion of Ukraine, the EU again imposed further sanctions, including on the energy sector. Whilst there was initial consensus sufficient to design these, the broadening-out to include an oil embargo was opposed predominantly by a single state, Hungary. Lithuania's foreign minister, Gabrielius Landsbergis, aired the frustration that 'the whole union is being held hostage by one member state' (Rankin, 2022). Several CEE states were able to gain concessions from an embargo on Russian oil from February 2023 (and the end of 2022 for imports by sea). In effect they succeeded in making the ban only partial. Imports via the Druzhba oil pipeline to Hungary, Slovakia and Czechia were initially exempt, as were those to Germany, but these ceased by the end of 2022 (Rankin, 2022). Croatia was also permitted some imports until the end of 2023, and Bulgaria the end of 2024 (Cahill, 2022). In August 2022 the Hungarian government signed a deal to increase imports from Russia (Preussen, 2022), and launched a domestic poster campaign featuring pictures of sanctions in the form of bombs punishing Hungary (Tidey, 2022).

Voluntary Decrease of Natural Gas Consumption during the 2022/2023 Winter

The Commission quickly proposed a plan to phase out Russian energy supplies before 2030 (European Commission, 2022a). This included demand-side responses and energy efficiency measures, along with increasing low volumes of natural gas in underground storages (Zachmann et al., 2021). Although member states did not experience shortages of natural gas supplies that would require employment of the solidarity mechanisms of the 2017 SoS Regulation, the Commission proposed a voluntary mechanism to decrease the chance of shortages and ensure enough gas within the EU in such a situation. The proposal was for a decrease of natural gas consumption of 15% during the winter of 2022/2023 when compared with the average of the previous five-year period (European Commission, 2022b). This was to be voluntary, but importantly would become mandatory in an emergency (Taylor, 2022b); this proposal was supported by Poland and Slovenia, which welcomed the common approach by the EU to challenges caused by Russia (Patricolo, 2022).

Not all member states were initially supportive of this proposal, and Portugal and Spain argued that as they did not import any gas from Russia their savings would not contribute to solving problems connected to this supplier (Kluth, 2022). Slovakia was opposed on the basis of the reliance on gas for industry (Jenčová, 2022). Hungarian Prime Minister Viktor Orbán criticised the proposal by claiming that it imposed solidarity on member countries and disadvantaged those states that had invested in storage as this could be used by 'irresponsible' countries with lower levels of stored gas (Orbán, 2022). These arguments were successful in forestalling any mandatory requirement without European Council approval, and member states agreed to a voluntary measure and their 'best efforts' (Council of the EU, 2022a). Some states also achieved an opt-out, including island states (geographic islands) and 'energy islands'. On the basis of the latter, the Baltic States received an exemption as their electricity system had not yet been synchronised with the rest of the EU (Council of the EU, 2022b). The EU managed to decrease gas consumption during the period between August 2022 and March 2023 by 17.7%, compared with the five-year average, surpassing its 15% goal (Abnett, 2023).

6.4 SHAPING GAS LEGISLATION

Besides proposing new policy initiatives in the area of energy security, CEE countries have been also active in shaping internal energy market legislation, especially in the natural gas sector. They influenced two main types of legislation: gas liberalisation (especially the third liberalisation package) and security of supply legislation proposed by the Commission as a direct response to the 2009 gas supply disruption. This section examines impact of CEE countries on these two types of legislation with a focus on anti-monopoly investigation against Gazprom that was connected to the internal market rules.

Negotiating the Third Liberalisation Package

Although the CEE countries have been mostly interested in energy security since accession, it was an internal market issue that presented the first major negotiation challenge. Soon after second internal energy market package legislation was adopted in 2003 and 2004, liberalising gas and electricity markets, respectively, discussion on future unbundling steps began. CEE countries demonstrated a variety of positions towards this. Whilst many member countries, supported by the Commission, wanted further liberalisation resulting in the complete separation of energy companies dealing with production, distribution, storage, and selling of natural gas and electricity (i.e., full unbundling), most CEE countries successfully opposed full unbundling.

The original proposal by the Commission called for a full unbundling as the only option within the third energy package. This was changed very soon after the Commission started preliminary talks with member states and other crucial stakeholders (energy companies, regulators, etc.) as it faced strong opposition. The second option introduced by the Commission in its revised third liberalisation package proposal allowed for much more flexibility between individual activities of energy companies. This, however, was still not satisfactory for eight member countries, including several from CEE that were able to create a blocking minority that gave them a strong negotiating position vis-à-vis the Commission. The result was a third option that allowed member states to change the structure of their energy companies only minimally compared with the second package (Herweg, 2017). The final third energy package of 2009 thus included three liberalisation options – from full unbundling (option one) that was adopted by Lithuania to one that represented very limited change (option three) adopted by Slovakia and several other CEE countries. Lithuania adopted the strictest liberalisation option predominantly due to foreign policy reasons. The country aimed to decrease the influence of Gazprom on its natural gas market, and had to bear the consequences in the form of higher natural gas prices as a result of worsening foreign relations with Russia (Adomaitis and Lannin, 2012).

The third option was a result of opposition from Bulgaria, Latvia and Slovakia together with Austria, France, Germany, Greece and Luxembourg (Euractiv, 2008). At that time the Commission already worked with two versions of unbundling that it wanted to include into the new legislation proposal: ownership unbundling and an independent system operator. This group of member states proposed their own, 'third' version of unbundling with an independent transmission operator. The group formed a blocking minority able to veto the proposal, and therefore the third option found its way into the Commission's proposal of the third liberalisation package. The main difference was that in the third option vertically integrated energy companies were allowed to keep distribution networks in their ownership (similar to the second option), but the links between the 'mother' company and the operator of the networks were much stronger (i.e., less unbundled). As a result, the third option (chosen by several EU member states) represented only a limited liberalisation through unbundling compared with the second package (Pielow et al., 2009).

Not all CEE countries were engaged in the liberalisation negotiations. For example, Czechia during the final negotiations of the third package held the presidency of the Council of the EU and therefore assumed a position of mediator (Mišík, 2015). Poland did not assume a specific position toward the package; however, it was very interested in the so-called Gazprom clause (see below). In February 2010 the Polish Ministry of Foreign Affairs invited the Commission to scrutinise the contract between Gazprom and the national energy company PGNiG. The Commission concluded that it was in breach of EU law in the third package, by preventing third-party access to the Yamal pipeline. This was used to justify the renegotiation of the contract to remove the destination clause forbidding the resale of Russian gas (EU Business, 2010). Similarly, the Commission played a role in amending a Bulgarian gas contract with Russia (Euractiv, 2010).

Response to the 2009 Supply Disruption: New Security of Supply Legislation

The 2009 gas supply disruption was the main catalyst of energy security development until 2022 fully reshaped EU climate and energy policy. The CEE countries supported the Commission's proposals for new legislation in this area as they considered it a key tool to increase their resilience against future supply disruptions.

Reacting to the 2009 gas supply disruption, the Commission proposed and the member states together with the European Parliament adopted the Security of Gas Supply Regulation 994/2010 (Official Journal of the European Union, 2010). This was an update to a 2004 Directive (2004/67/EC) that proved unable to prevent the crisis from happening. The new SoS Regulation created the backbone of EU's security of gas supply rules until it was replaced in 2017. However, despite the necessity to ramp up EU's efforts in the energy security area, during the negotiations the Regulation was opposed especially by the Netherland and Germany, with several other countries from Western Europe having reservations about common minimum standards on security of supplies and infrastructure. However, it was supported by CEE countries. Polish representatives were particularly active in the preparatory phase of the legislation within the European Parliament as well as during the Council discussions, creating a regional group of CEE countries supporting the Regulation and becoming the spokesperson for the region in this matter (Bocquillon and Maltby, 2017). Poland pushed for a stricter definition of energy emergency that the Commission would be empowered to declare. Most importantly, the country pursued a 10% decrease of regular supplies as a reason to declare an emergency, while West European member states supported the Commission's idea of a more severe 20% decrease as the crisis trigger. As a compromise, the Regulation gave the Commission the ability to proclaim emergency upon two countries' request (Bocquillon and Maltby, 2017).

The first SoS Regulation also introduced an information exchange mechanism to intergovernmental energy agreements between member states and third countries that was further developed in the 2012 Decision 994/2012/EU adopted by the Commission. Through this the Commission gained a right to check ex-post the fit of these agreements with internal market rules, enhancing its monitoring powers. This system proved unsuccessful in preventing member states from concluding energy agreements that were not in line with the internal market rules. Therefore, the Commission included in the new Decision 2017/684/EU an ex-ante system of checks. Within this new system, member states' entities were allowed to conclude LTCs with third parties only after their draft versions' alignment with EU's internal energy market rules was checked by the Commission. Not all states, however, were in favour of this new system – from within CEE, Hungary was one of the opponents that along with countries including Italy, Germany and France was able to form a blocking minority that led to changes that weakened the Commission's original proposal to be able to force revisions of contracts (Council of the EU, 2016; European Commission, 2016a). Very strong support for the Commission's proposal came from Poland and the Baltic States, which viewed the Commission as their ally in energy negotiations with Russia (Batzella, 2021, p. 756).

A 2017 Regulation (2017/1938) further revised the EU's Security of Gas Supply legislation, including the concept of regional risk groups (Official Journal of the European Union, 2017). During the drafting period, the Commission proposed nine groups (as opposed to the final thirteen groups clustered into four categories); however, its idea of fixed groups was replaced by risk groups depending on possible supply risks, an idea supported by member states (CEEP, 2018). Bulgaria unsuccessfully requested derogation from the rules due to high expected investments for required infrastructure that would fulfil the new criteria, and criticised what it perceived would be increased competences of the Commission granted by the new rules and the large bureaucratic load on national authorities (European Parliament, 2016).

Influence on Anti-monopoly Investigation against Gazprom

Lithuania was key to the legal challenge to Gazprom's activities in Europe, complaining to the Commission in January 2011 (Reuters, 2016b). Later in the year the Commission raided the offices of Gazprom as well as E.ON Ruhrgas and RWE (Germany), PGNiG (Poland) and OMV (Austria). The response by Gazprom was to adjust prices in its LTCs with companies in France, Germany, Slovakia, Italy and Austria. However, the Commission investigation continued, focusing on Gazprom's activities in Bulgaria, Czechia, Estonia, Hungary, Latvia, Lithuania, Poland and Slovakia, and resulted in charging Gazprom in 2015 with the abuse of its dominant position and the overcharging of eight countries by up to 40% (European Commission, 2015c). This was settled in 2018 after Gazprom committed to removing restrictions preventing CEE countries from re-exporting Russian gas (Bulgaria, Czechia, Estonia, Hungary, Latvia, Lithuania, Poland and Slovakia), with the Commission arguing that 'Gazprom has accepted that it has to play by our common European rules' (Rankin, 2018).

Opposition to the Nord Stream Gas Pipeline at the EU Level

Besides actively supporting new infrastructural projects within the EU, CEE countries – to a limited degree – also joined the discussion about new energy supplies to the EU. The most visible was Poland and its criticism towards Nord Stream gas pipelines, both the first and the second leg of the project.

The Nord Stream project was an EU priority included in 2000 TEN-E Guidelines and reconfirmed in the mid-2006 review (European Commission, 2009b). Polish opposition to Nord Stream I was clear from 2005 when the chair of the political party Civic Platform argued that it 'unambiguously violates the common interests of the European Union and its member states' (MosNews, 2005). Prime Minister Kaczynski compared the plans to the 1939 Molotov Ribbentrop pact (RFERL, 2006), and Foreign Minister Fotyga claimed that '[i]t is imperative for Poland and Central Eastern Europe to reduce dependency [on Russian energy resources] while it seems like the old member states would like to do the opposite' (Geden et al., 2006, p. 16). Foreign Minister Sikorski stated this was a case of Russia and Germany '[t]aking the decision first and consulting after [which] is not our idea of solidarity' (Deutsche Welle, 2006). In 2006 Poland vetoed a replacement to the 1997 EU-Russia Partnership and Cooperation Agreement, positioning the country as a regional actor advocating for less close relations with

Russia (Copsey, 2009), an opportunity for 'unprecedented leverage' (Schmidt-Felzmann, 2008, p. 177).

In the summer of 2008, a Polish initiative (led by a Polish member of the European Parliament and Parliament committee chairman, Marcin Libicki) was successful: the passing of a European Parliament report critical of the pipeline, demanding a positive environment assessment. With 542 out of 602 MEPs supporting the report (Europolitics, 2008) Aleks Szczerbiak described this as the 'major (and perhaps the greatest) Polish success . . . the resolution carried an important symbolic message that the project was a controversial one, and raised concerns outside Poland as well as within it' (2011, p. 74). However, MEPs rejected blocking construction without support from all Baltic Sea countries (PolskieRadio, 2008), and the pipeline received environmental approvals and began operating in 2011.

Poland used several approaches to voice its criticism towards the second leg of the pipeline. For example, the Polish Office of Competition and Consumer Protection objected first to Gazprom's joint venture with European energy companies in 2016 (German Uniper and BASF Wintershall, Anglo-Dutch Shell, Austrian OMV and French Engie) and later the financial agreement with these companies in 2017 citing anti-monopoly rules (Schmidt-Felzmann, 2018). In 2009 Gazprom's bid for an exemption from EU liberalisation legislation that meant that the company could use only 50% of the capacity of the OPAL (Ostsee-Pipeline-Anbindungsleitung) pipeline was rejected. This would have connected Nord Stream to the German mainland. However, in 2016 the Commission revised this policy and allowed Gazprom to also bid for the other 50% of the capacity alongside third parties (Yafimava, 2017), arguing intra alia that '[t]he increased utilisation of the OPAL pipeline that is likely to result from the changed scope of the exemption will further increase security of supply' (European Commission, 2016b, p. 14). This allowed Gazprom to increase its gas transit via Nord Stream I and consequently decrease transit via other pipelines, while providing precedents for further infrastructural development connected to the Nord Stream II pipeline (especially the EUGAL pipeline connecting to Czechia). Poland (with support of Latvia and Lithuania) challenged this decision at the European Court of Justice, arguing that it would harm energy security in CEE. In 2019 the Court sided with this appeal and overruled the Commission's 2016 decision, stating that it was 'in breach of the principle of energy solidarity' (ECJ, 2019). This represented a further shift towards the concrete incorporation of the concept of solidarity, 'as energy solidarity has previously been understood . . . largely as a policy guidance rather than a legal principle' (Yafimava, 2021, p. 2).

Together with the imposition of US sanctions from December 2019, this decision had a significant impact on slowing down the completion of Nord Stream II and the possible circumvention of Russian gas transit through Ukraine via the Brotherhood pipeline that would likely follow. However, it was not until February 2022 that the already finished second line of the Nord Stream pipeline was cancelled. This was followed by Russia reducing gas transit through the first line by 75% in June 2022, and completely in August, followed by damage to both legs that jeopardised their (re)start indefinitely (BBC, 2022b).

6.5 FINANCING

One of the main lessons from the 2009 gas supply disruption was that it was a shortage of gas pipeline interconnections, not of gas itself, that led full or partial interruptions of supplies via the Brotherhood pipeline to CEE countries (European Commission, 2009a). Therefore, the EU started a process of infrastructural development where it co-financed member states' energy projects, first through the European Energy Programme for Recovery (EEPR), which was designed not only to support infrastructural development but also to help member states with their recovery following the economic crisis of 2008–2010 (European Parliament and the Council, 2009c). This was later replaced by the Projects of Common Interest (PCI) mechanism, which created a list of infrastructural projects qualifying for EU support published by the Commission every two years (European Commission, 2015g; European Parliament and the Council, 2013). At the end of 2021 the Commission published its fifth list, one that sparked discussion due to its inclusion of fossil fuel projects (especially natural gas) in a period of volatile prices and increased instability of the gas market (European Commission, 2021g). CEE countries greatly benefitted from these mechanisms, and almost all new energy infrastructure developed within the region since the 2009 gas supply disruption was supported by the EU[1] (Oravcová and Mišík, 2018; Prontera and Plenta, 2020). This section examines how CEE countries influenced these mechanisms to provide support for projects they considered crucial for their energy security. It also discusses the positions of CEE countries towards the development of the post-pandemic recovery funds that, contrary to the previous mechanisms, focused on climate objectives of the EU, most importantly the 37% mandatory share of recovery funds dedicated to climate policy.

Influence on Amount Committed to EU Co-financing of Energy Projects

New legislation was not the only way in which the EU reacted to the challenges identified during the 2009 gas supply interruption. The Commission proposed a system of energy corridors aimed at improving energy security by developing new energy infrastructure with the help of EU funds. This was done in collaboration with member states; however, the Visegrad Group came up with its own corridor. To further strengthen the infrastructural development within the CEE region, the North-South Energy Corridor was proposed in September 2010 by the Visegrad Group. CEE Energy Ministers sent a letter successfully urging the Commission to

[1] See Chapter 4 on this issue, including discussion on Lithuania as the main exception.

include the corridor among the priority infrastructural projects to enable the CEE countries to receive EU financial support (Mišík, 2012). Of the €9.1 billion Connecting Europe Facility funding proposed for energy infrastructure in the EU, €6.7 billion was earmarked for projects in the CEE region (European Commission, 2012, p. 8).

Latvia, Poland and Lithuania were active in highlighting the vulnerability of the Baltic 'energy island' and the necessity of an EU response (Maltby, 2014). In February 2006, the Baltic States' leaders met and agreed on a 'declaration' and 'communiqué' (Baltic Prime Ministers, 2006) supporting the Commission's proposal for a 'new energy policy for Europe' and highlighting their lack of 'any gas and electricity interconnections with other EU member states' and 'that the energy security problem that affects the Baltic States should be addressed at [the] EU level'. In March 2006, the Commission committed to an objective of connecting the Baltic States as '[i]nterconnection is a crucial mechanism for solidarity' (European Commission, 2006). By 2008, following extensive lobbying from the Baltic States and Poland, the issue of the Baltics as an energy island was firmly on the agenda. In November the Commission adopted the Second Strategic Energy Review, in which the Baltic Energy Market Interconnection Plan (BEMIP) was identified as one of the six priority energy infrastructure projects (European Commission, 2008b, p. 4). In June 2009, the eight Baltic Sea member states – Denmark, Estonia, Finland, Germany, Lithuania, Latvia, Sweden and Poland – and the Commission signed a BEMIP memorandum of understanding, to identify, coordinate and contribute to infrastructure financing and implementation, and the European Economic Recovery Plan provided for substantial financial support to infrastructure projects in the region (European Commission, 2013b, p. 86).

A coalition of northern 'frugal' states insisted on conditionality for accessing the €724 billion of Recovery and Resilience Facility (RRF) funds (de la Porte and Jensen, 2021, p. 388). There was opposition from Visegrad Group countries regarding the rule of law conditionality (Fabbrini, 2022, p. 192), and Hungary and Poland initially vetoed the RRF package (France 24, 2020b). The result was a compromise in which a qualified majority of member states could block payments to members on rule of law grounds, and the Commission was empowered to design budgetary safeguards (Brunsden et al., 2020). All CEE states had their national plans approved by the Council, and all member states were required to commit a minimum of 37% of spending from the RRF to climate policy. The scale of funds was significant; Bulgaria, Romania and Croatia received RRF funding allocations of more than 10% of the national GDP in 2019 (European Parliament, 2022).

6.6 CLIMATE AMBITIONS

While CEE countries have proposed several energy security initiatives and supported many related Commission proposals, the situation has been different when it comes to EU climate policy. In this area most CEE countries presented reservations and opposition at the EU level, often arguing that energy security and climate targets are incompatible. For example, following rising tensions between Ukraine and Russia, Hungary's Viktor Orban blamed climate policy for increasing energy prices when he argued, 'We're most threatened by the European commissioner called Timmermans [the Commission vice-president in charge of the EU green deal].... He's threatening the people of Europe with high energy prices' (Rankin, 2021). This section examines CEE countries' activities at the EU in connection to climate goals, discussing their position towards the EU's 2020 and 2030 decarbonisation targets and towards the taxonomy of sustainable financing that categorises energy sources considered to be suitable for decarbonising the EU's economy.

Influence on the Taxonomy

In 2020 a discussion on sustainable financing of the energy sector started in the EU. The idea was to label certain energy sources as green to give investors greater clarity about which energy sources have long-term EU support. While the inclusion of some energy sources (renewables) and exclusion of others (coal, oil) was not challenged, the main discussion revolved around the inclusion of natural gas and nuclear energy (Schreiber et al., 2020). CEE countries were active in this negotiation. Czechia sided with Germany in successfully pushing for gas in the taxonomy[2] (Euractiv, 2022; France 24, 2022). During the discussion on nuclear energy, the Commission assumed a neutral position, while France, Hungary, Poland, Czechia, Romania, Slovakia and Slovenia were successful in lobbying in March 2021 to guarantee a role for nuclear energy in the decarbonised EU (Reuters, 2021c).

CEE supporters of nuclear energy made the argument that it represents a secure and climate-neutral energy source and proposed 'technological neutrality'. This concept was used to justify the utilisation of nuclear energy for reaching climate goals, that is, the decarbonisation of the electricity sector, including the financial support of the EU. Along with Poland, Czechia and Slovakia are the two most vocal regional supporters of the technology at the EU level, alternately hosting the European Nuclear Energy Forum, an annual platform for discussing nuclear energy within the EU. The CEE countries supported the Lisbon Treaty's provision guaranteeing member states control over their energy mix (Article 194, para. 2) and have used this article as an argument against any efforts to set common rules concerning the energy mix at the EU level that – in their view – could have limited the utilisation of nuclear technology, repeatedly stressing the necessity of continuing member state sovereignty over energy mix in European Council discussions (see, for example, European Council, 2019b).

[2] Albeit with some restrictions on how carbon intensive it is permitted to be.

Preferences on Renewables, Energy Efficiency and Emission Targets

The EU initially aimed to decrease emissions by 80–95% by 2050 compared with 1990, though the 2019 European Green Deal formalised a net zero 2050 goal, reaffirmed with the 2021 European Climate Law to accelerate an energy transition and meet international commitments. Member states agreed to two sets of mid-term sectoral targets until 2020 and 2030. These include increased renewable sources in the energy mix, increasing energy efficiency and decreasing carbon emissions. While Chapter 1 offers an overview of these goals and their development over time, this section outlines positions of CEE member states in these negotiations, and the impact on EU negotiations and the overall ambition of the final targets.

One of the main differences between the 2020 and 2030 targets was that while two of three 2020 goals were binding at the national level, the 2030 targets are binding at the EU level only and member states do not have a national obligation to achieve renewable and energy efficiency targets. Such a change was supported also by many (though not all) CEE countries that feared the negative impact of ambitious climate goals on their economies after their experience in the early to mid-2010s attempting to achieve the targets (see Chapter 3 on renewable policy dismantling in several CEE countries). CEE countries did not express strong positions towards the 2020 climate and energy package; most of their criticism was towards the GHG emissions target (Mišík, 2021). Whilst the Visegrad Group countries (Czechia, Hungary, Poland and Slovakia) were critical towards the 2020 package, they did not try to veto it (Braun, 2014), failed to mobilise a broad opposition (Skovgaard, 2013) and instead successfully focused on negotiating lower national emission targets (Braun, 2019). The Baltic States used energy security as the main argument when criticising emission reduction targets (Bocquillon and Maltby, 2017), though they did not prove to be influential actors in the negotiation process (Braun, 2014). Although Slovenia joined coordinating meetings with other CEE members, it was only a passive participant (Buchan, 2010) and did not pursue its own preferences. While Bulgaria and Romania did not formally oppose the 2020 targets, they dismantled renewable support policies after reaching their national goals (Davidescu et al., 2018).

In 2011 the Commission proposed a road map to a decarbonisation by 2050 (European Commission, 2011b). It took member states almost a decade to fully support such a goal. At the summer 2019 European Council the goal was discussed but not supported (European Council, 2019b), in part due to the opposition by four CEE countries (Czechia, Estonia, Hungary and Poland). In December 2019 members 'endorse[d] the objective of achieving a climate-neutral EU by 2050' despite opposition from Poland (although not mentioned by name), which '[could not] commit to implement this objective as far as it is concerned' (European Council, 2019a, p. 1). In contrast to the negotiation of the 2020 goals, many CEE states were openly critical towards the climate and energy targets negotiated in 2014, with all now formally involved in the negotiations. The EU's member states adopted climate and energy targets for 2030 in the October 2014 European Council (European Council, 2014), though the agreed targets were less ambitious than those proposed by the Commission. The renewable energy target was reduced during negotiations from 30 to 27%, and from binding at the national level to binding only at the EU level.

The negotiations of the 2030 climate and energy targets started almost immediately after the previous targets were adopted thanks to the push provided by the relative failure of the 2009 Copenhagen climate change conference (Parker et al., 2017) and following the 2011 Commission 2050 road map to decarbonise the EU's economy (European Commission, 2011b). Poland criticised plans by the supporters of ambitious 2030 targets immediately after they were proposed, playing a prominent role in the negotiations (Skovgaard, 2013). The country blocked the Commission's proposals in the Environmental Council and vetoed the road map at the 2011 European Council, arguing that this would be very costly for an economy in which electricity generation is based on coal (Nelsen and Simon, 2012). Poland was at the forefront of CEE criticism of the 2030 climate and energy package; however, many other countries from the region also questioned the need for this new package (Skjærseth, 2016). Poland, Bulgaria, Czechia, Hungary, Romania and Slovakia all opposed ambitious 2030 targets. Bulgaria and Romania shifted from a passive position in the 2020 negotiations, shortly after their EU accession, to an active opposition of the 2030 package. The Visegrad Group was a visible regional grouping within CEE during the negotiations of the 2030 package. It criticised the idea of renewable targets binding at both EU and national levels (Visegrad Group, 2014), a statement that gained attention throughout the EU (Braun, 2019). The group was very active during the negotiations, opposing ambitious targets and arguing that the level of renewables in the energy mix should reflect the capability of individual member states (Polish Presidency of the Visegrad Group, 2013). The group even prepared a 'Concept Paper on the Climate and Energy 2030 Vision' arguing that renewables within the group are limited by their high costs (ibid.). Besides Poland, Czechia was an especially strong opponent of a renewables target (European Commission, 2013c), claiming in a non-paper with the United Kingdom that national plans connected to the 2030 goals should 'only be sufficient to enable an assessment of collective progress, and should be significantly less prescriptive than is currently the case under the 2020 climate and energy package' (UK and CR non-paper, 2015, p. 4).

On the other hand, some CEE countries supported more ambitious climate and energy targets until 2030 and therefore 'there was no "eastern front"' with a united negotiating position (Mišík, 2021, p. 63). Member states presented their positions on the Commission's 2013 Green Paper (European Commission, 2013d) during the consultation process (European Commission, 2013c). Estonia and Slovenia supported Commission's proposal and together with eleven other member states published a paper calling for an ambitious decarbonisation policy that would provide long-term benefits (Green Growth Group, 2013). Lithuania also supported development of a binding renewables target at the national level (Geden and Fischer, 2014). The final version of the 2030 climate and energy package was a compromise that reflected positions of the main veto players, including Poland and several other CEE countries (Skjærseth, 2015). In climate policy, CEE countries continued to extract significant concessions and side-payments, including 'solidarity revenues' from the Emissions Trading System (10% allocated to the region, plus free allowances to their power sector) (Bocquillon and Maltby, 2017).

Preferences on Coal

At the 2018 UN COP24 climate conference in Poland, the Polish president argued that there was 'no plan today to fully give up on coal' and, in the same month regarding the 200 years of remaining coal supplies in the country, that it would be 'hard not to use them' (Gabbatiss, 2018b). At the same conference, a Solidarity and Just Transition Silesia Declaration drafted by the Polish presidency was signed by fifty-six states: 'Reaffirming that Parties to the Paris Agreement on climate change are taking into account the imperatives of a just transition of the workforce and the creation of decent work and quality jobs' (Polish Government, 2018). After the 'Platform for Coal Regions in Transition' was launched in 2018, Slovakia became part of this EU initiative together with nineteen other coal regions from other member states. Several other CEE countries have their coal regions included in this initiative – four in Poland (Silesia, Lower Silesia, Greater Poland, Lesser Poland), three in the Czech Republic (Moravia-Silesia, Usti, Karlovy Vary), two in Slovenia (Zasavska and Savinjsko-Šaleška) and one in Romania (Jiu Valley). The main goal of the Platform is to support transition of the coal regions to a post-coal future (Popp, 2019). A key EU tool for this is the €5 billion EU Just Transition Fund, increased to €19 billion in the 2021–2027 financial period (European Commission, 2022n). However, this initiative has been criticised by the European Court of Auditors. An assessment of €12.5 billion in seven coal-producing regions in Germany, Poland, Romania, Czechia and Spain concluded that 'EU support for coal regions achieved little for climate transition . . . EU financial assistance for coal regions has had a limited impact on both jobs and energy transition' (ECA, 2022a).

6.7 CONCLUSION

This chapter has explored the impact of CEE countries on EU's climate and energy policy. These countries have been active in energy security policy, proposing new initiatives and supporting those proposed by the Commission in the energy security area. In contrast, many countries opposed ambitious climate targets. However, CEE countries were not homogenous in their opposition of climate targets, with some support for more ambitious objectives, and whilst a preference is often to dilute their ambition it is rarely to block it altogether. At various points CEE countries have proposed specific initiatives, often invoking energy security concerns. A discursive strategy of Poland was to invoke 'solidarity', and the Baltic States their 'energy island'. The success of such overarching strategies was in transforming what were perceived as national and regional concerns, and instead highlighting them in terms of the problems posed by dependence on Russian energy for the EU as a whole (Maltby, 2014, p. 231). This strategy had some success after 2009, with a growing consensus on the risks posed by dependence on EU energy supplies that accelerated in 2022.

7

The Global Context

Decarbonisation, Pandemic and Invasion

7.1 INTRODUCTION

Within this chapter the book goes beyond the discussion on the CEE region and EU and provides an examination of how specific positions of CEE countries towards energy and climate policy fit within the global transition towards low-carbon economies (Aklin and Urpelainen, 2018; Child et al., 2018). The chapter examines global efforts to decarbonise with a focus on the Covid-19 pandemic and the full-scale Russian invasion of Ukraine, both of which have had a profound impact on energy sectors and efforts beyond Europe to increase energy security, including through a focus on domestic renewables and, to a lesser extent, on nuclear energy sources (Kuzemko et al., 2022; Szulecki and Overland, 2023; Zakeri et al., 2022). The main purpose is to discuss the relevance of the CEE region for the broader global energy transition, and the lessons the region can offer for discussion about how to approach the road towards achieving Paris Agreement commitments of dramatic emissions reductions (Bonsu, 2020; Deutch, 2020). As of October 2022, globally, eighty-eight countries, covering approximately 79% of global emissions, had adopted net-zero targets (UN, 2022a).

A link is created between our findings from the CEE region and international energy transitions and climate and energy policy, demonstrating that features of countries in CEE are not unique when placed in an international context. Energy security – the main energy policy issue for the CEE region for more than a decade – has become a European and global concern since February 2022 (Boute, 2022; Mišík, 2022), though the extent to which renewables, at least in the short term, are considered tools to achieve this varies, particularly within CEE (Osička and Černoch, 2022). It was the external shock in the form of Russian's 2022 invasion of Ukraine (Korosteleva, 2022), following more than fifteen years of CEE countries' efforts (see Chapter 6), that has resulted in a paradigm shift within the EU (European Council, 2022a, 2022b). As the CEE region implements the EU's climate and energy policies, whilst also shaping these, insights into the process of developing and implementing decarbonisation policy have been provided. The EU has also been widely considered, and self-identifies as, an international climate change policy leader (Oberthür and Dupont, 2021; Wurzel et al., 2019), so our analysis of how EU enlargement has shaped EU 2020, 2030 and broader climate and energy policy is a contribution to understanding the EU's international role and future prospects. The experience of CEE countries within the EU and their (limited) ability to influence the Union can serve as an example for other regional groups.

The chapter discusses the energy transition experience of CEE in the context of a global perspective (Hager and Stefes, 2016), examining the ability of the region to adapt and contribute to the expected significant changes associated with the global energy transition (Hefner, 2009; Petit, 2017), including its readiness for technological remodelling that the energy transition will bring (Rojey, 2009). This chapter engages with the broader international energy policy literature (Bradshaw, 2013; Goldthau, 2013; Petit, 2017), and that which focuses specifically on the analysis of energy transitions and issues of climate justice and the distribution of burdens and responsibilities (Sovacool and Dworkin, 2014), security of supply (and demand) concerns (Vivoda, 2022), and trade-offs regarding economic and environmental security objectives (Khan et al., 2021; Marti and Puertas, 2022). This discussion creates a basis for comparison with the CEE states within the EU, and challenges faced in achieving climate and energy goals. While the chapter draws generalisable conclusions about the CEE region, it considers specific country examples in highlighting different choices these countries made to balance their energy security and climate policy objectives and responsibilities. In this way the book contributes to the more general discussion of global energy transitions.

The chapter is divided into several sections. The following section looks at global energy transitions and the role of the EU (Fekete et al., 2021; Jankó et al., 2020). The third section focuses on issues connected to energy justice, and the EU's similar burden-sharing concept – especially when discussing ambitious climate goals and arguments about who should take the lead on energy transitions (Emodi et al., 2022; Levesque et al., 2021). The fourth section focuses on gas, whilst the fifth discusses coal phase-outs, given the urgency of this for the Paris Agreement (Keles and Yilmaz, 2020). While they are accelerating in the EU, many CEE countries face particular challenges to achieve this, similar to a number of emerging and developing countries that rely heavily on coal for electricity generation (Cardoso and Turhan, 2018). The sixth section examines the position of nuclear technology in electricity generation at the global level. Following the Fukushima nuclear disaster, many countries reversed pro-nuclear stances (Elliott, 2013; Joskow and Parsons, 2012), but a new wave of interest in nuclear technology as a tool to increase energy security emerged since 2022 (Caglar, 2022; Mathew, 2022).

7.2 GLOBAL ENERGY TRANSITION

The first part of this section examines climate change negotiations, starting with the 1997 Kyoto meeting and the role of different countries in leading these negotiations. The second part of this section discusses the global developments of the energy sector that is the major emitter of GHG. We primarily focus on the effects of the Covid-19 pandemic and also briefly consider Russia's invasion of Ukraine on the global energy system, energy consumption patterns, and emissions.

Climate Mitigation Negotiations

The global energy transition has been driven by the need to reduce emissions. In order to prevent irreversible changes to the Earth's climate, the international community adopted the Paris Agreement in 2016 (Rosen, 2015). Negotiations on the preceding Kyoto Protocol resulted in the first-ever effort to create a global consensus among countries to curb emissions in order to tackle climate change (Dogan et al., 2022). However, it focused on 'industrialised' states only; the relatively unambitious goals were missed; and the United States, crucial due to its significant emissions, never ratified the agreement (Morena, 2023). However, a breakthrough was the introduction of a burden-sharing scheme reflecting historic responsibilities and ability to pay (Böhringer, 2003, p. 463).

The Copenhagen climate agreement in 2009 failed to meet high expectations (van Eck and Feindt, 2022). The EU tried, unsuccessfully, to lead the negotiations and present its policies as a blueprint for other countries and regions; the EU's strategy of 'leading by example and ideational leadership failed to convince the world to support a binding treaty for top-down targets and timetables' (Parker et al., 2017, p. 249), and the summit 'marked a low point for EU climate leadership' (Kreienkamp et al., 2022, p. 739). This reflected the EU's internal challenges to agreeing on a 2020 energy and climate package during which several countries opposed ambitious climate targets (see Chapter 6). The negotiations leading to the 2015 Paris Agreement were dominated by the United States; however, the EU learnt how to pursue its own preferences more successfully, supporting 'a hybrid set up with bottom-up reduction pledges combined with a top-down review of performance' (Parker et al., 2017, p. 249). Here China contributed to the success, committing to a domestic cap on emissions (Hilton and Kerr, 2017).

The achievement was unanimity on the urgency of tackling climate change, and the necessity to reduce emissions in all countries for the first time, most importantly, to limit the rise of global temperature to 2°C compared with the pre-industrial period. The EU was part of a High Ambition coalition committed to a more ambitious 1.5°C target (Hoegh-Guldberg et al., 2019). Some 185 countries presented nationally determined climate plans in order to contribute to this goal (Dasandi et al., 2021); major emitters of GHG like the EU (European Commission, 2011b;

European Council, 2019a), Korea and Japan have committed to net zero by 2050, and China by 2060 (Normile, 2020). By late 2021 more than seventy countries had committed to net zero targets, representing 76% of total world emissions and including seventeen G20 countries, alone representing 69% of global domestic emissions (UN, 2021b).

The support of the United States for the Agreement was crucial as the country belongs among the top GHG emitters. However, soon after the United States ratified the agreement negotiated by the Obama administration, President Trump decided to withdraw from it (Zhang et al., 2017), citing economic competitiveness: 'What we don't do is punish the American people while enriching foreign polluters' (Harrabin, 2019). This raised questions about the future of the Agreement until the Biden administration re-joined in 2021 (Chemnick, 2021), and pledged carbon neutrality by 2050 and a 2030 emission reduction target of 65% compared with 2008 whilst 'expand [ing] American technologies, industries, and jobs' (White House, 2021).

Energy Transitions and Covid-19

The energy sector is at the centre of efforts to decrease GHG emissions as it is responsible for about 40% of emissions (WNA, 2022b). Despite global efforts to decrease emissions, they have steadily increased, except for 2020 when the Covid-19 pandemic caused an economic downturn and significantly decreased mobility (Zakeri et al., 2022). However, a year later the International Energy Agency estimated that emissions had reached a new record high, as the world 'experienced an extremely rapid economic recovery ... driven by unprecedented fiscal and monetary stimulus and a fast – although uneven – roll-out of vaccines' (IEA, 2022b, p. 3). The increased utilisation of coal in electricity generation was a significant factor behind this, rising by 6%. Difficult market and weather conditions limited the use of other types of fuel for electricity generation – natural gas prices rapidly increased throughout 2021 and most of 2022, and in 2022 hydroelectricity and nuclear power were negatively affected by climate change–driven high summer temperatures and low water levels.

Emissions increases were not evenly distributed among countries and regions. China was responsible for most of the growth of emissions (IEA, 2022b, p. 6), and was the only country that recorded economic growth during 2020 and 2021. In contrast to other advanced economies, the country's economic growth was slower than its electricity demand growth, indicating an increase in energy intensity of its economy during this period, with coal covering 56% of the demand growth (IEA, 2022b). At the global level, the IEA noted that 'certain advanced economies have emphasised decarbonisation measures in their economic recovery', and renewables recorded a new annual growth record in 2021. However, the post-pandemic recovery was also closely connected to increasing utilisation of fossil fuels (IEA, 2022b, p. 4), particularly outside the OECD countries.

Within the EU, although 2021 saw an annual increase of emissions by 6.5%, this followed a 10.8% emission reduction between 2019 and 2020, so an overall emissions reduction during the 2019–2021 period (Crippa et al., 2022). However, the post-pandemic economic recovery was also fuelled by increased utilisation of fossil fuels, especially the use of coal in the energy sector. This resulted in annual emissions intensity increasing by 20% (EEA, 2022). The EU is though predicted to return to the trend of long-term emission intensity decrease driven by the transition from fossil fuels to renewables in electricity generation – in 2021 the energy sector was 45% less carbon-intensive than in 1990 (ibid.). One of the main obstacles to energy transitions are high costs and the uneven starting line of different countries. Therefore, one of the main questions that international negotiations, and those within the EU, have had to address is how to achieve global emissions reductions among countries with different energy mix legacies (i.e., historical carbon emissions), energy mixes or economic performance. The following section examines these issues and increasing the deployment of renewables as the main tool to develop a carbon-neutral economy in the future.

7.3 ENERGY JUSTICE, BURDEN SHARING AND WORLDWIDE EMPLOYMENT OF RENEWABLES

Energy transitions are associated with costs that are unevenly distributed (Bogdanov et al., 2021). We can differentiate between uneven distributions of energy transition costs within individual societies – where different groups of people are impacted at various levels, causing problems related to energy poverty (Castaño-Rosa et al., 2019; Sovacool et al., 2016) – and between countries and/or regions. The latter is mainly characterised as the difference between a majority of advanced economies leading the energy transition – though variably as Australia, Canada and the United States during the Trump administration demonstrated – and key emerging economies that are less supportive of ambitious climate goals and argue that economic development requires access to cheap energy (Afful-Dadzie et al., 2020). Here we can see a link with some of the arguments that have been presented by CEE countries criticising ambitious climate goals proposed by the Commission and other EU members, especially those from Western Europe.

Energy justice at the global level 'involves the right of all to access energy services, regardless of whether they are citizens of more or less greatly developed economies' (Sovacool and Dworkin, 2014, p. 5). Emerging economies often invoke climate justice with regard to historical emissions: in 2015 Indian Prime Minister Narendra Modi stated to the UN General Assembly that 'the issue is of equity and justice ... You cannot condemn the developing world which is still at a very low carbon stage ... the principle of common but differentiated responsibilities is the bedrock of our collective enterprise' (Modi cited in Brar, 2015). Similarly, in 2021 China's Director of Climate Change at the Ministry of Ecology and Environment argued that Western countries should 'shoulder the responsibility' for climate action, as 'climate change today is a result of the past emissions. So there is no way developed countries can shake off their responsibilities' (Gao cited in ITV 2021). Indeed, the Global North was responsible for 92% of excess global GHG emissions as of 2015, and 'a small number of high-income countries have appropriated substantially more than their fair share of the atmospheric commons', resulting in 'a process of atmospheric colonisation' (Hickel, 2020, p. 403).

Emerging economies successfully argued for continued economic growth rather than emissions reductions (Goldthau et al., 2020). Advanced economies should lead the decarbonisation not only because of their historical GHG 'legacy', but also because this supported their economic development that has allowed them to switch to initially more expensive low carbon energy sources. This has been embedded at the core of international negotiations, with the Kyoto Protocol stating that countries take 'into account their common but differentiated responsibilities and their specific national and regional development priorities, objectives and circumstances' (UN, 1997). This echoes the EU's principle – at the March 2007 European Council, member states endorsed the EU's 20-20-20 targets and specified that each country should contribute to climate policy 'according to their differentiated responsibilities and respective capabilities' (European Council, 2007, p. 11).

Another important concept in connection with energy transition to net zero is burden sharing (Zhang and Shi, 2014). The question at the centre of this concept asks, 'How should the costs of climate change mitigation and adaptation be spread across countries and generations?' (Page, 2008, p. 556). The Paris Agreement includes Nationally Determined Contributions (NDCs), or national emission reduction pledges to achieve the common goal 'to reach global peaking of greenhouse gas (GHG) emissions as soon as possible and to undertake rapid reductions thereafter' (UN, 2015, p. 4). It is 'understood that the peaking of emissions will take longer for developing countries, and that emission reductions are undertaken on the basis of equity, and in the context of sustainable development and efforts to eradicate poverty, which are critical development priorities for many developing countries' (UN, 2023). As a result, Nationally Determined Contributions highlight 'how nations construct their own vulnerability, readiness for climate finance, good will, and culpability (or lack thereof) for climate change' and represent the 'stark contrasts in NDC discourses between North–South as well as historical emitters and emerging economies' (Mills-Novoa and Liverman, 2019, p. 10).

While developing nations present especially their own vulnerabilities vis-à-vis climate change, they mostly discuss mitigation tools in connection to external support. The discussion in NDCs thus reflects 'an ongoing debate about who will pay for global mitigation and adaptation efforts' (Mills-Novoa and Liverman, 2019, p. 11). This is not a new question; already in 2008 Page claimed that 'there is no single principle or approach at present that identifies developed countries and their citizens, cleanly and persuasively, as the entities that should shoulder the burden of mitigation and adaptation' (2008, p. 573). Despite a Paris Agreement pledge of $100 billion per year in international climate finance provided by wealthier countries for climate mitigation and adaptation, the target in 2020 was missed by $17 billion (CarbonBrief, 2022). Moreover, the UN's global stocktake 2021 policies in place would result in a 2.8°C temperature rise, and pledges for future policy would reduce to 2.4–2.6°C by the end of the century (UN, 2022a). A key barrier remains that of fair burden sharing (Leimbach and Giannousakis, 2019, p. 273). The UN's 27th annual Climate Change Conference (COP27) in 2022 reemphasised 'the importance of 'climate justice' ... [e]mphasizing that enhanced effective climate action should be implemented in a manner that is just and inclusive while minimizing negative social or economic impacts that may arise from climate action' (UN, 2022b, p. 1).

Renewables

Although renewables are crucial for the development of carbon-neutral economies, 'the large-scale deployment of renewable energy technologies has been limited by economic, socio-cultural, and institutional constraints' (Vanegas Cantarero, 2020, p. 1). Issues like costs of renewables (Heptonstall and Gross, 2021), limits of their social acceptance (Cousse, 2021; Cousse et al., 2020) or technical limitations (especially intermittency; Chen et al., 2021) have proven to be obstacles to their deployment. However, the International Energy Agency predicts that globally 'new renewable generation [will] cover almost 90% of additional electricity demand through 2025' (IEA, 2022c, p. 7).

Renewables and Energy Security

Renewable sources of energy are presented at the global level as a solution to two crucial contemporary energy policy issues: climate change and energy security. In the recent past there was a common understanding of a trade-off for policy-makers between these two (Brown and Huntington, 2008, p. 3510). However, increasingly they are considered to be synergistic, particularly in economically advanced states, though a key barrier is the economic capacity in emerging and developed economies, and failure of the former to mobilise jointly US$100 billion per year for 'meaningful mitigation action' in the latter (UN, 2022b, p. 6). The continuing relative higher price of renewables, especially in those countries that do not have a system of paying for carbon emission in place (as, for example, the EU ETS) remains a key barrier. The deployment of renewable energy globally remains at an early stage, with renewable energy sources in 2021 accounted for only 12% of global energy supply (IEA, 2022d).

Until recently, the role of renewables in supporting energy security is often more prominent internationally than within CEE (see Chapters 3 and 4, also Gökgöz and Güvercin, 2018; Sattich et al., 2022; Viviescas et al., 2019). In the EU prior to 2022, renewables were mainly connected to climate, as within the Energy Union initiative (European Commission, 2015a) and to a greater extent within the European Green Deal (European Commission, 2019; see Chapter 1). The link between energy security and renewables has been limited until 2022 (Mišík, 2016; Szulecki et al., 2016), when this argument was emphasised by the Commission (European Commission, 2022a). The connection between renewables and energy security was much stronger beyond the EU (Adenle et al., 2015). Hamed and Bressler argue that in Israel and Jordan renewables have been linked to energy independence and security (2019, p. 387), and in the case of China, the objective of increasing supply security is a 'major incentive for renewable energy deployment' (Wang et al., 2018, p. 193).

Investment in Renewable Energy

The argument against renewables within CEE relates to higher costs (Hernik et al., 2019). Opponents argue that higher employment of these energy sources would decrease economic growth due to the need to provide subsidies to their operators and finance energy transitions. Indeed, following the 2009 renewables directive, several CEE countries experienced a steep increase in renewable subsidies, which led to renewable policy dismantling in countries such as Bulgaria, Czechia, Romania and Slovakia (see Chapter 3), despite the link between renewables and higher economic costs in the region being contested (Marinaş et al., 2018). In 2022 the IEA argued that 'economic arguments in favour of cost-competitive and affordable clean technologies are now stronger' (IEA, 2022e) and that '[i]n all IEA scenarios, energy employment is set to grow, outweighing declines in fossil fuel jobs' (IEA, 2022f).

Investment in renewables is also on an upward trajectory globally, linked to the increased availability of sustainable finance, decreasing costs and policy and legislation. Estimates for 2022 were that US$1.4 trillion was invested in clean energy, with an average annual growth since 2015 of 2%, and 12% since 2020, with the highest investment from China ($380 billion) followed by the EU ($260 billion) (IEA, 2022g). In China between 2010 and 2021, renewable generation increased by 19.2% per year (Hawkins, 2023). In contrast, since the 2015 Paris Agreement, investment in fossil fuels has been 30% lower. However, the IEA estimates that what is needed by 2030 to be aligned with a net zero 2050 emissions scenario is annual energy investment of $4.6 trillion, more than tripling current investment (IEA, 2022g).

It is clear that the conception of a synergy between economic development and renewables, rather than a trade-off, is increasingly held. For example, Prime Minister Modi emphasised the investment potential: 'There are huge renewable energy deployment plans for the next decade. This is a big opportunity to invest in India.... We want to make India a global manufacturing hub in the renewable energy sector . . . we are showing to the world that sound environmental policies can also be sound economics' (cited in Dutta, 2020). The International Renewable Energy Agency envisages similar potential in Central and South Eastern Europe:

'The full deployment of renewable options [...] could raise the 2030 renewables share to 34%, cost-effectively' (IRENA, 2020, p. 9).

7.4 NATURAL GAS AS A BRIDGING FUEL

Natural gas has been considered a bridging fuel between high-carbon and low-carbon energy systems as it has the lowest fossil fuel emissions and is an attractive replacement for coal (Díaz et al., 2017; Gürsan and de Gooyert, 2021; McGlade et al., 2018). Woollacott argued that 'the expansion of natural gas over the past decade has played a significant role in bridging us toward a lower-emissions future' (2020, p. 9). However, this approach also has been criticised for delaying the transition toward a post-carbon economy (Hausfather, 2015) as investment is diverted and polices and energy systems locked in to a fossil fuel reliance. Following the 2009 gas supply disruption, CEE countries embarked on a path of natural gas infrastructure diversification supported by the EU (Prontera and Plenta, 2020), which was criticised for creating long-term interest (and thus also dependency) on natural gas. Similarly, projects like Nord Stream (I and II) were viewed as cementing EU's dependency on natural gas as well as on Russia as its main supplier (Herranz-Surrallés et al., 2022; Vihma and Wigell, 2016). However, this has changed rapidly since 2022. The immediate response by the Commission was to propose a full cut-off of Russian energy supplies before 2030 (European Commission, 2022a) and to decrease the EU's natural gas consumption during the 2022/2023 winter season by 15% compared with the average of the previous five-year period (Council of the EU, 2022a). A 19% reduction was achieved between August 2022 and January 2023 compared with the average between 2017 and 2021, through a combination of political will, policy coordination and the good fortune of a mild winter (Eurostat 2023f, see also above). The framing of gas as a bridge remains prominent.

7.5 COAL PHASING OUT/PHASING DOWN?

Coal fuelled the industrial revolution and became a synonymous with development and economic growth (Isoaho and Markard, 2020). However, it is also the energy source that produces most GHG emissions (Jaramillo et al., 2007), and a coal phase-out is considered the most effective way to decrease emissions (Rockström et al., 2017). Indeed, in 2021 Estonia, Poland, Cyprus and Greece recorded the highest emission intensity in the electricity sector among EU member states, linked to coal use (and shale oil in Estonia) (EEA, 2022). While there is an almost unanimous agreement within the EU that coal has to be phased out as soon as possible – and most EU member countries have already committed to this goal (Brauers et al., 2020) – the situation at the global level is more complex (see, for example, Lin and Raza, 2020). Of the forty-eight members of the Powering Past Coal Alliance at the end of 2022, committed to phasing out coal by 2030, twenty-one were EU members

(PPCA, 2023).[1] Whilst coal use is forecast to decline in the United States and EU, coal demand in India 'is set to continue to be the growth engine of global coal demand' (IEA, 2022a, p. 7). Indeed, coal still presents an important energy source, is responsible for 27% of global energy supply and almost 37% of electricity generation (Ritchie and Roser, 2022), and is key when discussing the ability of the international community to decrease GHG and develop a global carbon-neutral economy.

While the EU and other advanced economies are decreasing coal consumption, many developing countries, including India and China, have been building new coal capacity as a relatively inexpensive domestic source of electricity, improving their energy security and supporting economic development and energy access (Shearer et al., 2017; Zhao et al., 2017). Some 27 GW of new coal-fired capacity was commissioned worldwide in 2019, and while the pipeline for the new coal-fired power plants is shrinking, there was still more than 500 GW of capacity under different stages of development worldwide in the first half of 2019 (Shearer, 2019). China has the biggest coal generation fleet, responsible for 55% of the country's energy consumption in 2021, down from 70% in 2001 though also constituting a significant increase in volumes of coal used (EIA, 2022). Combined with the high share of industry in the country's GDP (39% compared with the global average of 30%), China's emissions intensity was the highest of major economies in 2021 (IEA, 2022b, p. 10). Whilst China is committed to peaking emissions in 2030, President Xi Jinping made it clear in 2022 that coal's phase-out will be gradual 'in a well-planned and phased way, in line with the principle of getting the new before discarding the old ... [and] [c]oal will be used in a cleaner and more efficient way' (cited in Bloomberg, 2022). He also noted that the use of coal 'would be hard to change in the short term' (cited in Hawkins, 2023). As China was responsible for 53% of global coal consumption in 2021, the country's climate commitments are key for a global energy transition (IEA, 2022a).

Increased electricity production in coal-fired power plants was considered a rapid solution to increased energy demand connected to the post-pandemic recovery, and was responsible for 40% of the global emissions increase between 2020 and 2021 (IEA, 2022b). Coal consumption increased 14% in 2021 compared with 2020 (IEA, 2022a). Moreover, due to the efforts to fight high electricity prices and strengthen energy security by means of domestic coal, the trend of increased use of coal continued in 2022 and was not limited to emerging economies. Although developed economies have stopped introducing new coal-fired generation capacities, several countries, including the United Kingdom, temporarily restarted their coal generation capacity to guarantee the stability of electricity grid during the winter of 2022/2023 (Davies, 2022). Moreover, the UK government even approved the first new coal mine in over three decades, criticised as a reversal of that country's climate goals a year after hosting the UN's climate conference in Glasgow (Reed, 2022).

[1] 9 member states had phased out coal by the end of 2021 (European Commission, 2022l).

In the EU the countries did not reverse coal phase-out plans (Kuzemko et al., 2020). However, although coal-fired power plants require the largest amount of carbon allowances due to their high levels of emissions, the price of natural gas as the primary alternative to coal was so high during 2022 and the second half of 2021 that coal represented a cheaper option.

Despite an overall understanding within the EU that coal needs to be excluded from the energy mix to fulfil common climate goals, coal remains an important energy source for a number of states. Six have not set a 2030 phase-out deadline, and as of late 2023, Poland had no phase-out deadline. Therefore, coal could be a part of EU's energy mix in the mid- to long-term perspective, unless financial support such as the EU's Just Transition Fund can contribute to accelerated coal phase-outs (European Commission, 2022l). In a parallel to the global discussions of distributing funding from wealthier states, the Just Transition Fund is envisaged to support less wealthy states and regions in the Union, where an energy transition 'cannot be sufficiently achieved by the Member States owing to the disparities in the levels of development of the various territories and to the backwardness of the least favoured territories, as well as to the limit on the financial resources of Member States and territories' (European Parliament and the Council, 2021c).

Decisions about what to fund remain contested. The European Court of Auditors analysed the first period of EU's financial and other support of these regions (2014–2020) during which €12.5 billion were allocated, and concluded that phasing out coal production was then sometimes offset by imports of it, or of other fossil fuels (European Court of Auditors, 2022, p. 4). It has also been argued that coal phase-out can have a negative impact on the EU's ETS system as once large capacities of coal-fired power plants are decommissioned, 'a sharp decrease in the demand for [allowances] is observed' (Anke et al., 2020, p. 9), requiring adjustments to the emissions cap. The current EU ETS reform, however, has focused on other sources of GHG emissions, including transport and building (Kurmayer, 2022d).

To improve the EU's energy security in 2022, the Commission's approach – supported by all member states – called for energy savings, improvement of energy efficiency, and higher employment of renewable energy sources as a way out of the energy crisis (European Commission, 2022a, 2022b). Whilst Germany temporarily restarted significant coal capacity (10 GW), postponed the decommissioning of another 4 GW (IEA, 2022a, p. 7) and planned a new lignite mine in the Rhineland (Pitel, 2023), this was set to be a temporary measure: in autumn 2022 the German economy minister reiterated a 2021 pledge to accelerate a national coal phase-out from 2038 to 2030, though by early 2023 this was confirmed only for the industrial region of North Rhine–Westphalia (Pitel, 2023). In April 2022 the EU imposed sanctions that banned Russian coal imports from August (Euronews, 2022), which meant that member states needed to find alternatives for 45% of coal consumption. New sources of coal were found, including in Indonesia, South Africa and Colombia (IEA, 2022a). Russia has sought out replacement markets;

India has very significantly increased imports of newly discounted Russian oil, from negligible amounts to nearly 1 million barrels per day; whilst China has more than tripled Russian LNG imports (Menon, 2022).

A 1.5°C-aligned energy transition has been estimated to require a very substantial increase in global investment in energy systems, US$1.6–3.8 trillion per year until 2050 (IPCC, 2018, p. 154). This investment may be driven in part by the risk of 'stranded assets' (Sovacool, 2016) leading to 'un-burnable carbon' (Newell and Simms, 2021), investment deterred by the beginning of the 'end of the fossil fuel age', reinforced by the Paris Agreement (Paterson, 2021). A fossil fuel divestment movement has moved from a social movement from 2012 to universities, financial and insurance institutions (Braungardt et al., 2019). In 2015 the Bank of England governor warned of 'stranded' fossil fuel assets (Carney cited in Clark, 2015), and from the mid-2010s there was a 'quiet revolution' seeking to integrate sustainable development into the fabric of the financial system' (UNEP, 2015, p. 4), increasingly including the 'advocacy of central banks for a climate-neutral economy' (Siderius, 2022, p. 5). Some of the world's major investment banks by the beginning of the 2020s had committed to no longer investing in coal or fossil fuels, and by the end of 2022, 121 central banks had joined the 'The Central Banks and Supervisors Network for Greening the Financial System' (NGFS, 2022). Significantly, the World Bank argues that 'Phasing down coal hinges on scaling up renewables' (World Bank, 2023), which requires investment.

There has been a major shift in energy infrastructure funding, and it was estimated that by 2019 $11 trillion of divestment commitments had been made (350.org, 2019). There has been a wave of divestments away from coal, including by the Japan Bank for International Cooperation (JBIC) in 2020, and in 2021 by the South Korean Export-Import Bank of Korea (KEXIM) and the Korea Trade Insurance Corporation (K-SURE) (Buckley, 2021). In 2021 the Chinese government also decided to cease all financing of overseas coal power plants (Reuters, 2022a), as did the G7 (G7, 2021). The European Investment Bank has gone further, ceasing the financing of all fossil fuels, including gas, by the end of 2021 (Ambrose and Henley, 2019), and in 2021 the US Department of the Treasury, as a major actor in a number of multilateral development banks, announced guidance that aims to 'promote ending international financing of carbon-intensive fossil fuel-based energy while simultaneously advancing sustainable development and a green recovery' (Segal and Bertez, 2021). At the 2021 Conference of the Parties (COP), the Glasgow Financial Alliance for Net Zero (GFANZ) was set up, with 450 organisations with $130 trillion of assets committed to net zero–aligned investments (UK Government, 2021). However, there remains criticism of what is categorised as 'green', including the 'illusory promises' and fantasies of carbon offsetting (Watt, 2021, p. 1083). In the first year of GFANZ it has been claimed that 'the 56 top banks ... provided at least US$269 billion to 102 of the major fossil fuel expanders' (Reclaim Finance, 2023, p. 7). Crucially, the phase-out of coal and other fossil fuels requires a shift in national investments away from fossil fuel subsidies. Despite a G20 commitment to phase these out in 2009, they were estimated at US$5.9 trillion in 2020 (6.8% of GDP; IMF, 2022). The European Court of Auditors estimated fossil fuel subsidies of €56 billion in the EU in 2019, representing only a marginal decrease from €58 billion in 2008; fifteen member states also subsidised fossil fuels more than renewable energy, including eight CEE states (ECA, 2022b, p. 30). This financial commitment is essential to overcome the challenge the World Bank highlights, that developing countries face: 'a triple penalty when transitioning to clean energy: They often pay more for electricity, cannot access clean energy projects, and are locked into fossil fuel dependency' (World Bank, 2023).

There are two main issues connected to utilisation of coal by developing countries that can be linked to arguments used by CEE countries: economic development and energy security. First, several CEE countries (with Poland at the forefront) have argued during negotiations of climate and energy targets for 2020 and 2030 that ambitious emission reduction goals would present significant costs for their energy systems and increase the price of electricity and slow economic development (Bento et al., 2017; Rybak and Rybak, 2021). This is closely connected to the discussion about burden sharing in connection to emission reduction (see above). Many emerging and developing economies remain dependent on coal (and other fossil sources), including India, Pakistan and China (IEA, 2022a; Lin and Raza, 2020). China aims to decarbonise by 2060 and have its carbon emissions peak by 2030, though a challenge will be to retire the 1,037 coal-fired power plants in operation in 2021, with only a fifth being relatively inefficient and having strong economic reasons to close these quickly (Cui et al., 2021). Moreover, China is developing internal infrastructure to improve access of its steel and power sectors to domestic coal, to dependency on coal imports and increasing the country's energy security (Gosens et al., 2022). Coal has also been presented by several CEE countries as a domestic source of energy that is able to guarantee (or even increase) energy security (Mata Pérez et al., 2019). Such arguments were used also in cases when a significant part of utilised coal was imported from abroad – as in Slovakia and Poland, the latter significantly dependent on Russian for coal imports. Both main issues are combined for India, with Modi in 2021 stating that '[e]nergy independence is vital for India's development' (cited in Bhatti, 2021).

7.6 GLOBAL ENERGY TRANSITIONS AND THE REBIRTH OF NUCLEAR ENERGY?

Since 2022 interest in nuclear energy has increased. Two major accidents had previously undermined its widespread adoption. Through the 1990s the Chernobyl disaster lingered over the nuclear industry, causing cancellation of nuclear programmes in several European countries (including Italy; Neresini and Lorenzet, 2016), and had a negative and lasting effect on nuclear construction globally before the 2000s saw increased interest in this technology (Csereklyei, 2014). Nuclear as a low-carbon technology started to be presented as a solution not only to energy generation needs but also to climate change challenges. In the late 2000s more than fifty countries without nuclear power plants were interested in starting nuclear programmes (Jewell, 2011). Due to uranium reserves being more evenly geographically distributed than oil and gas and better protected from commodity price fluctuation at the time, nuclear power was 'considered to provide a more secure, in both short- and long-term, supply of energy' whilst also being presented as a climate solution (Jewell, 2011, p. 1041).

However, the 2011 Fukushima disaster strengthened opposition towards nuclear energy within the EU and also worldwide and caused fierce debates about its future (Elliott, 2013). Even France, the main supporter of nuclear energy among West European countries, initially re-evaluated its nuclear policy (Joskow and Parsons, 2012), until the French president in 2020 stated that whilst there will be a reduction in its use, nuclear energy will 'remain the cornerstone of our strategic autonomy' (Reuters, 2020). Investment is a challenge though – in 2022, half of France's fifty-six reactors were offline, many because of corrosion at ageing plants (White, 2022). Outside of the EU, Switzerland re-evaluated its nuclear policy. In 2016 the country passed a new law – which was unsuccessfully challenged in a referendum organised by a right-wing populist party – to gradually phase out nuclear energy as individual nuclear power plants reach their expected lifespan, replaced by renewables and energy efficiency measures (Steffen and Patt, 2022). Delays and budgetary overruns have been recorded in all European nuclear projects (Paks 2 [Hungary], Flamanville 3 [France], Mochovce 3 and 4 [Slovakia], Hinkley Point C [United Kingdom]), which have contributed to a negative image of nuclear energy in parts of Europe.

Since 2022 nuclear energy started to again be considered as an important domestic source of energy, adding to energy security, providing overall stability of the electricity grid and protecting the public from price spikes caused by high prices of natural gas used in electricity generation. The International Atomic Energy Agency in 2021 revised its annual projections for global nuclear energy upwards for the first time since 2011, and further increased them in 2022, estimating a more than doubling of generating capacity by 2050 on the basis that '[d]riven by the impacts of climate change and the energy crisis, governments are reconsidering their portfolios in favour of nuclear power' (IAEA, 2022). As Kuzemko et al. note, under the current 'return to geopolitical framings of energy security' . . . renewables and nuclear are considered "home grown" and thereby as boosting independence' (Kuzemko et al., 2022, p. 4).

Several European countries – including Belgium, France, and the United Kingdom – announced plans to extend their nuclear fleet as a direct response (Kuzemko et al., 2022), and most CEE states have continued to make nuclear central to their national security and energy transition plans. Their main argument for support is connected to energy security. Nuclear energy is viewed in the region as a domestic source of energy despite requiring imported nuclear fuel – in most cases from Russia (Pan, 2023), and efforts to develop alternative nuclear fuels and to replace Russian suppliers have proved unsuccessful (Vlček, 2016). Arguments about the climate credentials of nuclear technology started to be presented by the nuclear supporters of the CEE region only since the second half of the 2010s, and the continuation, expansion and, in the case of Poland, development of nuclear energy are driven by the twin imperatives of climate targets and energy security concerns. For example, in 2022, the Polish government argued that developing nuclear energy was 'important for the entire country both in terms of energy transition, as well as security of energy supply' (Moskwa cited in Wolska, 2022).

Whilst thirteen reactors closed in the United States between 2013 and 2022, government financial support of $6 billion in 2021, and equivalent private funding, indicates a recommitment to the technology (McCormick, 2023), echoed by increasing public support – a majority favoured nuclear energy in 2022, for the first time since 2015 (Saad, 2022). In 2022 €50 billion was committed to extending the lifespan of existing plants and building at least six new reactors in France (White and Abboud, 2022). Even Japan started to re-evaluate its position towards nuclear energy. After the 2011 Fukushima nuclear disaster, all nuclear plants were temporarily shut down, and only partially restarted later. However, due to increased costs of electricity and warnings of electricity shortages, and as a response to energy security challenges, the country in 2022 considered extending the lifespan of existing plants (beyond the current sixty years), bringing idled plants back online and replacing decommissioned nuclear plants with new ones (Reuters, 2022b). In March 2022, for the first time since 2011, a narrow majority of the Japanese public (53%) supported a restart of nuclear reactors (compared with 44% in September 2021) (Stapczynski, 2022). At the end of 2022 the Japanese nuclear road map planned $1.1 trillion of investment and the restart of forty-five out of the fifty-four nuclear reactors still not operational eleven years after Fukushima (Sugiura and Inagaki, 2022). In 2022 the Japanese prime minister announced plans to restart idled plants and potentially build additional reactors because 'Russia's invasion of Ukraine has vastly transformed the world's energy landscape.... To overcome an imminent crisis caused of a power supply crunch, we must take the utmost steps to mobilise all possible policies in the coming years and prepare for any emergency' (cited in McCurry, 2022).

7.7 CONCLUSION

This chapter embedded the discussion of the CEE countries' energy and climate policy into a broader discussion on issues of decarbonisation and energy transition at the global level. The dynamics between EU member states, where several less economically advanced CEE countries are the main opponents of ambitious climate goals on the grounds of prioritising economic development, security of supply and fairer burden distribution, can be linked to discussions at the global level. Here there is a division between many Global North and Global South countries, with the latter often arguing – similarly to several CEE countries – that an energy transition towards low-carbon economies should be led by the rich countries (of the Global North), while a fair transition is one in which developing countries should get their opportunity in the short and medium term to develop their economies using less expensive, domestic fossil fuels.

Financing to provide climate mitigation and adaptation will need to be increased in scale and maintained in the long term. Whilst the increase in renewables globally, within the EU and within the CEE is encouraging, it needs to be backed by a sustained shift in financing away from fossil fuels and towards renewables and forms of Just Transition funding that mitigate the costs of the energy transition and deliver burden sharing. Key to energy transitions is political will, as noted in 2023 by the World Bank that 'a strong governmental commitment is key', echoed by the United Nations' Intergovernmental Panel on Climate Change that '[e]ffective climate action is enabled by political commitment [and] regulatory and economic instruments' (IPCC, 2022a). Without this the conclusion is that 'delayed mitigation and adaptation action would lock-in high-emissions infrastructure, raise risks of stranded assets and cost-escalation, reduce feasibility, and increase losses and damages' (IPCC, 2022a). Action will require a shared understanding of the public and key political and energy actors; as the Moroccan Minister of Energy Transition and Sustainable Development noted, 'The energy transition is not a luxury; it is a necessity' (Leila Benali cited in World Bank, 2023). There are signs that despite climate ambition and public support for it in CEE being lower than the EU average, there is little appetite to reverse necessary policies. Economic, societal and security drivers that may be coalescing to drive the more rapid energy transition required.

8

Conclusion

Following the end of communist regimes at the end of 1980s and beginning of 1990s, countries of Central and Eastern Europe embarked on a complex political and economic transition towards democracy and market economy. The European Union represented the material application of these ideas, and CEE countries applied for the membership throughout the 1990s with the aim to 'return to Europe', among the most developed liberal democratic societies and strongest global economies. This aim overshadowed all other goals and challenges that these countries had to overcome during this period, including a complex application process that required candidate countries to reform almost all sectors of their economies and often reform and stabilise their political institutions. There was strong elite and public support for EU membership, as a means to achieve overall stability of their democratic regimes and the strength of their market economies. With few having an extended previous experience of democracy, and most CEE states seeing short periods of democracy from 1918 replaced through coups in the 1920s and 1930s, the EU represented an opportunity to achieve and consolidate economic and political transitions despite the political and economic costs of accession.

However, the accession process did not deal with all issues to the same degree. Some policies (like agriculture, fisheries or competition) were highlighted, while others such as energy security as EU legislation and policy were largely absent. Other issues were effectively imposed by the acquis rather than negotiated, such as shutting down nuclear reactors considered by the international community to be unsafe (Oudenaren, 2001). CEE countries managed to negotiate only in terms of achieving a limited number of transition periods and derogations from the EU within their energy policy. While climate policy was not very developed during the 1990s, the closely connected EU environmental policy was adopted by the accession countries without major difficulties as they were motivated to improve environments negatively impacted by decades of communist regimes.

During the 1990s there was only limited development of policies in the CEE countries that were not connected to the EU membership applications. Whilst the Baltic States and Czechia experienced interruptions of Russian energy supplies, the region was characterised by a passive approach towards energy security before accession (and energy policy in general); the most important exception was a new Czech oil pipeline and contract with Norway to diversity its natural gas supply. Post-accession energy security began to be prioritised more generally in the region, and discussions at the EU level about energy security intensified (Mayer, 2008), particularly following a second major gas supply disruption in 2009.

Russian supplies were fully halted for almost three weeks in 2009 (European Commission, 2009a) and diversification of supplies and suppliers became a priority for the Commission and a number of member states, including those from CEE (Prontera and Plenta, 2020). However, whilst internal energy market integration was significant, with the Commission's investigation of Gazprom's monopolistic behaviour in CEE energy markets an important moment, competences related to external energy security stayed mostly in national hands and there was only limited development at the EU level of a common external energy policy (for example, the Commission's efforts to check the fit between long-term energy contracts between third countries and member states and internal market rules). Several member states continued to strengthen ties with their external energy suppliers, including Russia, despite the stated objective of diversification, and Russia's share of EU imports of natural gas between 2010 and 2020 increased from 30.6% to 38.2% (Eurostat, 2022c). For example, there was widespread support, including from Germany, for the development of the Nord Stream II pipeline to expand gas imports from Russia. This was criticised by many CEE countries that viewed this increased cooperation as a threat to their individual, regional and collective EU energy security. Only after Russia's full-scale invasion of Ukraine in February 2022 was there the necessary consensus to fundamentally re-evaluate energy relations with Russia.

Immediately after the invasion the Commission presented a plan of how to exclude Russian supplies from EU energy mix before 2030 (European Commission, 2022a) and later a plan of how to survive the winter of 2022/2023 without Russian natural gas supplies (European Commission, 2022b). Member states collectively agreed to lower their gas consumption over the winter and reduced gas consumption by nearly 20%, with states including Germany ceasing Russian gas imports (Abnett, 2023). The crisis began to emerge in mid-2021 as a response to – among other issues – the post-pandemic increase of demand and Gazprom's deliberate low injections into German underground storages (Mišík, 2022). The policy response had begun to emerge much earlier; in 2009 (Council of the EU, 2009), the member states collectively agreed, without referring to Russia, that '[e]nergy security is a key priority which needs to be enhanced by improving energy efficiency, diversifying energy suppliers, sources and supply routes, and promoting the Union's energy interests vis-à-vis third countries. In order to deliver on energy security, the

EU collectively, as well as each Member State, must be prepared to combine solidarity with responsibility.' The year 2022 represented the elevation of energy security to a top priority in the EU: there was a consensus amongst member states that the primary source of insecurity was reliance on imports of Russian fossil fuels, an alignment with the views generally held in CEE since 2006. Importantly, this discursive agreement was accompanied by decisive policy action.

8.1 TWO MAIN ARGUMENTS OF THE BOOK

This book examined climate and energy policies of the CEE countries and presented two main arguments. First, energy security is a long-standing concern in the region and has had priority over climate policy; second, despite this general observation, there are significant differences between CEE member states, and we cannot consider the region to be homogenous. Due to several factors – including experience of oil and natural gas supply disruptions, but also a result of a securitisation of the issue by political elites – CEE countries have been prioritising energy security over climate change mitigation goals. Generally, they have presented these two as a trade-off – the price of reaching more ambitious climate goals was in decreased energy security that was guaranteed by fossil fuels, mostly domestic, but including imported. Expensive renewable energy sources in this view not only would mean increased energy prices for the end consumers (including industry) but also would mean destabilisation of existing energy systems – both literally, in terms of electricity grid stability, and figuratively, in terms of decreased production in domestic coal mines or other parts of industry connected to fossil fuels.

CEE countries have become an increasingly diverse group, and an assertive set of member states since accession, quickly moved from almost uncritical support for major climate and energy initiatives at the EU level to actively attempting to shape the agenda and policy. This has been reflected in general preferences to prioritise energy security, including further integration and collective EU responses and in a general though increasingly differential preference for lower levels of climate ambition, including renewable energy targets.

8.2 RESEARCH QUESTIONS

The main research question of this book asked: What explains the shape, process and extent of energy transitions in CEE? To answer this question, a set of three sub-questions has been developed.

Following an introduction to climate and energy policy in the EU in general and the CEE region in particular, the second chapter developed a theoretical framework applied to climate and energy policy throughout the book. Chapters 3–5 applied this framework through an exploration of the first research sub-question – What drives energy and climate policy development in the CEE region? – with a focus on governance, foreign policy and state-society relations. Chapter 6 considered the second research sub-question – What effect does this region have on EU energy and climate policy, including the structural effect of EU enlargement and material effect on energy supplies and the impact of CEE countries attempting to upload their own policy preferences on EU climate and energy policy? Chapter 7 went beyond the EU and considered climate and energy policy from an international perspective to address the third research sub-question, to consider how these developments relate to the global context, drawing on parallels to, and lessons for, global energy transitions including those in the Global South.

Chapter 3 studied the development of energy governance in CEE countries related to EU accession and the evolution of the EU's internal energy market. In general, these countries were supportive of deeper integration, especially related to security of supplies – though most policy development was internal. Internal market and anti-monopoly legislation had a significant effect on reducing the control of Gazprom over existing infrastructure and energy companies, tackling long-term gas contracts and their restrictive destination clauses that prevented reselling, effectively blocking planned pipelines, as well as lowering prices through liberalising energy trade. Renewable energy policy, including through the 2009 renewable energy directive, was influential in stimulating a limited energy transition in CEE countries through legally binding national targets; however, renewable policies in several countries were subsequently dismantled (especially in Bulgaria, Czechia, Slovakia) due to high costs and lack of political will limiting development in the 2010s beyond the minimum required. Part of the explanation here is that in only a few instances (for example, Lithuania) were renewables connected to energy security issues; in most cases they remained lower priority environmental concerns.

Chapter 4 explored how the dependency of CEE countries on energy imports, particularly natural gas, shapes their climate and energy policy and their prioritisation of energy security over climate goals. In many CEE states, energy has been securitised to the extent that it is closely associated with national security, and prioritised as a result. The chapter explored different ways how EU members from the CEE region have focused on increasing their energy security by diversification of their energy infrastructure and exploiting various domestic sources of energy – including coal, renewables and nuclear – to decrease their dependency on Russia as their main energy supplier. A focus on achieving greater energy independence from Russia has driven, and been used to justify, continued high reliance on fossil fuels despite EU pressure. Paradoxically, nuclear energy is considered a domestic source of energy that serves to decrease dependency on Russia even by those CEE countries with nuclear power plants that are currently dependent on Russian fuel or, in Hungary's case, reliant on Russian funding and technology. Similarly, Poland has also been significantly reliant on coal imports from Russia despite framing coal as a means to achieve energy security.

Chapter 5 examined state-society relations and focused on the role of the civil society on climate and energy policy in the region, highlighting the considerable variation between states and contestation around the form and pace of energy transitions. A key difference remains the effect of structural energy market issues on public and political support. There is a general commitment to a 'Just Transition' away from fossil fuels, but in practice the political will to achieve this varies. Whilst most governments are committed to an increasingly rapid coal phase-out and economic restructuring to support affected employees and regions, other governments are attempting to delay this for as long as possible, citing economic and energy security concerns, and there remains public resistance and protests by trade unions against substantive pro-climate policy. A commonality is increased public concern with environmental and climate issues, with examples across the region of effective opposition to specific fossil fuel energy developments and in support of energy transition policies in general.

Chapter 6 examined activities of CEE countries and various preferences these countries pursue at the EU level, demonstrating their significant impact on EU climate and energy policy. Poland and the other Visegrad states (Slovakia, Hungary and Czechia), along with Romania and Bulgaria, have often shared preferences on lower climate targets, often reducing the ambition of negotiated outcomes rather than blocking them, though Poland has also vetoed a number of proposals and effectively opted out of the 2050 net-zero target. CEE states have also been active in initiating or supporting energy security proposals. The region has been the site of growing Commission intervention in energy security often at the request of these countries – against Gazprom, coordinating regional initiatives and investing in infrastructure.

In Chapter 7 the monograph went beyond the discussion on the CEE region and the EU and examined the links with global energy transitions. As a region it is a microcosm of common but differentiated responsibility and capacity also found in global climate negotiations and the Paris Agreement, with the EU implementing effort sharing in its renewable energy targets, its Covid-19 recovery plan for Europe, and the supplementary REPowerEU initiative to accelerate energy transitions and remove Russian energy imports whilst mitigating the social and economic challenges associated with them. The preferences and concerns of CEE countries – mostly those connected to climate ambitions – are present also at the global level where some developing and other countries argue in favour of short- to medium-term use of fossil fuels to ensure that economic development is not undermined, and argue in favour of a gradual energy transition. Key within the EU, and globally, is financial support from more to less economically developed states, to facilitate these efforts in a 'fair' way with the help of financial stimuli and other types of support. As explored in this book, the EU's funding has played a significant role in driving CEE energy transitions, with €724 billion in Covid-19 recovery funding to 2026, including a requirement that 37% is dedicated to climate measures. However, the European Investment Bank in 2023 estimated that to meet the EU's 2030 target of a 55% emissions reduction, €1 trillion per year of investment was needed, €356 billion per year more than the 2011–2020 annual average (European Investment Bank, 2023, p. 8).

A challenge that will dominate CEE, broader EU and international energy transition policy is the definition of a 'Just Transition' that balances economic and environmental goals, as well as incorporating energy security concerns: 'Equity remains a central element in the UN climate regime.... Distributional consequences within and between countries include shifting of income and employment during the transition from high- to low-emissions activities' (IPCC, 2022b), and this applies within and between countries and regions. This is particularly important as the phase-down and phase-out of fossil fuels expands and accelerates. As the UN's Intergovernmental Panel on Climate Change (IPCC) reported in 2022, all pathways to limiting warming to 1.5 or 2°C 'involve rapid and deep and in most cases immediate GHG emission reductions in all sectors' (2022b, p. 24), and 'attention to equity ... at all scales can build social trust, and deepen and widen support for transformative changes' (2022a, p. 43). Funding in the EU needs to be increased, including support to countries within CEE, and internationally. A $100 billion international fund was promised as part of the 2009 Copenhagen Climate conference, but it was $17 billion short by the original target date of 2020 (OECD, 2022). In November 2022 the UN's Secretary General called for wealthier countries to agree to a 'climate solidarity pact' to support climate mitigation and adaptation in lower-income countries (Hodgson, 2022).

8.3 THE WAY FORWARD

While this monograph presented a detailed account of climate and energy policy of the CEE countries, it also provides avenues for future research. First, the changes to these two policies caused by the Russian invasion of Ukraine are ongoing during the finalisation of this book in late 2023, and further significant changes as a result are inevitable. Future research should include a focus on the impact of the crisis, triggered by the invasion of Ukraine, on the CEE region. For example, nuclear energy is considered to be an answer not only to energy security, but also to climate challenges by several countries of the region (Kratochvíl and Mišík, 2020; Żuk, 2023); however, Russian fuel supplies are still crucial for several existing nuclear power plants in the region (Szulecki and Overland, 2023), and the future of Russia's involvement in Hungary's ongoing nuclear power plant construction is uncertain.

Second, future research shall focus on various paths of decarbonisation that will be chosen by CEE countries. While the pace of this process differs among these member states, the direction is clearly visible even in the least ambitious country of the group (Poland). However, the character of these transition pathways varies, with several CEE countries opting for nuclear energy while others focus more narrowly on renewables. A challenge that lies ahead is to facilitate national energy transitions that also guarantee stability and reliability of energy (particularly electricity) systems regionally, and across the whole EU. CEE states have become more active and influential in EU climate and energy policy-making, and the 2021 energy crisis and its consequences present an opportunity to shape the responses, continuing to highlight the importance, and definition, of 'security' and 'solidarity'.

It has taken a series of 'crises' in the EU to move from setting objectives of decreasing dependence on Russian energy to achieving these. CEE states have played a key role in the initial agenda and objective setting, with their concern about the negative effects of Russian energy dependence on economic, energy and national security diffusing incompletely before 2022 when a paradigmatic shift occurred that set the EU on a seemingly irreversible path to completely removing Russia as an energy partner in just a few years. However, the influence of CEE states is also on policy development. Repeated invocations of the importance of solidarity, and the source scale and appropriate response to threats to energy security, have found an increasingly sympathetic audience. CEE states framed their energy security as intertwined with that of the EU as a whole, demanding that the community act. Within the EU it was almost solely CEE that experienced Russian energy supply disruptions and market manipulation and political economic pressure by Russia. This process of securitisation, driven by political actors in the region along with support from the Commission, whilst incomplete before 2022, still contributed to a range of legislation that has provided CEE states a role within an increasingly common internal and external energy policy. 'Energy islands' have gradually been removed, a single energy market has continued to emerge, and by many quantitative measures energy security did increase despite rising dependence on Russian energy imports. The EU experienced significant challenges in the energy crisis of the winter of 2022/2023, including prices and associated economic challenges and rising inflation, but security of supply was maintained in the face of member state and EU boycotts, and Russia cutting off gas supplies to several member states. This was still an energy crisis, but policy responses since 2006, and 2009, meant that the EU was better able to weather the storm in the short term at least.

Energy transitions are significantly underway in all CEE states, but for many the main material, institutional and economic challenges of transformation lie ahead. For the EU, maintaining a sense of equitable effort sharing will be key to the political acceptability of increasingly ambitious climate goals, including sub-sectoral targets such as energy efficiency and renewables, and the essential phasing-out of fossil fuels.

Conceptually, the findings support the assumptions of those including Kuzemko (2014), Ciută (2009) and Kuus (2007) regarding the construction of 'threats' to security, and Campbell (2002), t'Hart (1993) and Hay (1996) in terms of the construction of 'crises'. Whether an energy 'threat' or energy 'crisis' exists is related to material indicators of the vulnerability of energy supplies, pricing, storage and diversification, and this in CEE is linked to material path dependencies of institutions, energy supplies and energy systems. The socio-technical systems literature including the work of Geels (e.g., 2014) usefully highlights the importance of the co-evolution of these, and the regime resistance to energy transitions (Ford and Newell, 2021). A perception of insecurity is also strongly informed by 'actors' history, identities, and strategic myths' (Ciută, 2009, p. 137).

The extent to which governments and other key energy actors conceive energy supplies and prices to be insecure, and frame that as such, affects the development of energy policy attitudes towards risk, and how best to insure against risk. In turn, this is a strong explanatory factor in accounting for the extent of political will to make energy policy changes at a national level and/or to upload these preferences at the EU level in an attempt to influence agenda-setting, policy-making and policy implementation. That environmental issues are often not considered a security issue or risk in many CEE countries does not mean that they will not be in the future. Whilst political and societal support for climate action is relatively lower in CEE, the region is not a homogenous bloc, and the book has identified rising concern about climate change, and in some cases an increasing understanding of domestic renewables as a source of energy security, and in others of economic opportunity. Economic, environmental and national security drivers will be crucial in determining the political will to accelerate energy transitions in CEE, and societal and political actors will be key to shaping the pace, form and character of energy transitions in the region towards 2050.

Bibliography

350.org, 2019. $11 trillion and counting. https://financingthefuture.platform350.org/wp-content/uploads/sites/60/2019/09/FF_11Trillion-WEB.pdf

Aalto, P., Nyyssönen, H., Kojo, M., Pal, P., 2017. Russian nuclear energy diplomacy in Finland and Hungary. *Eurasian Geogr. Econ.* 58, 386–417. https://doi.org/10.1080/15387216.2017.1396905

Abdelal, R. E., Tarontsi, S., 2013. *Energy Security in Europe (B): The Southern Corridor (No. 711– 033), Harvard Business School Supplement.* www.hbs.edu/faculty/Pages/item.aspx?num=39589

Abnett, K., 2022. EU brands Russian gas halt 'blackmail', working on response. Reuters, 27 April.

2023. EU cut winter gas use 18%, surpassing energy crisis goal. Reuters, 19 April.

Abraham, J., 2017. Just transitions for the miners: labor environmentalism in the Ruhr and Appalachian coalfields. *New Polit. Sci.* 39, 218–240. https://doi.org/10.1080/07393148.2017.1301313

Adenle, A. A., Azadi, H., Arbiol, J., 2015. Global assessment of technological innovation for climate change adaptation and mitigation in developing world. *J. Environ. Manage.* 161, 261–275. https://doi.org/10.1016/j.jenvman.2015.05.040

Adomaitis, N., Lannin, P., 2012. Baltic states, in EU, fight reliance on Russia gas. Reuters, 5 July.

Afful-Dadzie, A., Mallett, A., Afful-Dadzie, E., 2020. The challenge of energy transition in the Global South: the case of electricity generation planning in Ghana. *Renew. Sustain. Energy Rev.* 126, 109830. https://doi.org/10.1016/j.rser.2020.109830

Agencia za enegrijo, 2017. *Pomembnejši kazalniki na področju oskrbe z električno energijo in zemeljskim plinom za leto 2016*. Ljubljana.

Aklin, M., Urpelainen, J., 2018. *Renewables: The Politics of a Global Energy Transition*. MIT Press, Cambridge, MA.

Aktualita, 2013. Severní Čechy zaplnily nové billboardy CCG. Aktualita. https://web.archive.org/web/20131211062528/www.czechcoal.cz/cs/novinky/aktuality/2013/20130211.html

Al-Mansour, F., Sucic, B., Pusnik, M., 2014. Challenges and prospects of electricity production from renewable energy sources in Slovenia. *Energy* 77, 73–81. https://doi.org/10.1016/j.energy.2014.04.106

Ali, S. W., Sadiq, M., Terriche, Y., Naqvi, S. A. R., Hoang, L. Q. N., Mutarraf, M. U., Hassan, M. A., Yang, G., Su, C.-L., Guerrero, J. M., 2021. Offshore wind farm-grid integration: a review on infrastructure, challenges, and grid solutions. *IEEE Access* 9, 102811–102827. https://doi.org/10.1109/ACCESS.2021.3098705

Ambrose, J., Henley, J., 2019. European Investment Bank to phase out fossil fuel financing. *The Guardian*, 15 November.

Andersen, S. S., Goldthau, A., Sitter, N., 2017. *Energy Union: Europe's New Liberal Mercantilism?* Palgrave Macmillan, London.

Anderson, R. J., 2008. *Europe's Dependence on Russian Natural Gas: Perspectives and Recommendations for a Long-Term Strategy*. Garmisch-Partenkirchen.

Andoura, S., Hancher, L., van der Woude, M., 2010. *Towards a European Energy Community: A Policy Proposal by Jacques Delors*. Brussels.

Andreev, S. A., 2009. The unbearable lightness of membership. *Communist Post-Communist Stud.* 42, 375–393.

Angel, J., 2016. *Strategies of Energy Democracy*. Brussels.

Anke, C.-P., Hobbie, H., Schreiber, S., Möst, D., 2020. Coal phase-outs and carbon prices: interactions between EU emission trading and national carbon mitigation policies. *Energy Policy* 144, 111647. https://doi.org/10.1016/j.enpol.2020.111647

Argüelles, L., Anguelovski, I., Dinnie, E., 2017. Power and privilege in alternative civic practices: examining imaginaries of change and embedded rationalities in community economies. *Geoforum* 86, 30–41. https://doi.org/10.1016/j.geoforum.2017.08.013

Aslund, A., 2013. *How Capitalism Was Built: The Transformation of Central and Eastern Europe, Russia, the Caucasus, and Central Asia*. Cambridge University Press, Cambridge.

Augutis, J., Krikštolaitis, R., Pečiulytė, S., Konstantinavičiūtė, I., 2011. Sustainable development and energy security level after Ignalina NPP shutdown. *Technol. Econ. Dev. Econ.* 17, 5–21. https://doi.org/10.3846/13928619.2011.553930

Austvik, O. G., 2016. The Energy Union and security-of-gas supply. *Energy Policy* 96, 372–382. https://doi.org/10.1016/j.enpol.2016.06.013

B&S Europe, 2015. *Evaluation of PHARE [EU pre-accession] financial assistance to Bulgaria, Cyprus, Czech Republic, Estonia, Hungary, Latvia, Lithuania, Malta, Poland, Romania, Slovakia, Slovenia.*

Badera, J., Kocoń, P., 2014. Local community opinions regarding the socio-environmental aspects of lignite surface mining: experiences from central Poland. *Energy Policy* 66, 507–516. https://doi.org/10.1016/j.enpol.2013.11.048

Baev, P. K., Øverland, I., 2010. The South Stream versus Nabucco pipeline race: geopolitical and economic (ir)rationales and political stakes in mega-projects. *Int. Aff.* (Royal Inst. Int. Aff. 1944–) 86, 1075–1090.

Baker, L., Newell, P., Phillips, J., 2014. The political economy of energy transitions: the case of South Africa. *New Polit. Econ.* 19, 791–818. https://doi.org/10.1080/13563467.2013.849674

Balmaceda, M. M., 2008. Corruption, intermediary companies, and energy security: Lithuania's lessons for Central and Eastern Europe. *Probl. Post-Communism* 55, 16–28. https://doi.org/10.2753/PPC1075-8216550402

2013. *Politics of Energy Dependency: Ukraine, Belarus, and Lithuania between Domestic Oligarchs and Russian Pressure*. University of Toronto Press, Toronto.

Balthasar, A., Schreurs, M. A., Varone, F., 2020. Energy transition in Europe and the United States: policy entrepreneurs and veto players in federalist systems. *J. Environ. Dev.* 29, 3–25. https://doi.org/10.1177/1070496519887489

Baltic Pipe, 2021. Energinet estimates cost of Baltic Pipe delay at 80 million euro. 2 July. www.baltic-pipe.eu/energinet-energinet-estimates-cost-of-baltic-pipe-delay-at-80-million-euro/

Baltic Prime Ministers, 2006. Declaration of the Prime Ministers of Lithuania, Latvia, Estonia on security of supply in the Baltic States and common European energy policy. www.urm.lt/get_file.php?file=L2RhdGEvaHRocGQvaHRtbC91bXIvbS9tX2ZpbGVzL3dmaWxlcy9maWxlMTM4My5wZGY7RGVrbGFyYWNpamEyMDA2LnBkZjs7

Baltic Times, 2018. Lithuania broke its promise to Latvia over LNG terminal – former ambassador. 20 February.

Balzacq, T., 2005. The three faces of securitization: political agency, audience and context. *Eur. J. Int. Relations* 11, 171–201. https://doi.org/10.1177/1354066105052960

2010. A theory of securitization: origins, core assumptions, and variants, in: *Securitization Theory: How Security Problems Emerge and Dissolve*. Routledge, London, pp. 1–30.

Bankwatch, 2020. Czech Coal Commission likely to approve 2038 as coal phaseout date in key vote tomorrow. Bankwatch, 3 December. https://bankwatch.org/press_release/czech-coal-commission-likely-to-approve-2038-as-coal-phaseout-date-in-key-vote-tomorrow

Barber, T., 2018. Bulgaria puts reforms aside to focus on EU presidency. *Financial Times*, 10 January.

Barigazzi, J., Kijewski, L., 2022. EU's Russian oil ban stalls as Hungary holds up sanctions. Politico, 8 May.

Barnett, J., Adger, W. N., 2007. Climate change, human security and violent conflict. *Polit. Geogr.* 26, 639–655. https://doi.org/10.1016/j.polgeo.2007.03.003

Barnett, J., Burningham, K., Walker, G., Cass, N., 2010. Imagined publics and engagement around renewable energy technologies in the UK. *Public Underst. Sci.* 21, 36–50. https://doi.org/10.1177/0963662510365663

Batzella, F., 2018. *The Dynamics of EU External Energy Relations: Fighting for Energy*. Routledge, London.

2021. The role of the Commission in intergovernmental agreements in the field of energy: a foot in the door technique? *JCMS J. Common Mark. Stud.* 59, 745–761. https://doi.org/10.1111/jcms.13129

Bauer, M. W., Knill, C., 2012. Understanding policy dismantling: an analytical framework, in: Bauer, M. W., Jordan, A., Green-Pederson, C., Héritier, A. (Eds.), *Dismantling Public Policy*. Oxford University Press, Oxford, pp. 30–51.

Baun, M., Marek, D., 2013. *The New Member States and the European Union: Foreign Policy and Europeanization*. Routledge, London.

Bauwens, T., Devine-Wright, P., 2018. Positive energies? An empirical study of community energy participation and attitudes to renewable energy. *Energy Policy* 118, 612–625. https://doi.org/10.1016/j.enpol.2018.03.062

Bauwens, T., Gotchev, B., Holstenkamp, L., 2016. What drives the development of community energy in Europe? The case of wind power cooperatives. *Energy Res. Soc. Sci.* 13, 136–147. https://doi.org/10.1016/j.erss.2015.12.016

BBC, 2007. EU rejects Balkans nuclear plea. BBC News, 13 March. http://news.bbc.co.uk/2/hi/europe/6445795.stm

2009. Bulgaria urges return to nuclear. BBC News, 6 January. http://news.bbc.co.uk/2/hi/europe/7814477.stm

2011. Italy nuclear: Berlusconi accepts referendum blow. BBC News, 14 June. www.bbc.co.uk/news/world-europe-13741105

2012. Bulgaria bans shale gas drilling with 'fracking' method. BBC News, 19 January. www.bbc.com/news/world-europe-16626580

2022a. Russia to build two nuclear reactors in Hungary. BBC News, 27 August. www.bbc.com/news/world-europe-62695938

2022b. Nord Stream 1: how Russia is cutting gas supplies to Europe. BBC News, 29 September. www.bbc.com/news/world-europe-60131520

Beaussier, A.-L., Cabane, L., 2020. Strengthening the EU's response capacity to health emergencies: insights from EU crisis management mechanisms. *Eur. J. Risk Regul.* 11, 808–820. https://doi.org/10.1017/err.2020.80

Beckmann, V., Otto, I. M., Tan, R., 2015. Overcoming the legacy of the past? Analyzing the modes of governance used by the Polish agricultural producer groups. *Agric. Econ. (Czech Republic)* 61, 222–233. https://doi.org/10.17221/190/2014-AGRICECON

Béland, D., 2010. Reconsidering policy feedback: how policies affect politics. *Adm. Soc.* 42, 568–590. https://doi.org/10.1177/0095399710377444

Bell, S. E., Braun, Y. A., 2010. Coal, identity, and the gendering of environmental justice activism in central Appalachia. *Gend. Soc.* 24, 794–813. https://doi.org/10.1177/0891243210387277

Belyi, A. V., 2019. *Stepping on the Gas: Future-Proofing Estonia's Energy Market and Security*. International Centre for Defence and Security, Tallin.

Bento, J. P. C., Szczygiel, N., Moutinho, V., 2017. Fossil fuel power generation and economic growth in Poland. *Energy Sources, Part B Econ. Planning, Policy* 12, 930–935. https://doi.org/10.1080/15567249.2017.1324536

Bernardi, L., Morales, L., Lühiste, M., Bischof, D., 2018. The effects of the Fukushima disaster on nuclear energy debates and policies: a two-step comparative examination. *Env. Polit.* 27, 42–68. https://doi.org/10.1080/09644016.2017.1383007

Bernhard, M., 1993. Civil society and democratic transition in East Central Europe. *Polit. Sci. Q.* 108, 307–326. https://doi.org/10.2307/2152014

Bessi, A., Guidolin, M., Manfredi, P., 2021. The role of gas on future perspectives of renewable energy diffusion: bridging technology or lock-in? *Renew. Sustain. Energy Rev.* 152, 111673. https://doi.org/10.1016/j.rser.2021.111673

Bhatti, J., 2021. Making India energy-independent by 2047: a look at PM Modi's blueprint Down to Earth, 18 August. www.downtoearth.org.in/blog/energy-efficiency/making-india-energy-independent-by-2047-a-look-at-pm-modi-s-blueprint-78528

Biden, J., 2023. *President Biden's State of the Union Address*. www.whitehouse.gov/state-of-the-union-2023/

Binhack, P., Tichý, L., 2012. Asymmetric interdependence in the Czech-Russian energy relations. *Energy Policy* 45, 54–63. https://doi.org/10.1016/j.enpol.2012.01.027

Birchfield, V. L., Duffield, J. S., 2011. *Toward a Common European Union Energy Policy: Problems, Progress, and Prospects*. Palgrave Macmillan, New York.

Blondeel, M., Van de Graaf, T., Haesebrouck, T., 2020. Moving beyond coal: exploring and explaining the Powering Past Coal Alliance. *Energy Res. Soc. Sci.* 59, 101304. https://doi.org/10.1016/j.erss.2019.101304

Bloomberg, 2022. China won't rush its clean energy transformation, Xi says. Bloomberg, 16 October.

Boasson, E. L., Wettestad, J., 2013. *EU Climate Policy: Industry, Policy Interaction and External Environment*. Routledge, London.

Bocquillon, P., Maltby, T., 2017. The more the merrier? Assessing the impact of enlargement on EU performance in energy and climate change policies. *East European Politics* 33, 88–105. https://doi.org/10.1080/21599165.2017.1279605

Bodenhamer, A., 2016. King coal: a study of mountaintop removal, public discourse, and power in Appalachia. *Soc. Nat. Resour.* 29, 1139–1153. https://doi.org/10.1080/08941920.2016.1138561

Boersma, T., 2015. *Energy Security and Natural Gas Markets in Europe: Lessons from the EU and the United States*. Routledge, London.

Bogdanov, D., Ram, M., Aghahosseini, A., Gulagi, A., Oyewo, A. S., Child, M., Caldera, U., Sadovskaia, K., Farfan, J., De Souza Noel Simas Barbosa, L., Fasihi, M., Khalili, S., Traber, T., Breyer, C., 2021. Low-cost renewable electricity as the key driver of the global energy transition towards sustainability. *Energy* 227, 120467. https://doi.org/10.1016/j.energy.2021.120467

Böhringer, C., 2003. The Kyoto Protocol: a review and perspectives. *Oxford Rev. Econ. Policy* 19, 451–466. https://doi.org/10.1093/oxrep/19.3.451

Bonsu, N. O., 2020. Towards a circular and low-carbon economy: insights from the transitioning to electric vehicles and net zero economy. *J. Clean. Prod.* 256, 120659. https://doi.org/10.1016/j.jclepro.2020.120659

Boogaerts, A., Portela, C., Drieskens, E., 2016. One swallow does not make spring: a critical juncture perspective on the EU sanctions in response to the Arab Spring. *Mediterr. Polit.* 21, 205–225. https://doi.org/10.1080/13629395.2015.1125285

Borozan, S., Mateska, A. K., Krstevski, P., 2021. Progress of the electricity sectors in South East Europe: challenges and opportunities in achieving compliance with EU energy policy. *Energy Reports* 7, 8730–8741. https://doi.org/10.1016/j.egyr.2021.11.203

Börzel, T. A., Buzogány, A., 2010. Environmental organisations and the Europeanisation of public policy in Central and Eastern Europe: the case of biodiversity governance. *Env. Polit.* 19, 708–735. https://doi.org/10.1080/09644016.2010.508302

2019. Compliance with EU environmental law: the iceberg is melting. *Env. Polit.* 28, 315–341. https://doi.org/10.1080/09644016.2019.1549772

Börzel, T. A., Risse, T., 2007. Europeanization: the domestic impact of European Union politics, in: Jørgensen, K. E., Pollack, M., Rosamond, B. (Eds.), *The SAGE Handbook of European Union Politics*. SAGE Publications, London, pp. 483–504.

Börzel, T. A., Sedelmeier, U., 2017. Larger and more law abiding? The impact of enlargement on compliance in the European Union. *J. Eur. Public Policy* 24, 197–215. https://doi.org/10.1080/13501763.2016.1265575

Boute, A., 2022. Weaponizing energy: energy, trade, and investment law in the new geopolitical reality. *Am. J. Int. Law* 116, 740–751. https://doi.org/10.1017/ajil.2022.53

Bouzarovski, S., 2009. East-Central Europe's changing energy landscapes: a place for geography. *Area* 41, 452–463.

Bouzarovski, S., Bassin, M., 2011. Energy and identity: imagining Russia as a hydrocarbon superpower. *Ann. Assoc. Am. Geogr.* 101, 783–794. https://doi.org/10.1080/00045608.2011.567942

Bouzarovski, S., Konieczny, M., 2010. Landscapes of paradox: public discourses and policies in Poland's relationship with the Nord Stream pipeline. *Geopolitics* 15, 1–21. https://doi.org/10.1080/14650040903420362

Bouzarovski, S., Thomson, H., 2019. *Transforming Energy Poverty Policies in the European Union: Second Annual Report of the European Union Energy Poverty Observatory*. Brussels.

Bouzarovski, S., Tirado Herrero, S., 2015. The energy divide: integrating energy transitions, regional inequalities and poverty trends in the European Union. *Eur. Urban Reg. Stud.* 24, 69–86. https://doi.org/10.1177/0969776415596449

2017. Geographies of injustice: the socio-spatial determinants of energy poverty in Poland, the Czech Republic and Hungary. *Post-Communist Econ.* 29, 27–50. https://doi.org/10.1080/14631377.2016.1242257

Bouzarovski, S., Tirado Herrero, S., Petrova, S., Frankowski, J., Matoušek, R., Maltby, T., 2017. Multiple transformations: theorizing energy vulnerability as a socio-spatial

phenomenon. *Geogr. Ann. Ser. B, Hum. Geogr.* 99, 20–41. https://doi.org/10.1080/04353684.2016.1276733
Bouzarovski, S., Tirado Herrero, S., Petrova, S., Ürge-Vorsatz, D., 2016. Unpacking the spaces and politics of energy poverty: path-dependencies, deprivation and fuel switching in post-communist Hungary. *Local Environ.* 21, 1151–1170. https://doi.org/10.1080/13549839.2015.1075480
Bradshaw, M., 2013. *Global Energy Dilemmas*. Policy Press, London.
Brar, N., 2015. Need to ensure climate justice, says PM Modi at United Nations. NDTV.com. www.ndtv.com/india-news/need-to-ensure-climate-justice-says-pm-modi-at-united-nations-1223108
Brauers, H., Oei, P.-Y., 2020. The political economy of coal in Poland: drivers and barriers for a shift away from fossil fuels. *Energy Policy* 144, 111621. https://doi.org/10.1016/j.enpol.2020.111621
Brauers, H., Oei, P.-Y., Walk, P., 2020. Comparing coal phase-out pathways: the United Kingdom's and Germany's diverging transitions. *Environ. Innov. Soc. Transitions* 37, 238–253. https://doi.org/10.1016/j.eist.2020.09.001
Braun, M., 2014. EU climate norms in East-Central Europe. *JCMS J. Common Mark. Stud.* 52, 445–460. https://doi.org/10.1111/jcms.12101
2019. The Czech Republic's approach to the EU 2030 climate and energy framework. *Env. Polit.* 28, 1105–1123. https://doi.org/10.1080/09644016.2019.1625139
Braungardt, S., van den Bergh, J., Dunlop, T., 2019. Fossil fuel divestment and climate change: reviewing contested arguments. *Energy Res. Soc. Sci.* 50, 191–200. https://doi.org/10.1016/j.erss.2018.12.004
Bricout, A., Slade, R., Staffell, I., Halttunen, K., 2022. From the geopolitics of oil and gas to the geopolitics of the energy transition: Is there a role for European supermajors? *Energy Res. Soc. Sci.* 88, 102634. https://doi.org/10.1016/j.erss.2022.102634
Bridge, G., Bouzarovski, S., Bradshaw, M., Eyre, N., 2013. Geographies of energy transition: space, place and the low-carbon economy. *Energy Policy* 53, 331–340. https://doi.org/10.1016/j.enpol.2012.10.066
Brown, B., Spiegel, S. J., 2019. Coal, climate justice, and the cultural politics of energy transition. *Glob. Environ. Polit.* 19, 149–168. https://doi.org/10.1162/glep_a_00501
Brown, S. P. A., Huntington, H. G., 2008. Energy security and climate change protection: Complementarity or tradeoff? *Energy Policy* 36, 3510–3513. https://doi.org/10.1016/j.enpol.2008.05.027
Brugidou, M., Bouillet, J., 2023. *A Return to Grace for Nuclear Power in European Public Opinion? Some Elements of a Rapid Paradigm Shift*. Brussels.
Brulle, R. J., Norgaard, K. M., 2019. Avoiding cultural trauma: climate change and social inertia. *Env. Polit.* 28, 886–908. https://doi.org/10.1080/09644016.2018.1562138
Brunsden, J., Fleming, S., Khan, M., 2020. EU recovery fund: How the plan will work? *Financial Times*, 21 July.
Brutschin, E., 2015. Shaping the EU's energy policy agenda: the role of Eastern European countries, in: Tosun, J., Biesenbender, S., Schulze, K. (Eds.), *Energy Policy Making in the EU: Building the Agenda*. Springer, London, pp. 187–204. https://doi.org/10.1007/978-1-4471-6645-0_10
Brzozowski, A., 2020. Polish PM: Nord Stream 2 blows up EU energy policy 'from inside'. Euractiv.com. www.euractiv.com/section/all/short_news/polish-pm-nord-stream-2-blows-up-eu-energy-policy-from-inside/
Bublitz, A., Keles, D., Zimmermann, F., Fraunholz, C., Fichtner, W., 2019. A survey on electricity market design: insights from theory and real-world implementations of capacity remuneration mechanisms. *Energy Econ.* 80, 1059–1078. https://doi.org/10.1016/j.eneco.2019.01.030

Buchan, D., 2010. *Eastern Europe's Energy Challenge: Meeting Its EU Climate Commitments* (No. EV 55). Oxford.

Buckley, T., 2021. President Xi Jinping's profound United Nations General Assembly speech. The Institute for Energy Economics and Financial Analysis, 22 September. https://ieefa.org/resources/president-xi-jinpings-profound-united-nations-general-assembly-speech

Bulgarian Government, 2008. *Bulgarian Energy Strategy by 2020*. Draft version. Sofia. www.strategy.bg/FileHandler.ashx?fileId=1436

2011. *National Security Strategy of the Republic of Bulgaria*. Sofia. www.me.government.bg/files/useruploads/files/national_strategy1.pdf

2012. *Presentation of the Annual Report on the Absorption of EU Funds in the Republic of Bulgaria for 2011*. Sofia.

Bulgarian Ministry of Energy, 2011. *National Energy Strategy till 2020*. Sofia.

Bulgarian National Radio, 2016. Rumen Radev for Le Monde: Bulgaria must not be an enemy to Russia. https://bnr.bg/en/post/100772144

Burke, M. J., 2018. Shared yet contested: energy democracy counter-narratives. *Frontiers in Communications*, 3. https://doi.org/10.3389/fcomm.2018.00022

Burke, M. J., Stephens, J. C., 2018. Political power and renewable energy futures: a critical review. *Energy Res. Soc. Sci.* 35, 78–93. https://doi.org/10.1016/j.erss.2017.10.018

Burnham, A., Han, J., Clark, C. E., Wang, M., Dunn, J. B., Palou-Rivera, I., 2012. Life-cycle greenhouse gas emissions of shale gas, natural gas, coal, and petroleum. *Environ. Sci. Technol.* 46, 619–627. https://doi.org/10.1021/es201942m

Buschmann, P., Oels, A., 2019. The overlooked role of discourse in breaking carbon lock-in: the case of the German energy transition. *WIREs Clim. Chang.* 10, e574. https://doi.org/10.1002/wcc.574

Bush, G. W., 2006. *President Bush's State of the Union Address*. Washington, DC.

Business Insider, 2015. Czech Republic to expand brown coal mining program. 19 October.

Butler, E., 2011. The geopolitics of merger and acquisition in the Central European Energy market. *Geopolitics* 16, 626–654. https://doi.org/10.1080/14650045.2011.520866

2018. Central and Eastern European energy security: more than Russia, in: Ostrowski, W., Butler, E. (Eds.), *Understanding Energy Security in Central and Eastern Europe: Russia, Transition and National Interest*. Routledge, London.

Buzan, B., Wæver, O., Wilde, J. de, 1998. *Security: A New Framework for Analysis*. Lynne Rienner, Boulder, CO.

Buzogány, A., 2017. Illiberal democracy in Hungary: Authoritarian diffusion or domestic causation? *Democratization* 24, 1307–1325. https://doi.org/10.1080/13510347.2017.1328676

2021. Beyond Balkan exceptionalism: assessing compliance with EU law in Bulgaria and Romania. *Eur. Polit. Soc.* 22, 185–202. https://doi.org/10.1080/23745118.2020.1729048

Buzogány, A., Ćetković, S., 2021. Fractionalized but ambitious? Voting on energy and climate policy in the European Parliament. *J. Eur. Public Policy* 28, 1038–1056. https://doi.org/10.1080/13501763.2021.1918220

Buzogány, A., Cotta, B., 2022. Post-accession backsliding and European Union environmental policies. *Post-Communist Econ.* 34, 647–665. https://doi.org/10.1080/14631377.2021.1965361

Caglar, A. E., 2022. Can nuclear energy technology budgets pave the way for a transition toward low-carbon economy? Insights from the United Kingdom. *Sustainable Development* 31(1), 198–210.

Cahill, B., 2022. EU's latest sanctions on Russian Oil: What are they and will it work? Energy Post, 14 June. https://energypost.eu/eus-latest-sanctions-on-russian-oil-what-are-they-and-will-it-work/

Calvert, K., 2015. From 'energy geography' to 'energy geographies': perspectives on a fertile academic borderland. *Prog. Hum. Geogr.* 40, 105–125. https://doi.org/10.1177/0309132514566343

Campbell, J. L., 2002. Ideas, politics, and public policy. *Annu. Rev. Sociol.* 28, 21–38. https://doi.org/10.1146/annurev.soc.28.110601.141111

Capellán-Pérez, I., Johanisova, N., Young, J., Kunze, C., 2020. Is community energy really non-existent in post-socialist Europe? Examining recent trends in 16 countries. *Energy Res. Soc. Sci.* 61, 101348. https://doi.org/10.1016/j.erss.2019.101348

CarbonBrief, 2022. Analysis: US falling $32bn short on 'fair share' of $100bn climate-finance goal. www.carbonbrief.org/analysis-us-falling-32bn-short-on-fair-share-of-100bn-climate-finance-goal/

Cardoso, A., Turhan, E., 2018. Examining new geographies of coal: dissenting energyscapes in Colombia and Turkey. *Appl. Energy* 224, 398–408. https://doi.org/10.1016/j.apenergy.2018.04.096

Carley, S., Konisky, D. M., 2020. The justice and equity implications of the clean energy transition. *Nat. Energy* 5, 569–577. https://doi.org/10.1038/s41560-020-0641-6

Carmin, J., Vandeveer, S. D., 2004. Enlarging EU environments: Central and Eastern Europe from transition to accession. *Env. Polit.* 13, 3–24. https://doi.org/10.1080/09644010410001685119

Castaño-Rosa, R., Solís-Guzmán, J., Rubio-Bellido, C., Marrero, M., 2019. Towards a multiple-indicator approach to energy poverty in the European Union: a review. *Energy Build.* 193, 36–48. https://doi.org/10.1016/j.enbuild.2019.03.039

CEE Bankwatch Network, 2016. Croatia to drop controversial coal plant project, confirms minister. https://bankwatch.org/press_release/croatia-to-drop-controversial-coal-plant-project-confirms-minister

CEE Energy News, 2021. Slovenia: Coal phase-out premature for Chamber of Commerce and Industry. https://ceenergynews.com/electricity/slovenias-chamber-of-commerce-and-industry-believes-that-a-coal-phase-out-by-2033-is-premature/

2022. Lithuania and Latvia discuss acceleration of the Baltics' power synchronisation. https://ceenergynews.com/electricity/lithuania-and-latvia-discuss-acceleration-of-the-baltics-power-synchronisation/

CEEP, 2018. *Cross-Border Energy Cooperation in Central Europe*. Central Europe Energy Partners Policy Paper. Brussels.

Cehlár, M., Domaracká, L., Šimko, I., Puzder, M., 2015. Mineral resource extraction and its political risks, in: Majerník, M., Daneshjo, N., Bosák, M. (Eds.), *Production Management and Engineering Sciences*. CFC Press, London, pp. 39–43.

Černoch, F., Dančák, B., Kod'ousková, H., Leschenko, A., Ocelík, P., Osička, J., Šebek, V., Vlček, T., Zapletalová, V., 2012. *The Future of the Druzhba Pipeline as a Strategic Challenge for the Czech Republic and Poland*. Muni, Brno.

Černoch, F., Lehotský, L., Ocelík, P., Osička, J., Vencourová, Ž., 2019. Anti-fossil frames: examining narratives of the opposition to brown coal mining in the Czech Republic. *Energy Res. Soc. Sci.* 54, 140–149. https://doi.org/10.1016/j.erss.2019.04.011

Ćetković, S., Buzogány, A., 2016. Varieties of capitalism and clean energy transitions in the European Union: when renewable energy hits different economic logics. *Clim. Policy* 16, 642–657. https://doi.org/10.1080/14693062.2015.1135778

2019. The political economy of EU climate and energy policies in Central and Eastern Europe revisited: shifting coalitions and prospects for clean energy transitions. *Polit. Gov.* 7, 124–138. https://doi.org/10.17645/pag.v7i1.1786

2020. Between markets, politics and path-dependence: explaining the growth of solar and wind power in six Central and Eastern European countries. *Energy Policy* 139, 111325. https://doi.org/10.1016/j.enpol.2020.111325

Ćetković, S., Hagemann, C., 2020. Changing climate for populists? Examining the influence of radical-right political parties on low-carbon energy transitions in Western Europe. *Energy Res. Soc. Sci.* 66, 101571. https://doi.org/10.1016/j.erss.2020.101571

Chaisty, P., Whitefield, S., 2015. Attitudes towards the environment: Are post-Communist societies (still) different? *Env. Polit.* 24, 598–616. https://doi.org/10.1080/09644016.2015.1023575

Chatterton, P., Featherstone, D., Routledge, P., 2013. Articulating climate justice in Copenhagen: antagonism, the commons, and solidarity. *Antipode* 45, 602–620. https://doi.org/10.1111/j.1467-8330.2012.01025.x

Chemnick, J., 2021. U.S. officially rejoins Paris climate agreement. *Scientific American*. www.scientificamerican.com/article/u-s-officially-rejoins-paris-climate-agreement/

Chen, C., Yang, Z., Hu, G., 2021. Signalling the cost of intermittency: What is the value of curtailed renewable power? *J. Clean. Prod.* 302, 126998. https://doi.org/10.1016/j.jclepro.2021.126998

Child, M., Kemfert, C., Bogdanov, D., Breyer, C., 2019. Flexible electricity generation, grid exchange and storage for the transition to a 100% renewable energy system in Europe. *Renew. Energy* 139, 80–101. https://doi.org/10.1016/j.renene.2019.02.077

Child, M., Koskinen, O., Linnanen, L., Breyer, C., 2018. Sustainability guardrails for energy scenarios of the global energy transition. *Renew. Sustain. Energy Rev.* 91, 321–334. https://doi.org/10.1016/j.rser.2018.03.079

Chung, J.-B., Kim, E.-S., 2018. Public perception of energy transition in Korea: nuclear power, climate change, and party preference. *Energy Policy* 116, 137–144. https://doi.org/10.1016/j.enpol.2018.02.007

Chyong, C. K., Reiner, D .M., Aggarwal, D., 2023. Market power and long-term gas contracts: the case of Gazprom in Central and Eastern European gas markets. *Energy J.* 44.

Cicero, 2021. *Hungary External Review of 2020 Green Bond Allocation Reporting*. Oslo.

Cirtautas, A. M., Schimmelfennig, F., 2010. Europeanisation before and after accession: conditionality, legacies and compliance. *Eur. Asia. Stud.* 62, 421–441. https://doi.org/10.1080/09668131003647812

Ciută, F., 2009. Security and the problem of context: a hermeneutical critique of securitisation theory. *Rev. Int. Stud.* 35, 301–326. https://doi.org/10.1017/S0260210509008535

2010. Conceptual notes on energy security: Total or banal security? *Secur. Dialogue* 41, 123–144.

Clark, P., 2015. Mark Carney warns investors face 'huge' climate change losses. *Financial Times*, 29 September.

Client Earth, 2019. Huge court win as we block Polish coal-fired power station. Client Earth, 19 June. www.clientearth.org/latest/latest-updates/news/huge-court-win-as-we-block-polish-coal-fired-power-station/

Closson, S., 2009. Russia's key customer: Europe, in: Perovic, J., Orttung, R. W. (Eds.), *Russian Energy Power and Foreign*. Routledge, London.

Collier, M., 2018. Baltics, Poland vow electricity grids will be synchronized by 2025. eng.lsm.lv, 22 March. https://eng.lsm.lv/article/politics/diplomacy/baltics-poland-vow-electricity-grids-will-be-synchronized-by-2025.a272280/

Collins, J., Osborne, L., 2018. As coal mines shutter, Polish miners seek a way to adjust. DW.com, 6 December.

Cook, A., 2014. Greenpeace protests against Paks II nuclear power plant. *Financial Times.*, 30 January.

Copsey, N., 2009. Parliament and the making of Polish national preferences in the European Union, in: *The Global Crisis and the EU Responses: The Perspectives of the SBH Team Presidency*. 'Together for Europe' Research Centre, Budapest, pp. 218–232.

Copsey, N., Pomorska, K., 2010. Poland's power and influence in the European Union: the case of its eastern policy. *Comp. Eur. Polit.* 8, 304–326. https://doi.org/10.1057/cep.2009.3

2014. The influence of newer member states in the European Union: the case of Poland and the Eastern Partnership. *Eur. Asia. Stud.* 66, 421–443. https://doi.org/10.1080/09668136.2013.855391

Corner, A., Venables, D., Spence, A., Poortinga, W., Demski, C., Pidgeon, N., 2011. Nuclear power, climate change and energy security: exploring British public attitudes. *Energy Policy* 39, 4823–4833. https://doi.org/10.1016/j.enpol.2011.06.037

Correljé, A., van der Linde, C., 2006. Energy supply security and geopolitics: a European perspective. *Energy Policy* 34, 532–543. https://doi.org/10.1016/j.enpol.2005.11.008

Corry, O., 2011. Securitisation and 'riskification': second-order security and the politics of climate change. *Millennium* 40, 235–258. https://doi.org/10.1177/0305829811419444

Council of the EU, 1964. *Protocol of Agreement on Energy Problems, Official Journal 069: 1099–1100*. Brussels.

Council of the EU, 2006a. *Proposal for a European Energy Security Treaty Information by the Polish Delegation*. Brussels.

2006b. *Council Conclusions: 'A New Energy Policy for Europe' Contribution of the Energy Ministers to the 2006 Spring European Council*. Brussels.

2008. *Energy and Climate Change: Elements of the Final Compromise*. Brussels.

2009. *Presidency Conclusions 19/20 March 2009*. Brussels.

2014. *A Policy Framework for Climate and Energy in the Period from 2020 to 2030*. Brussels.

2016. *Outcome of the Council meeting*. 3472nd Council meeting. Transport, Telecommunications and Energy. Brussels.

2018. *Silesia Declaration on Solidarity and Just Transition*. Brussels.

2022a. *Council Regulation (EU) 2022/1369 of 5 August 2022 on Coordinated Demand-Reduction Measures for Gas*. Brussels.

2022b. *Member States Commit to Reducing Gas Demand by 15% Next Winter*. Brussels.

Cousse, J., 2021. Still in love with solar energy? Installation size, affect, and the social acceptance of renewable energy technologies. *Renew. Sustain. Energy Rev.* 145, 111107. https://doi.org/10.1016/j.rser.2021.111107

Cousse, J., Wüstenhagen, R., Schneider, N., 2020. Mixed feelings on wind energy: affective imagery and local concern driving social acceptance in Switzerland. *Energy Res. Soc. Sci.* 70, 101676. https://doi.org/10.1016/j.erss.2020.101676

Creamer, E., Eadson, W., van Veelen, B., Pinker, A., Tingey, M., Braunholtz-Speight, T., Markantoni, M., Foden, M., Lacey-Barnacle, M., 2018. Community energy: entanglements of community, state, and private sector. *Geogr. Compass* 12, e12378. https://doi.org/10.1111/gec3.12378

Crippa, M., Guizzardi, D., Banja, M., Solazzo, E., Muntean, M., Schaaf, E., Pagani F., Monforti-Ferrario, F., Olivier, J. G. J., Quadrelli, R., Risquez Martin, A., Taghavi-Moharamli, P., Grassi, G., Rossi, S., Oom, D., Branco, A., San-Miguel, J., Vignati, E., 2022. *CO_2 Emissions of All World Countries*. Joint Research Centre, Luxembourg. https://doi.org/10.2760/07904

Crisp, J., 2015. Joint gas buying on EU leaders' summit agenda. Euractiv, 4 March. www.euractiv.com/section/climate-environment/news/joint-gas-buying-on-eu-leaders-summit-agenda/

Crnčec, D., Penca, J., Lovec, M., 2023. The COVID-19 pandemic and the EU: From a sustainable energy transition to a green transition? *Energy Policy* 175, 113453. https://doi.org/10.1016/j.enpol.2023.113453

Crnčec, D., Sučić, B., Merše, S., 2021. Slovenia: drivers and challenges of energy transition to climate neutrality, in: Mišík, M., Oravcová, V. (Eds.), *From Economic to Energy Transition: Three Decades of Transitions in Central and Eastern Europe*. Springer International, Cham, pp. 247–282. https://doi.org/10.1007/978-3-030-55085-1_9

Croatian Government, 2017. *National Security Strategy*. Zagreb.

2009. *Energy Strategy of the Republic of Croatia*. Zagreb.

Csereklyei, Z., 2014. Measuring the impact of nuclear accidents on energy policy. *Ecol. Econ.* 99, 121–129. https://doi.org/10.1016/j.ecolecon.2014.01.010

Cui, R. Y., Hultman, N., Cui, D., McJeon, H., Yu, S., Edwards, M. R., Sen, A., Song, K., Bowman, C., Clarke, L., Kang, J., Lou, J., Yang, F., Yuan, J., Zhang, W., Zhu, M., 2021. A plant-by-plant strategy for high-ambition coal power phaseout in China. *Nat. Commun.* 12, 1468. https://doi.org/10.1038/s41467–021-21786-0

Culley, M. R., Ogley-Oliver, E., Carton, A. D., Street, J. C., 2010. Media framing of proposed nuclear reactors: an analysis of print media. *J. Community Appl. Soc. Psychol.* 20, 497–512. https://doi.org/10.1002/casp.1056

Czech Government, 2003. *Security Strategy*. Prague.

Dąbrowski, M., 2012. Shallow or deep Europeanisation? The uneven impact of EU Cohesion policy on the regional and local authorities in Poland. *Environ. Plan. C Gov. Policy* 30, 730–745. https://doi.org/10.1068/c1164r

Daigneault, P.-M., 2014. Reassessing the concept of policy paradigm: aligning ontology and methodology in policy studies. *J. Eur. Public Policy* 21, 453–469. https://doi.org/10.1080/13501763.2013.834071

Dannreuther, R., 2013. Geopolitics and international relations of resources, in: Dannreuther, R., Ostrowski, W. (Eds.), *Global Resources: Conflict and Cooperation*. Palgrave Macmillan UK, London, pp. 79–97. https://doi.org/10.1057/9781137349149_5

2015. Energy security and shifting modes of governance. *Int. Polit.* 52, 466–483. https://doi.org/10.1057/ip.2015.4

Dasandi, N., Graham, H., Lampard, P., Jankin Mikhaylov, S., 2021. Engagement with health in national climate change commitments under the Paris Agreement: a global mixed-methods analysis of the nationally determined contributions. *Lancet Planet. Heal.* 5, e93–e101. https://doi.org/10.1016/S2542–5196(20)30302-8

Dastan, S. A., 2018. Negotiation of a cross-border natural gas pipeline: an analytical contribution to the discussions on Turkish Stream. *Energy Policy* 120, 749–760. https://doi.org/10.1016/j.enpol.2018.03.012

Davidescu, S., Hiteva, R., Maltby, T., 2018. Two steps forward, one step back: renewable energy transitions in Bulgaria and Romania. *Public Adm.* 96, 611–625. https://doi.org/10.1111/padm.12522

Davies, R., 2022. National Grid asks UK coal power plants to be on standby this winter. *The Guardian*, 28 July.

de Almeida, L., 2019. SoS back-and-forth? Minimum v. exhaustive harmonization of the right to be protected customers in gas supply crises: Eni and Others. *Eur. Energy Environ. Law Rev.* 20, 92–100.

de Hauteclocque, A., Conti, I., Glachant, J. M., 2015. *From a Reactive to a Proactive EU Regulatory Framework for Long-Term Gas Import Contracts*. Florence School of Regulation, Florence.

de la Porte, C., Jensen, M. D., 2021. The next generation EU: an analysis of the dimensions of conflict behind the deal. *Soc. Policy Adm.* 55, 388–402. https://doi.org/10.1111/spol.12709

Dekanozishvili, M., 2023. *Dynamics of EU Renewable Energy Policy Integration*. Palgrave Macmillan, Cham.

Detraz, N., Betsill, M. M., 2009. Climate change and environmental security: for whom the discourse shifts. *Int. Stud. Perspect.* 10, 303–320. https://doi.org/10.1111/j.1528-3585.2009.00378.x

Deutch, J., 2020. Is net zero carbon 2050 possible? *Joule* 4, 2237–2240. https://doi.org/10.1016/j.joule.2020.09.002

Deutsche Welle, 2006. Poland hits out at Germany over gas partnership with Russia. DW.com, 1 May. www.dw-world.de/dw/article/0,,1986869,00.html

Díaz, P., Van Vliet, O., Patt, A., 2017. Do we need gas as a bridging fuel? A case study of the electricity system of Switzerland. *Energies* 10, 861. https://doi.org/10.3390/en10070861

Diez, T., von Lucke, F., Wellmann, Z., 2016. *The Securitisation of Climate Change: Actors, Processes and Consequences*. Routledge, London.

Dimitrova, A., 2002. Enlargement, institution-building and the EU's administrative capacity requirement. *West Eur. Polit.* 25, 171–190. https://doi.org/10.1080/713601647

Dimitrova, A., Buzogány, A., 2014. Post-accession policy-making in Bulgaria and Romania: Can non-state actors use EU rules to promote better governance? *JCMS* 52, 139–156. https://doi.org/10.1111/jcms.12084

Dimitrova, A., Toshkov, D., 2009. Post-accession compliance between administrative co-ordination and political bargaining. *Eur. Integr. – Online Pap.* 13, 1–18. https://doi.org/10.1695/2009019

Dimitrova, M., 2020. Krizevci is a convincing champion of EU funds and a pioneer in the transition to green energy. The Mayor.eu, 19 October. www.themayor.eu/en/a/view/krizevci-is-a-convincing-champion-of-eu-funds-and-a-pioneer-in-the-transition-to-green-energy-6152

Dinan, D., 2014. *Europe Recast: A History of European Union*. Palgrave Macmillan, London.

Dogan, E., Chishti, M. Z., Karimi Alavijeh, N., Tzeremes, P., 2022. The roles of technology and Kyoto Protocol in energy transition towards COP26 targets: evidence from the novel GMM-PVAR approach for G-7 countries. *Technol. Forecast. Soc. Change* 181, 121756. https://doi.org/10.1016/j.techfore.2022.121756

dpa, 2022. Czech Republic and Slovakia demand EU green label for nuclear energy. dpa.com, 11 January. https://energycentral.com/news/czech-republic-and-slovakia-demand-eu-green-label-nuclear-energy-0

Dubois, U., Saplacan, R., 2010. Public service perspectives on reforms of electricity distribution and supply: a modular analysis. *Ann. Public Coop. Econ.* 81, 313–356. https://doi.org/10.1111/j.1467-8292.2010.00413.x

Dunlap, R. E., 2013. Climate change skepticism and denial: an introduction. *Am. Behav. Sci.* 57, 691–698. https://doi.org/10.1177/0002764213477097

Dupont, C., 2016. *Climate Policy Integration into EU Energy Policy: Progress and Prospects*. Routledge, London. https://doi.org/10.4324/9781315751665

Dupont, C., Oberthür, S., 2015. *Decarbonization in the European Union: Internal Policies and External Strategies*. Springer, London.

Dutkevičová, T., 2013. Energy self-sufficient village Kněžice. 100% communities. www.100-res-communities.eu/national_leagues/clu_czec/best-practices/energy-self-sufficient-village-knezice

Dutta, S., 2020. India's green energy plan makes $20 billion business sense: PM Modi. *Times of India*, 27 November.

DW, 2011. Belgium aims to phase out nuclear power by 2025. DW.com, 31 October. www.dw.com/en/belgium-aims-to-phase-out-nuclear-power-by-2025/a-15500989

Dytrych, S., 2020. *Komunitní energetika českou vládu nezajímá*. Pro-Energy.
Easton, A., 2021. Turow: vast Polish coal mine infuriates the neighbours. BBC.com. www.bbc.com/news/world-europe-57484009
Eastring, 2018. The presentation of the feasibility study. Eastring, 20 September. www.eastring.eu/page.php?page=news&year=2018
EBRD, 2021. Bohunice International Decommissioning Support Fund. EBRD. www.ebrd.com/what-we-do/sectors/nuclear-safety/bohunice.html
ECA, 2017. *EU Must Cut Emissions and also Adapt to Climate Change, Warn Auditors*. Luxembourg.
2022a. *EU Support for Coal Regions Achieved Little for Climate Transition*. Luxembourg.
2022b. *Energy Taxation, Carbon Pricing and Energy Subsidies*. Luxembourg.
ECJ, 2019. *The General Court Annuls the Commission Decision Approving the Modification of the Exemption Regime for the Operation of the OPAL Gas Pipeline*. Luxembourg.
EEA, 2022. Greenhouse gas emission intensity of electricity generation in Europe. EEA, 2 June. www.eea.europa.eu/en/analysis/indicators/greenhouse-gas-emission-intensity-of-1
Egenhofer, C., Alessi, M., Georgiev, A., Fujiwara, N., 2011. *The EU Emissions Trading System and Climate Policy towards 2050: Real Incentives to Reduce Emissions and Drive Innovation?* Brussels.
EIA, 2018. *Petroleum and Other Liquids*. Washington, DC.
2022. *Country Analysis Executive Summary: China*. Washington, DC.
Eicke, L., Weko, S., Apergi, M., Marian, A., 2021. Pulling up the carbon ladder? Decarbonization, dependence, and third-country risks from the European carbon border adjustment mechanism. *Energy Res. Soc. Sci.* 80, 102240. https://doi.org/10.1016/j.erss.2021.102240
Eikeland, P. O., 2011. The Third Internal Energy Market Package: New power relations among member states, EU institutions and non-state actors? *J. Common Mark. Stud.* 49, 243–263. https://doi.org/10.1111/j.1468-5965.2010.02140.x
EJAtlas, 2016. Plomin Power Station Unit C, Croatia. https://ejatlas.org/print/plomin-power-station-unit-c-croatia
2018. Gubin Brody lignite mine, Poland. https://ejatlas.org/conflict/the-gubin-brody-lignite-mine-poland
2019a. Wind farm licensing cases. https://ejatlas.org/conflict/public-participation-in-a-wind farm-licensing-case
2019b. Pungesti's resistance to Chevron gas fracking. *Global Atlas of Environmental Justice*. https://ejatlas.org/conflict/resistance-to-shale-gas-fracking
Elliott, D., 2013. *Fukushima: Impacts and Implications*. Palgrave Macmillan, Basingstoke.
Emmerich, P., Hülemeier, A.-G., Jendryczko, D., Baumann, M. J., Weil, M., Baur, D., 2020. Public acceptance of emerging energy technologies in context of the German energy transition. *Energy Policy* 142, 111516. https://doi.org/10.1016/j.enpol.2020.111516
Emodi, N. V., Okereke, C., Abam, F. I., Diemuodeke, O. E., Owebor, K., Nnamani, U. A., 2022. Transport sector decarbonisation in the Global South: a systematic literature review. *Energy Strateg. Rev.* 43, 100925. https://doi.org/10.1016/j.esr.2022.100925
Energy Bulletin, 2005. Former Secretary of Defense testifies before Senate on peak oil. www2.energybulletin.net/node/11014
2020. Crowd investing for solar roofs in Križevci. https://energy-cities.eu/wp-content/uploads/2020/07/Krizevci_crowdfunding-solarPV_2020_en.pdf
2010. National Report Bulgaria. www.csd.bg/artShow.php?id1/415199
2019. Eastring gone wild. https://energy-europe.eu/economy/eastring-gone-wild/

2019. Poland's top court blocks coal plant. www.energy-reporters.com/environment/polands-top-court-blocks-coal-plant/

ENTSOG, 2021. *Union-Wide Simulation of Gas Supply and Infrastructure Disruption Scenarios (SoS Simulation)*. Brussels.

Epstein, R. A., Jacoby, W., 2014. Eastern enlargement ten years on: Transcending the East-West divide? *J. Common Mark. Stud.* 52, 1–16. https://doi.org/10.1111/jcms.12089

ERR, 2022. Latvia to initially join Paldiski LNG terminal. news.err.ee. https://news.err.ee/1608571222/latvia-to-initially-join-paldiski-lng-terminal

Escribano, G., González-Enríquez, C., Lázaro-Touza, L., Paredes-Gázquez, J., 2023. An energy union without interconnections? Public acceptance of cross-border interconnectors in four European countries. *Energy* 266, 126385. https://doi.org/10.1016/j.energy.2022.126385

Estonian Government, 2017. *National Defence Strategy*. Tallin.

EU Business, 2010. Russia, Poland gas deal 'in line with EU law'. www.eubusiness.com/news-eu/poland-russia-gas.6tj

Euracoal, 2022. Poland. https://euracoal.eu/info/country-profiles/poland/

Euractiv, 2008. Eight EU states oppose unbundling, table 'third way'. www.euractiv.com/section/energy/news/eight-eu-states-oppose-unbundling-table-third-way/

2010. Commission urges Bulgaria to change Gazprom clause. www.euractiv.com/section/energy/news/commission-urges-bulgaria-to-change-gazprom-clause/

2012. Poland Blocks EU's Zero-Carbon Plan. www.euractiv.com/section/climate-environment/news/poland-blocks-eu-s-zero-carbon-plan/

2014. Finland and Estonia to build LNG terminals. www.euractiv.com/section/energy/news/finland-and-estonia-to-build-lng-terminals/

2015. Hungary says EU authorised its nuclear fuel supply deal with Russia. www.euractiv.com/section/energy/news/hungary-says-eu-authorised-its-nuclear-fuel-supply-deal-with-russia/

2022. Germany takes firm pro-gas stance in green taxonomy feedback to EU. www.euractiv.com/section/energy-environment/news/germany-takes-firm-pro-gas-stance-in-green-taxonomy-feedback-to-eu/

2023. Polish parliament votes 700 metre rule for wind turbines. www.euractiv.com/section/energy-environment/news/polish-parliament-votes-700-metre-rule-for-wind-turbines/

Euratom, 1957. *Consolidated Version of the Treaty Establishing the European Atomic Energy Community*. Brussels.

EurObserv'ER, 2023. 21st annual overview barometer, 28 February. www.eurobserv-er.org/21st-annual-overview-barometer/

Eurofound, 2019. *Future of Manufacturing: Energy Scenario: Employment Implications of the Paris Climate Agreement*. Luxembourg.

Euronews, 2022. EU embargo on Russian coal comes into force. www.euronews.com/my-europe/2022/08/11/eu-embargo-on-russian-coal-comes-into-force

European Commission, 1968. *First Guidelines for a Community Energy Policy: Memorandum Presented by the Commission to the Council, Bulletin of the European Communities, Supplement to No. 12-1968, COM (68) 1040 Final*. Brussels.

1995. *For a European Union Energy Policy*. Green Paper. Brussels.

1997. *Agenda 2000: Commission Opinion on Romania's Application for Membership of the European Union*. Brussels.

2005. *The Attitudes of European Citizens towards Environment: Special Eurobarometer 217*. Brussels.

2006. *Green Paper: A European Strategy for Sustainable, Competitive and Secure Energy*. Brussels.

2007. *An Energy Policy for Europe*. Brussels.
2008a. *Special Eurobarometer 295 Attitudes of European Citizens towards the Environment*. Brussels.
2008b. *Second Strategic Energy Review*. Brussels.
2009a. *The January 2009 Gas Supply Disruption to the EU: An Assessment*. Brussels.
2009b. *Ex-post Evaluation of the Trans-European Energy Networks (TEN-E) Funding Programme 2000–2006*. Brussels.
2010a. *Energy Infrastructure Priorities for 2020 and Beyond*. Brussels.
2010b. *Economic Recovery: Second Batch of 4-Billion-Euro Package Goes to 43 Pipeline and Electricity Projects*. Brussels.
2011a. *Energy Roadmap 2050 Impact Assessment Part 1 Including Part I of Annex 1 Scenarios: Assumptions and Results*. Brussels.
2011b. *A Roadmap for Moving to a Competitive Low Carbon Economy in 2050*. Brussels.
2012. *Connecting Europe: The Energy Infrastructure for Tomorrow*. Brussels.
2013a. *Member State's Energy Dependence: An Indicator-Based Assessment*. Brussels.
2013b. *On the Implementation of the European Energy Programme for Recovery*. Brussels.
2013c. *Green Paper 2030: Main Outcomes of the Public Consultation*. Brussels.
2013d. *Green Paper: A 2030 Framework for Climate and Energy Policies*. Brussels.
2014a. *In-Depth Study of European Energy Security*. Brussels.
2014b. *European Energy Security Strategy*. Brussels.
2014c. *Report on the Implementation of Regulation (EU) 994/2010 and Its Contribution to Solidarity and Preparedness for Gas Disruptions in the EU*. Brussels.
2014d. *Communication from the Commission to the European Parliament and the Council on the Short Term Resilience of the European Gas System*. Brussels.
2014e. *Report on the Findings of the Baltics and Finland Focus Group*. Brussels.
2015a. *A Framework Strategy for a Resilient Energy Union with a Forward-Looking Climate Change Policy* 1–21. https://doi.org/10.1017/CBO9781107415324.004
2015b. *Energy Poverty and Vulnerable Consumers in the Energy Sector across the EU: Analysis of Policies and Measures*. Brussels.
2015c. *Antitrust: Commission Sends Statement of Objections to Gazprom for Alleged Abuse of Dominance on Central and Eastern European Gas Supply Markets*. Brussels.
2015d. *End of Energy Isolation in the Baltics: How the Gas Interconnector Poland-Lithuania (GIPL) Works*. Brussels.
2015e. *First Gas Interconnector between Poland and Lithuania Ends Energy Isolation of the Baltic States*. Brussels.
2015f. *Special Eurobarometer 435, Climate Change*. Brussels.
2015g. *Commission Delegated Regulation (EU) 2016/89 of 18 November 2015 Amending Regulation (EU) No 347/2013 of the European Parliament and of the Council as Regards the Union List of Projects of Common Interest*. Brussels.
2016a. *Report on the Application of the Decision 994/2012/EU Establishing an Information Exchange Mechanism on Intergovernmental Agreements between Member States and Third Countries in the Field of Energy*. Brussels.
2016b. *Commission Decision of 28.10.2016 on Review of the Exemption of the Ostseepipeline-Anbindungsleitung from the Requirements on Third Party Access and Tariff Regulation Granted under Directive 2003/55/EC*. Brussels.
2017a. *State Aid: Commission Clears Investment in Construction of Paks II Nuclear Power Plant in Hungary*. Brussels.
2017b. *Special Eurobarometer 459, September 2017: Climate Change*. Brussels.
2017c. *European Unconventional Oil and Gas Assessment*. Brussels.

2017d. *Indicators for Monitoring Progress towards Energy Union Objectives: A Fully Integrated Internal Energy Market, Wholesale Market Functioning*. Brussels.
2018a. Launch of the EU Energy Poverty Observatory (EPOV). https://ec.europa.eu/energy/en/events/launch-eu-energy-poverty-observatory-epov
2018b. *Data on the Budgetary and Technical Implementation of the European Energy Programme for Recovery*. Brussels.
2018c. *Nuclear Safety and Decommissioning*. Brussels.
2018d. *Electricity Directive: Options on Regulated Prices, Energy Poverty and Vulnerable Customers: A Non-paper from the Commission*. Brussels.
2019a. *The European Green Deal*. Brussels.
2019b. *Extension of Liquefied Natural Gas (LNG) Terminal: Increasing Poland and EU's Energy Security*. Brussels.
2019c. *Energy Union: EU Invests to Upgrade Polish Liquefied Natural Gas Terminal in Swinoujście*. Brussels.
2019d. *State Aid: Commission Approves Public Support for Croatian LNG Terminal at Krk Island*. Brussels.
2019e. *Special Eurobarometer 490 Summary Climate Change Survey Requested by the European Commission*. Brussels. https://doi.org/10.2834/00469
2019f. *RE:START: Strategy for Economic Restructuring of Czech Coal Regions*. Brussels.
2020a. *On the Implementation of the European Energy Programme for Recovery and the European Energy Efficiency Fund*. Brussels.
2020b. 2020 *Report on the State of the Energy Union Pursuant to Regulation (EU) 2018/1999 on Governance of the Energy Union and Climate Action*. Brussels.
2020c. *An EU-Wide Assessment of National Energy and Climate Plans*. Brussels.
2020d. *Assessment of the Final National Energy and Climate Plan of Czechia*. Brussels.
2020e. *Assessment of the Final National Energy and Climate Plan of Poland*. Brussels.
2020f. *Assessment of the Final National Energy and Climate Plan of Hungary*. Brussels.
2020g. *Assessment of the Final National Energy and Climate Plan of Romania*. Brussels.
2020h. *Assessment of the Final National Energy and Climate Plan of Slovakia*. Brussels.
2020i. *Assessment of the Final National Energy and Climate Plan of Slovenia*. Brussels.
2020j. *Baltic States and Poland Sign €720 Million Grant Agreement for the Baltic Synchronisation Project*. Brussels.
2020k. *Gas Interconnector Poland-Lithuania: Works in Progress*.
2020l. *Executite Summary of Poland's National Energy and Climate Pland for the Years*, 2021–2030. Warsaw.
2020m. *European Semester 2020: 2020 Country Reports Annexes D*. Brussels.
2020n. 'Indicators and Data', EU Energy Poverty Observatory. https://energy-poverty.ec.europa.eu/observing-energy-poverty/national-indicators_en
2021a. *From Where Do We Import Energy?* https://ec.europa.eu/eurostat/cache/infographs/energy/bloc-2c.html
2021b. *European Green Deal: Commission Proposes Transformation of EU Economy and Society to Meet Climate Ambitions*. https://transport.ec.europa.eu/news-events/news/european-green-deal-commission-proposes-transformation-eu-economy-and-society-meet-climate-ambitions-2021-07-14_en
2021c. *Data on the Budgetary and Technical Implementation of the European Energy Programme for Recovery*. Brussels.
2021d. *Funding for PCIs*. https://energy.ec.europa.eu/topics/infrastructure/projects-common-interest/funding-projects-common-interest_en
2021e. *Special Eurobarometer 513 Climate Change*. Brussels.

2021f. *Commission Proposes New EU Framework to Decarbonise Gas Markets, Promote Hydrogen and Reduce Methane Emissions*. Brussels.
2021g. *Annex VII to Regulation (EU) No 347/2013*. Brussels.
2022a. *REPowerEU: Joint European Action for More Affordable, Secure and Sustainable Energy*. Brussels.
2022b. *Save Gas for a Safe Winter*. Brussels.
2022c. *EU Emission Trading System*. https://climate.ec.europa.eu/eu-action/eu-emissions-trading-system-eu-ets_en
2022d. *Modernisation Fund*. https://ec.europa.eu/clima/eu-action/funding-climate-action/modernisation-fund_en
2022e. *What Is the Innovation Fund?* https://ec.europa.eu/clima/eu-action/funding-climate-action/innovation-fund/policy-development_en
2022f. *NER 300 Programme*. https://ec.europa.eu/clima/eu-action/funding-climate-action/ner-300-programme_en
2022g. *Innovation Fund Progress Report*. Brussels.
2022h. *Third Call for Large-Scale Projects*. https://climate.ec.europa.eu/eu-action/eu-funding-climate-action/innovation-fund/calls-proposals/large-scale-calls_en
2022i. *EU Energy in Figures: Statistical Pocketbook 2022*. Brussels.
2022j. *Commission Delegated Regulation (EU) 2022/564*. Brussels.
2022k. *The Just Transition Mechanism: Making Sure No One Is Left Behind*. https://commission.europa.eu/strategy-and-policy/priorities-2019-2024/european-green-deal/finance-and-green-deal/just-transition-mechanism_en
2022l. *The Just Transition Fund*. https://commission.europa.eu/funding-tenders/find-funding/eu-funding-programmes/just-transition-fund_en
2022m. *Flash Eurobarometer 514: EU's Response to the Energy Challenges*. Brussels.
2022n. *Energy Emergency: Preparing, Purchasing and Protecting the EU Together*. Brussels.
2023a. *Energy Union Indicators Webtool*. https://energy.ec.europa.eu/data-and-analysis/energy-union-indicators-webtool_en
2023b. *European Climate Infrastructure and Environment Executive Agency*. https://cinea.ec.europa.eu/programmes/life_en#life2014
2023c. *Coal Regions in Transition*. https://energy.ec.europa.eu/topics/oil-gas-and-coal/eu-coal-regions/initiative-coal-regions-transition_en
2023d. *Energy Prices and Costs in Europe*.
2023e. *Quarterly Report on European Gas Markets with Focus on Price Developments in 2022*. Brussels.
2023f. *New Reports Highlight 3rd Quarter Impact of Gas Supply Cuts*. https://energy.ec.europa.eu/news/new-reports-highlight-3rd-quarter-impact-gas-supply-cuts-2023-01-13_en
European Community, 1986. *Single European Act*. Brussels.
European Council, 2003. *European Security Strategy*. Brussels.
2007. *Council Conclusions, March 2007*. Brussels.
2008. *European Council Conclusions, December 2008*. Brussels.
2014. *European Council (23 and 24 October 2014) – Conclusions*. Brussels.
2016. *Shared Vision, Common Action: A Stronger Europe. A Global Strategy for the European Union's Foreign and Security Policy*. Brussels.
2019a. *European Council Meeting (12 December 2019) – Conclusions*. Brussels.
2019b. *European Council Meeting (20 June 2019) – Conclusions*. www.consilium.europa.eu/media/39922/20-21-euco-final-conclusions-en.pdf
2022a. *European Council Meeting (24 and 25 March 2022) – Conclusions*. Brussels.
2022b. *European Council Meeting (20 and 21 October 2022) – Conclusions*. Brussels.

European Court of Auditors, 2016. *EU Nuclear Decommissioning Assistance Programmes in Lithuania, Bulgaria and Slovakia: Some Progress Made since 2011, but Critical Challenges Ahead*. Luxembourg.

2022. *EU Support to Coal Regions: Limited Focus on Socio-economic and Energy Transition*. Luxembourg.

European Investment Bank, 2023. *Investment Report 2022/23 Key Findings*. Luxembourg.

European Parliament, 2016. *Reasoned Opinion of the National Parliament of the Republic of Bulgaria on the Proposal for a Regulation of the European Parliament and of the Council Concerning Measures to Safeguard the Security of Gas Supply and Repealing Regulation (EU) No 994/2010*. Brussels.

2021a. *Inrternal Energy Market*. Brussels.

2021b. *Financing the Trans-European Networks*. Brussels.

2022. *EU Recovery Instrument*. Brussels.

European Parliament and the Council, 2009a. *Directive 2009/28/EC of the European Parliament and of the Council of 23 April 2009 on the Promotion of the Use of Energy from Renewable Sources*. Brussels.

2009b. *Directive 2009/29/EC of the European Parliament and of the Council of 23 April 2009 Amending Directive 2003/87/EC so as to Improve and Extend the Greenhouse Gas Emission Allowance Trading Scheme of the Community*. Brussels.

2009c. *Regulation (EC) No 663/2009 of the European Parliament and of the Council of 13 July 2009 Establishing a Programme to Aid Economic Recovery by Granting Community Financial Assistance to Projects in the Field of Energy*. Brussels.

2013. *Regulation (EU) No 347/2013 of the European Parliament and of the Council of 17 April 2013 on Guidelines for Trans-European Energy Infrastructure*. Brussels.

2018. *Directive (EU) 2018/2001 of the European Parliament and of the Council of 11 December 2018 on the Ppromotion of the Use of Energy from Renewable Sources*. Brussels.

2021a. *Regulation (EU) 2021/241 of 12 February 2021 Establishing the Recovery and Resilience Facility*. Brussels.

2021b. *European Climate Law*. Brussels.

2021c. *Regulation (EU) 2021/1056 of the European Parliament and of the Council of 24 June 2021 Establishing the Just Transition Fund*. Brussels.

Europolitics, 2008. MEPs squabble over Nord Stream pipeline. Europolitics. www.europolitics.info/meps-squabble-over-nord-stream-pipeline-artr147856-10.html

Eurostat, 2021. *Energy Statistical Country Data Sheet*. Brussels.

2022a. Renewable energy statistics. https://ec.europa.eu/eurostat/statistics-explained/index.php?title=Renewable_energy_statistics

2022b. Energy production and imports. https://ec.europa.eu/eurostat/statistics-explained/index.php?title=Energy_production_and_imports

2022c. Energy production and imports, January 2022. https://ec.europa.eu/eurostat/statistics-explained/index.php?title=Energy_production_and_imports

2023a. EU energy mix and import dependency. https://ec.europa.eu/eurostat/web/products-eurostat-news/-/edn-20220209-1

2023b. Share of renewable energy more than doubled between 2004 and 2021. https://ec.europa.eu/eurostat/statistics-explained/index.php?title=Renewable_energy_statistics#Share_of_renewable_energy_more_than_doubled_between_2004_and_2021

2023c. Share of energy from renewable sources. https://ec.europa.eu/eurostat/databrowser/view/NRG_IND_REN__custom_5097043/default/table?lang=en

2023d. Greenhouse gas emissions by source sector (source: EEA). https://ec.europa.eu/eurostat/cache/metadata/en/env_air_gge_esms.htm

2023e. Annual inflation down to 6.9% in the euro area. https://ec.europa.eu/eurostat/documents/2995521/16324910/2-19042023-AP-EN.pdf/ff3d6b28-9c8f-41cd-714f-d1fd38afob15

2023f. EU gas consumption decreased by 19%. https://ec.europa.eu/eurostat/web/products-eurostat-news/w/DDN-20230221-1

eustream, 2011. Projekt reverzného toku plynu je dokončený.

2021. Annual report 1 August 2020–31 July 2021. Bratislava.

Fabbrini, F., 2022. The legal architecture of the economic responses to COVID-19: EMU beyond the pandemic. *JCMS J. Common Mark. Stud.* 60, 186–203. https://doi.org/10.1111/jcms.13271

Fagan, A., 2004. *Environment and Democracy in the Czech Republic: The Environmental Movement in the Transition Process*. Edward Elgar Publishing, Cheltenham. https://doi.org/10.4337/9781845420604

Fagan, A., Buzogány, A., 2022. Beyond Europeanization: political ecology and environmentalism in Central and Eastern Europe. *Env. Polit.* 31, 1203–1213. https://doi.org/10.1080/09644016.2022.2147652

Falkner, G., Treib, O., 2008. Three worlds of compliance or four? The EU-15 compared to new member states. *J. Common Mark. Stud.* 46, 293–313. https://doi.org/10.1111/j.1468-5965.2007.00777.x

Fawn, R., 2006. The Temelín nuclear power plant and the European Union in Austrian–Czech relations. *Communist Post-Communist Stud.* 39, 101–119. https://doi.org/10.1016/j.postcomstud.2005.12.001

Fekete, H., Kuramochi, T., Roelfsema, M., Elzen, M. den, Forsell, N., Höhne, N., Luna, L., Hans, F., Sterl, S., Olivier, J., van Soest, H., Frank, S., Gusti, M., 2021. A review of successful climate change mitigation policies in major emitting economies and the potential of global replication. *Renew. Sustain. Energy Rev.* 137, 110602. https://doi.org/10.1016/j.rser.2020.110602

Fernandez, R., Palazuelos, E., 2014. A political economy approach to the European Union gas model: continuities and changes. *JCMS J. Common Mark. Stud.* 52, 495–511. https://doi.org/10.1111/jcms.12113

Ferris, N., 2021. More renewables does not have to mean higher electricity bills. Energy Monitor. www.energymonitor.ai/policy/market-design/more-renewables-does-not-have-to-mean-higher-electricity-bills

Financial Times, 2021. Carbon pricing: twists on the winding road to net zero. *Financial Times*, 29 December.

2022. Germany fires up coal plants to avert gas shortage as Russia cuts supply. *Financial Times*, 19 June.

Finke, D., 2017. Underneath the culture of consensus: transparency, credible commitments and voting in the Council of Ministers. *Eur. Union Polit.* 18, 339–361. https://doi.org/10.1177/1465116517709972

Fischhendler, I., Nathan, D., Boymel, D., 2015. Marketing renewable energy through geopolitics: solar farms in Israel. *Glob. Environ. Polit.* 15, 98–120. https://doi.org/10.1162/GLEP_a_00300

Fisher, S., 2006. *Political Change in Post-Communist Slovakia and Croatia: From Nationalist to Europeanist*. Palgrave, London.

Fitzgerald, J., 2012. The messy politics of 'clean coal': the shaping of a contested term in Appalachia's energy debate. *Organ. Environ.* 25, 437–451. https://doi.org/10.1177/1086026612466091

Fleck, A., 2022. Here's where energy poverty is felt most in Europe. World Economic Forum. www.weforum.org/agenda/2022/11/energy-poverty-in-europe-heating-gas/

Fleming, R., 2019. A legal perspective on gas solidarity. *Energy Policy* 124, 102–110. https://doi.org/10.1016/j.enpol.2018.09.037

Ford, A., Newell, P., 2021. Regime resistance and accommodation: toward a neo-Gramscian perspective on energy transitions. *Energy Res. Soc. Sci.* 79, 102163. https://doi.org/10.1016/j.erss.2021.102163

Foy, H., 2014. Poland on course for battle on new EU climate change targets. *Financial Times*, 1 October.

France 24, 2009. Russia agrees to higher oil transit fees with Ukraine's Naftogaz. www.france24.com/en/20091229-russia-agrees-higher-oil-transit-fees-with-ukraines-naftogaz

2018. Greenpeace ends Polish coal-plant protest. France 24, 29 November. www.france24.com/en/20181129-greenpeace-ends-polish-coal-plant-protest

2020a. Romania's mining heartland faces up to post-coal future. France 24, 3 December. www.france24.com/en/live-news/20201203-romania-s-mining-heartland-faces-up-to-post-coal-future

2020b. Hungary says it blocked EU budget over migration 'blackmail'. France 24, 18 November. www.france24.com/en/europe/20201118-hungary-says-it-blocked-eu-budget-over-migration-blackmail

2022. Paris, Berlin 'agree to disagree' on French push to label nuclear energy green. France 24, 7 January. www.france24.com/en/europe/20220107-paris-berlin-agree-to-disagree-on-french-push-to-label-nuclear-energy-green

Franki, V., Višković, A., 2015. Energy security, policy and technology in South East Europe: presenting and applying an energy security index to Croatia. *Energy* 90, 494–507. https://doi.org/10.1016/j.energy.2015.07.087

Frantál, B., Malý, J., 2017. Close or renew? Factors affecting local community support for rebuilding nuclear power plants in the Czech Republic. *Energy Policy* 104, 134–143. https://doi.org/10.1016/j.enpol.2017.01.048

Fraune, C., Knodt, M., 2018. Sustainable energy transformations in an age of populism, post-truth politics, and local resistance. *Energy Res. Soc. Sci.* 43, 1–7. https://doi.org/10.1016/j.erss.2018.05.029

Fridays for Future, 2022. Map. https://fridaysforfuture.org/action-map/map/

Friends of the Earth, 2021. Oil shale plant halted in Estonia after youth activists' court case. https://friendsoftheearth.eu/news/shale-oil-plant-halted-in-estonia/

Friends of the Earth Europe, 2015. We are the limits! Anti-coal protests across Czech Republic. https://friendsoftheearth.eu/news/we-are-the-limits-anti-coal-protests-across-czech-republic/

Fuller, S., McCauley, D., 2016. Framing energy justice: perspectives from activism and advocacy. *Energy Res. Soc. Sci.* 11, 1–8. https://doi.org/10.1016/j.erss.2015.08.004

G7, 1992. Economic Declaration: Working Together for Growth and a Safer World. https://g7g20-documents.org/fileadmin/G7G20_documents/1992/G7/Germany/Leaders/1%20Leaders'%20Language/Economic%20Declaration%20-%20Working%20Together%20for%20Growth%20and%20a%20Safer%20World_08071992.pdf

2021. Carbis Bay G7 summit communiqué: our shared agenda for global action to build back better. www.whitehouse.gov/briefing-room/statements-releases/2021/06/13/carbis-bay-g7-summit-communique/

Gabbatiss, J., 2018a. Poland broke law by logging ancient forest, rules EU court. *The Independent*, 17 April.

2018b. COP24: Poland shows no signs of breaking coal addiction despite toxic air and warnings of climate disaster. *The Independent*, 8 December.

Gál, Z., 2021. From economic transformation to energy transition: the legacy of thirty years of post-communist development, in: Mišík, M., Oravcová, V. (Eds.), *From Economic to*

Energy Transition: Three Decades of Transitions in Central and Eastern Europe. Springer International, Cham, pp. 29–61. https://doi.org/10.1007/978-3-030-55085-1_2

Galbreath, D. J., Lašas, A., 2011. The 'Baltic' factor in EU–Russian relations: in search of coherence and co-operation in an era of complexity. *J. Contemp. Eur. Stud.* 19, 261–272. https://doi.org/10.1080/14782804.2011.580914

Ganev, V. I., 2014. The legacies of 1989: Bulgaria's year of civic anger. *J. Democr.* 25, 33–45.

Gatto, A., 2022. The energy futures we want: a research and policy agenda for energy transitions. *Energy Res. Soc. Sci.* 89, 102639. https://doi.org/10.1016/j.erss.2022.102639

Gawlikowska-Fyk, A., 2019. Poland: coping with the challenges of decarbonization and diversification, in: Godzimirski, J. M. (Ed.), *New Political Economy of Energy in Europe: Power to Project, Power to Adapt*. Springer International, Cham, pp. 195–214. https://doi.org/10.1007/978-3-319-93360-3_8

Geden, O., Fischer, S., 2014. *Moving Targets: Negotiations on the EU's Energy and Climate Policy Objectives for the Post-2020 Period and Implications for the German Energy Transition*. Berlin.

Geden, O., Marcelis, C., Maurer, A., 2006. *Perspectives for the European Union's External Energy Policy*. Berlin.

Geels, F. W., 2005. Processes and patterns in transitions and system innovations: refining the co-evolutionary multi-level perspective. *Technol. Forecast. Soc. Change* 72, 681–696. https://doi.org/10.1016/j.techfore.2004.08.014

2010. Ontologies, socio-technical transitions (to sustainability), and the multi-level perspective. *Res. Policy* 39, 495–510. https://doi.org/10.1016/j.respol.2010.01.022

2014. Regime resistance against low-carbon transitions: introducing politics and power into the multi-level perspective. *Theory Cult. Soc.* 31, 21–40. https://doi.org/10.1177/0263276414531627

Geels, F. W., Berkhout, F., van Vuuren, D. P., 2016. Bridging analytical approaches for low-carbon transitions. *Nat. Clim. Chang.* 6, 576–583. https://doi.org/10.1038/nclimate2980

Geels, F. W., Sovacool, B., Schwanen, T., Sorrell, S., 2017. Sociotechnical transitions for deep decarbonization. *Policy Forum* 357, 1242–1244.

Geiger, J., 2023. Germany will need to hold onto coal power for longer. OilPrice.com, 16 January. https://oilprice.com/Latest-Energy-News/World-News/Germany-Will-Need-To-Hold-Onto-Coal-Power-For-Longer.html

Geny, F., 2010. Can unconventional gas be a game changer in European gas markets? Working paper, Oxford Institute for Energy Studies, Oxford.

Genys, D., Krikštolaitis, R., 2017. Switching political nuclear energy preferences, changing public attitude. *Balt. J. Law Polit.* 10, 225–243. https://doi.org/10.1515/bjlp-2017-0018

Godzimirski, J. M., 2013. *Russian Energy in a Changing World: What Is the Outlook for the Hydrocarbons Superpower?* Routledge, London.

2016. *EU Leadership in Energy and Environmental Governance: Global and Local Challenges and Responses*. Palgrave, London.

Gökgöz, F., Güvercin, M. T., 2018. Energy security and renewable energy efficiency in EU. *Renew. Sustain. Energy Rev.* 96, 226–239. https://doi.org/10.1016/j.rser.2018.07.046

Goldberg, S. M., 2011. Security of supply in the context of European energy market liberalisation: a brief overview. *Int. Bus. Law J.* 433–462.

Goldman, G. T., Berman, E., Halpern, M., Johnson, C., Kothari, Y., Reed, G., Rosenberg, A. A., 2017. Ensuring scientific integrity in the age of Trump. *Science* 80(355), 696–698. https://doi.org/10.1126/science.aam5733

Goldthau, A., 2013. *The Handbook of Global Energy Policy*. Wiley, London.

2016. *Assessing Nord Stream 2: Regulation, Geopolitics & Energy Security in the EU, Central Eastern Europe & the UK*. London.
2018. *The Politics of Shale Gas in Eastern Europe: Energy Security, Contested Technologies and the Social Licence to Frack*. Cambridge University Press, Cambridge.
Goldthau, A., Eicke, L., Weko, S., 2020. The global energy transition and the Global South, in: Hafner, M., Tagliapietra, S. (Eds.), *The Geopolitics of the Global Energy Transition*. Springer International, Cham, pp. 319–339. https://doi.org/10.1007/978-3-030-39066-2_14
Goldthau, A., Sitter, N., 2015. *A Liberal Actor in a Realist World: The European Union Regulatory State and the Global Political Economy of Energy*. Oxford University Press, Oxford. https://doi.org/10.17159/1727-3781/2017/v20i0a1681
Goldthau, A., Sovacool, B. K., 2016. Energy technology, politics, and interpretative frames: shale gas fracking in Eastern Europe. *Glob. Environ. Polit.* 16, 50–69. https://doi.org/10.1162/GLEP_a_00375
Gonzalez-Salazar, M. A., Kirsten, T., Prchlik, L., 2018. Review of the operational flexibility and emissions of gas- and coal-fired power plants in a future with growing renewables. *Renew. Sustain. Energy Rev.* 82, 1497–1513. https://doi.org/10.1016/j.rser.2017.05.278
Gosens, J., Turnbull, A. B. H., Jotzo, F., 2022. China's decarbonization and energy security plans will reduce seaborne coal imports: results from an installation-level model. *Joule* 6, 782–815. https://doi.org/10.1016/j.joule.2022.03.008
Gotev, G., 2015. *Seven EU Countries Oppose Nord Stream*. Brussels.
Götz, R., 2007. *Russian Gas and European Energy Security*. Stiftung Wissenschaft und Politik, Berlin.
Government of the Czech Republic, 2022. *Programové prohlášení vlády*. Prague.
2019. *Transformácia uhoľného regiónu horná Nitra*. Bratislava.
Government of Slovenia, 2021. Slovenia joins the Powering Past Coal Alliance initiative. www.gov.si/en/news/2021-11-05-slovenia-joins-the-powering-past-coal-alliance-initiative/
Grant, Z. P., Tilley, J., 2019. Fertile soil: explaining variation in the success of Green parties. *West Eur. Polit.* 42, 495–516. https://doi.org/10.1080/01402382.2018.1521673
Gravey, V., Jordan, A., 2016. Does the European Union have a reverse gear? Policy dismantling in a hyperconsensual polity. *J. Eur. Public Policy* 23, 1180–1198. https://doi.org/10.1080/13501763.2016.1186208
Gravey, V., Jordan, A. J., 2020. Policy dismantling at EU level: reaching the limits of 'an ever-closer ecological union'? *Public Adm.* 98, 349–362. https://doi.org/10.1111/padm.12605
Gray, D., 1995. *Reforming the Energy Sector in Transition Economies: Selected Experience and Lessons*. Washington, DC.
Green Growth Group, 2013. *Going for Green Growth: The Case for Ambitious and Immediate EU Low Carbon Action*. www.gov.uk/government/publications/going-for-green-growth-the-case-for-ambitious-and-immediate-eu-low-carbon-action
Grigas, A., 2013a. Energy policy: the Achilles heel of Baltic States, in: Grigas, A., Kasekamp, A., Maslauskaite, K., Zorgenfreija, L. (Eds.), *The Baltic States in the EU: Yesterday, Today and Tomorrow*. Notre Europe – Jacques Delors Institute, Paris.
2013b. *The Politics of Energy and Memory between the Baltic States and Russia*. Routledge, London.
Gritsenko, D., 2018. Explaining choices in energy infrastructure development as a network of adjacent action situations: the case of LNG in the Baltic Sea region. *Energy Policy* 112, 74–83. https://doi.org/10.1016/j.enpol.2017.10.014
Groenleer, M. L. P., Van Schaik, L. G., 2007. United we stand? The European Union's international actorness in the cases of the International Criminal Court and the Kyoto

Protocol. *JCMS J. Common Mark. Stud.* 45, 969–998. https://doi.org/10.1111/j.1468-5965.2007.00756.x

Gros, D., Steinherr, A., 2004. *Economic Transition in Central and Eastern Europe: Planting the Seeds.* Cambridge University Press, Cambridge. https://doi.org/10.1017/CBO9780511805646

Grubler, A., Wilson, C., Nemet, G., 2016. Apples, oranges, and consistent comparisons of the temporal dynamics of energy transitions. *Energy Res. Soc. Sci.* 22, 18–25. https://doi.org/10.1016/j.erss.2016.08.015

Gündüzyeli, E., Flisowska, J., 2020. Poland goes all out on coal rescue against EU's higher climate goal. Euractiv, 23 December. www.euractiv.com/section/energy/opinion/poland-goes-all-out-on-coal-rescue-against-eus-higher-climate-goal/

Gurgul, H., Lach, Ł., 2011. The role of coal consumption in the economic growth of the Polish economy in transition. *Energy Policy* 39, 2088–2099.

Gürsan, C., de Gooyert, V., 2021. The systemic impact of a transition fuel: Does natural gas help or hinder the energy transition? *Renew. Sustain. Energy Rev.* 138, 110552. https://doi.org/10.1016/j.rser.2020.110552

Gürtler, K., Postpischil, R., Quitzow, R., 2019. The dismantling of renewable energy policies: the cases of Spain and the Czech Republic. *Energy Policy* 133, 110881. https://doi.org/10.1016/j.enpol.2019.110881

Gustafson, T., 2020. *The Bridge: Natural Gas in a Redivided Europe.* Harvard University Press, Cambridge, MA.

Haber, H., 2018. Liberalizing markets, liberalizing welfare? Economic reform and social regulation in the EU's electricity regime. *J. Eur. Public Policy* 25, 307–326. https://doi.org/10.1080/13501763.2016.1249012

Hager, C., Stefes, C. H., 2016. *Germany's Energy Transition: A Comparative Perspective.* Palgrave Macmillan, New York.

Hamed, T. A., Bressler, L., 2019. Energy security in Israel and Jordan: the role of renewable energy sources. *Renew. Energy* 135, 378–389. https://doi.org/10.1016/j.renene.2018.12.036

Hancher, L., Marhold, A., 2019. A common EU framework regulating import pipelines for gas? Exploring the Commission's proposal to amend the 2009 Gas Directive. *J. Energy Nat. Resour. Law* 37, 289–303. https://doi.org/10.1080/02646811.2019.1569873

Hanley, S., Vachudova, M. A., 2018. Understanding the illiberal turn: democratic backsliding in the Czech Republic. *East Eur. Polit.* 34, 276–296. https://doi.org/10.1080/21599165.2018.1493457

Harper, J., 2018. Poland's pro-coal government goes green. DW, 5 September. www.dw.com/en/polands-pro-coal-government-goes-green/a-45357008

Harrabin, R., 2019. Paris Agreement: Trump confirms US will leave climate accord. BBC. www.bbc.co.uk/news/world-us-canada-50165596

Hart, P.'t, 1993. Symbols, rituals and power: the lost dimensions of crisis management. *J. Contingencies Cris. Manag.* 1, 36–50. https://doi.org/10.1111/j.1468-5973.1993.tb00005.x

Haughton, T., 2007. When does the EU make a difference? Conditionality and the accession process in Central and Eastern Europe. *Polit. Stud. Rev.* 5, 233–246. https://doi.org/10.1111/j.1478-9299.2007.00130.x

2011. Half full but also half empty: conditionality, compliance and the quality of democracy in Central and Eastern Europe. *Polit. Stud. Rev.* 9, 323–333. https://doi.org/10.1111/j.1478-9302.2010.00220.x

Haughton, T., Malová, D., 2007. Emerging patterns of EU membership: drawing lessons from Slovakia's first two years as a member state. *Politics* 27, 69–75. https://doi.org/10.1111/j.1467-9256.2007.00281.x

Hauser, P., Heinrichs, H. U., Gillessen, B., Müller, T., 2018. Implications of diversification strategies in the European natural gas market for the German energy system. *Energy* 151, 442–454. https://doi.org/10.1016/j.energy.2018.03.065

Hausfather, Z., 2015. Bounding the climate viability of natural gas as a bridge fuel to displace coal. *Energy Policy* 86, 286–294. https://doi.org/10.1016/j.enpol.2015.07.012

Hawker, G., Bell, K., Gill, S., 2017. Electricity security in the European Union: the conflict between national capacity mechanisms and the single market. *Energy Res. Soc. Sci.* 24, 51–58. https://doi.org/10.1016/j.erss.2016.12.009

Hawkins, A., 2023. China ramps up coal power despite carbon neutral pledges. *The Guardian*, 23 April.

Hay, C., 1996. Narrating crisis: the discursive construction of the 'winter of discontent'. *Sociology* 30, 253–277. https://doi.org/10.1177/0038038596030002004

Heffron, R. J., McCauley, D., 2018. What is the 'just transition'? *Geoforum* 88, 74–77. https://doi.org/10.1016/j.geoforum.2017.11.016

Hefner, R. A., 2009. *The Grand Energy Transition: The Rise of Energy Gases, Sustainable Life and the Next Great Expansion*. Wiley, New York.

Heinrich, A., 2018. Securitisation in the gas sector: energy security debates concerning the example of the Nord Stream pipeline, in: Szulecki, K. (Ed.), *Energy Security in Europe: Divergent Perceptions and Policy Challenges*. Springer International, Cham, pp. 61–91. https://doi.org/10.1007/978-3-319-64964-1_3

Heisenberg, D., 2005. The institution of 'consensus' in the European Union: formal versus informal decision-making in the Council. *Eur. J. Polit. Res.* 44, 65–90. https://doi.org/10.1111/j.1475-6765.2005.00219.x

Helm, D., 2007. *The New Energy Paradigm*. Oxford University Press, Oxford. https://doi.org/10.1108/17506220910970623

Heptonstall, P. J., Gross, R. J. K., 2021. A systematic review of the costs and impacts of integrating variable renewables into power grids. *Nat. Energy* 6, 72–83. https://doi.org/10.1038/s41560-020-00695-4

Hernik, J., Noszczyk, T., Rutkowska, A., 2019. Towards a better understanding of the variables that influence renewable energy sources in eastern Poland. *J. Clean. Prod.* 241, 118075. https://doi.org/10.1016/j.jclepro.2019.118075

Herranz-Surrallés, A., 2016. An emerging EU energy diplomacy? Discursive shifts, enduring practices. *J. Eur. Public Policy* 23, 1386–1405. https://doi.org/10.1080/13501763.2015.1083044

2017. Energy diplomacy under scrutiny: parliamentary control of intergovernmental agreements with third-country suppliers. *West Eur. Polit.* 40, 183–201. https://doi.org/10.1080/01402382.2016.1240406

Herranz-Surrallés, A., Solorio, I., Fairbrass, J. (Eds.), 2022. *Renegotiating Authority in EU Energy and Climate Policy*. Routledge, London.

Herweg, N., 2017. *European Union Policy-Making: The Regulatory Shift in Natural Gas Market Policy*. Palgrave Macmillan, London.

Hewitt, R. J., Bradley, N., Baggio Compagnucci, A., Barlagne, C., Ceglarz, A., Cremades, R., McKeen, M., Otto, I. M., Slee, B., 2019. Social innovation in community energy in Europe: a review of the evidence. *Front. Energy Res.* 7. https://doi.org/10.3389/fenrg.2019.00031

Hickel, J., 2020. Quantifying national responsibility for climate breakdown: an equality-based attribution approach for carbon dioxide emissions in excess of the planetary boundary. *Lancet Planet. Heal.* 4, e399–e404. https://doi.org/10.1016/S2542–5196(20)30196-0

Hilton, I., Kerr, O., 2017. The Paris Agreement: China's 'new normal' role in international climate negotiations. *Clim. Policy* 17, 48–58. https://doi.org/10.1080/14693062.2016.1228521

Hilton, J., 2018. Bulgarian coal communities face dark times. DW.com, 27 December. www.dw.com/en/bulgarian-coal-communities-face-dark-times/a-46825497

Hiteva, R. P., Maltby, T., 2014. Standing in the way by standing in the middle: the case of state-owned natural gas intermediaries in Bulgaria. *Geoforum* 54, 120–133. https://doi.org/10.1016/j.geoforum.2014.04.006

Hodge, B.-M. S., Jain, H., Brancucci, C., Seo, G.-S., Korpås, M., Kiviluoma, J., Holttinen, H., Smith, J. C., Orths, A., Estanqueiro, A., Söder, L., Flynn, D., Vrana, T. K., Kenyon, R. W., Kroposki, B., 2020. Addressing technical challenges in 100% variable inverter-based renewable energy power systems. *WIREs Energy Environ.* 9, e376. https://doi.org/10.1002/wene.376

Hodgson, C., 2022. COP27: UN chief calls for rich countries to agree 'climate solidarity pact'. *Financial Times*, 7 November.

Hoegh-Guldberg, O., Jacob, D., Taylor, M., Guillén Bolaños, T., Bindi, M., Brown, S., Camilloni, I. A., Diedhiou, A., Djalante, R., Ebi, K., Engelbrecht, F., Guiot, J., Hijioka, Y., Mehrotra, S., Hope, C. W., Payne, A. J., Pörtner, H.-O., Seneviratne, S. I., Thomas, A., Warren, R., Zhou, G., 2019. The human imperative of stabilizing global climate change at 1.5°C. *Science* 365(6459). https://doi.org/10.1126/science.aaw6974

Hofmann, S. C., Staeger, U., 2019. Frame contestation and collective securitisation: the case of EU energy policy. *West Eur. Polit.* 42, 323–345. https://doi.org/10.1080/01402382.2018.1510197

Högselius, P., 2012. *Red Gas*. Palgrave Macmillan, London.

Holesch, A., Kyriazi, A., 2022. Democratic backsliding in the European Union: the role of the Hungarian-Polish coalition. *East Eur. Polit.* 38, 1–20. https://doi.org/10.1080/21599165.2020.1865319

Holmgren, S., Pever, M., Fischer, K., 2019. Constructing low-carbon futures? Competing storylines in the Estonian energy sector's translation of EU energy goals. *Energy Policy* 135, 111063. https://doi.org/10.1016/j.enpol.2019.111063

Holz, F., Sogalla, R., von Hirschhausen, C. R., Kemfert, C., 2022. Energy supply security in Germany can be guaranteed even without natural gas from Russia: special issue on the war in Ukraine. DIW focus. www.diw.de/de/diw_01.c.839511.de/publikationen/diw_focus/2022_0007/energy_supply_security_in_germany_can_be_guaranteed_even_without_natural_gas_from_russia.html

Hope, K., 2014. Bulgarians see Russian hand in anti-shale protests. *Financial Times*, 30 November.

Hosli, M. O., Mattila, M., Uriot, M., 2011. Voting in the Council of the European Union after the 2004 enlargement: a comparison of old and new member states. *J. Common Mark. Stud.* 49, 1249–1270. https://doi.org/10.1111/j.1468-5965.2011.02196.x

Hubbert, M. K., 1956. Nuclear energy and the fossil fuels. Shell Development Company, Exploration and Production Research Division, Houston, TX. www.energycrisis.com/Hubbert/1956/1956.pdf

Huber, R. A., 2020. The role of populist attitudes in explaining climate change skepticism and support for environmental protection. *Env. Polit.* 29, 959–982. https://doi.org/10.1080/09644016.2019.1708186

Huber, R. A., Fesenfeld, L., Bernauer, T., 2020. Political populism, responsiveness, and public support for climate mitigation. *Clim. Policy* 20, 373–386. https://doi.org/10.1080/14693062.2020.1736490

Hungarian Government, 2012. *National Security Strategy*. Budapest.

Huntington, S. P., 1993. *The Third Wave: Democratization in the Late Twentieth Century*. University of Oklahoma Press, Norman.

Huysmans, J., 2011. What's in an act? On security speech acts and little security nothings. *Secur. Dialogue* 42, 371–383.

IAEA, 2021. *Nuclear Power Reactors in the World*. Vienna.

2022. IAEA Projections for Nuclear Power Growth Increase for Second Year Amid Climate, Energy Security Concerns. www.iaea.org/newscenter/pressreleases/iaea-projections-for-nuclear-power-growth-increase-for-second-year-amid-climate-energy-security-concerns

iDnes, 2022. Podpora jádra stoupá. Měli bychom být soběstační, říkají Češi v průzkumu. iDnes. www.idnes.cz/ekonomika/domaci/podpora-jaderne-energie-v-cr.A221128_122236_ekonomika_ric

IEA, 2016. *Energy Policies of IEA Countries: Poland 2016 Review*. Paris.

2017. *Coal 2017: Analysis and Forecasts to 2022*. Paris.

2018. *Slovak Republic: 2018 Review*. Paris.

2022a. *Coal 2022: Analysis and Forecast to 2025*. Paris.

2022b. *Global Energy Review: CO_2 Emissions in 2021*. Paris.

2022c. *Renewables*. Paris.

2022d. *Energy System Overview*. www.iea.org/reports/energy-system-overview

2022e. *World Energy Outlook 2022: Executive Summary*. Paris.

2022f. *World Energy Employment: Executive Summary*. Paris.

2022g. *World Energy Investment 2022*. Paris.

IMF, 2022. *Fossil Fuel Subsidies*. www.imf.org/en/Publications/WP/Issues/2023/08/22/IMF-Fossil-Fuel-Subsidies-Data-2023-Update-537281

Immergut, E. M., 2006. Historical-institutionalism in political science and the problem of change, in: Wimmer, A., Kössler, R. (Eds.), *Understanding Change: Models, Methodologies and Metaphors*. Palgrave Macmillan UK, London, pp. 237–259. https://doi.org/10.1057/9780230524644_17

The Independent, 2021. Polish miners, power workers, protest shift away from coal. Via AP News, 9 June.

2022. Czech Republic to end coal use by 2033, boost nuclear power. *The Independent*, 7 January.

Industriall, 2021. Trade unions protest in Sofia against the lack of clear vision on a just transition in Bulgaria. https://news.industriall-europe.eu/Article/656

Innovation and Networks Executive Agency, 2021. First Croatian LNG terminal officially inaugurated in Krk island. https://cinea.ec.europa.eu/news-events/news/first-croatian-lng-terminal-officially-inaugurated-krk-island-2021-01-29_en

Intellinews, 2020. French Orano to join $8bn nuclear power plant expansion project in Romania. www.intellinews.com/french-orano-to-join-8bn-nuclear-power-plant-expansion-project-in-romania-195122/

IPCC, 2014. *Climate Change 2014: Mitigation of Climate Change*. Cambridge.

2018. Global warming of 1.5°C. www.ipcc.ch/site/assets/uploads/sites/2/2022/06/SPM_version_report_LR.pdf

2022a. *Headline Statements*. www.ipcc.ch/report/ar6/syr/resources/spm-headline-statements/

2022b. *Climate Change 2022, Mitigation of Climate Change, Summary for Policymakers*. Geneva.

IRENA, 2020. *Renewable Energy Prospects for Central and South-Eastern Europe Energy Connectivity*. Abu Dhabi.

2021. *Renewable Energy and Jobs: Annual Review 2021*. Abu Dhabi.

Isaacs, R., Molnar, A., 2017. Island in the neoliberal stream: energy security and soft re-nationalisation in Hungary. *J. Contemp. Eur. Stud.* 25, 107–126. https://doi.org/10.1080/14782804.2016.1198688

Isoaho, K., Markard, J., 2020. The politics of technology decline: discursive struggles over coal phase-out in the UK. *Rev. Policy Res.* 37, 342–368. https://doi.org/10.1111/ropr.12370

ITV, 2021. Western countries 'shoulder responsibility' for climate change action. www.itv.com/news/2021-10-18/western-countries-shoulder-responsibility-for-climate-change-action

Iyer, G., Ledna, C., Clarke, L., Edmonds, J., McJeon, H., Kyle, P., Williams, J. H., 2017. Measuring progress from nationally determined contributions to mid-century strategies. *Nat. Clim. Chang.* 7, 871–874. https://doi.org/10.1038/s41558–017-0005-9

Jack, V., 2022. Energy emergency revives Estonia's polluting oil shale industry. Politico, 28 August. www.politico.eu/article/energy-emergency-revives-estonias-polluting-oil-shale-industry/

Jackson, J., 2023. Polish backpedal on windfarms put EU funds at risk. EUobserver, 31 January. https://euobserver.com/green-economy/156661

Jahn, D., 2021. Quick and dirty: how populist parties in government affect greenhouse gas emissions in EU member states. *J. Eur. Public Policy* 28, 980–997. https://doi.org/10.1080/13501763.2021.1918215

Jamasb, T., Pollitt, M., 2005. Electricity market reform in the European Union: review of progress toward liberalization & integration. *Energy J.* 26, 11–41.

Jamasmie, C., 2016. Bulgaria coal miners stay underground to protest layoffs, delayed salaries. Mining.com, 12 October. www.mining.com/bulgaria-coal-miners-stay-underground-to-protest-layoffs-delayed-salaries/

Janda, K., 2018. Slovak electricity market and the price merit order effect of photovoltaics. *Energy Policy* 122, 551–562. https://doi.org/10.1016/j.enpol.2018.07.021

Janeliūnas, T., 2009. Lithuanian energy strategy and its implications on regional cooperation, in: Spruds, A., Rostoks, T. (Eds.), *Energy: Pulling the Baltic Sea Region Together or Apart?* Latvian Institute of International Affairs, Riga, pp. 190–222.

2021. Energy transformation in Lithuania: aiming for the grand changes, in: Mišík, M., Oravcová, V. (Eds.), *From Economic to Energy Transition: Three Decades of Transitions in Central and Eastern Europe*. Springer International, Cham, pp. 283–313. https://doi.org/10.1007/978-3-030-55085-1_10

Jänicke, M., Quitzow, R., 2016. Multi-level reinforcement in European climate and energy governance: mobilizing economic interests at the sub-national levels. *Environmental Policy and Governance*, 27, 122–136. https://doi.org/10.1002/eet.1748

Jankó, F., Drüszler, Á., Gálos, B., Móricz, N., Papp-Vancsó, J., Pieczka, I., Pongrácz, R., Rasztovits, E., Dezső, Z. S., Szabó, O., 2020. Recalculating climate change consensus: the question of position and rhetoric. *J. Clean. Prod.* 254, 120127. https://doi.org/10.1016/j.jclepro.2020.120127

Jaramillo, P., Griffin, W. M., Matthews, H. S., 2007. Comparative life-cycle air emissions of coal, domestic natural gas, LNG, and SNG for electricity generation. *Environ. Sci. Technol.* 41, 6290–6296. https://doi.org/10.1021/es063031o

Jarosz, A., 2011. Rola Unii Europejskiej w sporze o gazociąg północny. Komentarze w prasie polskiej i niemieckiej. *Rocz. Pol.* https://doi.org/10.35757/RPN.2011.19.07

Jasanoff, S., Simmet, H. R., 2017. No funeral bells: public reason in a 'post-truth' age. *Soc. Stud. Sci.* 47, 751–770. https://doi.org/10.1177/0306312717731936

JAVYS, 2019. *Decommissioning of Nuclear Facilities: A1 Nuclear Power Plant*. Bratislava.

2023. Spoločnosť JAVYS uskutočnila v roku 2022 päť prepráv vyhoretého jadrového paliva a zabezpečovala päť prepráv čerstvého jadrového paliva. www.javys.sk/sk/informacny-servis/aktuality-tlacove-spravy-napisali-o-nas/tlacove-spravy/2057-spolocnost-javys-uskutocnila-v-roku-2022-pat-preprav-vyhoreteho-jadroveho-paliva-a-zabezpecovala-pat-preprav-cerstveho-jadroveho-paliva

Jenčová, I., 2022. Európa bude šetriť plynom za cenu veľkých ústupkov. Euractiv.sk, 27 July.

Jenkins, K. E. H., Sovacool, B. K., Błachowicz, A., Lauer, A., 2020. Politicising the just transition: linking global climate policy, Nationally Determined Contributions and targeted research agendas. *Geoforum* 115, 138–142. https://doi.org/10.1016/j.geoforum.2020.05.012

Jewell, J., 2011. Ready for nuclear energy? An assessment of capacities and motivations for launching new national nuclear power programs. *Energy Policy* 39, 1041–1055. https://doi.org/10.1016/j.enpol.2010.10.041

Jewell, J., Vinichenko, V., Nacke, L., Cherp, A., 2019. Prospects for powering past coal. *Nat. Clim. Chang.* 9, 592–597. https://doi.org/10.1038/s41558-019-0509-6

Jeziorski, M., 2006. *Gas Pains*. Warsaw.

Jirušek, M., 2020. The attitude of the Visegrad Group countries towards Russian infrastructural projects in the gas sector. *Energy Policy* 139, 111340. https://doi.org/10.1016/j.enpol.2020.111340

Jirušek, M., Kuchyňková, P., Vlček, T., 2020. Business as usual or geopolitical games? Russian activities in energy sector of the Czech Republic, in: Holzer, J., Mareš, M. (Eds.), *Czech Security Dilemma: Russia as a Friend or Enemy?* Palgrave, London, pp. 117–150.

Jirušek, M., Vlček, T., Henderson, J., 2017. Russia's energy relations in Southeastern Europe: an analysis of motives in Bulgaria and Greece. *Post-Soviet Aff.* 33, 335–355. https://doi.org/10.1080/1060586X.2017.1341256

Jonek-Kowalska, I., 2022. Multi-criteria evaluation of the effectiveness of energy policy in Central and Eastern European countries in a long-term perspective. *Energy Strateg. Rev.* 44, 100973. https://doi.org/10.1016/j.esr.2022.100973

Jones, D., Brown, S., Czyżak, P., Broadbent, H., Bruce-Lockhart, C., Dizon, R., Ewen, M., Fulghum, N., Copsey, L., Candlin, A., Rosslowe, C., Fox Disclaimer, H., 2023. *European Electricity Review 2023*. London.

Jordan, A., Bauer, M. W., Green-Pedersen, C., 2013. Policy dismantiling. *J. Eur. Public Policy* 20, 795–805. https://doi.org/10.1080/13501763.2013.771092

Jordan, A., Huitema, D., van Asselt, H., Rayner, T., Berkhout, F., 2010. *Climate Change Policy in the European Union: Confronting the Dilemmas of Mitigation and Adaptation?* Cambridge University Press, Cambridge. https://doi.org/10.1017/CBO9781139042772

Jordan, A. J., Moore, B., 2020. *Durable by Design? Policy Feedback in a Changing Climate*. Cambridge University Press, Cambridge. https://doi.org/10.1017/9781108779869

Joskow, P. L., Parsons, J. E., 2012. The future of nuclear power after Fukushima. *Econ. Energy Environ. Policy* 1, 99–114.

JRC, 2018. *EU Coal Regions: Opportunities and Challenges Ahead*. Brussels.

2021. *Recent Trends in EU Coal, Peat and Oil Shale Regions*. Brussels.

Judge, A., Maltby, T., 2017. European Energy Union? Caught between securitisation and 'riskification'. *Eur. J. Int. Secur.* 2, 179–202. https://doi.org/10.1017/eis.2017.3

Kallemets, K., 2016. Economic sustainability of Estonian shale oil industry until 2030. *Oil Shale* 33, 272.

Kalt, T., 2021. Jobs vs. climate justice? Contentious narratives of labor and climate movements in the coal transition in Germany. *Env. Polit.* 30, 1135–1154. https://doi.org/10.1080/09644016.2021.1892979

Kama, K., 2016. Contending geo-logics: energy security, resource ontologies, and the politics of expert knowledge in Estonia. *Geopolitics* 21, 831–856. https://doi.org/10.1080/14650045.2016.1210129

Kaminski, I., 2018. Poland's coal habit draws new fire as UN climate talks begin. Clim. Docket. www.climateliabilitynews.org/2018/12/02/poland-coal-un-climate-katowice/

Karimi, F., Toikka, A., 2018. General public reactions to carbon capture and storage: Does culture matter? *Int. J. Greenh. Gas Control* 70, 193–201. https://doi.org/10.1016/j.ijggc.2018.01.012
Katinas, V., Markevicius, A., Perednis, E., Savickas, J., 2014. Sustainable energy development: Lithuania's way to energy supply security and energetics independence. *Renew. Sustain. Energy Rev.* 30, 420–428. https://doi.org/10.1016/j.rser.2013.10.033
Keles, D., Yilmaz, H. Ü., 2020. Decarbonisation through coal phase-out in Germany and Europe: impact on emissions, electricity prices and power production. *Energy Policy* 141, 111472. https://doi.org/10.1016/j.enpol.2020.111472
Kemfert, C., Präger, F., Braunger, I., Hoffart, F. M., Brauers, H., 2022. The expansion of natural gas infrastructure puts energy transitions at risk. *Nat. Energy* 7, 582–587. https://doi.org/10.1038/s41560–022-01060-3
Khan, I., Hou, F., Irfan, M., Zakari, A., Le, H. P., 2021. Does energy trilemma a driver of economic growth? The roles of energy use, population growth, and financial development. *Renew. Sustain. Energy Rev.* 146, 111157. https://doi.org/10.1016/j.rser.2021.111157
Khan, M., 2021. The EU's electricity market and why soaring gas prices are driving bills higher. *Financial Times*, 14 October. www.ft.com/content/f37d2a36-4609-4b3e-9795-064b6d459676
Khrushcheva, O., Maltby, T., 2016. The future of EU-Russia energy relations in the context of decarbonisation. *Geopolitics* 21, 799–830. https://doi.org/10.1080/14650045.2016.1188081
Kikstra, J. S., Vinca, A., Lovat, F., Boza-Kiss, B., van Ruijven, B., Wilson, C., Rogelj, J., Zakeri, B., Fricko, O., Riahi, K., 2021. Climate mitigation scenarios with persistent COVID-19-related energy demand changes. *Nat. Energy* 6, 1114–1123. https://doi.org/10.1038/s41560–021-00904-8
Kilian, B., Elgström, O., 2010. Still a green leader? The European Union's role in international climate negotiations. *Coop. Confl.* 45, 255–273.
Kingsley, T., 2021. 'Utopian fantasy': Hungary's Orban attacks EU climate change policy in latest spat. *The Independent*, 21 October. www.independent.co.uk/climate-change/climate-change-hungary-eu-b1942790.html
Kirchner, E., Berk, C., 2010. European energy security co-operation: between amity and enmity. *JCMS J. Common Mark. Stud.* 48, 859–880. https://doi.org/10.1111/j.1468-5965.2010.02077.x
Klare, M. T., 2009. *Rising Powers, Shrinking Planet: The New Geopolitics of Energy*. Henry Holt, New York.
Klemetti, L., Mäkinen, H., 2022. New sources of natural gas for Finland: the Balticconnector pipeline and LNG imports, in: Liuhto, K. (Ed.), *The Future of Energy Consumption, Security and Natural Gas: LNG in the Baltic Sea Region*. Springer International, Cham, pp. 275–307. https://doi.org/10.1007/978-3-030-80367-4_10
Klevas, V., Streimikiene, D., Grikstaite, R., 2007. Sustainable energy in Baltic States. *Energy Policy* 35, 76–90. https://doi.org/10.1016/j.enpol.2005.10.009
Kluth, A., 2022. Europe is faking solidarity, and Putin knows it. Bloomberg, 27 July. www.bloomberg.com/opinion/articles/2022-07-27/european-union-gas-deal-shows-fake-solidarity-and-putin-knows-it#xj4y7vzkg
Knill, C., Tosun, J., Bauer, M. W., 2009. Neglected faces of Europeanization: the differential impact of the EU on the dismantling of domestic policies. *Public Adm.* 87, 519–537. https://doi.org/10.1111/j.1467-9299.2009.01768.x
Kochanek, E., 2019. Regional cooperation on gas security in Central Europe. *Polityka Energ. – Energy Policy J.* 22, 19–38. https://doi.org/10.33223/epj/103667
Kopecký, P., Mudde, C., 2002. The two sides of Euroscepticism: party positions on European integration in East Central Europe. *Eur. Union Polit.* 3, 297–326. https://doi.org/10.1177/1465116502003003002

2003. Rethinking civil society. *Democratization* 10, 1–14. https://doi.org/10.1080/13510340312331293907

Kopp, S.-D., 2015. *Politics, Markets and EU Gas Supply Security: Case Studies of the UK and Germany*. Springer, Wiesbaden.

Korkmaz, D., 2018. Is the EU a great power? The case of natural gas, in: Heiskala, R., Aro, J. (Eds.), *Policy Design in the European Union: An Empire of Shopkeepers in the Making?* Springer International, Cham, pp. 217–251. https://doi.org/10.1007/978-3-319-64849-1_10

Korosteleva, J., 2022. The implications of Russia's invasion of Ukraine for the EU energy market and businesses. *Br. J. Manag.* 33, 1678–1682. https://doi.org/10.1111/1467-8551.12654

Kotek, P., Selei, A., Takácsné Tóth, B., Felsmann, B., 2023. What can the EU do to address the high natural gas prices? *Energy Policy* 173, 113312. https://doi.org/10.1016/j.enpol.2022.113312

Kovacevic, A., 2009. *The Impact of the Russia–Ukraine Gas Crisis in South Eastern Europe*. Oxford.

Kovács, Z., 2014. Hungarian public left in the dark over decision to build new reactors at Paks nuclear power plant. *Budapest Beacon*, 17 January. https://budapestbeacon.com/hungarian-public-left-in-the-dark-over-decision-to-build-new-reactors-at-paks-nuclear-power-plant/

Kozlova, M., Overland, I., 2022. Combining capacity mechanisms and renewable energy support: a review of the international experience. *Renew. Sustain. Energy Rev.* 155, 111878. https://doi.org/10.1016/j.rser.2021.111878

Kramer, J. M., 2004. EU enlargement and the environment: six challenges. *Env. Polit.* 13, 290–311. https://doi.org/10.1080/09644010410001685245

Kratochvíl, P., Mišík, M., 2020. Bad external actors and good nuclear energy: media discourse on energy supplies in the Czech Republic and Slovakia. *Energy Policy* 136, 111058.

Kreienkamp, J., Pegram, T., Coen, D., 2022. Explaining transformative change in EU climate policy: multilevel problems, policies, and politics. *J. Eur. Integr.* 44, 731–748. https://doi.org/10.1080/07036337.2022.2072838

Krupnik, S., Wagner, A., Koretskaya, O., Rudek, T. J., Wade, R., Mišík, M., Akerboom, S., Foulds, C., Smith Stegen, K., Adem, Ç., Batel, S., Rabitz, F., Certomà, C., Chodkowska-Miszczuk, J., Denac, M., Dokupilová, D., Leiren, M. D., Ignatieva, M. F., Gabaldón-Estevan, D., Horta, A., Karnøe, P., Lilliestam, J., Loorbach, D., Mühlemeier, S., Nemoz, S., Nilsson, M., Osička, J., Papamikrouli, L., Pellizioni, L., Sareen, S., Sarrica, M., Seyfang, G., Sovacool, B., Telešienė, A., Zapletalová, V., von Wirth, T., 2022. Beyond technology: a research agenda for social sciences and humanities research on renewable energy in Europe. *Energy Res. Soc. Sci.* 89, 102536. https://doi.org/10.1016/J.ERSS.2022.102536

Kruyt, B., van Vuuren, D. P., de Vries, H. J. M., Groenenberg, H., 2009. Indicators for energy security. *Energy Policy* 37, 2166–2181. https://doi.org/10.1016/j.enpol.2009.02.006

Kuchler, M., 2017. Post-conventional energy futures: rendering Europe's shale gas resources governable. *Energy Res. Soc. Sci.* 31, 32–40. https://doi.org/10.1016/j.erss.2017.05.028

Kuchler, M., Bridge, G., 2018. Down the black hole: sustaining national socio-technical imaginaries of coal in Poland. *Energy Res. Soc. Sci.* 41, 136–147. https://doi.org/10.1016/j.erss.2018.04.014

Kulovesi, K., Oberthür, S., 2020. Assessing the EU's 2030 Climate and Energy Policy Framework: incremental change toward radical transformation? *Rev. Eur. Comp. Int. Environ. Law* 29, 151–166. https://doi.org/10.1111/reel.12358

Kunze, C., Becker, S., 2015. Collective ownership in renewable energy and opportunities for sustainable degrowth. *Sustain. Sci.* 10, 425–437.

Kurmayer, N. J., 2022a. Germany's first LNG terminal is open for business. Euractiv.com, 17 December. www.euractiv.com/section/energy/news/germanys-first-lng-terminal-is-open-for-business/

2022b. Germany and five other EU countries commit to solidarity as blackouts loom. Euractiv.com, 27 June. www.euractiv.com/section/energy/news/germany-and-five-other-eu-countries-commit-to-solidarity-as-blackouts-loom/

2022c. Berlin makes U-turn, backs joint gas purchasing at EU level. Euractiv.com, 4 October. www.euractiv.com/section/energy/news/berlin-makes-u-turn-backs-joint-gas-purchasing-at-eu-level/

2022d. EU approves CO_2 tax on heating and transport, softened by new social climate fund. Euractiv.com, 18 December. www.euractiv.com/section/emissions-trading-scheme/news/eu-agrees-co2-tax-on-heating-and-transport-fuels-softened-by-new-social-climate-fund/

Kuus, M., 2007. *Geopolitics Reframed: Security and Identity in Europe's Eastern Enlargement.* Palgrave Macmillan, New York.

Kuzemko, C., 2014. Ideas, power and change: explaining EU–Russia energy relations. *J. Eur. Public Policy* 21, 58–75. https://doi.org/10.1080/13501763.2013.835062

Kuzemko, C., Blondeel, M., Dupont, C., Brisbois, M. C., 2022. Russia's war on Ukraine, European energy policy responses & implications for sustainable transformations. *Energy Res. Soc. Sci.* 93, 102842. https://doi.org/10.1016/j.erss.2022.102842

Kuzemko, C., Bradshaw, M., Bridge, G., Goldthau, A., Jewell, J., Overland, I., Scholten, D., Van de Graaf, T., Westphal, K., 2020. Covid-19 and the politics of sustainable energy transitions. *Energy Res. Soc. Sci.* 68, 101685. https://doi.org/10.1016/j.erss.2020.101685

Kuzemko, C., Lockwood, M., Mitchell, C., Hoggett, R., 2016. Governing for sustainable energy system change: politics, contexts and contingency. *Energy Res. Soc. Sci.* 12, 96–105. https://doi.org/10.1016/j.erss.2015.12.022

LaBelle, M., 2009. Expanding opportunities: strategic buying of utilities in new EU member states. *Energy Policy* 37, 4672–4678. https://doi.org/10.1016/j.enpol.2009.06.022

LaBelle, M., Goldthau, A., 2014. Escaping the valley of death? Comparing shale gas technology policy prospects to nuclear and solar in Europe. *J. World Energy Law Bus.* 7, 93–111. https://doi.org/10.1093/jwelb/jwt020

LaBelle, M., Horwitch, M., 2013. The breakout of energy innovation: accelerating to a new low carbon energy system, in: Goldthau, A. (Ed.), *The Handbook of Global Energy Policy*, Wiley Online Books.

LaBelle, M. C., 2017. In pursuit of energy justice. *Energy Policy* 107, 615–620. https://doi.org/10.1016/j.enpol.2017.03.054

Lahiri-Dutt, K., 2016. The diverse worlds of coal in India: energising the nation, energising livelihoods. *Energy Policy* 99, 203–213. https://doi.org/10.1016/j.enpol.2016.05.045

Lamb, W. F., Antal, M., Bohnenberger, K., Brand-Correa, L. I., Müller-Hansen, F., Jakob, M., Minx, J. C., Raiser, K., Williams, L., Sovacool, B. K., 2020. What are the social outcomes of climate policies? A systematic map and review of the ex-post literature. *Environ. Res. Lett.* 15, 113006.

Latvian Government, 2005. *National Security Strategy*. Riga.

2006. *Guidelines for Development of Energy Sector for 2007–2016*. Riga.

2008. *National Security Strategy*. Riga.

2011. *National Security Strategy*. Riga.

2015. *National Security Strategy*. Riga.

2020. *Latvia's National Energy and Climate Plan 2021–2030*. Riga.

Le Billon, P., Lujala, P., Singh, D., Culbert, V., Kristoffersen, B., 2021. Fossil fuels, climate change, and the COVID-19 crisis: pathways for a just and green post-pandemic recovery. *Clim. Policy* 21, 1347–1356. https://doi.org/10.1080/14693062.2021.1965524

Le Coq, C., Paltseva, E., 2014. EU-Russia gas relationship at a crossroads, in: Oxenstierna, S., Tynkkynen, V.-P. (Eds.), *Russian Energy and Security up to 2030*. Routledge, London, pp. 59–78.

Lehotský, L., Černoch, F., Osička, J., Ocelík, P., 2019. When climate change is missing: media discourse on coal mining in the Czech Republic. *Energy Policy* 129, 774–786. https://doi.org/10.1016/j.enpol.2019.02.065

Lehtveer, M., Pelakauskas, M., Ipbüker, C., Howells, M., Rogner, H.-H., Das, A., Toomet, O.-S., Tkaczyk, A. H., 2016. Estonian energy supply strategy assessment for 2035 and its vulnerability to climate driven shocks. *Environ. Prog. Sustain. Energy* 35, 469–478. https://doi.org/10.1002/ep.12240

Leimbach, M., Giannousakis, A., 2019. Burden sharing of climate change mitigation: global and regional challenges under shared socio-economic pathways. *Clim. Change* 155, 273–291. https://doi.org/10.1007/s10584–019-02469-8

LETA, 2022. Liquefied natural gas terminal idea progresses in Latvia. Baltic News Network, 20 April. https://bnn-news.com/liquefied-natural-gas-terminal-idea-progresses-in-latvia-234039

Levesque, A., Pietzcker, R. C., Baumstark, L., Luderer, G., 2021. Deep decarbonisation of buildings energy services through demand and supply transformations in a 1.5°C scenario. *Environ. Res. Lett.* 16, 054071. https://doi.org/10.1088/1748-9326/abdf07

Li, L., Taeihagh, A., 2020. An in-depth analysis of the evolution of the policy mix for the sustainable energy transition in China from 1981 to 2020. *Appl. Energy* 263, 114611. https://doi.org/10.1016/j.apenergy.2020.114611

Lin, B., Raza, M. Y., 2020. Coal and economic development in Pakistan: a necessity of energy source. *Energy* 207, 118244. https://doi.org/10.1016/j.energy.2020.118244

Lippert, B., Umbach, G., Wessels, W., 2001. Europeanization of CEE executives: EU membership negotiations as a shaping power. *J. Eur. Public Policy* 8, 980–1012. https://doi.org/10.1080/13501760110098314

Lis, A., Stankiewicz, P., 2017. Framing shale gas for policy-making in Poland. *J. Environ. Policy Plan.* 19, 53–71. https://doi.org/10.1080/1523908X.2016.1143355

Lithuanian Government, 2002. *National Security Strategy*. Vilnius.

2012. *National Security Strategy*. Vilnius.

2017. *National Security Strategy*. Vilnius.

Lockwood, M., 2018. Right-wing populism and the climate change agenda: exploring the linkages. *Env. Polit.* 27, 712–732. https://doi.org/10.1080/09644016.2018.1458411

Lockwood, M., Kuzemko, C., Mitchell, C., Hoggett, R., 2017. Historical institutionalism and the politics of sustainable energy transitions: a research agenda. *Environ. Plan. C Polit. Sp.* 35, 312–333. https://doi.org/10.1177/0263774X16660561

Lofstedt, R., 2008. Are renewables an alternative to nuclear power? An analysis of the Austria/Slovakia discussions. *Energy Policy* 36, 2226–2233. https://doi.org/10.1016/j.enpol.2007.11.022

Loisel, R., Alexeeva, V., Zucker, A., Shropshire, D., 2018. Load-following with nuclear power: market effects and welfare implications. *Prog. Nucl. Energy* 109, 280–292. https://doi.org/10.1016/j.pnucene.2018.08.011

Lowitzsch, J., Hoicka, C. E., van Tulder, F. J., 2020. Renewable energy communities under the 2019 European Clean Energy Package: Governance model for the energy clusters of the future? *Renew. Sustain. Energy Rev.* 122, 109489. https://doi.org/10.1016/j.rser.2019.109489

LRT, 2019. Swedish court upholds arbitration ruling in Lithuania's dispute with Gazprom. LRT.it, 4 July. www.lrt.lt/naujienos/news-in-english/19/1075565/swedish-court-upholds-arbitration-ruling-in-lithuania-s-dispute-with-gazprom

Macalister, T., 2000. Look east: Doors open to majors. *The Guardian*, 14 November.

MacDowall, A., 2012. Bulgaria's grand slam energy plans: two down, South Stream to go. *Financial Times*, 3 April. www.ft.com/content/beb4140e-b639-37e1-a57f-5c9444878cfa

Mahoney, J., Thelen, K., 2010. *Explaining Institutional Change: Ambiguity, Agency, and Power*. Cambridge University Press, Cambridge.

Makszimov, V., 2022. Solar industry 'shocked' by Hungarian government's suspension of feed-in. Euractiv.com, 17 October. www.euractiv.com/section/politics/news/solar-industry-shocked-by-hungarian-governments-suspension-of-feed-in/

Maldini, P., Pauković, D., 2015. *Croatia and the European Union. Changes and Development*. Routledge, London.

Maltby, T., 2013. European Union energy policy integration: a case of European Commission policy entrepreneurship and increasing supranationalism. *Energy Policy* 55, 435–444. https://doi.org/10.1016/j.enpol.2012.12.031

2014. European energy security policy-making in the context of EU enlargement: the role of newer member states as agenda-setters. PhD thesis, University of Manchester.

2015. Between amity, enmity and Europeanisation: EU energy security policy and the example of Bulgaria's Russian energy dependence. *Eur. Asia. Stud.* 67, 809–830. https://doi.org/10.1080/09668136.2015.1046817

Manowska, A., Osadnik, K. T., Wyganowska, M., 2017. Economic and social aspects of restructuring Polish coal mining: focusing on Poland and the EU. *Resour. Policy* 52, 192–200. https://doi.org/10.1016/j.resourpol.2017.02.006

Marcinkiewicz, K., 2006. The European Energy Security Treaty: let us respond together to energy threats. *Financial Times*.

Marcinkiewicz, K., Tosun, J., 2015. Contesting climate change: mapping the political debate in Poland. *East Eur. Polit.* 31, 187–207. https://doi.org/10.1080/21599165.2015.1022648

Marinaş, M.-C., Dinu, M., Socol, A.-G., Socol, C., 2018. Renewable energy consumption and economic growth: causality relationship in Central and Eastern European countries. *PLoS ONE* 13, e0202951.

Marktanner, M., Salman, L., 2011. Economic and geopolitical dimensions of renewable vs. nuclear energy in North Africa. *Energy Policy* 39, 4479–4489. https://doi.org/10.1016/j.enpol.2010.12.047

Marshall, J. P., 2016. Disordering fantasies of coal and technology: carbon capture and storage in Australia. *Energy Policy* 99, 288–298. https://doi.org/10.1016/j.enpol.2016.05.044

Marti, L., Puertas, R., 2022. Sustainable energy development analysis: energy trilemma. *Sustain. Technol. Entrep.* 1, 100007. https://doi.org/10.1016/j.stae.2022.100007

Martin, R., Sunley, P., 2010. *The Place of Path Dependence in an Evolutionary Perspective on the Economic Landscape*. Edward Elgar, Cheltenham. https://doi.org/10.4337/9781849806497.00010

Mata Pérez, M. de la E., Scholten, D., Smith Stegen, K., 2019. The multi-speed energy transition in Europe: opportunities and challenges for EU energy security. *Energy Strateg. Rev.* 26, 100415. https://doi.org/10.1016/j.esr.2019.100415

Mathew, M. D., 2022. Nuclear energy: a pathway towards mitigation of global warming. *Prog. Nucl. Energy* 143, 104080. https://doi.org/10.1016/j.pnucene.2021.104080

Matláry, J. H., 1997. *Energy Policy in the European Union*. Macmillan Education UK, London. https://doi.org/10.1007/978-1-349-25735-5

Mattila, M., 2008. Voting and coalitions in the Council after the enlargement, in: Naurin, D., Wallace, H. (Eds.), *Unveiling the Council of the European Union: Games Governments Play in Brussels*. Palgrave Macmillan UK, London, pp. 23–35. https://doi.org/10.1057/9780230583788_2

2009. Roll call analysis of voting in the European Union Council of Ministers after the 2004 enlargement. *Eur. J. Polit. Res.* 48, 840–857. https://doi.org/10.1111/j.1475-6765.2009.01850.x

Mayer, S. M., 2008. Path dependence and Commission activism in the evolution of the European Union's external energy policy. *J. Int. Relations Dev.* 11, 251–278. https://doi.org/10.1057/jird.2008.12

Mazák, J., Diviák, T., 2018. Transactional activism without transactions: network perspective on anti-corruption activism in the Czech Republic. *Soc. Mov. Stud.* 17, 203–218. https://doi.org/10.1080/14742837.2017.1404904

McCauley, D., Heffron, R., 2018. Just transition: integrating climate, energy and environmental justice. *Energy Policy* 119, 1–7. https://doi.org/10.1016/j.enpol.2018.04.014

McCormick, M., 2023. US nuclear enjoys revival as public and private funding pours in. *Financial Times,* 1 January. www.ft.com/content/f3c6f333-bc2e-4694-963a-7084e438905a

McCright, A. M., Dunlap, R. E., Marquart-Pyatt, S. T., 2016. Political ideology and views about climate change in the European Union. *Env. Polit.* 25, 338–358. https://doi.org/10.1080/09644016.2015.1090371

McCurry, J., 2022. Japan eyes return to nuclear power more than a decade after Fukushima disaster. *The Guardian,* 25 August.

McDonald, M., 2013. Discourses of climate security. *Polit. Geogr.* 33, 42–51. https://doi.org/10.1016/j.polgeo.2013.01.002

McEnchroe, T., 2020. 61 percent of Czechs support nuclear energy, survey shows. https://english.radio.cz/61-percent-czechs-support-nuclear-energy-survey-shows-8702325

McGlade, C., Pye, S., Ekins, P., Bradshaw, M., Watson, J., 2018. The future role of natural gas in the UK: A bridge to nowhere? *Energy Policy* 113, 454–465. https://doi.org/10.1016/j.enpol.2017.11.022

McGowan, F., 2011. Putting energy insecurity into historical context: European responses to the energy crises of the 1970s and 2000s. *Geopolitics* 16, 486–511. https://doi.org/10.1080/14650045.2011.520857

2014. Regulating innovation: European responses to shale gas development. *Env. Polit.* 23, 41–58. https://doi.org/10.1080/09644016.2012.740939

McWilliams, B., Zachmann, G., 2022. *European Union Demand Reduction Needs to Cope with Russian Gas Cuts*. Brussels.

Meadowcroft, J., 2009. What about the politics? Sustainable development, transition management, and long term energy transitions. *Policy Sci.* 42, 323. https://doi.org/10.1007/s11077–009-9097-z

Melichar, J., 2018. Will Slovak coal giant benefit from EU's clean energy transition efforts? Euractiv.com, 11 June. www.euractiv.com/section/energy/opinion/will-slovak-coal-giant-benefit-from-eus-clean-energy-transition-efforts/

Menon, S., 2022. Ukraine crisis: Who is buying Russian oil and gas? BBC, 23 May. www.bbc.com/news/world-asia-india-60783874

Mezősi, A., Felsmann, B., Kerekes, L., & Szabó, L., 2020. Coexistence of nuclear and renewables in the V4 electricity system: friends or enemies? *Energy Policy*, 140, 111449.

Mete, G., 2020a. The energy mix: decarbonisation and natural gas in EU energy policy, in: *Energy Transitions and the Future of Gas in the EU: Subsidise or Decarbonise* (pp. 37–89). https://doi.org/10.1007/978-3-030-32614-2_3

2020b. *Energy Transitions and the Future of Gas in the EU: Subsidise or Decarbonise*. Palgrave, London.

Meyer, M., Moder, C., Neumayr, M., Vandor, P., 2020. Civil Society and Its Institutional Context in CEE. *Volunt. Int. J. Volunt. Nonprofit Organ.* 31, 811–827. https://doi.org/10.1007/s11266-019-00106-7

MFA Poland, 2014. *Roadmap towards an Energy Union for Europe*. Non-paper addressing the EU's energy dependency challenges. Warsaw.
Mihók, P., 2020. Understanding political institutional support for completing the Mochovce nuclear power plant. *Prog. Nucl. Energy* 120, 103192. https://doi.org/10.1016/j.pnucene.2019.103192
Mikulska, A., Kosinski, E., 2018. Explaining Poland's coal paradox. Forbes, 28 March. www.forbes.com/sites/thebakersinstitute/2018/03/28/explaining-polands-coal-paradox/
Miller, C. A., Iles, A., Jones, C. F., 2013. The social dimensions of energy transitions. *Sci. Cult. (Lond).* 22, 135–148. https://doi.org/10.1080/09505431.2013.786989
Mills-Novoa, M., Liverman, D. M., 2019. Nationally Determined Contributions: material climate commitments and discursive positioning in the NDCs. *WIREs Clim. Chang.* 10, e589. https://doi.org/10.1002/wcc.589
Milne, R., 2022. Lithuania becomes first EU country to end imports of Russian gas. *Financial Times*, 3 April. www.ft.com/content/efcadd5a-b192-4567-a991-56cd6fd83dae
Minas, S., Ntousas, V., 2018. *EU Climate Diplomacy: Politics, Law and Negotiations*. Routledge, London.
Ministerstwo Gospodarki, 2014. *Polish Nuclear Power Programme*. Warsaw.
Ministry of Economy of the Slovak Republic, 2014. *Energy Policy of the Slovak Republic*. Bratislava.
2015. *Rozhodnutie č.23/2015 Ministerstva hospodárstva SR*. Bratislava.
Ministry of Energy, 2019. *Draft Integrated Energy and Climate Plan of the Republic of Bulgaria*. Sofia.
2021. *Integrated Energy and Climate Plan of the Republic of Bulgaria*. Sofia.
Ministry of Energy of Poland, 2021. Energy of Poland until 2040. www.gov.pl/attachment/62a054de-0a3d-444d-a969-90a89502df94
Ministry of Energy of the Republic of Lithuania, 2015. LitPol Link to receive EUR 27 million of EU funding. https://enmin.lrv.lt/en/news/litpol-link-to-receive-eur-27-million-of-eu-funding
Ministry of Energy of the Republic of Lithuania, 2018. *National Energy Independence Strategy*. Vilnius.
Ministry of National Development, 2012. *National Energy Strategy 2030*. Budapest.
Ministry of Trade and Industry of the Czech Republic, 2015a. *Státní energetická koncepce*. Prague.
2015b. *National Action Plan for the Development of the Nuclear Energy Sector in the Czech Republic*. Praha.
2019. *National Energy and Climate Plan of the Czech Republic*. European Commission. energy.ec.europa.eu/system/files/2020-03/cs_final_necp_main_en_0.pdf
Mišík, M., 2010. Security first: energy policy in the new member states of the European Union, in: Malová, D. (Ed.), *From Listening to Action: New Member States in the EU*. Devín Publishing House, Bratislava, pp. 101–129.
2012. Crisis as remedy? The 2009 gas crisis and its influence on the increase of energy security within Visegrad Group countries. *Int. Issues Slovak Foreign Policy Aff.* 21, 56–72.
2015. The influence of perception on the preferences of the new member states of the European Union: the case of energy policy. *Comp. Eur. Polit.* 13, 198–221. https://doi.org/10.1057/cep.2013.9
2016. On the way towards the Energy Union: position of Austria, the Czech Republic and Slovakia towards external energy security integration. *Energy* 111, 68–81. https://doi.org/10.1016/j.energy.2016.05.056
2019. *External Energy Security in the European Union: Small Member States' Perspective*. Routledge, London. https://doi.org/10.4324/9781351106535

2021. When the accession legacy fades away: Central and Eastern European countries and the EU renewables targets. *The International Spectator* 56(3), 56–70. https://doi.org/10.1080/03932729.2021.1932137

2022. The EU needs to improve its external energy security. *Energy Policy* 165, 112930. https://doi.org/10.1016/j.enpol.2022.112930

Mišík, M., Nosko, A., 2017. The Eastring gas pipeline in the context of the Central and Eastern European gas supply challenge. *Nat. Energy* 2, 844–848. https://doi.org/10.1038/s41560–017-0019-6

2023a. Post-pandemic lessons for EU energy and climate policy after the Russian invasion of Ukraine: introduction to a special issue on EU green recovery in the post-Covid-19 period. *Energy Policy* 177, 113546. https://doi.org/10.1016/j.enpol.2023.113546

2023b. Each one for themselves: exploring the energy security paradox of the European Union. *Energy Res. Soc. Sci.* 99, 103074. https://doi.org/10.1016/j.erss.2023.103074

Mišík, M., Oravcová, V., 2020. Energy governance in Slovakia, in: Knodt, M., Kemmerzell, J. (Eds.), *Handbook of Energy Governance in Europe*. Springer International, Cham, pp. 1–29. https://doi.org/10.1007/978-3-319-73526-9_27–1

Mišík, M., Oravcová, V. (Eds.), 2021a. *From Economic to Energy Transition: Three Decades of Transitions in Central and Eastern Europe*. Palgrave Macmillan, Cham. https://doi.org/10.1007/978-3-030-55085-1

2021b. Introduction: Central and Eastern European perspectives on energy transition, in: Mišík, M., Oravcová, V. (Eds.), *From Economic to Energy Transition: Three Decades of Transitions in Central and Eastern Europe*. Palgrave Macmillan, Cham, pp. 1–25. https://doi.org/10.1007/978-3-030-55085-1_1

2022. Ex ante governance in the European Union: energy and climate policy as a 'test run' for the post-pandemic recovery. *Energy Policy* 167, 113076. https://doi.org/10.1016/J.ENPOL.2022.113076

Mišík, M., Prachárová, V., 2016. Before 'independence' arrived: interdependence in energy relations between Lithuania and Russia. *Geopolitics* 21, 579–604. https://doi.org/10.1080/14650045.2015.1113402

2021. Perfect compliance? Nuclear power in Central and Eastern Europe and the EU membership, in: Mišík, M., Oravcová, V. (Eds.), *From Economic to Energy Transition: Three Decades of Transitions in Central and Eastern Europe*. Palgrave Macmillan, Cham, pp. 429–456. https://doi.org/10.1007/978-3-030-55085-1_15

Mocek, P., Pieszczek, M., Swiadrowski, J., Kapusta, K., Wiatowski, M., Stanczyk, K., 2016. Pilot-scale underground coal gasification (UCG) experiment in an operating mine 'Wieczorek' in Poland. *Energy* 111, 313–321.

Modern Power Systems, 2016. Completion of NordBalt and LitPol closes the Baltic Ring. www.modernpowersystems.com/features/featurecompletion-of-nordbalt-and-litpol-closes-the-baltic-ring-4847289/

Moravcsik, A., Vachudova, M., 2005. Preferences, power and equilibrium: the causes and consequences of EU enlargement, in: Schimmelfenning, F., Sedelmeier, U. (Eds.), *The Politics of European Union Enlargement: Theoretical Approaches*. Routledge, London, pp. 198–209.

Morena, E., 2023. The climate brokers: philanthropy and the shaping of a 'US-compatible' international climate regime, in: Aykut, S., Maertens, L. (Eds.), *The Climatization of Global Politics*. Springer International, Cham, pp. 41–62. https://doi.org/10.1007/978-3-031-17895-5_3

Morgan, S., 2019. EU climate deal falls at summit, four countries wield the axe. Euractiv.com, 20 June. www.euractiv.com/section/energy-environment/news/eu-climate-deal-falls-at-summit-four-countries-wield-the-axe/

Morris, A., 2021. Is Bulgaria ready to give up coal? DW.com, 10 November. www.dw.com/en/is-bulgaria-ready-to-give-up-coal/a-59716811

Moscow Times, 2014. Polish miners protest against cheap Russian coal by blocking train. *Moscow Times*, 24 September. www.themoscowtimes.com/2014/09/24/polish-miners-protest-against-cheap-russian-coal-by-blocking-train-a39716

MosNews, 2005. Poland calls Baltic gas pipeline Russian German conspiracy. MosNews.com, 5 August. www.mosnews.com/money/2005/08/05/polandpipeline.shtml

MTVSZ, 2020. Közösségi energia. https://mtvsz.hu/kozossegi-energia

Müller, N., Teixidó, J. J., 2021. The effect of the EU ETS free allowance allocation on energy mix diversification: the case of Poland's power sector. *Clim. Policy* 21, 804–822. https://doi.org/10.1080/14693062.2020.1870914

Müller, W. C., 2017. Rejecting nuclear energy: from party competition accident to state doctrine, in: Müller, W. C., Thurner, P. W. (Eds.), *The Politics of Nuclear Energy in Western Europe*. Oxford University Press, Oxford, pp. 98–124.

Müller, W. C., Thurner, P. W., 2017. *The Politics of Nuclear Energy in Western Europe*. Oxford University Press, Oxford.

Murmann, J. P., 2006. *Knowledge and Competitive Advantage: The Coevolution of Firms, Technology, and National Institutions*. Cambridge University Press, Cambridge.

Murphy, K., 2017. 'Clean' coal power plants: Matt Canavan hints at government subsidy. *The Guardian*, 2 February.

Naftogaz, 2022. *Resilience. Victory. Recovery. Naftogaz Annual Report 2021*. Kyiv.

Natorski, M., Pomorska, K., 2017. Trust and decision-making in times of crisis: the EU's response to the events in Ukraine. *JCMS J. Common Mark. Stud.* 55, 54–70. https://doi.org/10.1111/jcms.12445

Nelsen, A., 2015. Poland's shale gas revolution evaporates in face of environmental protests. *The Guardian*, 12 January.

Nelsen, A., Simon, F., 2012. Poland defies Europe over 2050 low-carbon roadmap. Euractiv.com, 8 March. www.euractiv.com/section/development-policy/news/poland-defies-europe-over-2050-low-carbon-roadmap/

Neresini, F., Lorenzet, A., 2016. Can media monitoring be a proxy for public opinion about technoscientific controversies? The case of the Italian public debate on nuclear power. *Public Underst. Sci.* 25, 171–185.

Neslen, A., 2018. Spain to close most coal mines in €250m transition deal. *The Guardian*, 26 October.

Neuman, M., 2017. The Visegrád group as a vehicle for promoting national interests in the European Union: the case of the Czech Republic. *Polit. Cent. Eur.* 13, 55–67. https://doi.org/10.1515/pce-2016-0022

Neuwahl, N., Kovacs, C., 2021. Hungary and the EU's rule of law protection. *J. Eur. Integr.* 43, 17–32. https://doi.org/10.1080/07036337.2020.1717484

Newell, P., Mulvaney, D., 2013. The political economy of the 'just transition'. *Geogr. J.* 179, 132–140. https://doi.org/10.1111/geoj.12008

Newell, P., Simms, A., 2021. How did we do that? Histories and political economies of rapid and just transitions. *New Polit. Econ.* 26, 907–922. https://doi.org/10.1080/13563467.2020.1810216

NGFS, 2022. Membership. www.ngfs.net/en/about-us/membership

Normile, D., 2020. China's bold climate pledge earns praise – but is it feasible? *Science* 370 (6512), 17–18. https://doi.org/10.1126/science.370.6512.17

Nosko, A., 2013. Energy security in transition: coping with energy import dependence in the Czech Republic, Slovakia and Hungary. PhD dissertation, Central European University.

Nosko, A., Mišík, M., 2017. No united front: the political economy of energy in Central and Eastern Europe, in: Andersen, S. S., Goldthau, A., Sitter, N. (Eds.), *Energy Union* (pp. 201–222). Palgrave Macmillan, London. https://doi.org/10.1057/978-1-137-59104-3_12

Notes from Poland, 2022. Support for nuclear energy in Poland almost doubles in a year [WWW Document]. https://notesfrompoland.com/2022/12/05/support-for-nuclear-energy-in-poland-almost-doubles-in-a-year/

Noutcheva, G., Bechev, D., 2008. The successful laggards: Bulgaria and Romania's accession to the EU. *East Eur. Polit. Soc.* 22, 114–144. https://doi.org/10.1177/0888325407311793

Novak, B., 2015. Legislative committee approves bill to classify Paks II project for 30 years. *Budapest Beacon*, 27 February. https://budapestbeacon.com/legislative-committee-approves-bill-classify-paks-ii-project-30-years/

Novinite, 2014. Chevron to Explore a Fifth Romanian Location for Shale Gas. www.novinite.com/articles/159901/Chevron+to+Explore+a+Fifth+Romanian+Location+for+Shale+Gas

2019. Protest in front of KEVR building because of the electricity, heating and hot water price increase. www.novinite.com/articles/198227/Protest+in+front+of+KEVR+Building+Because+of+the+Electricity%2C+Heating+and+Hot+Water+Price+Increase

2021. Bulgaria may have new nuclear reactor in ten years. www.novinite.com/articles/207671/Bulgaria+May+Have+New+Nuclear+Reactor+in+Ten+Years

2023. Bulgaria's Ecominister: We are not prepared with an alternative to coal plants. www.novinite.com/articles/218653/Bulgaria's+Ecominister%3A+We+are+Not+Prepared+with+an+Alternative+to+Coal+Plants

Novinky.cz, 2019. Babiš: Není možné dostat klima do pozice náboženství, že se nesmí létat letadly. www.novinky.cz/clanek/domaci-babis-neni-mozne-dostat-klima-do-pozice-nabozenstvi-ze-se-nesmi-letat-letadly-40296782

NSE, 2009. CEZ opens public tender for contractor of nuclear units. www.nsenergybusiness.com/news/newscez_opens_public_tender_for_contractor_of_nuclear_units_090803/

Obama, B., 2009. Transcript: Obama's speech on renewable energy policy. *New York Times*, 23 October. www.nytimes.com/2009/10/24/us/politics/24obama.text.html

Oberthür, S., 2016. Where to go from Paris? The European Union in climate geopolitics. *Glob. Aff.* 2, 119–130. https://doi.org/10.1080/23340460.2016.1166332

Oberthür, S., Dupont, C., 2021. The European Union's international climate leadership: Towards a grand climate strategy? *J. Eur. Public Policy* 28, 1095–1114. https://doi.org/10.1080/13501763.2021.1918218

Oberthür, S., Tänzler, D., Wright, E., Khandekar, G., 2022. *European Foreign Policy in a Decarbonising World: Challenges and Opportunities*. Routledge, London.

Ocelík, P., Osička, J., Zapletalová, V., Černoch, F., Dančák, B., 2017. Local opposition and acceptance of a deep geological repository of radioactive waste in the Czech Republic: a frame analysis. *Energy Policy* 105, 458–466. https://doi.org/10.1016/j.enpol.2017.03.025

OECD, 2022. *Climate Finance Provided and Mobilised by Developed Countries in 2016–2020: Insights from Disaggregated Analysis*. https://read.oecd.org/10.1787/286dae5d-en?format=pdf

Oels, A., 2013. Rendering climate change governable by risk: from probability to contingency. *Geoforum* 45, 17–29. https://doi.org/10.1016/j.geoforum.2011.09.007

Oettinger, G., 2011. Speech of Commissioner Oettinger at the Conference on the occasion of the opening of ACER Ljubljana, 3 March. European Commission Press Corner. https://ec.europa.eu/commission/presscorner/detail/en/SPEECH_11_145

Official Journal of the European Union, 2010. *Regulation (EU) 994/2010*. Brussels.

2017. *Regulation (EU) 2017/1938 Concerning Measures to Safeguard the Security of Gas Supply*. Brussels.

2018. *Regulation (EU) 2018/1999 of the European Parliament and of the Council of 11 December 2018 on the Governance of the Energy Union and Climate Action*. Brussels.
Olabi, A. G., Onumaegbu, C., Wilberforce, T., Ramadan, M., Abdelkareem, M. A., Al-Alami, A. H., 2021. Critical review of energy storage systems. *Energy* 214, 118987. https://doi.org/10.1016/j.energy.2020.118987
Open Access Government, 2019. Hungary plans to ditch coal by 2030 and become fully reliant on renewable energy. www.openaccessgovernment.org/hungary-plans-to-ditch-coal-by-2030-and-become-fully-reliant-on-renewable-energy/55057/
Oravcová, V., Mišík, M., 2018. EU funds and limited cooperation: energy infrastructure development in the Visegrad Group. *Int. Issues Slovak Foreign Policy Aff.* 27, 11–26.
Oravcová, V., Yakovenko, K., Mišík, M., 2022. Complete but fragmented: research on energy in Central and Eastern Europe. *Energies* 15(17), 6185. https://doi.org/10.3390/en15176185
Orbán, K., 2016. NGOs contest Paks II permit. *Budapest Beacon*, 30 September. https://budapestbeacon.com/environmental-groups-to-contest-paks-ii-environmental-permit/
Orbán, V., 2022. Speech by Prime Minister Viktor Orbán at the 31st Bálványos Summer Free University and Student Camp. https://2015-2022.miniszterelnok.hu/speech-by-prime-minister-viktor-orban-at-the-31st-balvanyos-summer-free-university-and-student-camp/
Orenstein, M. A., Kelemen, R. D., 2017. Trojan horses in EU foreign policy. *JCMS J. Common Mark. Stud.* 55, 87–102. https://doi.org/10.1111/jcms.12441
Orttung, R. W., Perovic, J., 2012. Energy security, in: Mauer, V., Cavelty, M. D. (Eds.), *Handbook of Security Studies*. Routledge, Abingdon.
Osička, J., Černoch, F., 2017. Anatomy of a black sheep: the roots of the Czech Republic's pro-nuclear energy policy. *Energy Res. Soc. Sci.* 27, 9–13. https://doi.org/10.1016/j.erss.2017.02.006
2022. European energy politics after Ukraine: the road ahead. *Energy Res. Soc. Sci.* 91, 102757. https://doi.org/10.1016/j.erss.2022.102757
Osička, J., Černoch, F., Zapletalová, V., Lehotský, L., 2021. Too good to be true: sugarcoating nuclear energy in the Czech national energy strategy. *Energy Res. Soc. Sci.* 72, 101865. https://doi.org/10.1016/j.erss.2020.101865
Osička, J., Kemmerzell, J., Zoll, M., Lehotský, L., Černoch, F., Knodt, M., 2020. What's next for the European coal heartland? Exploring the future of coal as presented in German, Polish and Czech press. *Energy Res. Soc. Sci.* 61, 101316. https://doi.org/10.1016/j.erss.2019.101316
Osička, J., Ocelík, P., 2017. Natural gas infrastructure and supply patterns in Eastern Europe: trends and policies. *Energy Sources, Part B Econ. Planning, Policy* 12, 358–364. https://doi.org/10.1080/15567249.2015.1136971
Ostrowski, W., 2020. The twenty years' crisis of European energy security: Central and Eastern Europe and the US. *Geopolitics*, 1–23. https://doi.org/10.1080/14650045.2020.1835863
Oudenaren, J. Van, 2001. The limits of coditionality: nuclear reactor safety in Central and Eastern Europe 1994–2001. *Int. Polit.* 38, 467–498.
Overland, I., 2019. The geopolitics of renewable energy: debunking four emerging myths. *Energy Res. Soc. Sci.* 49, 36–40. https://doi.org/10.1016/j.erss.2018.10.018
Pachocka, M., 2016. Understanding the Visegrad Group states' response to the migrant and refugee crisis 2014+ in the European Union. *Yearb. Polish Eur. Stud.* 101–132.
Page, E. A., 2008. Distributing the burdens of climate change. *Env. Polit.* 17, 556–575. https://doi.org/10.1080/09644010802193419
Pakalkaitė, V., Posaner, J., 2019. The Baltics: between competition and cooperation, in: Godzimirski, J. M. (Ed.), *New Political Economy of Energy in Europe: Power to Project, Power to Adapt*. Springer International, Cham, pp. 215–237. https://doi.org/10.1007/978-3-319-93360-3_9

Pan, Y., 2023. Managing the atomic divorce: the challenges of East Central Europe' s nuclear energy decoupling from Russia. *Electr. J.* 36, 107241. https://doi.org/10.1016/j.tej.2023.107241

Panarello, D., Gatto, A., 2023. Decarbonising Europe: EU citizens' perception of renewable energy transition amidst the European Green Deal. *Energy Policy* 172, 113272. https://doi.org/10.1016/j.enpol.2022.113272

Parker, C. F., Karlsson, C., 2018. The UN climate change negotiations and the role of the United States: assessing American leadership from Copenhagen to Paris. *Env. Polit.* 27, 519–540. https://doi.org/10.1080/09644016.2018.1442388

Parker, C. F., Karlsson, C., Hjerpe, M., 2017. Assessing the European Union's global climate change leadership: from Copenhagen to the Paris Agreement. *J. Eur. Integr.* 39, 239–252. https://doi.org/10.1080/07036337.2016.1275608

Paterson, M., 2021. The end of the Fossil Fuel Age'? Discourse politics and climate change political economy. *New Polit. Econ.* 26, 923–936. https://doi.org/10.1080/13563467.2020.1810218

Patricolo, C., 2019. Hungary to phase out coal by 2030. Emerging Europe. https://emerging-europe.com/news/hungary-to-phase-out-coal-by-2030/

2022. Member states agree to reduce gas demand by 15%[WWW Document]. ceenergy-news.com, 26 July. https://ceenergynews.com/eu-affairs/member-states-agree-to-reduce-gas-demand-by-15/

Pavlínek, P., Pickles, J., 2000. *Environmental Transitions: Transformation and Ecological Defence in Central and Eastern Europe*. Routledge, London.

Pavlović, D., Banovac, E., Vištica, N., 2018. Defining a composite index for measuring natural gas supply security: the Croatian gas market case. *Energy Policy* 114, 30–38. https://doi.org/10.1016/j.enpol.2017.11.029

Pech, L., Scheppelle, K. L., 2017. Illiberalism within: rule of law backsliding in the EU. *Cambridge Yearb. Eur. Leg. Stud.* 19, 3–47. https://doi.org/10.1017/cel.2017.9

Pelinka, A., 1983. The nuclear power referendum in Austria. *Elect. Stud.* 2, 253–261. https://doi.org/10.1016/S0261-3794(83)80032-8

Peng, D., Poudineh, R., 2019. Electricity market design under increasing renewable energy penetration: misalignments observed in the European Union. *Util. Policy* 61, 100970. https://doi.org/10.1016/j.jup.2019.100970

Perrone, G., 2019. *The Security of Natural Gas Supplies in the European Union Policy*. Rome.

Peseckyte, G., 2022. Lithuania now fully independent of Russian energy. Euractiv.com, 24 May. www.euractiv.com/section/politics/short_news/lithuania-now-fully-independent-of-russian-energy/

Petit, V., 2017. *The Energy Transition: An Overview of the True Challenge of the 21st Century*. Springer, London.

Petrova, S., 2014. *Communities in Transition: Protected Nature and Local People in Eastern and Central Europe*. Routledge, London.

Pew, 2020. Science and scientists held in high esteem across global publics. Pew Research Center, 29 September. www.pewresearch.org/science/2020/09/29/science-and-scientists-held-in-high-esteem-across-global-publics/

Pickles, J., Smith, A., 1998. *Theorizing Transition: The Political Economy of Post-Communist Transformations*. Routledge, London.

Piebalgs, A., 2008. Energy Security in the Baltic Sea Region Speech at the Baltic Sea Regional Business Forum. https://ec.europa.eu/commission/presscorner/detail/en/speech_08_296

Pielow, J.-C., Brunekreeft, G., Ehlers, E., 2009. Legal and economic aspects of ownership unbundling in the EU. *J. World Energy Law Bus.* 2, 96–116. https://doi.org/10.1093/jwelb/jwp001

Pierson, P., 2000. Increasing returns, path dependence, and the study of politics. *Am. Polit. Sci. Rev.* 94, 251–267. https://doi.org/10.2307/2586011

Pinker, A., Argüelles, L., Fischer, A., Becker, S., 2020. Between straitjacket and possibility: energy initiatives and the politics of regulation. *Geoforum* 113, 14–25. https://doi.org/10.1016/j.geoforum.2020.04.016

Pitel, L., 2023. German village becomes climate flashpoint over 'painful' coal revival. *Financial Times*, 11 January. www.ft.com/content/abb4e299-f10d-421a-b107-ee686c701dc2

Pivarnyik, B., 2017. MVM spends $3.8 million promoting Paks II. *Budapest Beacon.*, 15 September. https://budapestbeacon.com/mvm-spends-3-8-million-promoting-paks-ii/

Plumer, B., 2018. Covering climate talks in the heart of Poland's coal country. *New York Times*, 19 December.

Podoba, J., 1998. Rejecting green velvet: transition, environment and nationalism in Slovakia. *Env. Polit.* 7, 129–144. https://doi.org/10.1080/09644019808414376

Polanecký, K., Haverkamp, J., 2011. *Energy of the Future? Nuclear Energy in Central and Eastern Europe*. Prague.

Polish Government, 2003. *National Security Strategy*. Warsaw.

2007. *National Security Strategy*. Warsaw.

2013. *Strategy of Development of the National Security System of the Republic of Poland 2022*. Warsaw.

2018. *Solidarity and Just Transition Declaration*. Warsaw.

2020. *National Security Strategy*. Warsaw.

Polish Presidency of the Visegrad Group, 2013. *Visegrad 4 Integration & Cohesion*. Warsaw.

Pollak, J., Schubert, S., Kreutler, M., 2016. *Energy Policy of the European Union*. Palgrave, London.

Pollitt, M. G., 2012. The role of policy in energy transitions: lessons from the energy liberalisation era. *Energy Policy* 50, 128–137. https://doi.org/10.1016/j.enpol.2012.03.004

2019. The European single market in electricity: an economic assessment. *Rev. Ind. Organ.* 55, 63–87. https://doi.org/10.1007/s11151–019-09682-w

Polska Zielona Sieć, 2014. Czeczott power plant open letter to Mitsui. http://dlaklimatu.pl/wp-content/uploads/2014/06/Czeczott-power-plant-open-letter-to-Mitsui-FINAL.pdf

PolskieRadio, 2008. European Parliament passes report critical of North Stream. www2.polskieradio.pl/eo/dokument.aspx?iid=86547

Popp, R., 2019. A just transition of European coal regions. E3G. https://justtransitionforall.com/wp-content/uploads/2022/09/E3G_2019_Stakeholder_Mappings_European_Coal_Regions_Final-1.pdf

Portela, C., Pospieszna, P., Skrzypczyńska, J., Walentek, D., 2021. Consensus against all odds: explaining the persistence of EU sanctions on Russia. *J. Eur. Integr.* 43, 683–699. https://doi.org/10.1080/07036337.2020.1803854

Pöyry Management Consulting, 2018. *Independent Economic Analysis of the Long-Term Liquefied Natural Gas Import Solution to the Republic of Lithuania*. Oxford.

PPCA, 2022. PPCA members. Powering Past Coal Alliance. www.poweringpastcoal.org/members

2023. Our Members. Powering Past Coal Alliance. https://poweringpastcoal.org/members/

Praks, P., Kopustinskas, V., 2019. Node importance analysis of a gas transmission network with evaluation of a new infrastructure by ProGasNet, in: Luiijf, E., Žutautaitė, I., Hämmerli, B. M. (Eds.), *Critical Information Infrastructures Security*. Springer International, Cham, pp. 3–16.

Prăvălie, R., Bandoc, G., 2018. Nuclear energy: between global electricity demand, worldwide decarbonisation imperativeness, and planetary environmental implications. *J. Environ. Manage.* 209, 81–92. https://doi.org/10.1016/j.jenvman.2017.12.043

Preussen, W., 2022. Hungary signs new gas deal with Gazprom. Politico, 31 August. www.politico.eu/article/hungary-signs-deal-with-gazprom-over-additional-gas/

Prontera, A., Plenta, P., 2020. Catalytic Power Europe and gas infrastructural policy in the Visegrad countries. *Energy Policy* 137, 111189. https://doi.org/10.1016/j.enpol.2019.111189

PWEA, 2019. Customers will select RES: less expensive and cleaner. http://psew.pl/wp-content/uploads/2019/06/Przysz%C5%820%C5%9B%C4%87-morskiej-energetyki-wiatrowej-w-Polsce-raport.pdf

2020. Wind of hope for Poland's Green Deal. http://psew.pl/en/2020/08/25/wind-of-hope-for-polands-green-deal/

Radio Free Europe, 2019. Bulgaria seeks funding for second nuclear power plant. www.rferl.org/a/bulgaria-seeks-funding-for-second-nuclear-power-plant/29815609.html

Ragwitz, M., Steinhilber, S., Breitschopf, B., Resch, G., Panzer, C., Ortner, A., Busch, S., 2012. *Shaping an Effective and Efficient European Renewable Energy Market*. Karlsruhe.

Rahvaalgatus, 2017. Eesti vajab põlevkivienergeetikast väljumise strateegiat ehk PÕXITit. https://rahvaalgatus.ee/initiatives/e05abc15-5e49-4205-bfb3-520ed6caf057

Ralev, R., 2021. Slovenia to complete coal phase-out by 2033 – govt minister. SEE News. https://seenews.com/news/slovenia-to-complete-coal-phase-out-by-2033-govt-minister-753858

Rankin, J., 2018. EU settles seven-year Gazprom dispute without imposing fine. *The Guardian*, 24 May.

2021. EU considers natural gas purchase in response to surging energy prices. *The Guardian*, 12 October.

2022. Hungary 'holding EU hostage' over sanctions on Russian oil. *The Guardian*, 16 May.

Rečka, L., Ščasný, M., 2016. Impacts of carbon pricing, brown coal availability and gas cost on Czech energy system up to 2050. *Energy* 108, 19–33. https://doi.org/10.1016/j.energy.2015.12.003

2017. Impacts of reclassified brown coal reserves on the energy system and deep decarbonisation target in the Czech Republic. *Energies* 10(12), 1947. https://doi.org/10.3390/en10121947

2018. Brown coal and nuclear energy deployment: effects on fuel-mix, carbon targets, and external costs in the Czech Republic up to 2050. *Fuel* 216, 494–502. https://doi.org/10.1016/j.fuel.2017.12.034

Reclaim Finance, 2023. Throwing fuel on the fire: GFANZ financing of fossil fuel expansion . https://reclaimfinance.org/site/wp-content/uploads/2023/01/Throwing-fuel-on-the-fire-GFANZ-financing-of-fossil-fuel-expansion.pdf

Reed, S., 2022. Britain approves new coal mine despite climate concerns. *New York Times*, 8 December.

REKK, 2018. *Self-Assessment and Development Options for the Slovenian Gas Wholesale Market*. Budapest.

Renn, O., Marshall, J. P., 2016. Coal, nuclear and renewable energy policies in Germany: from the 1950s to the 'Energiewende.' *Energy Policy* 99, 224–232. https://doi.org/10.1016/j.enpol.2016.05.004

RESCOOP, 2023. Our members. www.rescoop.eu/members

Reuters, 2012a. Romanian coal miners protest over pay. 8 March.

2012b. Bulgarians protest, seek moratorium on shale gas. 14 January.

2013. Update 1: Poland says will not tax shale gas output until 2020. 22 May.

2016a. Polish firms concede defeat in search for shale gas riches. 12 October.

2016b. EU's anti-monopoly case against Russia's Gazprom. 25 October.

2018a. Slovak court orders detained Greenpeace activists to stay in custody. 2 December.

2018b. Bulgarian miners march to protect coal production. 29 November.

2019. Bulgaria seeks investors to build Belene nuclear plant. 11 March.
2020. France's Macron says nuclear will remain key energy source. 8 December.
2021a. Hoping for cheaper gas to come, Europe reverses Russian link to tap storage. 30 December.
2021b. Hungary gets 5-year payment delay on Russian-led nuclear plant project. 29 April (corrected).
2021c. EU climate policy risks sidelining nuclear power, seven countries say. 24 March.
2021d. Estonian prime minister pledges break with far-right past. 26 January.
2022a. China's overseas coal ban sees 15 projects cancelled. 21 April.
2022b. Japan turns back to nuclear power to tackle energy crisis. 16 December.
2023. Bulgarian lawmakers back coal plants with vote to roll back green targets. 12 January.
RFERL, 2006. EU criticizes Poland's Nazi pipeline comment. Radio Free Europe Radio Liberty. www.rferl.org/content/article/1068083.html
2022. Orban requests increase in Russian gas imports during meeting with Putin. Radio Free Europe Radio Liberty. www.rferl.org/a/hungary-orban-putin-russia-gas/31681502.html
Rilska, B., 2012. *The Price of Gas Remains Unclear Three Days before the Signing of the Contract with 'Gazprom.'* Dnevnik.
Ritchie, H., Roser, M., 2022. Electricity mix. Our World in Data. https://ourworldindata.org/electricity-mix
Rixen, T., Viola, L. A., 2014. Putting path dependence in its place: toward a taxonomy of institutional change. *J. Theor. Polit.* 27, 301–323. https://doi.org/10.1177/0951629814531667
Rockström, J., Gaffney, O., Rogelj, J., Meinshausen, M., Nakicenovic, N., Schellnhuber, H. J., 2017. A roadmap for rapid decarbonization. *Science* 355(6331), 1269–1271. https://doi.org/10.1126/science.aah3443
Rodríguez-Fernández, L., Fernández Carvajal, A. B., Ruiz-Gómez, L. M., 2020. Evolution of European Union's energy security in gas supply during Russia–Ukraine gas crises (2006–2009). *Energy Strateg. Rev.* 30, 100518. https://doi.org/10.1016/j.esr.2020.100518
Rodríguez-Gómez, N., Zaccarelli, N., Bolado-Lavín, R., 2016. European ability to cope with a gas crisis: comparison between 2009 and 2014. *Energy Policy* 97, 461–474. https://doi.org/10.1016/j.enpol.2016.07.016
Roeben, V., 2018. *Towards a European Energy Union: European Energy Strategy in International Law.* Cambridge University Press, Cambridge. https://doi.org/10.1017/9781316529720
Rohracher, H., Späth, P., 2013. The interplay of urban energy policy and socio-technical transitions: the eco-cities of Graz and Freiburg in retrospect. *Urban Stud.* 51, 1415–1431. https://doi.org/10.1177/0042098013500360
Rojey, A., 2009. *Energy and Climate: How to Achieve a Successful Energy Transition.* Wiley, New York.
Romanian Government, 2007. *National Security Strategy.* Bucharest.
2016. *Romanian Energy Strategy 2016–2030, with an Outlook to 2050 (Executive Summary).* Sofia.
2020. *National Defence Strategy 2020–2024.* Bucharest.
Rosen, A. M., 2015. The wrong solution at the right time: the failure of the Kyoto protocol on climate change. *Polit. Policy* 43, 30–58. https://doi.org/10.1111/polp.12105
Rosslowe, C., 2020. EU ETS emissions 2019: Europe's coal power collapse exposes steel plants as Europe's biggest emitters. Ember, 7 April. https://ember-climate.org/insights/research/eu-ets-emissions-2019/
Roth, M., 2011. Poland as a policy entrepreneur in European external energy policy: Towards greater energy solidarity vis-à-vis Russia? *Geopolitics* 16, 600–625. https://doi.org/10.1080/14650045.2011.520865

Ruble, I., 2017. European Union energy supply security: the benefits of natural gas imports from the Eastern Mediterranean. *Energy Policy* 105, 341–353. https://doi.org/10.1016/j.enpol.2017.03.010

Ruiz, I. B., 2018. Lobbyists push fossil fuels at COP24. DW, 12 December. www.dw.com/en/lobbyists-push-fossil-fuels-at-climate-talks/a-46671775

Rumelt, R. P., 1995. Inertia and transformation, in: Montgomery, C. A. (Ed.), *Resource-Based and Evolutionary Theories of the Firm: Towards a Synthesis*. Springer US, Boston, pp. 101–132. https://doi.org/10.1007/978-1-4615-2201-0_5

Russian Government, 2009. *Energy Strategy of Russia for the Period up to 2030*. Moscow.

Ruzzenenti, F., Wagner, A., 2018. Efficiency and the rebound effect in the hegemonic discourse on energy. *Nat. Cult.* 13, 356–377. https://doi.org/10.3167/nc.2018.130303

Rybak, A., Rybak, A., 2021. Methods of ensuring energy security with the use of hard coal: the case of Poland. *Energies* 14(18), 5609. https://doi.org/10.3390/en14185609

Saad, L., 2022. Americans divided on nuclear energy. Gallup, 20 May. https://news.gallup.com/poll/392831/americans-divided-nuclear-energy.aspx

Sadurski, W., 2004. Accession's democracy dividend: the impact of the EU enlargement upon democracy in the new member states of Central and Eastern Europe. *Eur. Law J.* 10, 371–401. https://doi.org/10.1111/j.1468-0386.2004.00222.x

Saether, B., Isaksen, A., Karlsen, A., 2011. Innovation by co-evolution in natural resource industries: the Norwegian experience. *Geoforum* 42, 373–381. https://doi.org/10.1016/j.geoforum.2011.01.008

Sánchez Nicolás, E., 2022. Campaigners challenge €13bn proposed gas projects. EUobserver, 7 June. https://euobserver.com/green-economy/155114

Sarlos, G., 2015. Risk perception and political alienism. *Cent. Eur. J. Public Policy* 8, 93–111.

Sarrica, M., Brondi, S., Cottone, P., Mazzara, B. M., 2016. One, no one, one hundred thousand energy transitions in Europe: the quest for a cultural approach. *Energy Res. Soc. Sci.* 13, 1–14. https://doi.org/10.1016/j.erss.2015.12.019

Sattich, T., Morgan, R., Moe, E., 2022. Searching for energy independence, finding renewables? Energy security perceptions and renewable energy policy in Lithuania. *Polit. Geogr.* 96, 102656. https://doi.org/10.1016/j.polgeo.2022.102656

Sauer, N., 2019. Poland's coal miners: 'EU climate proposals terrify us'. ClimateHomeNews.com, 24 September. www.climatechangenews.com/2018/09/24/poland-coal-miners-eu/

Schimmelfennig, F., 2001. The community trap: liberal norms, rhetorical action, and the eastern enlargement of the European Union. *Int. Organ.* 55, 47–80. https://doi.org/10.1162/002081801551414

2005. Strategic calculation and international socialization: membership incentives, party constellations, and sustained compliance in Central and Eastern Europe. *Int. Organ.* 59, 827–860.

Schimmelfennig, F., Sedelmeier, U., 2004. Governance by conditionality: EU rule transfer to the candidate countries of Central and Eastern Europe. *J. Eur. Public Policy* 11, 661–679. https://doi.org/10.1080/1350176042000248089

2005. *Europeanization of Central and Eastern Europe*. Cornell University Press, Ithaca, NY.

Schmidt, A., 2020. From Intermarium to the Three Seas Initiative: the implications of the Polish orientation over the Central and Eastern European region on Hungarian foreign policy, in: Bogdanova, O., Makarychev, A. (Eds.), *Baltic-Black Sea Regionalisms: Patchworks and Networks at Europe's Eastern Margins*. Springer International, Cham, pp. 149–168. https://doi.org/10.1007/978-3-030-24878-9_10

Schmidt-Felzmann, A., 2008. All for one? EU member states and the Union's common policy towards the Russian Federation. *J. Contemp. Eur. Stud.* 16, 169–187. https://doi.org/10.1080/14782800802309771

2011. EU member states' energy relations with Russia: conflicting approaches to securing natural gas supplies. *Geopolitics* 16, 574–599. https://doi.org/10.1080/14650045.2011.520864

2018. *The Commercial Deals Connected with Gazprom's Nord Stream 2: A Review of Strings and Benefits Attached to the Controversial Russian Pipelines*. Warsaw.

Schreiber, P., Pinson, L., Can Ileri, E., Jeandon, J., 2020. Behind the curtains: when the gas and nuclear lobbies reshape the EU sustainable taxonomy. ReclaimFinance.org media briefing, August. https://reclaimfinance.org/site/en/2020/08/25/behind-the-curtains-when-the-gas-and-nuclear-lobbies-reshape-the-eu-sustainable-taxonomy/

Schubert, D. K. J., Thuß, S., Möst, D., 2015. Does political and social feasibility matter in energy scenarios? *Energy Res. Soc. Sci.* 7, 43–54. https://doi.org/10.1016/j.erss.2015.03.003

Scislowska, M., 2018. Ahead of climate talks, Poles are divided over coal mining. AP News, 27 November. https://apnews.com/article/coal-mining-international-news-katowice-science-technology-15b849ca072f47f7b79e220d32b28124

Sedelmeier, U., 2005. *Constructing the Path to Eastern Enlargement: The Uneven Policy Impact of EU Identity*. Manchester University Press, Manchester.

2011. Europeanisation in new member and candidate states. *Living Rev. Eur. Gov.* 6, 1–52. https://doi.org/10.12942/lreg-2006-3

2012. Is Europeanisation through conditionality sustainable? Lock-in of institutional change after EU accession. *West European Politics* 35, 20–38. https://doi.org/10.1080/01402382.2012.631311

Segal, S., Bertez, C. 2021. Drilling down on Treasury's new fossil fuel energy guidance for multilateral development banks. CSIS, 19 August. www.csis.org/analysis/drilling-down-treasurys-new-fossil-fuel-energy-guidance-multilateral-development-banks

Selei, A., Takácsné Tóth, B., 2022. A modelling-based assessment of EU supported natural gas projects of common interest. *Energy Policy* 166, 113045. https://doi.org/10.1016/j.enpol.2022.113045

Sencar, M., Pozeb, V., Krope, T., 2014. Development of EU (European Union) energy market agenda and security of supply. *Energy* 77, 117–124. https://doi.org/10.1016/j.energy.2014.05.031

Seputyte, M., 2014. Lithuania grabs LNG in effort to curb Russian dominance. Bloomberg, 27 October. www.bloomberg.com/news/articles/2014-10-27/lithuania-grabs-lng-in-effort-to-curb-russian-dominance#xj4y7vzkg

Seyfang, G., Park, J. J., Smith, A., 2013. A thousand flowers blooming? An examination of community energy in the UK. *Energy Policy* 61, 977–989. https://doi.org/10.1016/j.enpol.2013.06.030

Shearer, C., 2019. How plans for new coal are changing around the world. CarbonBrief.org, 13 August. www.carbonbrief.org/guest-post-how-plans-for-new-coal-are-changing-around-the-world/

Shearer, C., Fofrich, R., Davis, S. J., 2017. Future CO_2 emissions and electricity generation from proposed coal-fired power plants in India. *Earth's Futur.* 5, 408–416. https://doi.org/10.1002/2017EF000542

Shotter, J., Huber, E., 2019. Can Poland wean itself off coal? *Financial Times*, 3 May. www.ft.com/content/674ce754-6b9b-11e9-80c7-60ee53e6681d

Siddi, M., 2017. The EU's gas relationship with Russia: solving current disputes and strengthening energy security. *Asia Eur. J.* 15, 107–117. https://doi.org/10.1007/s10308-016-0452-3

Siderius, K., 2022. An unexpected climate activist: central banks and the politics of the climate-neutral economy. *J. Eur. Public Policy*, 1–21. https://doi.org/10.1080/13501763.2022.2093948

Sikorski, R., 2012. *Minister of Foreign Affairs Annual Address 2012*. Warsaw.

Sillak, S., Kanger, L., 2020. Global pressures vs. local embeddedness: the de- and restabilization of the Estonian oil shale industry in response to climate change (1995–2016). *Environ. Innov. Soc. Transitions* 34, 96–115. https://doi.org/10.1016/j.eist.2019.12.003

Siqueira, D. S., de Almeida Meystre, J., Hilário, M. Q., Rocha, D. H. D., Menon, G. J., da Silva, R. J., 2019. Current perspectives on nuclear energy as a global climate change mitigation option. *Mitig. Adapt. Strateg. Glob. Chang.* 24, 749–777. https://doi.org/10.1007/s11027–018-9829-5

Sivek, M., Jirásek, J., Kavina, P., Vojnarová, M., Kurková, T., Bašová, A., 2020. Divorce after hundreds of years of marriage: prospects for coal mining in the Czech Republic with regard to the European Union. *Energy Policy* 142, 111524. https://doi.org/10.1016/j.enpol.2020.111524

Sivek, M., Vlček, T., Kavina, P., Jirásek, J., 2017. Lifting lignite mining limits: correction of the Czech Republic energy policy. *Energy Sources, Part B Econ. Planning, Policy* 12, 519–525. https://doi.org/10.1080/15567249.2016.1219789

Sjursen, H., Rosén, G., 2017. Arguing sanctions: on the EU's response to the crisis in Ukraine. *JCMS J. Common Mark. Stud.* 55, 20–36. https://doi.org/10.1111/jcms.12443

Skalamera, M., 2018. Revisiting the Nabucco Debacle. *Probl. Post-Communism* 65, 18–36. https://doi.org/10.1080/10758216.2016.1188015

Skjaerseth, J. B., 2015. EU climate and energy policy: demanded or supplied?, in: Bang, G., Underdal, A., Andresen, S. (Eds.), *The Domestic Politics of Global Climate Change: Key Actors in International Climate Cooperation*. Edward Elgar, Cheltenham.

2016. Linking EU climate and energy policies: policy-making, implementation and reform. *Int. Environ. Agreements Polit. Law Econ.* 16, 509–523. https://doi.org/10.1007/s10784–014-9262-5

2018. Implementing EU climate and energy policies in Poland: policy feedback and reform. *Env. Polit.* 27, 498–518. https://doi.org/10.1080/09644016.2018.1429046

2021. Towards a European Green Deal: the evolution of EU climate and energy policy mixes. *Int. Environ. Agreements Polit. Law Econ.* 21, 25–41. https://doi.org/10.1007/s10784–021-09529-4

Skjaerseth, J. B., Eikeland, P. O., Gulbrandsen, L. H., Jevnaker, T., 2016. *Linking EU Climate and Energy Policies: Decision-Making, Implementation and Reform*. Edward Elgar, Cheltenham. https://doi.org/10.4337/9781785361289

Skjaerseth, J. B., Wettestad, J., 2008. Implementing EU emissions trading: Success or failure? *Int. Environ. Agreements Polit. Law Econ.* 8, 275–290. https://doi.org/10.1007/s10784–008-9068-4

2010. Fixing the EU emissions trading system? Understanding the post-2012 changes. *Glob. Environ. Polit.* 10, 101–123. https://doi.org/10.1162/GLEP_a_00033

Skovgaard, J., 2013. The limits of entrapment: the negotiations on EU reduction targets, 2007–11. *JCMS J. Common Mark. Stud.* 51, 1141–1157. https://doi.org/10.1111/jcms.12069

2014. EU climate policy after the crisis. *Env. Polit.* 23, 1–17. https://doi.org/10.1080/09644016.2013.818304

Slovak Government, 2005. *Security Strategy of the Slovak Republic 2005*. Bratislava.

2019. *Európskej únii chýba vízia, zhodli sa P. Pellegrini a A. Babiš*. Bratislava.

2019. *Integrated National Energy and Climate Plan for 2021 to 2030*. Bratislava.

Slovenia Times, 2019. Ministry with proposal for community-owned solar power plants. https://sloveniatimes.com/ministry-with-proposal-for-community-owned-solar-power-plants/

Slovenian Government, 2010. *National Security Strategy*. Ljubljana.

2022. Slovenia concludes deal on the supply of natural gas from Algeria. Republic of Slovenia, 15 November. www.gov.si/en/news/2022-11-15-slovenia-concludes-deal-on-the-supply-of-natural-gas-from-algeria/

Sydney Morning Herald, 2009. EU warns Slovakia against reopening nuclear plant. 13 January. www.smh.com.au/world/eu-warns-slovakia-against-reopening-nuclear-plant-20090113-7fbz.html

Smil, V., 2003. *Energy at the Crossroads: Global Perspectives and Uncertainties*. MIT Press, Cambridge.

2008. Moore's curse and the great energy delusion. AEI.org, 19 November. www.aei.org/articles/moores-curse-and-the-great-energy-delusion/

2016. Examining energy transitions: a dozen insights based on performance. *Energy Res. Soc. Sci.* 22, 194–197. https://doi.org/10.1016/j.erss.2016.08.017

Smith, A., Stirling, A., Berkhout, F., 2005. The governance of sustainable socio-technical transitions. *Res. Policy* 34, 1491–1510. https://doi.org/10.1016/j.respol.2005.07.005

Sokołowski, J., Frankowski, J., Mazurkiewicz, J., Lewandowski, P., 2022. Hard coal phase-out and the labour market transition pathways: the case of Poland. *Environ. Innov. Soc. Transitions* 43, 80–98. https://doi.org/10.1016/j.eist.2022.03.003

Sorbello, P., Oliva, E., 2012. Nuclear energy in Bulgaria: strategic implications for the EU and Russia. *Eur. Perspect.* 4, 35–55.

Sotirov, M., Lovric, M., Winkel, G., 2015. Symbolic transformation of environmental governance: implementation of EU biodiversity policy in Bulgaria and Croatia between Europeanization and domestic politics. *Environ. Plan. C Gov. Policy* 33, 986–1004. https://doi.org/10.1177/0263774X15605925

Sovacool, B. K., 2014. Cornucopia or curse? Reviewing the costs and benefits of shale gas hydraulic fracturing (fracking). *Renew. Sustain. Energy Rev.* 37, 249–264. https://doi.org/10.1016/j.rser.2014.04.068

2016. How long will it take? Conceptualizing the temporal dynamics of energy transitions. *Energy Res. Soc. Sci.* 13, 202–215. https://doi.org/10.1016/j.erss.2015.12.020

Sovacool, B. K., Cooper, C., Parenteau, P., 2011. From a hard place to a rock: questioning the energy security of a coal-based economy. *Energy Policy* 39, 4664–4670. https://doi.org/10.1016/j.enpol.2011.04.065

Sovacool, B. K., Dworkin, M. H., 2014. *Global Energy Justice: Problems, Principles, and Practices*. Cambridge University Press, Cambridge.

Sovacool, B. K., Heffron, R. J., McCauley, D., Goldthau, A., 2016. Energy decisions reframed as justice and ethical concerns. *Nat. Energy* 1, 16024. https://doi.org/10.1038/nenergy.2016.24

Spasić, V., 2020. Slovenia to phase out coal by 2050 – draft NECP. Balkan Green Energy News, 7 February. https://balkangreenenergynews.com/slovenia-to-phase-out-coal-by-2050-draft-necp/

Spencer, T., Fazekas, D., 2013. Distributional choices in EU climate policy: 20 years of policy practice. *Clim. Policy* 13, 240–258. https://doi.org/10.1080/14693062.2013.745111

Spendzharova, A., Versluis, E., 2013. Issue salience in the European policy process: What impact on transposition? *J. Eur. Public Policy* 20, 1499–1516. https://doi.org/10.1080/13501763.2013.781802

Sperling, J., Webber, M., 2019. The European Union: security governance and collective securitisation. *West Eur. Polit.* 42, 228–260. https://doi.org/10.1080/01402382.2018.1510193

Šprajc, P., Bjegović, M., Vasić, B., 2019. Energy security in decision making and governance: methodological analysis of energy trilemma index. *Renew. Sustain. Energy Rev.* 114, 109341. https://doi.org/10.1016/j.rser.2019.109341

Stapczynski, S., 2022. Most Japanese back nuclear for first time since Fukushima. Bloomberg, 27 March. www.bloomberg.com/news/articles/2022-03-28/most-japanese-back-nuclear-power-for-first-time-since-fukushima#xj4y7vzkg

Statista, 2023. Share of gas supply from Russia in Europe in 2021, by selected country. www.statista.com/statistics/1201743/russian-gas-dependence-in-europe-by-country/

Stefanini, S., 2018a. Hungary wants end to coal power by 2030. Climate Home News, 20 November. www.climatechangenews.com/2018/11/20/hungary-wants-end-coal-power-2030/

2018b. Big coal no more: the industry once ruled Europe. Now it's struggling to survive. Politico, 20 March. www.politico.eu/article/coal-lobby-electricity-energy-union-big-coal-no-more/

Steffen, B., Patt, A., 2022. A historical turning point? Early evidence on how the Russia-Ukraine war changes public support for clean energy policies. *Energy Res. Soc. Sci.* 91, 102758. https://doi.org/10.1016/j.erss.2022.102758

Steinmo, S., Thelen, K. A., Longstreth, F., 1992. *Structuring Politics: Historical Institutionalism in Comparative Analysis*. Cambridge University Press, Cambridge.

Stern, J. P., 1998. *Competition and Liberalization in European Gas Markets: Towards a Continental European Model*. London.

Stop Elektrowni Północ, 2022. About us. https://stopep.org/

Streeck, W., Thelen, K., 2005. *Beyond Continuity: Institutional Change in Advanced Industrial Economies*. Oxford University Press, Oxford.

Štreimikienė, D., 2016. Review of financial support from EU Structural Funds to sustainable energy in Baltic States. *Renew. Sustain. Energy Rev.* 58, 1027–1038. https://doi.org/10.1016/j.rser.2015.12.306

Streimikiene, D., Ciegis, R., Grundey, D., 2007. Energy indicators for sustainable development in Baltic States. *Renew. Sustain. Energy Rev.* 11, 877–893. https://doi.org/10.1016/j.rser.2005.06.004

Stritzel, H., 2007. Towards a theory of securitization: Copenhagen and beyond. *Eur. J. Int. Relations* 13, 357–383. https://doi.org/10.1177/1354066107080128

Stulberg, A. N., 2015. Out of gas? Russia, Ukraine, Europe, and the changing geopolitics of natural gas. *Probl. Post-Communism* 62, 112–130. https://doi.org/10.1080/10758216.2015.1010914

Sugiura, E., Inagaki, K., 2022. Japan approves nuclear energy U-turn to avert crisis. *Financial Times*, 22 December.

Sullivan, F., 2016. Lavrov's Budapest visit: Hungary urges 'pragmatic cooperation' between EU and Russia. *Hungary Today*, 26 May. https://hungarytoday.hu/lavrovs-budapest-visit-hungary-urges-pragmatic-cooperation-eu-russia-62653/

Supreme Audit Office, 2017. *Funkcjonowanie górnictwa węgla kamiennego w latach 2007–2015 na tle założeń programu rządowego*. Warsaw.

Sýkora, L., Bouzarovski, S., 2012. Multiple transformations. *Urban Stud.* 49, 43–60.

Szabo, J., Fabok, M., 2020. Infrastructures and state-building: comparing the energy politics of the European Commission with the governments of Hungary and Poland. *Energy Policy* 138, 111253. https://doi.org/10.1016/j.enpol.2020.111253

Szczerbiak, A., 2011. *Poland within the European Union: New Awkward Partner or New Heart of Europe?* Routledge, Abingdon.

Szép, V., 2020. New intergovernmentalism meets EU sanctions policy: the European Council orchestrates the restrictive measures imposed against Russia. *J. Eur. Integr.* 42, 855–871. https://doi.org/10.1080/07036337.2019.1688316

Szőke, E., 2023. Hungary to loosen its rules on deployment of wind turbines. ceenergynews.com, 9 February. https://ceenergynews.com/renewables/hungary-to-loosen-its-rules-on-deployment-of-wind-turbines/

Szul, R., 2011. Geopolitics of natural gas supply in Europe: Poland between the EU and Russia. *Eur. Spat. Res. Policy* 18, 47–67. https://doi.org/10.2478/v10105-011-0012-1

Szulecka, J., Szulecki, K., 2022. Between domestic politics and ecological crises: (de)legitimization of Polish environmentalism. *Env. Polit.* 31, 1214–1243. https://doi.org/10.1080/09644016.2019.1674541

Szulecki, K., 2018a. Conceptualizing energy democracy. *Env. Polit.* 27, 21–41. https://doi.org/10.1080/09644016.2017.1387294

(Ed.), 2018b. *Energy Security in Europe: Divergent Perceptions and Policy Challenges*. Palgrave Macmillan, London.

2020. Securitization and state encroachment on the energy sector: politics of exception in Poland's energy governance. *Energy Policy* 136, 111066. https://doi.org/10.1016/j.enpol.2019.111066

Szulecki, K., Fischer, S., Gullberg, A. T., Sartor, O., 2016. Shaping the 'Energy Union': between national positions and governance innovation in EU energy and climate policy. *Clim. Policy* 16, 548–567. https://doi.org/10.1080/14693062.2015.1135100

Szulecki, K., Kusznir, J., 2018. Energy security and energy transition: securitisation in the electricity sector, in: Szulecki, K. (Ed.), *Energy Security in Europe: Divergent Perceptions and Policy Challenges*. Springer International, Cham, pp. 117–148. https://doi.org/10.1007/978-3-319-64964-1_5

Szulecki, K., Overland, I., 2020. Energy democracy as a process, an outcome and a goal: a conceptual review. *Energy Res. Soc. Sci.* 69, 101768. https://doi.org/10.1016/j.erss.2020.101768

2023. Russian nuclear energy diplomacy and its implications for energy security in the context of the war in Ukraine. *Nat. Energy* 8, 413–421.

Szulecki, K., Szulecka, J., 2017. Polish Environmental Movement 1980–2017: (De)legitimization, politics & ecological crises (No. 6 – November 2017), ESPRi Working Paper.

Talus, K., 2012. Winds of change: long-term gas contracts and changing energy paradigms in the European Union, in: Kuzemko, C., Belyi, A. V., Goldthau, A., Keating, M. F. (Eds.), *Dynamics of Energy Governance in Europe and Russia*. Palgrave Macmillan UK, London, pp. 227–242. https://doi.org/10.1057/9780230370944_12

Taylor, K., 2022a. Germany, Netherlands call for joint EU gas purchasing ahead of next winters. Euractiv.com, 12 October. www.euractiv.com/section/energy/news/germany-netherlands-call-for-joint-eu-gas-purchasing-ahead-of-next-winters/

2022b. EU-27 approves demand gas reduction plan after power struggle with Brussels. Euractiv.com, 26 July. www.euractiv.com/section/energy/news/eu-27-approves-demand-gas-reduction-plan-after-power-struggle-with-brussels/

Taylor, S., 2006. Aggressive Poles lose friends and influence. Politico, 22 March. www.politico.eu/article/aggressive-poles-lose-friends-and-influence/

Tchalakov, I., Hristov, I., 2019. The Bulgarian nuclear sector in transition: adopted Russian technology, state sovereignty and accession to the EU. *Environ. Innov. Soc. Transitions* 32, 107–121. https://doi.org/10.1016/j.eist.2019.03.008

Tchalakov, I., Mitev, T., 2019. Energy dependence behind the Iron Curtain: the Bulgarian experience. *Energy Policy* 126, 47–56. https://doi.org/10.1016/j.enpol.2018.11.008

Temper, L., Avila, S., Bene, D. Del, Gobby, J., Kosoy, N., Billon, P. Le, Martinez-Alier, J., Perkins, P., Roy, B., Scheidel, A., Walter, M., 2020. Movements shaping climate futures: a systematic mapping of protests against fossil fuel and low-carbon energy projects. *Environ. Res. Lett.* 15. https://doi.org/10.1088/1748-9326/abc197

Thaler, P., Pakalkaite, V., 2021. Governance through real-time compliance: the supranationalisation of European external energy policy. *J. Eur. Public Policy* 28, 208–228. https://doi.org/10.1080/13501763.2020.1712462

Thomas, N., 2016. Czech coal group OKD files for insolvency. *Financial Times*, 3 May.
Tidey, A., 2022. Ukraine war: Hungary comparing EU sanctions on Russia to bombs is 'inappropriate'. Euronews, 19 October. www.euronews.com/my-europe/2022/10/19/hungary-comparing-eu-sanctions-on-russia-to-bombs-is-inappropriate-says-eu-commission
Todorov, S., 2020. Bulgaria protesters take to streets over new environment threat. Balkan Insight, 26 June. https://balkaninsight.com/2020/06/26/bulgaria-protesters-take-to-streets-over-new-environment-threat/
Törőcsik, Á., Selei, A., 2018. *Cross-Border Energy Cooperation in Central Europe: The Case of Hungary*. Budapest.
Toshkov, D. D., 2017. The impact of the Eastern enlargement on the decision-making capacity of the European Union. *J. Eur. Public Policy* 24, 177–196. https://doi.org/10.1080/13501763.2016.1264081
Tosun, J., 2011. When the grace period is over: assessing the new member states' compliance with EU requirements for oil stockholding. *Energy Policy* 39, 7156–7164. https://doi.org/10.1016/j.enpol.2011.08.035
Tosun, J., Biesenbender, S., Schulze, K., 2015. *Energy Policy Making in the EU: Building the Agenda*. Springer-Verlag, London.
Tranter, B., Booth, K., 2015. Scepticism in a changing climate: a cross-national study. *Glob. Environ. Chang.* 33, 154–164. https://doi.org/10.1016/j.gloenvcha.2015.05.003
Treib, O., 2014. Implementing and complying with EU governance outputs. *Living Rev. Eur. Gov.* 9, 1–47. https://doi.org/10.12942/lreg-2014-1
Trokoudi, A., 2017. The security of gas supply under the (EU) Regulation 994/2010 and the recent proposal for its amendment, in: Hancher, L., Metaxas, A. (Eds.), *EU Energy Law and Policy: A South European Perspective*. Claeys and Casteels, Deventer.
Tromans, S., 2019. State support for nuclear new build. *J. World Energy Law Bus.* 12, 36–51. https://doi.org/10.1093/jwelb/jwy035
Tsebelis, G., 2002. *Veto Players: How Political Institutions Work*. Princeton University Press, Princeton, NJ.
Tsiropoulos, I., Nijs, W., Tarvydas, D., Ruiz Castello, P., 2020. Towards net-zero emissions in the EU energy system by 2050, JRC Technical Reports. https://doi.org/10.2760/081488
Tusk, D., 2014. A united Europe can end Russia's energy stranglehold. *Financial Times*, 21 April.
Tutak, M., Brodny, J., 2022. Renewable energy consumption in economic sectors in the EU-27: the impact on economics, environment and conventional energy sources. A 20-year perspective. *J. Clean. Prod.* 345, 131076. https://doi.org/10.1016/j.jclepro.2022.131076
TVP World, 2018. Shale gas extraction in Poland unprofitable: finance ministry. 29 November.
UK and CR non-paper, 2015. European Governance of EU Energy Policy goals.
UK Government, 2014. *Estimated Impacts of Energy and Climate Change Policies on Energy Prices and Bills: 2014*. London.
UK Government, 2021. *Fact Sheet: Net Zero-Aligned Financial Centre*. London.
Ullman, R. H., 1983. Redefining security. *Int. Secur.* 8, 129–153. https://doi.org/10.2307/2538489
UN, 1992. *United Nations Framework Convention on Climate Change*. New York.
1997. *Kyoto Protocol to the United Nations Framework on Climate Change*. New York.
2015. *Paris Agreement*. New York.
2021a. Global coal to clean power transition statement. UN Climate Change Conference UK 2021. https://ukcop26.org/global-coal-to-clean-power-transition-statement/
2021b. *Addendum to the Emissions Gap Report 2021*. New York.

2022a. *The Closing Window: Climate Crisis Calls for Rapid Transformation of Societies. Emissions Gap Report 2022*. United Nations Environment Programme. https://wedocs.unep.org/bitstream/handle/20.500.11822/40874/EGR2022.pdf?sequence=1&isAllowed=y
2022b. *Sharm el-Sheikh Implementation Plan*. New York.
2023. National Determined Contributions. https://climatepromise.undp.org/news-and-stories/NDCs-nationally-determined-contributions-climate-change-what-you-need-to-know
UNEP, 2015. *The Financial System We Need*. New York.
UNFCCC, 2016. *Just Transition of the Workforce, and the Creation of Decent Work and Quality Jobs*. New York.
Unruh, G. C., 2000. Understanding carbon lock-in. *Energy Policy* 28, 817–830.
Ürge-Vorsatz, D., Miladinova, G., Paizs, L., 2006. Energy in transition: from the Iron Curtain to the European Union. *Energy Policy* 34, 2279–2297.
Ürge-Vorsatz, D., Tirado Herrero, S., 2012. Building synergies between climate change mitigation and energy poverty alleviation. *Energy Policy* 49, 83–90.
Valdés Lucas, J. N., Escribano Francés, G., San Martín González, E., 2016. Energy security and renewable energy deployment in the EU: liaisons dangereuses or virtuous circle? *Renew. Sustain. Energy Rev.* 62, 1032–1046.
Van de Graaf, T., Haesebrouck, T., Debaere, P., 2018. Fractured politics? The comparative regulation of shale gas in Europe. *J. Eur. Public Policy* 25, 1276–1293. https://doi.org/10.1080/13501763.2017.1301985
Van der Vleuten, E., 2004. Infrastructures and societal change: a view from the large technical systems field. *Technol. Anal. Strateg. Manag.* 16, 395–414. https://doi.org/10.1080/0953732042000251160
van Eck, C. W., Feindt, P. H., 2022. Parallel routes from Copenhagen to Paris: climate discourse in climate sceptic and climate activist blogs. *J. Environ. Policy Plan.* 24, 194–209. https://doi.org/10.1080/1523908X.2021.2000376
van Munster, R., 2009. *Securitizing Immigration, Securitizing Immigration*. Palgrave Macmillan UK, London.
van Veelen, B., van der Horst, D., 2018. What is energy democracy? Connecting social science energy research and political theory. *Energy Res. Soc. Sci.* 46, 19–28.
Vanegas Cantarero, M. M., 2020. Of renewable energy, energy democracy, and sustainable development: a roadmap to accelerate the energy transition in developing countries. *Energy Res. Soc. Sci.* 70, 101716. https://doi.org/10.1016/j.erss.2020.101716
Vanhercke, B., Verdun, A., 2022. The European Semester as Goldilocks: macroeconomic policy coordination and the recovery and resilience facility. *JCMS J. Common Mark. Stud.* 60, 204–223. https://doi.org/10.1111/jcms.13267
Vanttinen, P., 2022. Finland to open first LNG terminal. Euractiv.com, 10 June. www.euractiv.com/section/energy-environment/news/finland-to-open-first-lng-terminal/
Vasev, N., 2017. Governing energy while neglecting health: the case of Poland. *Health Policy (New. York)*. 121, 1147–1153. https://doi.org/10.1016/j.healthpol.2017.09.008
Vedby Rasmussen, M., 2004. 'It sounds like a riddle': security studies, the war on terror and risk. *Millennium* 33, 381–395. https://doi.org/10.1177/03058298040330020601
Verbong, G., Geels, F., 2007. The ongoing energy transition: lessons from a socio-technical, multi-level analysis of the Dutch electricity system (1960–2004). *Energy Policy* 35, 1025–1037. https://doi.org/10.1016/j.enpol.2006.02.010
Vihalemm, T., Keller, M., 2016. Consumers, citizens or citizen-consumers? Domestic users in the process of Estonian electricity market liberalization. *Energy Res. Soc. Sci.* 13, 38–48. https://doi.org/10.1016/j.erss.2015.12.004

Vihma, A., Wigell, M., 2016. Unclear and present danger: Russia's geoeconomics and the Nord Stream II pipeline. *Glob. Aff.* 2, 377–388. https://doi.org/10.1080/23340460.2016.1251073

Vilemas, J., 1995. Nuclear energy in Lithuania: present status and hopes for the future. *Energy Policy* 23, 719–722. https://doi.org/10.1016/0301-4215(94)00009-T

Visegrad Group, 2014. *Joint Statement of the 21st Meeting of the Ministerst of Environment of the Visegrad Group Countries, the Republic of Bulgaria and Romania*. Bratislava.

Visegrad Group, 2016. *Joint Statement of the Heads of Governments of the V4 Countries*. Bratislava.

Viviescas, C., Lima, L., Diuana, F. A., Vasquez, E., Ludovique, C., Silva, G. N., Huback, V., Magalar, L., Szklo, A., Lucena, A. F. P., Schaeffer, R., Paredes, J. R., 2019. Contribution of Variable Renewable Energy to increase energy security in Latin America: complementarity and climate change impacts on wind and solar resources. *Renew. Sustain. Energy Rev.* 113, 109232. https://doi.org/10.1016/j.rser.2019.06.039

Vivoda, V., 2022. LNG export diversification and demand security: A comparative study of major exporters. *Energy Policy* 170, 113218. https://doi.org/10.1016/j.enpol.2022.113218

Vlček, T., 2016. Critical assessment of diversification of nuclear fuel for the operating VVER reactors in the EU. *Energy Strateg. Rev.* 13–14, 77–85. https://doi.org/10.1016/j.esr.2016.08.006

Vlček, T., Jirušek, M., 2019. Comparison with Russian operations in the sector of natural gas: the case of Gazprom, in: Vlček, T., Jirušek, M. (Eds.), *Russian Oil Enterprises in Europe: Investments and Regional Influence*. Springer International, Cham, pp. 211–232.

Vogler, J., 2017. The challenge of the environment, energy, and climate change, in: Hill, C., Smith, M., Vanhoonacker, S. (Eds.), *International Relations and the European Union*. Oxford University Press, Oxford.

von der Leyen, U., 2023. Davos 23: Special Address by Ursula von der Leyen, President of the European Commission. World Economic Forum, 17 January. www.weforum.org/agenda/2023/01/davos-23-special-address-by-ursula-von-der-leyen-president-of-the-european-commission/

von Homeyer, I., Oberthür, S., Dupont, C., 2022. Implementing the European Green Deal during the evolving energy crisis. *JCMS J. Common Mark. Stud.* 60, 125–136. https://doi.org/10.1111/jcms.13397

von Lucke, F., 2021. Principled pragmatism in climate policy? The EU and changing practices of climate justice. *Polit. Geogr.* 86, 102355. https://doi.org/10.1016/j.polgeo.2021.102355

Wagner, A., 2015. Shale gas: energy innovation in a (non-)knowledge society: a press discourse analysis. *Sci. Public Policy* 42, 273–286. https://doi.org/10.1093/scipol/scu050

Wagner, A., Grobelski, T., Harembski, M., 2016. Is energy policy a public issue? Nuclear power in Poland and implications for energy transitions in Central and East Europe. *Energy Res. Soc. Sci.* 13, 158–169. https://doi.org/10.1016/j.erss.2015.12.010

Wagner, B., Hauer, C., Schoder, A., Habersack, H., 2015. A review of hydropower in Austria: past, present and future development. *Renew. Sustain. Energy Rev.* 50, 304–314. https://doi.org/10.1016/j.rser.2015.04.169

Waldholz, R., 2018. Smothered by smog, activists are urging Poland to reconsider coal. Public Radio International, 11 December. https://theworld.org/stories/2018-12-11/smothered-smog-activists-are-urging-poland-reconsider-coal

Walsh, M., 2019. Community energy in Hungary and Czechia. www.foeeurope.org/sites/default/files/climate_justice/2019/community_energy_in_hungary_and_czechia_briefing.pdf

Wang, B., Wang, Q., Wei, Y.-M., Li, Z.-P., 2018. Role of renewable energy in China's energy security and climate change mitigation: an index decomposition analysis. *Renew. Sustain. Energy Rev.* 90, 187–194. https://doi.org/10.1016/j.rser.2018.03.012

Wang, J., Kim, S., 2018. Comparative analysis of public attitudes toward nuclear power energy across 27 European countries by applying the multilevel model. *Sustain.* 10(5), 1518. https://doi.org/10.3390/su10051518

Wang, X., Lo, K., 2021. Just transition: a conceptual review. *Energy Res. Soc. Sci.* 82, 102291. https://doi.org/10.1016/j.erss.2021.102291

Wang, Z., Paavola, J., 2023. Resilience of the EU ETS to contextual disturbance: the case of EU enlargement and its impact on ETS policymaking dynamics. *Env. Polit.* 32, 69–89. https://doi.org/10.1080/09644016.2022.2043072

Washington Post, 2018. State of the Union 2018. www.washingtonpost.com/politics/2018/live-updates/trump-white-house/fact-checking-and-analysis-of-trumps-state-of-the-union-2018-address/about-that-war-on-beautiful-clean-coal/?noredirect=on

Watt, R., 2021. The fantasy of carbon offsetting. *Env. Polit.* 30, 1069–1088. https://doi.org/10.1080/09644016.2021.1877063

Weiner, C., 2019. Diversifying away from Russian Gas: the case of Poland. *Outlines Glob. Transform. Polit. Econ. Law* 12, 138–163. https://doi.org/10.23932/2542-0240-2019-12-2-138-163

2021. Pathways for a low-carbon electricity system in Poland and Hungary, in: Mišík, M., Oravcová, V. (Eds.), *From Economic to Energy Transition: Three Decades of Transitions in Central and Eastern Europe*. Springer International, Cham, pp. 211–245.

Weiner, C., Szép, T., 2022. The Hungarian utility cost reduction programme: an impact assessment. *Energy Strateg. Rev.* 40, 100817. https://doi.org/10.1016/j.esr.2022.100817

Wettestad, J., 2014. Rescuing EU emissions trading: mission impossible? *Glob. Environ. Polit.* 14, 64–81. https://doi.org/10.1162/GLEP_a_00229

White, S., 2022. Power plant shutdowns hinder France's 'nuclear adventure. *Financial Times*, 29 May.

White, S., Abboud, L., 2022. Macron restarts France's 'nuclear adventure' with plans for 6 reactors. *Financial Times*, 10 February.

White House, 2021. Executive Order on Catalyzing Clean Energy Industries and Jobs through Federal Sustainability. www.whitehouse.gov/briefing-room/presidential-actions/2021/12/08/executive-order-on-catalyzing-clean-energy-industries-and-jobs-through-federal-sustainability/

WHO, 2022. Air Pollution. www.who.int/news-room/fact-sheets/detail/ambient-(outdoor)-air-quality-and-health

Wilczek, M., 2020. Construction of Poland's first nuclear power plant to begin in 2026. Notes from Poland, 16 June. https://notesfrompoland.com/2020/06/16/construction-of-polands-first-nuclear-power-plant-to-begin-in-2026/

Williams, M. J., 2008. (In)security studies, reflexive modernization and the risk society. *Coop. Confl.* 43, 57–79.

WNA, 2021a. Nuclear power in Czech Republic. World Nuclear Association. https://world-nuclear.org/information-library/country-profiles/countries-a-f/czech-republic.aspx

2021b. Nuclear power in Lithuania. World Nuclear Association. www.world-nuclear.org/information-library/country-profiles/countries-g-n/lithuania.aspx

2022a. Nuclear power in Poland. World Nuclear Association. https://world-nuclear.org/information-library/country-profiles/countries-o-s/poland.aspx

2022b. Carbon dioxide emissions from electricity. World Nuclear Association. https://world-nuclear.org/information-library/energy-and-the-environment/carbon-dioxide-emissions-from-electricity.aspx

Wolska, A., 2022. Poland's road to nuclear: Will it pay off? Euractiv.com, 29 February. https://eu-sysflex.com/polands-road-to-nuclear-will-it-pay-off/

Woollacott, J., 2020. A bridge too far? The role of natural gas electricity generation in US climate policy. *Energy Policy* 147, 111867. https://doi.org/10.1016/j.enpol.2020.111867
World Bank, 2023. *Breaking Down Barriers to Clean Energy Transition*. Washington, DC.
Woźniakowski, T. P., Maatsch, A., Miklin, E., 2021. Rising to a challenge? Ten years of parliamentary accountability of the European Semester. *Polit. Gov.* 9. https://doi.org/10.17645/pag.v9i3.4690
Wunderlich, J.-U., 2020. Positioning as normative actors: China and the EU in climate change negotiations. *JCMS J. Common Mark. Stud.* 58, 1107–1123. https://doi.org/10.1111/jcms.13019
Wurzel, R. K. W., Liefferink, D., Di Lullo, M., 2019. The European Council, the Council and the member states: changing environmental leadership dynamics in the European Union. *Env. Polit.* 28, 248–270. https://doi.org/10.1080/09644016.2019.1549783
WWF, 2021. Coal comfort: Bulgarian recovery plan makes green gains, but stalls on coal exit – ball is in EC's court. World Wide Fund, 11 November. https://wwfcee.org/news/coal-comfort-bulgarian-recovery-plan-makes-green-gains-but-stalls-on-coal-exit-ball-is-in-ecs-court
Xinhua, 2019. Ecologists protest against coal dependency in Poland. 14 May. www.xinhuanet.com/english/2019-05/14/c_138058256.htm
Yafimava, K., 2017. *The OPAL Exemption Decision: Past, Present, and Future*. Oxford.
2021. *The OPAL Exemption Decision: A Comment on the Advocate General's Opinion on Its Annulment and Its Implications for the Court of Justice Judgement and OPAL Regulatory Treatment*. Oxford.
Youngs, R., 2009. *Energy Security: Europe's New Foreign Policy Challenge*. Routledge, London.
Zachmann, G., McWilliams, B., Sgaravatti, G., 2021. *How Serious Is Europe's Natural Gas Storage Shortfall?* Brussels.
Zachová, A., 2021a. Czech coal mining regions confronted with 'hidden' energy poverty. Euractiv.com, 22 February. www.euractiv.com/section/energy-environment/news/czech-coal-mining-regions-confronted-with-hidden-energy-poverty/
2021b. Czech health minister backs coal mining phase-out 'as soon as possible. Euractiv.com, 19 January. www.euractiv.com/section/air-pollution/news/czech-health-minister-backs-coal-mining-phase-out-as-soon-as-possible/
Zakeri, B., Paulavets, K., Barreto-Gomez, L., Echeverri, L. G., Pachauri, S., Boza-Kiss, B., Zimm, C., Rogelj, J., Creutzig, F., Ürge-Vorsatz, D., Victor, D. G., Bazilian, M. D., Fritz, S., Gielen, D., McCollum, D. L., Srivastava, L., Hunt, J. D., Pouya, S., 2022. Pandemic, war, and global energy transitions. *Energies* 15(17), 6114. https://doi.org/10.3390/en15176114
Zeng, S., Streimikiene, D., Baležentis, T., 2017. Review of and comparative assessment of energy security in Baltic States. *Renew. Sustain. Energy Rev.* 76, 185–192. https://doi.org/10.1016/j.rser.2017.03.037
Zhang, H.-B., Dai, H.-C., Lai, H.-X., Wang, W.-T., 2017. U.S. withdrawal from the Paris Agreement: reasons, impacts, and China's response. *Adv. Clim. Chang. Res.* 8, 220–225. https://doi.org/10.1016/j.accre.2017.09.002
Zhang, Y., Shi, H.-L., 2014. From burden-sharing to opportunity-sharing: unlocking the climate negotiations. *Clim. Policy* 14, 63–81. https://doi.org/10.1080/14693062.2014.857979
Zhao, C., Zhang, W., Wang, Y., Liu, Q., Guo, J., Xiong, M., Yuan, J., 2017. The economics of coal power generation in China. *Energy Policy* 105, 1–9. https://doi.org/10.1016/j.enpol.2017.02.020
Zhelyazkova, A., Kaya, C., Schrama, R., 2017. Notified and substantive compliance with EU law in enlarged Europe: evidence from four policy areas. *J. Eur. Public Policy* 24, 216–238. https://doi.org/10.1080/13501763.2016.1264084

Żuk, P., 2023. Soft power and the media management of energy transition: analysis of the media narrative about the construction of nuclear power plants in Poland. *Energy Reports* 9, 568–583. https://doi.org/10.1016/j.egyr.2022.11.192

Żuk, P., Żuk, P., 2022a. National energy security or acceleration of transition? Energy policy after the war in Ukraine. *Joule* 6, 709–712. https://doi.org/10.1016/j.joule.2022.03.009

2022b. The Turów Brown Coal Mine in the shadow of an international conflict: surveying the actions of the European Union Court of Justice and the populist policies of the Polish government. *Extr. Ind. Soc.* 10, 101054. https://doi.org/10.1016/j.exis.2022.101054

Index